PARAPOLITICS

PARAPOLITICS
Toward the City of Man

RAGHAVAN IYER

New York Oxford
OXFORD UNIVERSITY PRESS
1979

Library of Congress Cataloging in Publication Data
Iyer, Raghavan Narasimhan. Parapolitics. Includes index.
1. Political science. 2. State, The. I. Title.
JA71.I94 320 79-11800 ISBN 0-19-502596-2

Printed in the United States of America

To heroic pioneers
and humble exemplars
everywhere

PREFACE

Parapolitics involves continuous rethinking of the foundations as well as the frontiers of conventional politics. The societies of the future will require a courageous transcendence of our habitual ways of marking the contours of politics. This implies a critical distance from the facts, a fearless recognition of the costs of commitment in different spheres, and a cheerful look at limits and possibilities in the never-ending quest for the City of Man.

The City of Man may be discerned at three levels. First of all, it is an ideal conception. Any polis or moral community is an imperfect embodiment of *Civitas Humana.* Secondly, there is a nascent sense of global community emerging in our own time; the City of Man is an embryo struggling to be born. Thirdly, with the dissolution of moral traditions in many societies today, basic political concepts should be reconsidered in the light of the existing City of Man. Politics must be renovated parapolitically–within a matrix which allows politics to reform and transcend itself. The City of Man could use parapolitical conceptions to nurture its own vision of growth and fulfillment.

The conceptual basis of this work was germinated during a leisurely period of teaching political philosophy at Oxford. Its existential standpoint was developed over a decade of teaching in the United States, where all problems, for better and for worse, are larger than life (as known elsewhere). The pertinacity of the author's ethical commitments may be ascribed to his Indian upbringing. Much of the material here has been presented in a variety of contexts, including meetings sponsored by the Fund for the Republic, the Club of Rome, and other agencies. The author is indebted for comments on particular chapters to the late Professor John Plamenatz of Oxford, Professor James Joll of London, Professor Alan Gewirth of Chicago, and the late Robert Hutchins.

While the author alone is responsible for the views expressed, all who have perused this work have helped to enhance the concord between its contrapuntal facets.

Readers who are too disconcerted by the present to contemplate a radically different future may find some fuel for indignation. The book is especially dedicated to those bored with the prevailing ideologies but excited about the uncharted future. Neither a treatise on parapolitics nor an agenda for the City of Man, it offers a dialectical bridge between them to stimulate constructive thought on issues of common concern.

Santa Barbara R.N.I.
March 10, 1979

ACKNOWLEDGMENTS

Portions of Chapters 3, 6, 7, 11, 13, 14, and 15 have been published in *Center Diary* (Fund for the Republic), *Existential Humanist Psychology* (Brooks/Cole), *The Center Magazine* (Fund for the Republic), *Archiv für Rechte–Und Sozial Philosophie, Indian & Foreign Review, Growth II* (Capricorn Books), *L'Europe en l'an 2000* (Fayard), *Darmstadter Blatter, Looking Forward: The Abundant Society* (Fund for the Republic), and *The Future Is Tomorrow* (Mouton).

CONTENTS

PARAPOLITICS

I

POLITICS AND PARAPOLITICS

Men make the truth serve the pursuit of appearances, while appearances are given them for the pursuit of truth.

CLAUDE DE SAINT-MARTIN

The seventeenth century seemed to mark a radical break with medieval thought, the beginning of a new mode of rational and empirical inquiry that reached its height in the Enlightenment and continued through the nineteenth century into our own time. Some have sought a metaphysically and ethically neutral language in which social and political matters may be properly investigated, mainly with the aid of reason and in the light of experience. Human nature, in this view, possesses a fundamentally stable structure, discovered by careful observation and introspective awareness, or deduced from some more comprehensive rational theory of the universe. A correct analysis of the constants and variables in man, the unified structure of nature, and the unfolding process of history would enable us to explain human behavior and to arrive at indisputable conclusions concerning solutions to social and political problems. It has also been assumed that social and psychological phenomena are subject to ascertainable laws and that the paths of history and human behavior are predictable. Today we can see more clearly that the scientific iconoclasm and the expectations of an earlier epoch were somewhat naïve, that the turning points in European thought were not as sharp as imagined, and that an underlying continuity may be discerned. Even the boldest modern thinkers were more influenced by earlier conceptions than they realized. Above all, what we imagine to be invariable laws or universal truths are often inflated, sometimes vacuous, generalizations bound up with our presuppositions (neither fully provable nor wholly falsifiable) concerning God, Nature, Man, and History. The ghosts of discarded ideas are still with us, as Ibsen suggested, and we are subtly influenced by concepts and attitudes that we only too readily reject. If we are alienated from past tradition, we are not godlike spectators who stand outside time but rather unhappy men and women enslaved by new myths, imagining our loneliness to be a state of freedom.

Political and social theory may be seen as an indispensable prerequisite to the study of politics, as a pedagogic abstraction from the complex tradition of a political society, or merely as a specialized branch of political science with its own normative concerns and rarefied modes of philosophical analysis. All three views coexist among political scientists, with changing proportions of adherents. Even among those who regard political thought as fundamental to political science, there are radical differences of standpoint, as to whether the inquiry into ideas and concepts is an art or a science, whether it involves philosophical rigor or historical insight, and what is the most appropriate mode of analysis or synthesis. In regard to all such matters of basic disagreement, there have been significant shifts in attitude in the past decade. There is a noticeable decline in dogmatism among protagonists of divergent methods, and a fresh concern to discover a more humane and balanced approach to a protean subject, burdened by a medley of tools borrowed from cognate fields.

Political concepts need to be considered historically as well as analytically if their deceptive ambiguity and shifting meanings are to be appreciated. The polis or *samiti* was originally seen as a community of men, a society of moral and rational agents. If every man has some innate recognition of the true and of the good, enriched by active participation in a theater of political interaction, then a community of citizens is a moral community. It necessarily rests upon and reinforces social sympathy born of self-awareness and a shared consciousness of "the species nature," the common humanity and essential similarity, of individuals in diverse roles and situations. With this perspective, it is possible to derive a viable conception of the common good or public welfare from the individual's pursuit of the good in the company of other men and women. This humane pursuit requires a reasoned reflection upon oneself in relation to others and an imaginative empathy with a wide range of individuals. The notion of the common good could also be derived from some conception of the universe as a moral order and man's place in that order, an exalted view of Natural Law or of the polis as a microcosm of the macrocosm. Yet, such metaphysical underpinnings do not logically commit one to any medieval or modern organic view of the community as an entity, with a will, a life, a moral path, and a destiny of its own. The moral universe is compatible with ethical individualism if its social or metaphysical support is rightly comprehended.

The Greek conception of the polis as a moral order presupposed the possibility of a growing moral consensus, even an objective morality, without necessarily entailing any attempt to deduce moral values from social facts. It rather meant that the integrity and intelligibility of the cosmic order could envisage and explain a common human nature, capable of indefinite growth or perfectibility. The objective nature of morality could be reconciled with subjective views of the good by making a continuing distinction between the relativity (and partiality) of actual perceptions of the true and the good, and a postulated absolute truth and goodness. The postulate was needed, if for no other reason, as an incentive to moral growth, as a way of assuring the corrigibility in principle of human error, ignorance, and weakness. In this model, the stress is upon the exemplification of virtues by individuals instead of universilizable moral rules which could be applied to each act. The basic ethical term is the 'good'–the notions of 'right' and 'ought' are derivative. In Roman and Christian thought, however, the main emphasis shifted to laws, rules, and the rightness of acts. Both for Cicero and Saint Augustine, a moral community was necessarily one governed by civil laws, modeled upon the Natural Law. Uniformity of laws secured universality at the price of a conformity that was rigid in comparison with the more informal consensus implicit in the intuitionist and reasoned conceptions of Socrates and Plato. The subsequent centuries of medieval moral theology showed a recurrent tension between subjective intuitionism, reinforced by divine "grace" and human "faith," and objective universalism, bolstered by an imposing teleology.

Since the seventeenth century, there has been a preoccupation with the autonomy of the individual coincident with the rise of propertied democracy, individualism, and social atomism, and a glorification of rights and interests. Socialism and communism have often had to invoke some form of social and historical determinism to minimize the theoretical priority accorded to free will and individual autonomy. The notion of the common good has usually become identified in collectivist thought with an organic view of the community, or the assigning of historical and social reality to the collective interests of a class, race, nation, or empire. Methodological collectivism may be combined with ethical individualism. Indeed, this preference has become the reigning theme in Western thought—a significant stress on statistical determinism in the social sciences together with an insistent relativism in ethics. In contemporary *theoria* and *praxis,* we seem to have no firm basis for the conception of a moral community, unless we are already committed to some theological view of morality or a quasi-medieval conception of community.

The problem then remains: Can we now revive the notion of a moral community and provide a purely rational basis for it, without leaning toward extreme social determinism, without an appeal to sectarian religious belief, and without losing the gains in tolerance that have accrued from different forms of relativism? Can we rescue morality from the abyss of subjectivism and liberate the notion of community from the jungle of ideology? Can we secure the benefit of something less rigid than Kant's categorical imperative and at the same time more elevating than a merely utilitarian concern with the measurable consequences of particular decisions, thereby avoiding the Scylla of Natural Law metaphysics and the Charybdis of rampant moral relativism? Such questions are more easily asked than answered, but even the asking of them is vitally important in times when moral evasion becomes intellectually respectable. If a stable social morality could be successfully established by an appeal to reason, it would have important consequences for public policy and for current controversies on practical issues. Any rationalist ethic, especially one which purports to provide the basis of an objective morality which is universally valid and socially necessary, must include a definition of rationality. Rationality commonly means selecting the most efficient available means to achieving a rationally acceptable end, and an end is rationally acceptable if it cannot be shown to be irrational in any way. Rationality makes sense only when we already have ends, i.e., some preferences and desires must already exist for reason to operate at all. Rationality of means is the best policy in that it is the one most likely to achieve our ends and least likely to cost us too much–by comparison with alternative methods. The rationality of particular ends can only be justified in relation to further ends.

The idea of a moral community suggests a broader and more meaningful conception of politics than that found in most contemporary discussions. The notion that a person can act as a moral and rational agent, demonstrating a freedom to identify and choose among several possible alternatives, not all of which may have been already accepted or applied within the community, may seem irrelevant to modern mass politics. Given the generous hospitality in classical thought to this optimistic view of man, it is not surprising to find the etymological equation of the free citizen (*politikos*) and full participation in the moral life of the community (*polis*). Nor is it incongruous to find the noble expectation in ancient thought that from the creative participation of citizens in a continuous discussion of common ends there could emerge a minimal moral consensus and some degree of self-transcendence, credible commitments to the common good, and an increasing measure of self-enlightenment. Contemporary images and feelings about politics call attention chiefly to the compulsive manipulations of insecure persons in positions of power. This is partly a reflection of the progressive narrowing through several centuries of the content given to the conception of the political. Institutional modes of stabilizing political authority and power have weakened the open-textured sense of community which enhanced the polis and encouraged citizens to participate in meaningful roles. The regulated but abused invitation to acquire external status has restricted the horizon of individual growth. When the claims of imperial authority and national sovereignty are enlisted as ideological aids to the institutional infrastructure and the pressures of habitual conformity obscure the vital interstices of social life, it becomes difficult for men and women to believe in the rational basis of legal rights and effective participation in public life.

Modernity may even be seen as disguised medievalism. Medieval feudalism generated and confirmed a widespread dependence on institutional definitions of rights and authority. Citizens lost the moral protection afforded by the Ciceronian distinction between public and private in a civil society. They generally became dependent for self-reference upon a status accorded them within stagnant and hierarchical formulations of human nature in the name of an inaccessible *Civitas Dei.* Members of the *Civitas Terrena* had duties to fulfill in consonance with legally specified modes, but those with administrative authority–ecclesiastics and monarchs–appropriated the role of specifying the goals of community life and of interpreting the requirements of the common good. Since the eighteenth century, such institutional formulations of collective ends have been couched in secular language and buttressed by the monopolistic claims to formal authority of nation-states, armed with the military and economic power of technological societies. Sterile conceptions of mass society have emerged in which not only individual thought and identity are lost but the very right of individual valuation and validation is eclipsed by utilitarian definitions of the good. The result has been the indefinite enlargement of popular demands and hopes in highly structured modern societies, while the relevance of political activity to universal human needs has noticeably diminished. Terms like "nation" and "public interest" shroud a highly complex and overstrained political life in which leading roles are taken by those with skill and expertise in manipulating the System while displaying a modicum of ability to pursue the goals deemed important. A basic tension has arisen between the shared identity of the members of civil society and the irrational wills of those who gain office and dominate political life. To convince other people of their entitlement to govern, the politicians–now a much narrowed class of technicians–rely on stylized role performance. To convince others that what they want is what everyone wants, these political performers often resort to propagandizing popular emotions. This expedient becomes a substitute for deliberation and offers a convenient mask for those who wish to hide their sense of impotence in politics and their inability to participate effectively in the democratic process. In place of the politics of reason, which requires dialogue and consensus, there runs rampant a chaotic politics of power and bargaining, with its recourse to manipulation, propaganda, and intimidation. The politics of vision, rooted in a concern with fusing *theoria* and *praxis,* has been wholly obscured by the pseudo-politics of the management of illusions, consisting of little more than a facility for adopting any currently fashionable methodology and applying it as a technique of self-promotion.

No wonder a deep mistrust of politics and politicians has become an entrenched mode of popular thinking, and many are afraid of power while also losing touch with "the self in us that draws to the standard of all wise and beautiful things." Only when the credibility of political leaders becomes unduly suspect or when their amorality is transparent, as during the Suez crisis, the Czech uprising, or the Watergate scandal, does a persistent questioning of official pronouncements become widespread. People may temporarily show the inherent human propensity to demand reasons for the denial of legitimate preferences and seek to examine political decisions in the light of broader principles of justification. When "politics as usual" is far removed from the constructive dialectic of dialogue that is vital to a moral community, political leaders have no qualms in making shallow and immoral appeals to *raison d'état* when threatened with the loss of power and privilege.

The contemporary bifurcation of ethical and political standards is aggravated by encumbering politics with a whole set of concepts adapted to the ritual justification of current institutional practices. Politics is arbitrarily circumscribed in terms of external characteristics of the supposedly sovereign state, statutory law, and routinized practices. The exercise of coercive power is often presented as the central political act, evoking in turn the revolutionary obsession with justifiable violence in the name of a political cause. The tendency to define politics ostensively leads to further bewilderment when little effort is made to clarify and distinguish such basic political concepts as force, power, and authority, or freedom, liberty, and community. Political interaction could become meaningful to the extent to which men share common allegiances or stable beliefs or come under common rules, seeking common ends by humane means, and especially when they recognize their commonality in the process. External institutions, rules and laws, codifications of beliefs, and systems of concepts can at best serve as aids to reflection, but they cannot create a sense of community where there is none. Communities are effectively established by persons through voluntary activity, shared obligations, and the continuously rediscovered bonds among them. They could be permanently shattered by the illusory allegiances which people foster through token gestures or empty words, thus becoming enmeshed in traps of their own collective making. This is the irony and also the tragedy of contemporary politics.

Any community of human beings will seek diverse ways of invoking or affirming commonality. For example, there is the similarity that arises out of the very nature of being human. Individuals may be proudly aware of their intrinsic status, that they are born free and can exercise the power to think, to choose, and to create. A vital community of free persons will be secure in the shared awareness of an innate freedom which none can confer and none abrogate, which one could forget but of which one could be repeatedly reminded. Furthermore, one could remind oneself, especially if one is trying to throw off those psychological chains that are even greater fetters upon freedom than any external constraints. The politics of freedom significantly hinges upon what human beings think of themselves. Instead of striving to discipline all persons by common agreement in relation to a stipulated definition, it is better to assume that as long as men are men, they can choose to define themselves. A creative community should and must be self-defining. Self-conscious persons will define themselves in words and deeds through their dynamic conceptions of themselves and of each other. This is common sense, all too often overlooked and costly to forget. We cannot lay down and stipulate commonality for all men, although it has been repeatedly tried and may sometimes seem unavoidable in particular contexts.

Politics is inseparable from life–from human concerns, moral considerations, religious and secular beliefs, modes of living, inherited myths, dreams and nightmares; from preconceptions and presuppositions about fundamental issues, transcendental themes, and values; and from distinctions between right and wrong, good and evil, pleasure and pain, freedom and tyranny, egotism and altruism. Ultimate questions, even if unanswerable, are never irrelevant to the politics of free men. Even if persons will never agree about God, Nature, and the Self, they must agree to disagree. Although they may show diverse and muddled ways of expressing their presuppositions, they could hold contrasting or incompatible presuppositions and still agree about human needs, human excellence, and human welfare. This agreement need not be entire or even significant but only sufficient for the purpose of handling specific questions with self-respect and mutual forbearance as well as some reverence for the dignity of all persons. When political actors entertain specific questions relevant to decision making, they must also be in a position to respect others with radically different presuppositions regarding God, Nature, and Man. Political thinkers since the seventeenth century have been so concerned to secularize the vocabulary of politics and ethics as a result of the historic battles between Church and State, that they have been unconsciously led to smuggle notions of the sacred into the seemingly neutral and allegedly scientific or philosophical language of modern politics. The referential terms of political discourse–the State, society, and citizen–as well as whole clusters of political and ethical concepts, even with a recognizable descriptive or factual content, retained accretions of meaning from discarded beliefs, inherited values, obsolete dogmas, and the transmitted psychology of past human encounters.

On the physical plane, every person has had a million ancestors over a thousand years. On the intellectual and cultural level, the very words we use hark back to Sanskrit and the family of Indo-Aryan languages, to the ancient Greeks and the Roman Empire, to the Middle Ages and its peculiar problems and divisions that have left their scars and residues in language. We also have ties with the Renaissance and its heroic attempt to replace static concepts by fresh ideas that affirmed the Promethean capacity to create a new world commensurate with a noble vision of man, as in Pico della Mirandola's oration *On the Dignity of Man,* which laid the basis for modern humanism. We are especially linked to the complacent nineteenth century and its tragic aftermath. Words became infected with the ideologies of political movements on behalf of classes, élites, ruling classes, empires, and nations, and as a result we have inherited a welter of "isms"–liberalism, socialism, communism, fascism, and their prolific bastard progeny. No "ism" is a logically complete and self-consistent system of ideas. Its spurious claim to completeness converts it into an ideology which can win followers and reconcile them to losses and setbacks. An ideology is a form of imposition of holy writ by a putative expert on any doctrinal "ism," whether he or she be the guardian of a party or a church, the head of a nation or a program, or any leader who engages in an inefficient form of bossism and resorts intermittently to force, treachery, and trickery to secure compliance. This collusion initially seems adequate but in time becomes hard-hearted and precarious, and must eventually end. Demoralization results from imposition by force or fraud in lieu of inducement through a consistent appeal to the unrestricted use of reason, to common experience, and to shared insights.

The proud hope of the eighteenth century was to enlighten the minds of all men in conditions of freedom in a political society wherein every man shared in shaping his own destiny and that of all others. Politics was seen as an instrument of deliberate transformation, based upon an enduring consensus in determining the ends of society, the appropriate means in relation to those ends, and the rational ordering of individual values and collective priorities. This meant gaining control over the allocation of resources and achieving some valid sense of meaning and purpose to life in a political society–the tangible feeling that one belonged to a community of persons who shared goals and aspirations as well as trials and tribulations, who had a common inheritance either from their own historical ancestors or from the whole heritage of humanity, and a firm basis for looking forward to the future with some optimism. This involved facing the world with the confidence that the future was not wholly outside one's control, that one did not have to be entirely in the hands of any malign force or fate. The Enlightenment initiated an epoch in which it became meaningful for human beings to ask questions of themselves in relation to the world, of their own society in relation to mankind and history, and of themselves as citizens in relation to other citizens in a variety of roles, functioning under rules and also in the free space of human encounter. As creative agents with contrary views, conflicting plans, and colliding wills, persons can nonetheless strive to agree, in spite of disagreement, sufficiently to survive, to coexist, and to cooperate for some larger purpose wherein one might see beyond oneself and transcend the tyranny of the immediate.

Every human being has wants, preferences, and a fund of experiences from which each can draw insights and through which each can understand the experiences of others. All persons can make common reference to basic needs and wants. But what are basic needs? What are the basic wants? People cannot and need not agree, because no one can lay down a table of priorities unless one is saying, in effect, that others have to believe what one believes. A person who does not understand the difference between truth and victory, or between freedom and status, has not begun to individuate. Anyone who has repeatedly made the distinction knows its continual relevance. The moral problem is ever with every person. The language of politics could elevate the quality of human life when individuals learn to ask not merely about the statistics of wars, inflation, and recession, but also about the rightness and wrongness of decisions in relation to war and unemployment. These questions are inconvenient to men and women who need votes to be elected, and who also want, after they are elected, to be loved. It is difficult to expect people to love those who send many of their sons to fight in the prime of youth in a war that is meaningless to them and which they have not chosen. Such are the moral ambiguities of human beings, which give rise to the moral and political contradictions of a political society.

In any complex society men and women assume many roles and relate to each other in terms of these roles. Rules must apply to these formal relationships for the sake of making them manageable. Even in a complex democratic society, every man is a stranger to every other, and another man becomes relevant only when he is a threat. Today people are too easily threatened to see themselves as members of a moral community. They do not understand who they are; they do not know where they are going; they do not understand what is happening around them; and they do not like what they see. This unites all human beings. And yet the negative unity of all people in distress, this commonality in pain, is not a sufficient basis for overcoming estrangement. Locke thought, with pre-Freudian optimism, that men do not regard others as strangers when they can bring together their individual interests. Today, few people know what their immediate or common interests are. Short-term interests seem less important to many than long-term interests, but the most perceptible interest is in survival–not physical but psychological. This implies the need to belong, the desire to make sense of the world, and the wisdom to connect disparate events. Knowledge and language become real only when they involve meaningful self-reference and expanding self-knowledge. The ultimate reality is not a differentiation of subjects and objects. There is always a parapolitics that cannot be stated in the language of comparison and contrast. There is a real need to rethink the problem of the One and the Many in the political orbit, the problem of integration and unification.

A grand ideal, based upon a myth of illusory perfection centered in the past, may either stimulate actual advance in the present or merely result in somnolent self-deception and prolonged delusion. The historical materialist may plausibly attempt to reduce such historical myths to the status of meretricious but misleading disguises for economic and material objectives. Even if such reductionists are right–and reductionism is too easy a device to deploy in place of imaginative understanding–myths and symbols, concepts and ideals may exercise an influence of their own and undeniably affect the further evolution of thoughts and situations. The Populist enthusiasm for agrarian communism, though based upon an idealization of the past, indirectly influenced the decision of the Bolshevik government to make the common ownership of village lands the basis of the new agrarian system. What matters is not so much the historical accuracy of every myth, but the very fact that it was widely conceived as a living reality. Even if men could dispense wholly with myths, they could not readily conceive reality apart from the clusters of concepts which they hold. A historical life-ideal may be seen as any shared concept of excellence which men project into the past or the future. The vision of the golden age, the *kritayugam* or the reign of Kronos, may be centered on happiness or innocence or peace or the mere absence of constraint in human society. Alternatively, a cultural ideal may be concerned with death rather than life, with redemption rather than earthly fulfillment. The monastic ideal of poverty may overshadow the secular goal of material prosperity, and while the pastoral ideal may abandon culture for nature, the apostolic ideal abandons both for virtue and heavenly rest. The chivalric ideal incorporates the element of self-sacrifice, which is even more fundamental to the Bodhisattva (or *sannyasin*) ideal of renunciation that has had such a persisting influence in the East. In the course of history men have turned from retrospective to millennial ideals, and have often shown a ruthlessness in securing the compliance of others, thus shattering the very basis of a moral community.

The tradition of political thought that began in the teachings of Pythagoras and Plato came to an end in the theories of Marx and Mao. The traditional hierarchy of thought and action, contemplation and labor, philosophy and politics, was effectually inverted. The myth of socialized humanity in which the State will wither away shares with the idealized Athenian polis the denial of any division between rulers and ruled, and the universal enjoyment of leisure in a condition of comparative freedom. In an ideal society, classless and stateless, the lives of men and women may be devoted to aims higher than drudgery or political conflict. Meanwhile, the Socratic faith in dialogue has been partially displaced by the Marxian identification of action with violence. Today we know better what we are fighting *against* than what we are fighting for. The spiritual homelessness of modern man may be partly traced back to the Cartesian rift between man and the world, cognition and reality. We are poignantly conscious of the consequences of secularization, the shift from metaphysical notions of nature to a mundane philosophy of history, the connection between the liberal's concern with receding freedom and the conservative's anxiety about receding authority or tradition in a world structured by neither. We also know too well the crisis of culture in a mass society in which leisure time is used for consumption and entertainment rather than self-perfection or even self-cultivation. The world revolution is seen by orthodox Marxists as the decisive, apocalyptic act by which estranged man changes himself by changing the world, his inward division healed, his essential human nature released and renewed.

Our acceptance of Marxism, in its simpler or maturer formulation, depends not on the truth or falsity of its so-called scientific propositions but on whether we regard Marx's picture of the historical and social process as plausible and, ultimately, on whether we share his presuppositions about man and nature. To say this is to admit that he was a serious and systematic thinker, a daring secular metaphysician who deserves the sort of consideration that we might accord to Hobbes or Hegel, Spinoza or Rousseau. Marx stands to Hegel rather as Aristotle does to Plato, though he went much further than Aristotle in departing from his philosophical mentor. Political theories may be regarded not merely as speculative truths but also as propagandist devices to secure the acceptance or rejection of actual politics and systems. Marx went so much further in his prescriptive than in his explanatory function that he may plausibly be viewed as a latter-day prophet, the founder of a new secular religion. He stands in relation to Feuerbach rather as Aquinas to Aristotle. Altogether, his basic ideas were derivative, yet he expounded his original systematization more in the accents of a scientific expert than those of a religious oracle.

Marx was a moralist rather than a moral philosopher. The *Communist Manifesto* is the portrait of a civilization and a system felt to be iniquitous in its basic structure, standing condemned in the eyes of the detached spectator while also awaiting merited destruction by the heroic revolutionary. Traditional moral philosophy is an inquiry into the nature of the good, an intellectual discipline that proceeds from methodological doubt and a philosophical suspension of commitment. In this sense Marx was not a moral philosopher. Like Gandhi, he reversed the traditional primacy of *vita contemplativa* over the *vita activa* to such an extent that he dismissed contemplation without action as sterile, though he himself, unlike Gandhi, was a *philosophe* and a propagandist rather than an actor on the world's stage. Marxism shares with Augustinianism its totality of scope, its attempt to provide an all-inclusive view of reality. Marx might be called a metaphysical system-builder, but metaphysics since Aristotle bears many resemblances to theology and has been directly influenced by it, and has often found place for the God-idea. Metaphysics before Hegel concentrated on nature to the exclusion of history, whereas Marxism, like medieval Christianity, views all existence under the umbrella of history, framed by a temporalized pre-history at one end (primitive communism or paradise lost) and temporalized post-history at the other (future communism or paradise regained). Marx had the crucial concept of a total regeneration of man, corresponding to the Christian theme of salvation.

In *The Holy Family,* Marx says that the possessing class and the proletarian class represent one and the same human self-alienation. While the former is smug in its self-alienation and apprehends it as its own power, the latter feels crushed in its alienation and sees in it its own impotence. Marx's vision of society as a system in conflict, "a split self writ large," is religious or metaphysical rather than scientific. The ancient Hermetic axiom that man is the microcosm of the macrocosm is dramatically employed to draw men out, not from their blind restlessness, but from their mute complacency. Marx's historicism prevented him from pursuing his early philosophy to its logical conclusion and from asking fundamental questions about the ends of life and the deepest human urges that were frustrated under the competitive, acquisitive craze of the capitalist system. This prevented him from considering whether the regeneration of man would automatically take place with a total change of system from capitalism to communism. His millennial dream was a powerful myth centered on the future without adequate basis in the historical reality he was so concerned to reveal. Perfectionism and idealization, moralism and violence, ideologies and "isms," are all the strange bed-fellows and destructive enemies of a living ideal of human perfectibility.

It is important in this context to notice the different path taken by those social critics in the nineteenth century who showed concern not merely with capitalism but with industrialism itself, making aesthetic and moral protest against the ugliness and degradation in modern society–Ruskin, Rossetti, Morris, Pater, and Yeats. In an age of practical achievement when national ideals became increasingly materialistic, the life of the imagination asserted its claim against the social order, defending the sanctity of spontaneous creative activity. It was partly as a reaction to the Industrial Revolution that the word "artist" acquired a broader meaning than that of "artisan." In one of Beerbohm's cartoons Jowett, the Master of Balliol, is shown watching Rossetti at work on a large mural of some Arthurian legend. He asks Rossetti what they are going to do with the Grail when they find it (a very reasonable question to the respectable Victorian moralists). The Grail stood for all those values which need no utilitarian justification. Victorian culture, which served as the ideological superstructure of bourgeois capitalism in an era of expansion, also produced within itself its own antithesis. The Romantics sought refuge from industrialism in art and it was natural, though sad, that their apotheosis–art as a basis of moral protest–should have ended up in almost religious worship of art for its own sake. As aesthetic standards were threatened by industrialism, there was an overcompensation in the tendency to judge religion, morals, and society by purely aesthetic standards.

Marx saw the degradation of labor under capitalism as the result of economic exploitation, but Ruskin went further in seeing the dehumanization of the individual who was made to work with the precision of machines and to starve his powers of feeling and imagination. Marx held out against commercial values and asserted the dignity of man in his labor theory of value, but he did not see the deeper changes in the meaning of work that had resulted under industrialization and the ubiquity of utilitarianism. To Ruskin it was the degradation of the workman into a machine that was the real source of class hatred, making a mockery both of charity from the rich or the State and of any improvement of material conditions. Saint-Simon had singled out specialization as the momentous social phenomenon introduced by industrialism. To Ruskin and Morris the iniquity of division of labor was critically relevant to their aesthetic. Morris invited misunderstanding by insisting that every man shall be an artist, although his faith in every man's creative potential is essential to the socialist creed. Morris, like Marx, was led to justify a violent revolution to overthrow a society based on material power, postponing the fulfillment of his private vision until after the decisive victory. The utopian socialism of Morris became Marxist in its militant program during the unavoidable struggle, while the so-called scientific socialism of Marx became utopian in its anarchist dream of the ultimate aftermath of the revolution. If most revolutionaries could not help becoming romantic in their apotheosis of reason, some Romantics could not help becoming revolutionary in the cause of art. A creative response to the fertility of ideas and theories is far more fruitful than a pietistic deference to daunting tradition. The difference between a sophisticated and a crude Platonist, Hegelian, or Marxist is enormous, yet most political disputes in practice display much futile shadow-boxing, resulting in a caricature of the views of influential thinkers or theories.

Existentialism, the rebellion of the philosopher against philosophy itself, is one possible answer to a desperate situation in which the old metaphysical questions appear to be meaningless. Individual action, with its own quality of commitment, its being *engagé,* holds out the hope, not of solving any problems, but of making it possible to live with them without becoming, as Sartre once put it, a *salaud,* a hypocrite. The *Angst* of the existentialist is like the *tapas* of the *karma-yogin.* The self-suffering and practical commitment of which Gandhi spoke is a species of *tapas* unconcerned with, even skeptical about, ultimate enlightenment. Kafka describes the man who, if he wants to stand his ground at all, must give battle to the forces of both the past and the future, falling into the dream of a realm beyond the fighting-line, the timeless, spaceless empyrean cherished by the classical philosophers in India, the Taoists in China, and Plato and Parmenides in Greece. The parallelogram of forces in the battlefield between past and future should result in a diagonal force, to use an ancient metaphor for the activity of thought. For the thinking man *Kurukshetra,* the region of conflict, becomes *Dharmakshetra,* the realm of responsibility. Thanks to his teacher, Arjuna can assume the standpoint of Sanjaya, thus merging the roles of participant and spectator. The participant in the contest can aspire to the position of the umpire in Kafka's parable, but he may also die of exhaustion, oblivious to his original intentions and aware only of the interval in time which, while he lives, is the ground on which he must stand.

Dialectical logic can become the basis of self-questioning, through which a man may existentially integrate his life and his thinking. This demands that he show a willingness to examine all his presuppositions, and not be concerned merely with the orderly movement from premises to conclusions. Socratic dialogue seems to display a friendly impatience, a chiding tone of voice, a cool contempt for the vulgarity of instant certainty–wanting to come quickly to a conclusion which looks demonstrably true and may be useful in gaining worldly success, social status, and power over others. These crude preoccupations are irrational foes to the process of becoming a true individual, to the attainment of psychological maturity and the mellow ripening of wisdom. For centuries most political thinkers have too readily assumed that human nature is a fixed and unchanging essence, moved by unalterable laws–a form of secular determinism or materialistic Calvinism. We must hold to an open view of human nature if every person is to be seen, in a Godwinian sense, as a perfectible being capable of indefinite growth which precludes a static and final perfection. This was known during the ancient beginnings of political and ethical inquiry, but has become largely irrelevant both in contemporary academic life and in the mass media of our time. Men and women may be weak, but within a moral community it is always meaningful for them to wish to grow strong. And as long as people find meaningful the ideal and the hope of growing and perfecting themselves, their lives will have meaning. So, too, with world history. If enough individuals can find it around and within themselves, they can lend some of that meaning to the empty lives of many others.

Although words have progressively shrunk in significance and vitality during the long history of language, at the same time the social context, the human content, and the range of expectations in the arena of politics have continuously broadened. We are herein confronted with the central paradox of post-Enlightenment politics. The nation-state is not a polis and it is not a moral community. The State is not sovereign in the grandiose medieval sense or early modern conception, however much the holy oil of justification may be poured upon the nation-state in the name of some secular theory of social contract, tacit consent or general will, democratic centralism or popular sovereignty, welfare liberalism or brokerage pluralism. Most modern theories tend to be utilitarian or teleological, cloaking the dubious assumption that people are intelligent enough to seek and secure their own interests and the dangerous unstated presumption that they are always foolish enough to be successfully deceived in regard to their immediate and long-term interests. Like Hegel, Nietzsche thought that most men are victims of history, acted upon while pretending to be agents. Most men do not or perhaps cannot become strong enough to prevail over the unscrupulous and willful. When they use morality, it is hypercritical, for the sake of condemning others, and hypocritical, fostering a hollow self-righteousness. They do not find strength and inspiration in their own lives, and fail in setting themselves standards that would help to release their heroic potential. As long as every man is not a hero seeking to become king over himself, it is empirically unavoidable and contingently the case that some will take advantage of others. There is an acute weakness of will on the part of the many, and consequent attempts to compensate by looking for some Delphic Knife by which all problems could be instantly solved by a superman or savior. At the same time, such a leader is required to consult the desires of each, conform to the expectations of all, and gratify the passions of every person giving allegiance even while they impose contrary, volatile, and impossible demands upon him. As the ratios of expectations to results are intolerably inflated in modern politics, frustration becomes ubiquitous and the hope for human fulfillment seems chimerical.

Every human being is involved in a dynamic process of continual acceptance and reacceptance, identification and reidentification of authorities. In our time authority has broken down because the individual does not have an effective sense of self-determination. In this regard the rulers are not different from the ruled. In a democratic society those in positions of power are meant to be very much like the persons over whom they rule. Given that fact, with the decline of institutionalized authority and the weakening of formal modes of securing allegiance, the recovery of initiative is a challenge to the capacity of every citizen. Each must become an effective moral agent capable of translating his own conception of the good into a social goal sharable by many others. Every person participates potentially in a larger self that includes all selves. All men and women have a potential beyond their present power of action. The term "power" is etymologically connected with the verb *pouvoir.* In its derivative use as a substantive, it tends to foster the illusion that there is a determinate quantum of energy or power available to human beings in any society. If this is fixed, as people tended to think in the seventeenth-century climate of Newtonian physics and mechanics, power can be distributed solely through zero-sum games in which the gain of one must be the loss of another. If any group or person is to augment power, this must take power away from some other group or person. Such static thinking has contributed its share to the protracted tragedy of politics, and can be seen most poignantly in international affairs, especially in recent decades. Sinners of the world should unite—they have nothing to lose but their guilt. Even those who are warped by the competitive mentality may heal themselves and seek a richer conception of self-identity and self-satisfaction.

In classical political thought there was a concern to locate authority beyond anything that anyone could appropriate, either in wisdom or in justice, or, as in the Platonic Agathon—the supreme Good which is beyond definition. The Agathon can accommodate as many formulations as there are human beings, and every person can make his own report. As there will always be a transcending or conceivable good beyond the good(s) of particular individuals, the Agathon is ineffable and indefinable, and necessarily transcends the spatial and temporal limits of finite powers of perception. Justice is the primary application of the ruling conception of transcendental good to the political and social realms. It is hardly surprising that we find a pervasive awe before Justice in all societies from ancient times. Justice is always involved with that which the law cannot even attempt—to recognize the intractable problem of ethically reducing the ontological gap between the unique and the universal, and yet make constant approximations to satisfactory resolution. Justice is necessarily transcendental and therefore unattainable. But for the very reason that it is unattainable, credible approximations to it are critically important. Problems that are difficult to solve need not be shelved by individuals, while societies cannot evade them. No institutions work exactly in accordance with all expectations. At best, they attempt to fulfill stated intentions and conform to minimal expectations. When institutions become incapable of meeting the minimums, or altogether lose contact with their original intentions, then it becomes imperative for individuals to see beyond institutions. In so doing, they give themselves the opportunity to transcend the social structure, the impersonal rules and formal roles that restrict human encounter, and to explore those avenues of politics that are not entirely contained within structured relations.

Politics is the self-conscious articulation and continuous pursuit by human beings of shared or common (yet controvertible) ends in a civil society by a variety of means, ranging from coercive sanctions to rational persuasion and voluntary cooperation. A civil society is a historical and geographical collection of individuals organized in accordance with a set of laws and rules, at least some of which are equally binding upon all.

The wide range of political activity consistent with this broad definition of politics can be seen in the varied elements of politics it incorporates. First of all, self-conscious articulation points to the need for deliberation, while continuous pursuit requires a strong element of will. Deliberation and will sustain articulation and pursuit, together constituting a form of initiative or creative intervention in human affairs. Secondly, speech is necessary for the articulation of political ends. When employed to pursue shared or common but controvertible ends, it requires forums of dialogue and rational persuasion in order to be effective and relevant. Political dialogue, however fruitful, can never eliminate the gap between itself and political practice which frequently requires immediate action based upon incomplete knowledge. But its benefits to individual and collective life may extend far beyond the specifics of policy choices by introducing the element of rational self-transcendence in the political arena. A third element of politics is the familiar use of coercion, which must not be equated with brute force. It may operate in very subtle ways through social responses to informal rules as well as through statutory laws and enforced sanctions. A fourth element, the protection of individual claims, derives from the possibilities of deliberation and will, speech and coercion. Without this protection further elements could not be even minimally operative, in view of the multiple ends and conflicting choices of the political arena.

The shared or common nature of the ends pursued constitutes a fifth and quintessential element of politics, the promotion of social welfare. The welfare sought may be perceived on either a short- or long-term basis. Critical to this pursuit is the extent of participation, itself a sixth element which evokes the ethical and democratic conceptions of the Greek polis as well as the populist aspirations of Enlightenment politics. Participation may occur on several levels, in diverse modes, and according to distinct but variable ratios. The undefined and ever-evolving nature of participation is indicated by a seventh element, the preparation and continuous education for effective participation. Civic or political education may appeal to a patriotic sense of community, to participation in a "civil religion," or to the most exalted conceptions of human wisdom and compassion. If politics is to be more than the mere pursuit of individual or sectional interests, and is to become constructive as well as effective, then the eighth element will be the adjudication, coordination, and reconciliation of competing claims, public programs, and common objectives. A related but less controversial element, the ninth, is the promotion of conditions of healthy coexistence. These conditions may take the familiar forms of order and stability represented by legal structures, conventional values, or traditional symbols of authority. Yet the preservation of order may require the introduction of change and innovation, albeit in response to a crisis, but which also allows for a large measure of human growth and social regeneration. A tenth element is implicit within the definition, having to do with the legitimacy as well as the limitation of concern with a collective order. Parapolitics is an explicit way of legitimizing, encouraging, and sanctifying individual freedom and fulfillment. This stems from the unbounded capacities of individuals to enrich their social environment through inspired and self-chosen modes of cooperation within existing political structures.

To recognize a variety of means and modalities in political activity is simultaneously to recognize the existing facts of political life and also the *ante rem* and *post rem* character of politics. Different types of politics can be identified by diverse ends and contrasting means; a mechanical or institutional categorization of political patterns will not suffice. Politics is a distinctively human activity involving a broad range of insufficiently understood powers. The effects of political action can be appraised in terms of the tentatively definable characteristics and potentials of humanity as well as by changes in material and social conditions secured through political means. If types of politics are to be distinguished, the enumeration of distinctive ends and means must allow at every point for a potentially inexhaustible range of human powers and activities. The abilities of persons to imagine alternative states of societies and to engage in self-definition through their changing conceptions of what it means to be human, are as much a part of the political spectrum as any imitative reassertion of some familiar mode of self-aggrandizement. With these qualifications in mind, we may delineate six types of politics (see Figure 1).

The Politics of Perfectibility could be identified with the possibilities of self-direction, self-actualization, and self-transcendence. The distinction between means and ends would give way to a movement toward perfectibility through a mastery of the Dialectic of Transcendence. Here, a continuing process of affirmation, negation, and transformation provides a basis for identifying apt approximations to the Good for individuals and societies.

More familiar, at least on the level of an ideal, would be the Politics of Reason with its reliance upon deliberation, dialogue, and consensus. Within identifiable constraints, the Dialectic of Reason can become the basis of universalization, allocation, and choice in political life. The methods of political economy must be reconciled with the principles of political ethics, in a global as well as a national context.

The Politics of Welfare places stress on equalization, optimization, and maximization and is the painfully controversial basis of much contemporary politics. Bound up as much with human sympathy as with rationality, it moves through a Dialectic of Revolution that encompasses conflict, precipitation, and redistribution, variables little understood though endlessly analyzed.

More convenient but less far-sighted is the Politics of Stability, which relies on the available means of coercion, conciliation, and coexistence, and stresses the Logic of Contraction. The degrees of stability sought may vary, but since stability in a dynamic universe is an elusive goal, the Politics of Stability must compensate for its own emphasis upon centripetal forces by recognizing reluctantly the Logic of Expansion. Otherwise, unacknowledged involvement with the centrifugal forces of nature will vitiate political endeavors.

On the other hand, the Politics of Power, with its reliance on manipulation, propaganda, and persuasion, tends to pursue the Logic of Expansion through short-sighted methods of political action. The crude acquisition of power tends to overreach itself and

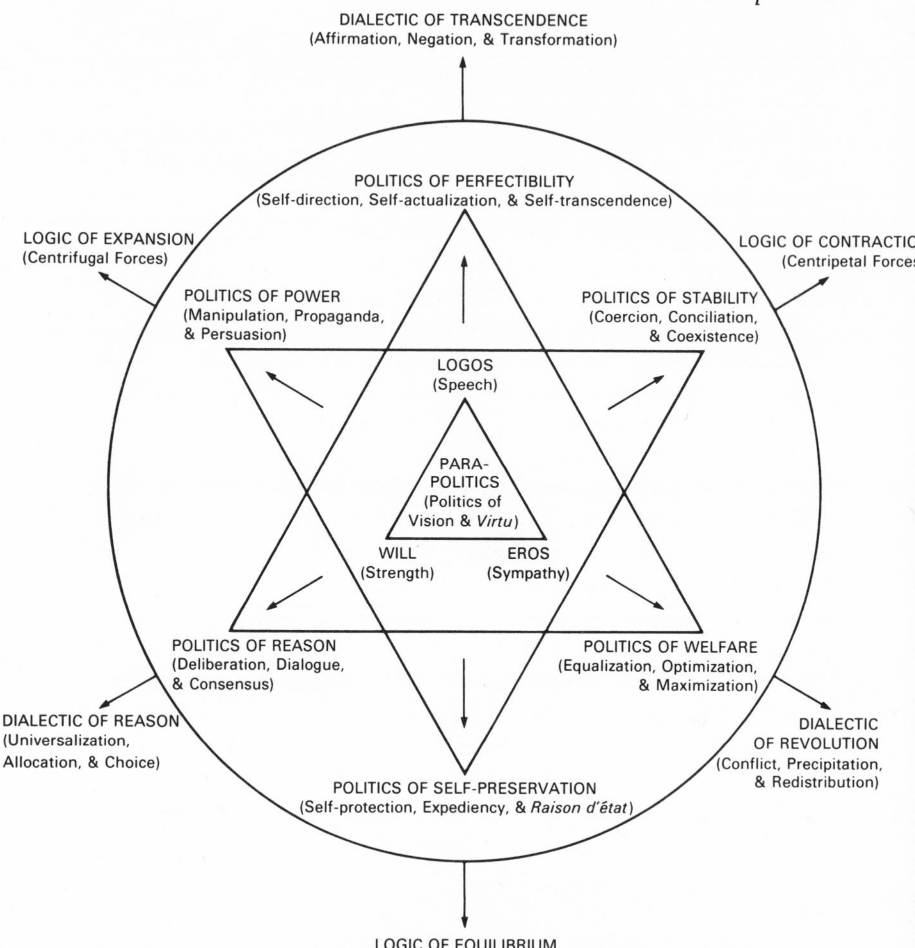

Figure 1. Six dimensions of politics

dissipate when the centrifugal forces exceed the cohesive power of the whole and are replaced by the coalescence of disparate contracting fragments of former structures.

The Politics of Self-Preservation, centered upon self-protection, expediency, and appeals to *raison d'état,* is preoccupied with the Logic of Equilibrium and a search for homeostasis. Paradoxically, it is marked by deficiency of imagination as well as by sporadic exemplifications of a worldly wisdom that echoes higher possibilities.

Parapolitics is beyond all of these, though partially present in each of them. The Politics of Vision is directed away from the politics of the past and the present, and represents a decisive break with the Politics of Stability, Power, and Self-Preservation.

Parapolitics signifies the imaginative application of seminal ideas vitalizing political theory and practice; the elaboration of fundamental principles into paradigms of relationships among persons and between civil means and humane ends; the quest for political understanding and action based upon expanding self-awareness; and the ever-receding perspective of ideals rooted in the ethics, metaphysics, and psychology of self-transcendence.

CRITICAL DISTANCE

This open-ended characterization of parapolitics includes a variety of elements, each capable of multiple instantiations within an evolving series of conceptual relations. First of all, the imaginative application of ideas suggests the effective insertion of unconstrained creativity into the concrete contexts of social life, bounded by spatial, temporal, and energic parameters. Critical distance as a detached awareness of expanding frontiers, fluctuating contours, and interstitial spaces, can help to overcome the inexorable pressures of linear time. Although parapolitics is dimensionless, it is the vital core from which the six dimensions of politics may be seen in proper perspective, together with the triple dialectic and the threefold logic of contraction, expansion, and equilibrium. The Politics of Vision and *Virtu* involves universal benevolence, constructive formulation, and creative action. It also requires a skill in timing that is the mature fruit of noetic discernment, a degree of inward detachment from spatio-temporal limitations, and a wise deliberation joined with compassion and *sophrosyne.* The true statesman, like the conventional political leader, will necessarily exercise *dianoia* in approximating solutions to emergent problems. He will also continually aspire to the transcendent *noesis* that reconciles the Many and the One, archetypally expressed by Plato in the relationship of Agathon and the Cave (Chapter 2).

Secondly, the appeal to seminal ideas can be apprehended only by paying attention to the parapolitical relations between men and institutions, not merely by chronicling systemic change or by making moralistic appeals in terms of a closed conception of human nature. There is evidence of a new mode of maturity in human consciousness and a contemporary concern with parapolitical freedom, which makes irrelevant many of the clichés of Left and Right. People with different presuppositions about the world and human nature, and with divergent convictions about political methods and the political process itself, may accept undogmatic formulations of such historic political principles as Natural Law, Tolerance and Civility, and Equality (Chapters 3, 4, and 5). Thirdly, a recognition of the dialectical elusiveness of such conceptions is a prerequisite for vitalizing political theory and practice. This suggests that in the politics of the future, credibility will belong primarily to those who command non-violently, who effortlessly exemplify authority beyond the limits of any formal power structure. It lies with those who can speak authentically of the existential needs of Individuation (Chapter 6), rather than those who trade in promises of satisfaction of temporary wants. The study of who gets what, when, and how, will have to be supplanted by an understanding of parapolitics which, in classical terms, involves the potency of Logos and the activity of Eros, philosophical clarity and psychological freedom. By maintaining and encouraging a sense of critical distance, the parapolitical statesman could provide appropriate leadership without requiring allegiance to any dogma. It was from this exalted standpoint that Philo Judaeus saw the politician as a soothsayer, "the interpreter of the dreams of men."

COSTS OF COMMITMENT

A fourth element in parapolitics, the elaboration of fundamental principles into paradigms, exacts both intellectual and ethical costs of commitment in order to preserve the universality of principles while meeting the challenges of events. Contemporary humanistic psychologists, like classical philosophers, acknowledge the incompleteness of all formulations and the indeterminacy of human growth. This recognition is rarely to be found among the popularizers and proponents of social and political theories, with their uncriticized predilections toward comfortable judgments derived from the scientific shibboleths of the seventeenth century, the sociological pseudo-laws of the eighteenth century, and the utilitarian ethics of the nineteenth. Too many commentators on political thought are so anesthetized by sophistic dichotomies, Aristotelian methods, and a decrepit form of Humean skepticism, that they can neither generate the Socratic starting point of genuine inquiry nor experience the higher flights of political imagination. This is shown in the surfeit of lackluster analyses offered by ex-colonialists and nationalists alike of the problems of Democracy and Liberty in Emerging Polities (Chapter 11). It demands moral courage and intellectual confidence to appreciate alternative world-views and systems of thought, or to grasp other men's visions before reinforcing the popular illusions of the present through hasty criticism. At the very least, the constructive use of political theory should communicate a sufficient awareness of many conceptual languages, the different levels of abstraction, mutations in central assumptions, the interaction between ideas and events, the logical and sociological functions of concepts with their identifiable core and indefinite boundaries, and the use of models to enlarge and deepen self-consciousness. But much more is expected of political theorists and spokesmen who would liberate themselves from old trappings and ideological encumbrances in renewing such conceptions as *Civitas Dei* and the Classless Society (Chapter 10).

In political thought we are faced with the problem of reconciling radically different ways of looking at the world, profoundly divergent conceptions of human possibilities and social transformation, incompatible yet unfalsifiable presuppositions, irreconcilable and unprovable beliefs. The relationships between ontology and epistemology, *theoria* and *praxis,* sociology and psychology, are crucial to political visions that see the same facts differently, and yet have a decisive impact upon our practical expectations, our hopes and our fears, and our self-conscious efforts. All political proposals and programs attempt to restructure relationships among persons, a fifth element of parapolitics, and are therefore inherently subject to ethical appraisal. In the case of individual reformers, sensitivity to moral complexities becomes The Revolutionary's Burden (Chapter 7). Revolutionaries and planners alike assert their proposals in defiance of those who impose restrictive conditions upon human potentials. This points to The Fundamental Revolution: From Élitism to Equality (Chapter 12). Sixthly, parapolitics is concerned with the relationships between civil means and humane ends, and requires both an integrative formulation of the relation between Means and Ends (Chapter 8) and the preservation of political rationality in the turbid confluence of Technology and Politics (Chapter 9). In every political society–even where a closed system of beliefs is the basis of common allegiance–the questioning of priorities, ultimate ends, and immediate goals requires commitment to collective self-understanding with credible individual self-reference in a climate of relative freedom, equality, civility, and fraternity.

LIMITS AND POSSIBILITIES

Inescapable limits may be perceived as offering opportunities as well as obstacles, thereby precluding excuses and alibis which foster crippling limitations on human possibility and initiative. Parapolitics implies, seventhly, the quest for political understanding and action based upon expanding self-awareness, an endeavor which requires a renewed discernment of meanings in received and recent formulations. Croce once put the question, "What is living and what is dead in the philosophy of Hegel?" This question might be raised of all political theories and concepts, of our inherited beliefs and conventional allegiances, and also of the social sciences and philosophical schools that still dominate our universities. Varied answers are possible, indeed desirable, but the universe of discourse must belong to those who can put themselves in the position not only of the Platonist, Thomist, Hegelian, or Marxist, but also of anarchists from Godwin to Gandhi, recent dialecticians from Lenin to Mao, apostles of modernity and iconoclasts of our time. The emergence of significant Global Pointers (Chapter 13) poses an enormous challenge to the synthetic powers and integrity of political imagination and social planning. The boundaries between the political and the non-political are being redrawn constantly in the light of changing human expectations. Political science is the greatest borrower among intellectual disciplines, and yet there is deep truth and continuity in the classical idea of political wisdom as the product of architectonic imagination. Its exercise is the Promethean task *par excellence* for those engaged in a continual process of self-definition within a theater of collective interaction that includes the worst and the best in human life.

To explore the possibilities for the global society of the future involves rethinking the apparent limits, preoccupations, and methods of past and present. Vital concerns such as The Future of Europe (Chapter 14) in relation to the other continents must be pursued in a context of post-colonial mondialism but with a lively appreciation of cultural resources. Tom Paine remarked that the religion of the future would strip away all the accretions upon that which was in the beginning. The social structure of the future will have some consonance with what has been forgotten and overlooked, once it is divested of the extravagances of the past and we have relinquished the superstructure of mummeries. The window within the immortal soul of man was the source of parapolitical vision in antiquity. Every person may give birth to insight, whether or not he or she has the good fortune of Meno. Each one has access to wisdom, whether or not a trained philosopher: what one is able to bring forth on any occasion is not all that one knows or all that could be released where there is love and trust.

An eighth element in parapolitics is the ever-receding perspective of ideals and goals. A stark paradox of the present is that, as State government grows and as bureaucratic planning expands, there is a concurrent and increasing alienation from the traditional centers of political action and decision making. These conditions require ecological and functional rather than merely territorial conceptions, so that private and public leadership may collaborate in many informal agencies, merging planning and implementation in a single activity. Implementation of public policy options, such as the provision of a guaranteed annual income as part of An Unfinished Dream (Chapter 16) of universal fulfillment, challenges the traditional limiting assumptions regarding role differentiation, economic position, and social status. The emergence of new forms of local participation has fostered cooperative experimentation in tapping unexplored human possibilities within The Community of Strangers (Chapter 15). This will necessitate some form of "civil religion" within *Civitas Humana,* compatible with many creeds, focused upon a rich conception of human potentials for self-actualization, and based upon the recognition of ontological plenty and existential scarcity. This constitutes a ninth element, the need for ideals rooted in the ethics, metaphysics, and psychology of self-transcendence. The political challenge of the future is constantly sharpened by the psychological terror of violent revolution and international confrontation, by anomie and civic disintegration, and by the inability of institutions to evoke genuine responsiveness. The passage from confusion to order–*Ex Chaos Cosmopolis* (Chapter 17)–depends upon a reconciliation of human differences within a vision of God, Man, Nature, and History. Diversity may be the celebration of unmanifest unity.

Politics has been perennially tormented by the tension between *Civitas Dei* and *Civitas Terrena,* with its dichotomous thinking and dualistic perspective. The alternative, integrative standpoint has always existed, but its proponents are few and far between and its recognizable practitioners too rare to be celebrated in the Epimethean language of recorded history. This is hardly surprising, considering its exacting nature. The truest benefactors of the human race have known through contemplation that the deeper one's roots in a transtemporal vision, sedulously maintained through detachment and deliberation, the sharper the eye for essentials and the more precise the direction of compassionate intelligence toward the meeting of human needs in the concrete contexts of everyday life. Those who sound the rumors or shrill alarms of war often strike the death knell but for themselves and the decadent structures that cling to the psychology of doom. Instead of wasteful, irresolvable disputation about the relevance of the Kingdom of Heaven to human beings on earth, lovers of humanity could see beyond the claims of class and race, sect and creed, to the continual, if incomplete, incarnation of *Civitas Dei* into an unfinished *Civitas Humana,* in the midst of earthly cities where "ignorant armies clash by night."

> The rest is silence. . . . Catastrophe will come; or worse than catastrophe, slow mouldering and withering into Hades.

> But if you can fix some conception of a true human state of life to be striven for—life, good, for all men, as for yourselves; if you can determine some honest and simple order of existence; following those trodden ways of wisdom, which are pleasantness, and seeking her quiet and withdrawn paths, which are peace;—then, and so sanctifying wealth into "commonwealth," all your art, your literature, your daily labours, your domestic affection, and citizen's duty, will join and increase into one magnificent harmony. You will know then how to build, well enough; you will build the stone well, but with flesh better; temples not made with hands, but riveted of hearts; and that kind of marble, crimson-veiled, is indeed eternal.[1]

1. John Ruskin, *Unto This Last and Traffic,* New York, Appleton-Century-Crofts, 1967, pp. 126-27.

I

CRITICAL DISTANCE

To be sure, man's life is a business which does not deserve to be taken too seriously; yet we cannot help being in earnest with it, and there's the pity. Still, as we are here in this world, no doubt, for us the becoming thing is to show this earnestness in a suitable way. ATHENIAN STRANGER

2

AGATHON AND THE CAVE

Great Magnet! Thy hidden power
Draws us ever onward to spaces anew.
Secret in the earth thy life forces waken
Stirrings and whispers that the ear cannot hear;
Later will come birth in the fullness of thy splendour.
All that has been shall lend to what comes after,
All that will come lies hidden in thy promise.

DRUID HYMN TO THE SUN

In the ratiocinative climate of our age of analysis, Plato's myths have sometimes been dismissed as mere poetic fantasies. Some have even suggested that they were employed to cover deficiencies in his chain of reasoning. As a result, his philosophy and political thought have not been properly grasped by his critics. Our difficulty in relation to the most creative spirits, the progenitors of fertile traditions of thought, is that almost anything said in response to their wisdom is more a truth about ourselves than about them. This problem takes on a specific form in regard to the mature apprehension of Plato, who employs modes of reasoning that have evident points of contact with our ordinary language and mundane encounters. His appeal to experience connects with our everyday life, and even when he speaks of illumination he does not, like some mystics, see it as the special prerogative of a privileged few, but grounds it as a permanent possibility in human nature itself. He is concerned with the varied conditions under which any person may attain to the highest insight. Because of his flexible methodology, our critical capacities are tested at many levels, especially in our courage to think afresh and our readiness to feel anew.

Platonism is hardly the same as the original oral teaching of

Plato, just as Christian theology is rather different from the unwritten teaching of Jesus. Many people unwittingly define their responses to Platonic thought and imagery in terms of their own traumas in bringing together the noetic and the psychic, the ardor of the sovereign self for the Agathon and the craving of the fugitive soul for the fleeting *agathos*. From the Platonic standpoint, there is no need to reject the process of becoming, although there is an ontological basis for adopting criteria which may identify higher and lower levels of reality. "Higher" means closer to the One, the homogeneous and the noumenal. It is that which gives a more inclusive perspective, a wider vision, and a greater strength. It also provides a continual stimulus to growth. "Lower" means a static localization of perspective, an oppressive confinement within territoriality and temporality. Such criteria are philosophically important to Plato, but there is nothing in them to justify a harsh repudiation of earthly beauty by religious votaries in the throes of repressive discipline.

In relation to any political thinker who refers to the transcendental as well as the temporal, it would be wise to adopt the attitude of mind intimated by Simone Weil in her *Notebooks:* "If I light an electric torch at night out of doors, I don't judge its power by looking at the bulb but by seeing how many objects it lights up. The brightness of a source of light is appreciated by the illumination it projects upon non-luminous objects."[1] The value of a transcendental outlook is known by the amount of illumination it throws upon the things of this world. As Saint Paul wrote, "Things visible are evidence of things invisible." Although this is what people often refuse to recognize because they are preoccupied with external marks, the essential virtue of anything is only partly manifested outside and around it. If, on the other hand, the light thrown on earthly things is overlooked on the pretext that spiritual values are alone important, there is the danger of having a non-existent treasure. Transcendental values are realized only when exemplified through social interaction. Philosophically, the rejection of two plausible alternatives is crucial to Platonic thought in its pristine form—common-sense realism and subjective idealism. As an objec-

1. Simone Weil, *First and Last Notebooks,* London, Oxford University Press, 1970, pp. 115-16.

tive idealist, Plato held that as a result of reflection upon abstract and noumenal realities, one is better able to reorder the realm of the concrete and the phenomenal. Herein lies the strength and continuing relevance of Platonic thought.

This is paradigmatically expressed in Plato's best-known myth, the "quaint parable" with which the Seventh Book of the *Republic* opens. In the Allegory of the Cave, Plato intimates that there is a truth beyond sense, pertaining to the eternal noumena which underlie earthly phenomena, a deeper realm of reality which cannot be adequately apprehended except by the philosopher who has been initiated into the Blessed Mysteries mentioned in *Phaedrus.* To realize fully the distinction between the intuitive and integrative standpoint of the true seer and the shared delusions of most men is to seize the parapolitical standpoint. This is the initial and critical step forward from the region of ignorance and flux toward the realm of correct cognition of noumenal realities. Our common tragedy lies in our refusal to recognize that we live in a condition of perpetual imprisonment, clinging tenaciously to the sights and sounds of earthly life, mistaking slavery for freedom and shadows for realities. The Allegory begins with a graphic picture of the abject condition of the majority of mankind. We are like chained slaves living in an underground den which has its mouth open toward the light. Here we have been from childhood, unable to see or to move beyond, constrained by the chains from even turning our heads around. Above and behind us a fire is blazing at a distance, but between the fire and ourselves there is a low wall like the screen behind which marionette players shelter to foster illusions. There are also men who carry implements of every kind which rise above this wall, images of men and animals and various objects. Some of these bearers speak; others remain silent. We are like the strange prisoners in this den who see only shadows of themselves, of one another, and of figures and objects–all of which the fire throws on the wall of the cave in front of us. We cannot distinguish voices from the echoes emanating from the surrounding darkness.

Given this picture, we might think that if only the prisoners were released from their chains by some external agency, they would cease to mistake shadows for realities and would automatically be disabused of their former errors. The Allegory shows that no such simple deliverance from illusions is possible. When any of the prisoners is liberated and compelled suddenly to stand up, turn around, and look toward the light, he will at first suffer excruciating pain. Further, the glare will disorient him and he will be unable to see even the shadows he formerly invested with reality. If he is told that what he saw before was an illusion and that he is now approaching real existence with clearer vision, he will be perplexed. He will continue to fancy that the shadows he saw for so long were truer than the objects which are now revealed. If he is compelled to look straight at the light, the pain in his eyes will induce him to turn away and take refuge in the objects of vision that have acquired a false but seemingly greater reality than the things which are now being shown to him. If he is dragged up the steep ascent and forced into the presence of the sun, his eyes will be dazzled and he will not be able to see anything at all. The liberated prisoner will need time to grow accustomed to the sight of the upper world. He will first see the shadows best, then the reflections of men and objects in the water, and then the objects themselves. Eventually he will gaze upon the light of the moon and the stars by night. At last he will be able to glimpse the sun. He will come to see that the sun is the generative source and guardian of the visible world and in this sense the cause of all that he and his fellows had been accustomed to behold. He would remember his old habitation and the delusions of his fellow prisoners, pity them, and congratulate himself on the change in himself and in his position. He would no longer care for the honors conferred upon one another by the ignorant prisoners on the basis of who were the quickest to observe the passing shadows. The first test that the liberated prisoner has to face is to become accustomed to his new condition and to forsake his long-cherished illusions. The second is to see the unity of all things. The third is to show compassion toward his fellow prisoners and not merely to revel in his own liberation. The fourth is to detach himself completely from the false valuations and hierarchical distinctions made by the dwellers in the den. His fifth and most difficult trial comes if he compels himself to re-enter the cave of darkness, for he would appear ridiculous to the prisoners who still cling to former illusions centered on the shadows. They would say that he had become blind to realities since leaving the cave, that it is better not even to think of ascending, that no ascent is possible, and that they would be entitled to put to death anyone who tried to free another and lead him up to the light.

The Allegory explains that the prison-house is the world of sight, the light of the fire is the power of seeing, and the journey upward is the ascent of the soul into the intellectual world. The shadows seen in the natural world, unlike the shadows of the cave, are reflections of real things rather than of images of real things. In the world of knowledge the archetypal idea of the Good, the Agathon, appears last of all and is seen with strain. It is only then inferred to be the universal source of all things beautiful and right; the parent of the orb of light in this visible world and the immediate source of reason and truth in the intellectual world; the power upon which the eye must be fixed in private and public life in order to act rationally. It is not surprising, we are told, that those who attain to this beatific vision are usually unwilling to descend to mundane affairs; for their souls are ever hastening into the upper world where they desire to dwell. Those who do descend from divine contemplations to the underground den will not find it easy to deal with those who have never yet seen the fire of the cave, much less the Agathon, the transcendental Good. The bewilderment of the eyes, physical as well as mental, is of two kinds and arises either from coming out of the light or from going into it. The plight of the soul as soon as it emerges from darkness into the light is to be pitied, and there is no reason to laugh at the condition of the soul which has come out of the brighter life and is unable to see because unaccustomed to the dark. We are told in the *Sophist* (254A):

> ELEATIC STRANGER The Sophist takes refuge in the darkness of Not-being, where he is at home and has the knack of feeling his way; and it is the darkness of the place that makes him so hard to perceive.
>
> THEAETETUS That may well be.
>
> ELEATIC STRANGER Whereas the Philosopher, whose thoughts constantly dwell upon the nature of reality, is difficult to see because his region is so bright; for the eye of the vulgar soul cannot endure to keep its gaze fixed on the divine.

It is equally wrong to think that we can put sight into blind eyes or knowledge into the soul, which were not there before. Yet, Cornford reminds us:

> The theory of Anamnesis was put forward to escape the sophistic dilemma; either we know a thing, and then there is no need to look for it; or we do not know it, and then we cannot know what we are looking for. The dilemma assumed that the only choice is between complete knowledge and blank ignorance. *Anamnesis provides for degrees of knowledge between these two extremes.*[2]

Just as the eye was unable to turn from darkness to the light without the whole body also turning, so, too, it is only by the movement of the whole soul that the instrument of knowledge can be turned from the world of Becoming toward that of Being, and can learn by degrees to endure the sight of the good and the true. Whereas the other virtues can be implanted by habit and exercise, the virtue of wisdom or of spiritual sight contains a divine element which is the identifying property or function of the soul. Sensual pleasures, like leaden weights, drag down the soul and turn its vision upon the things below, but if the soul is released from earthly impediments, the faculty of seeing the truth comes into full play.

Every detail of the Allegory of the Cave is significant. The entire Allegory could be interpreted in several ways–mystically, psychologically, or politically. It was Plato's genius that he could give us a parable replete with noetic wisdom, rich in symbolism, and suggestive of several seminal interpretations. His method was to descend from universals to particulars, to use his insight into the process of Becoming to derive lessons for personal and social life. He exemplified the ancient Hermetic maxim: "As above, so below." Recent interpreters have concentrated on the political moral to be drawn from the parable, and some since Nietzsche have wrongly regarded it as the poetic rationalization of a particular political outlook designed to make the philosopher acceptable in a polis. Plato explicitly states that the founders of the city must induce the best minds to continue ascending until they arrive at

2. Francis Macdonald Cornford, *Principium Sapientiae,* New York, Harper Torchbooks, 1965, p. 52.

the highest truth or ultimate good and then make them descend once more into the den and partake of honors and labors for which they do not care. They must become the benefactors of the entire community. They are not obliged to share in the toils of politics, but they must now share the fruits of their vision with their fellow men. Being Just Men, they will comply with the demands compassion makes upon them. The State in which the rulers are the most reluctant to exercise power is always the best. They alone command real authority, which requires a whole-hearted and single-minded concern with the good of all, excluding any self-protective preoccupation.

The upward ascent, which involves pain and struggle, will only be valid because of an exact correspondence between levels of reality, modes of knowing, and states of being. Who a man is reflects and determines what he really knows, which is connected with what he regards as real. Man determines what, and to what degree, things, objects of desire, and values will be real for him. To this extent, it is tempting to agree with Protagoras that man is the measure of all things. But as a reality-assigning agent, man is confronted with the philosophical question which Protagoras, a sophist and epistemological relativist, did not face: What is it about the world of nature that allows the existence of such a reality-assigning agent? There must be a sense in which there is a reality independent of individual minds and wills. There is also a subtle interplay between the reality that cannot be wholly grasped by the individual, and his own capacity to make that reality come alive through the self-conscious exercise of his reality-assigning function. He is able to grow in a direction that is in harmony with the whole of nature. If a man truly embodies what is implicit in the ascent from the Cave, he must realize the extent to which time and nature are on his side. He must prevail, but this idea of prevailing is much subtler and more elusive than any crude conception of survival or power. His moral growth is marked by an increase in the intensity and potency of his power of thought and ideation. The crucial assumption is that the mind of man, at any stage, is engaged in a mode of participation in planes of awareness divided into objects existing in relation to interdependent categories of space, time, and perception.

There are four stages of cognition on the Divided Line that may be viewed in this way (see Figure 2). At the lowest level are instantaneity and localization, the prison of the here and now. To be caught up in them is to be so lacking in critical distance from a given setting that nothing else can be seen. This mole-like life is restless, fantasy-ridden, and competitive in the extreme. It is often characterized through analogies with rodents or insects. At this level of existence, we engage in activities demeaning to the human status and even abdicate the privilege of being human. Such analogies usually tend to malign animals, because people cannot do what animals do with the natural precision of instinct. Nonetheless, this stage of consciousness is quite recognizable. Above it lies a second stage, which is much more dangerous than the first because it is the realm of pseudo-absolutization. It is characterized by opinions and ideologies that are only relatively true and therefore relatively false. The knowledge gained by comparison and contrast is contingent and not necessarily true. Many questions relative to space and time arise. Suppose someone advances the view that it is human nature to be selfish. One might ask what makes him say this? Where did he pick it up? What does it mean to him? How does he interpret it? Such questions begin to bring out the relativity of such assertions. Human beings at this stage, however, do not like the relativity of their opinions to be shown and tend to convey their assertions without qualification, as if they were totally true. They are made to look like immutable maxims, although, if they were, they would give strength and enable individuals or societies to maintain themselves without need of constant reinforcement. They would not leave people afraid of questions, or unable to consider the possibility of other ways of formulating similar truths. But pseudo-absolutization goes with dogmatism of the most insecure kind, which must be reinforced from outside by polls and by power, by this, that, and the other.

In the third stage, there are still limitations of space and time, but with a relative freedom from the here and now, and a cleaving to universal generalizations of given axioms. The supreme example is mathematics. Yet even the most central axioms in mathematics are conventional, and are based upon apparently arbitrary assumptions. In the third stage the degree of freedom from the relativities

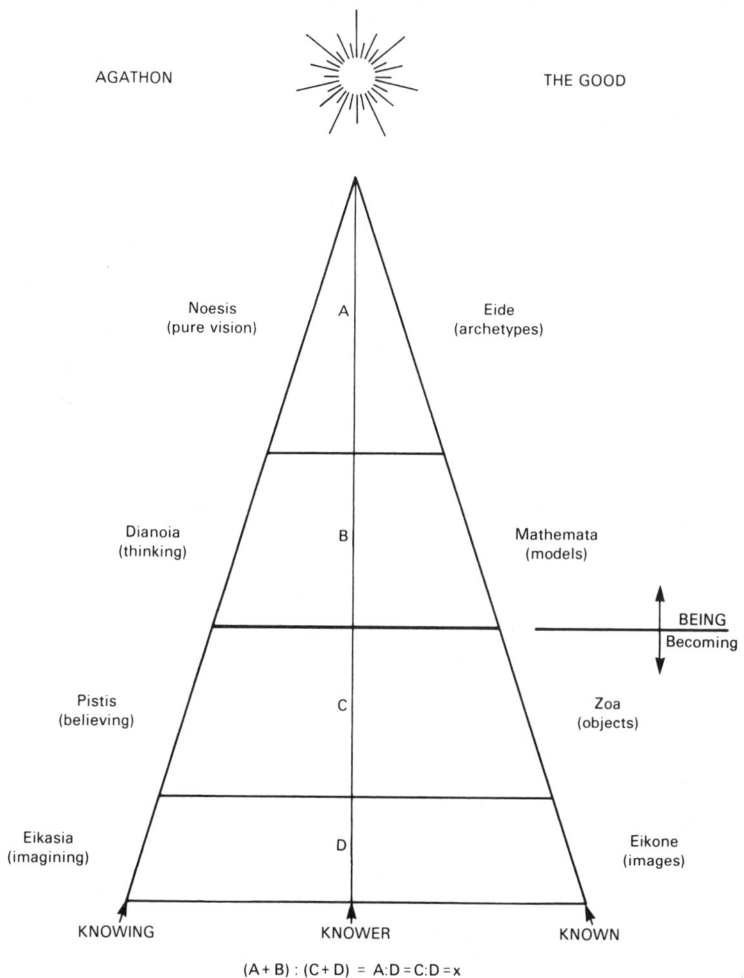

Figure 2. The divided line

of space and time may be secured at the cost of being unaware of lurking presuppositions which can act as mental blinders. This problem can be mitigated by critical distance wherein assumptions serve as aids to further questioning, leading to their step-by-step removal by treating them as hypotheses and stairways of ascent until the fourth stage is reached, or at least sensed. The fourth stage is *noesis,* in which there is almost total freedom from the ordinary limitations of space and time. There is a need to be flexible in formulation to progress beyond the third stage. But once the fourth stage is entered, there is a ready recognition that what is true without qualification can only be incompletely articulated or partially intimated at lesser levels. It can be embodied, but only imperfectly. Stenzel has described how, "Just as, in the strict sense, there cannot be an *appearance* of the Good, so, in the end, there cannot be *opinion* about it; the true Good can never become an object of δόξα [opinion] because it is an unconditional final end."[3]

The common feature of the Allegory of the Cave and the Divided Line is that, while in one way they point toward perfectibility, they also point to the redemptive principle that the less imperfect have access to more constructive ways of using and treating imperfections. This is crucial to parapolitics. The more a man grows toward perfection, the more patient he can be with imperfection, and the more innovative he can be in putting it to some use. He can be a wise and loving teacher able to teach anyone. He believes in the possibility and the magic of growth in each person, and can work within a person's range of aptitudes, helping his pupil to take a constructive view and make creative use of limits and conditions. Below the hidden summit, existences at each level of being and knowledge are as shadows cast by a magic lantern upon a colorless screen. These things cognized are therefore as real to him as himself. The practical problem of parapolitics is to discern the degree of reality which things possess while they move through the phenomenal world. This cannot be done so long as the only instrumentalities available are those wholly conditioned by the finite field of material limitations. On whatever plane political imagination may be acting, the observer and the elements on that plane constitute

3. Julius Stenzel, *Plato's Method of Dialectic,* ed. D. J. Allen, London, Russell and Russell, 1964, p. 49.

for the time being an apparent enclosure of reality. Together they not only provide a necessary basis for immediate action but also intimate future possibilities of enlightenment. What is true of individuals could apply to entire societies through a series of progressive awakenings that surpasses in scope any rationalist teleology or revolutionary utopianism. The painful movement culminating in the vision of the Agathon is only possible through a continuous articulation of the will in the service of universal sympathy. The ascent from the Cave requires a marriage of truth and love, of concentration and faith, which produces wisdom. If specific forms of politics are arts of the possible at particular stages in the dialectical process, then parapolitics involves the science of channeling the unbounded potential of the Agathon into particular contexts and situations within the Cave (see Figure 3).

The entire political moral of the parable bears a close resemblance to the pathway of the soul ever preparing itself for the perfect service of humanity. The parable also conveys the mystical teaching that, as the soul is initiated into the higher realms of being, it experiences a sense of strangeness, a new birth, until it has become accustomed to the sights and sounds of its higher plane of consciousness and becomes wholly indifferent to the lower impulses of earthly life. During the ascent the mystic comes to adore the Agathon, the invisible Sun, which gives sustenance to the whole universe, and to perceive the unity of all life and being. At the same time, the mystic who has chosen the path of renunciation, and not of liberation, must preserve his vision of the unity of the unseen universe while moving among the shadows of earthly existence–to bring back the soul's memory of its inward ascent and spiritual faculties while coping with the limitations of embodied existence in a phenomenal world. These truths pertain not merely to the mystic but to the psychological evolution of humanity. We are so overpowered by shadowy attractions and images that we needlessly shut ourselves from the light of archetypal ideas. Our earth–Plato's den–is only "the footstool of man in his ascension to higher regions," the vestibule

> . . . to glorious mansions,
> Through which a moving crowd forever press.

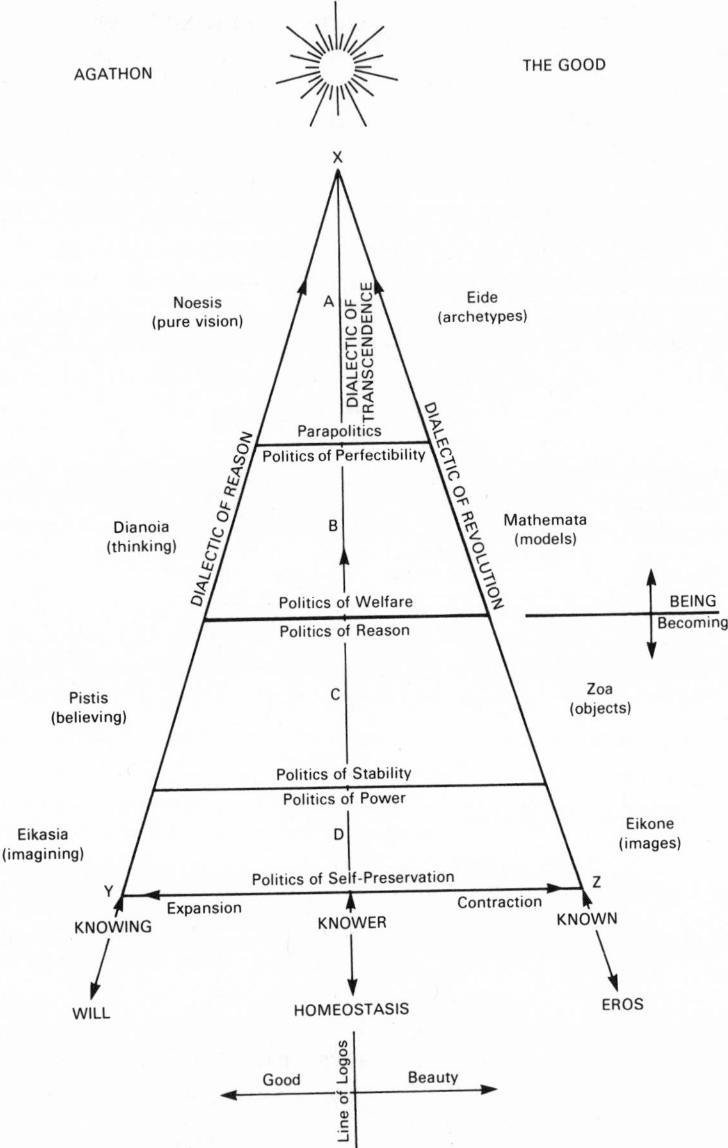

Figure 3. Politics and Agathon

The *Phaedo,* with its allusions to planes of reality and appropriate states of consciousness, generalizes at a psychological level the supernal truth underlying the Allegory of the Cave. In the *Republic* we are given the political and ethical corollary of this mystical truth. The ineffable and indefinable Agathon is beyond all conceptions of the good in the polis, and yet is ever relevant to each captive of the Cave, struggling in the darkness of mental obscuration and obstructed vision. The ethical and political redemption of persons and societies rests upon the existence of courageous predecessors who entered the light of the Agathon and cared enough to return to convey the promise and the possibility of freedom.

3
THE OPEN TEXTURE OF NATURAL LAW

It is reasonable to regard particular constitutions as "additions" to the one constitution agreeable to nature—just as civil laws are "additions" to the right reason of nature, and just as the political man is an "addition" to the man who lives in agreement with nature. PHILO JUDAEUS

The parapolitical conception of Natural Law is common to the cultures of the major civilizations as well as to the thought-patterns of less complex societies. It has recently been singled out as peculiarly empty. In the 1920s the economic historian, J. H. Clapham, designated the traditional categories of economic theory as empty boxes, useless though not intrinsically vacuous. In the 1950s there emerged several variants of the view that most of the basic categories of traditional political theory are empty of significance and may be dispensed with, at any rate in their older versions and former uses. Logical positivists declared that the concept of Natural Law is wholly empty of empirical content and cognitive meaning. Legal positivists contended that the concept is empty of operative force and practical import. Historians of ideas and sociologists have indicated that the concept is empty of precise connotation and unambiguous clarity. Political scientists have also assumed that the concept is empty of contemporary relevance and even theoretical value. For some of the early linguistic philosophers, the evident truth about Natural Law was essentially that, if introduced into any political controversy, it did not seem to change anything very much.

The argument that the concept of Natural Law is empty of empirical content rests upon the view that terms like "nature," "human nature," and "moral order" are confusing, misleading, and even dangerous abstractions. The claim is that the very generality of Natural Law breeds vagueness and generates disagreements which not only cannot be resolved but are fruitless and unmanageable. The concept is bereft of objective empirical referents and is burdened with a metaphysical flavor and a religious fervor that make it irrelevant to the quest for specificity in jurisprudence and effective communication in politics and society. A Natural Law assertion cannot be verified or falsified in experience, and disputants disagree not only on how much evidence is sufficient to verify or falsify it, but even as to what evidence would be relevant.

Let us take telling examples of Natural Law assertions:

"All beings seek self-preservation." (factual-seeming)
"All human beings are entitled to survive." (evaluative)
"A human being cannot seek self-preservation and with consistency deny the same right or urge to another." (a seemingly logical truth)
"All human beings are equally entitled to freedom of choice, thought, speech, and action." (evaluative)–liberty, negative or positive.
"All human beings are equally entitled to some minimal respect worthy of human stature." (evaluative)–minimal egalitarianism.
"All human beings are entitled to equal respect and equal opportunities of self-expression and self-fulfillment." (evaluative)–strict egalitarianism.
"No human being should act toward another in a manner that he or she would not wish anyone else to act toward him or her." (evaluative)–the Golden Rule.

Clearly, all these typical Natural Law assertions do not have the same logical status. In general, such assertions are not merely definitions of "man" or decisions of principle, and they certainly are not contingent truths. If we could correctly characterize them we might be in a position to show that the criticism of the logical positivists is irrelevant rather than false. Natural Law assertions are often about what a human being *must* be assumed to be, or how human beings *must* be treated if we are to assign abiding, universal, and meaningful status to being human; that is, if we are to regard all human beings (biologically defined) as rational and moral agents, or if we are to differentiate decisively between the human and other species of beings without detaching man entirely from nature. Feuerbach saw more clearly than anyone else what a theory of human nature must involve; sadly, Marx did not. It is important to concede that the word *must* necessarily introduces a metaphysical (a non-empirical as well as non-evaluative) element into every careful formulation of Natural Law. This notion of *must* or necessity is difficult to discard in moral and political philosophy as well as in the social and natural sciences. The function of *must* in formulations of Natural Law lies in the ambitious attempt to combine the notions of "it," "ought," and "can"–existence, norm, and potentiality. The theory of Natural Law apparently violates the Humean-Moorean canon that we cannot derive an "ought" from an "is," that merely because we say that x is the essential or defining characteristic of man, from such an assertion we cannot deduce a statement about what man ought to do. This is perfectly clear, and we do not need to commit the naturalist fallacy. Yet there would be no point in saying that man is x if we did not also imply that man is capable of y, that man is capable of being treated as a moral agent and as an object of praise and blame. The concept of Natural Law implicitly refers to the necessary conditions of human existence in the context of nature and society (pre-political, political, and parapolitical), but it also points to the undefined possibilities and shifting frontiers of human capacity and moral growth.

Inasmuch as the concept of Natural Law contains a minimal element, it is an attempt at the definition of "man" and the articulation of the foundations of human existence in a social and cosmic context. Insofar as it contains a maximal element, it is plainly metaphysical, passing beyond the boundaries of presently verifiable experience. However, between minimal and maximal ranges of meaning, the concept touches upon generally shared (or at least sharable) notions of human self-awareness, felt needs and ideals, common feelings of deprivation, self-alienation, and moral autonomy, as well as mutually recognizable signs of striving after a deeper and larger fulfillment than is capable of conceptualization. Natural Law has often been articulated with a stress on features that seem to be defined with dogmatic certainty, but essentially it expresses a deep sense of wonder, reverence, and agnosticism as to the unknown possibilities of human growth. It provides the needed critical distance from the dogmas of historicism, empiricism, and positivism (with their disguised metaphysics concerning the meaning of history, the finality of sense-experience, and the intelligibility of ordinary language within a particular social and legal system, culture, or polity at any given time).

The argument that the concept of Natural Law is empty of operative force rests upon the view that since the term "law" must be defined in terms of physical sanctions enforceable within the polity, consequently, the dependence of Natural Law upon theological, transcendental, or non-physical sanctions deprives the concept of the status of "law." But even positive law, though backed by coercive authority, relies for its effective and continuing operation upon a large measure of conformity, upon social sanctions, public opinion, and the internalization of externally determined obligations. This internalization is not merely a matter of civic status but reflects, however dimly and intermittently, a recognition of the moral stature of man and the conduct appropriate to a rational and self-conscious agent, endowed with a measure of free will and capable of choosing, deciding, assenting, and withdrawing support. Such a recognition lies behind Locke's deliberate shift from conscience to interest as the basis of human respect, Bentham's vain search for a clear and decisive criterion of choice and political action, Hume's reference to transubstantiation in the exchange of promises, and Durkheim's account of the transference of sanctity from religious to political and social acts. The notion of obligation, though attached to man-made laws, is prior to them, as Hobbes recognized. Otherwise it cannot be relied upon. It must be grounded in the nature of man.

The Enlightenment conception of progress did not make immediate or exclusive reference to nation-states, but was centered upon universal growth in knowledge and freedom, leading to a gradual reduction of inequalities within the conditions of all societies. Comtean positivism reduced this quest to the discovery and application of some single method of unification, amenable to institutionalization. When this method was applied to law, it became legal positivism. The first professor of modern jurisprudence, John Austin, declared law to be a command by a sovereign to a subject. He argued that this defining characteristic of law is backed by physical, psychological, and moral sanctions. The moral and psychological sanctions are unnecessary as long as the central authority behind the laws can apply physical sanctions inflicting penalties upon violators. Hence law is assured of continuance, can act as a stabilizing force, and will be the last appeal when men disagree. In any organized political community there must be a determinate, coercive, central, supreme, and sovereign authority that is the pillar of the legal system. In English history before James I, reliance was mostly placed upon common law. In Roman law, the emphasis was upon the term *lag,* having to do with laying down and collecting. To lay down a rule is to formulate it, making it into a formal rule. To state it is to make it statutory, because once stated by an appropriate procedure under an acceptable mode of authorization, it is binding upon those to whom it applies. The other function of *lag,* collecting, serves when a number of rules in society have achieved sufficient specificity to be assembled together, restated, and codified, thus reducing the multiplicity of precedents and practices, informal rules and conflicting laws. Law, however, cannot be understood merely with reference to external sanctions. It requires a certain necessary connection between the internal responses of individuals and the external sanctions prescribed. This link is crucial if law is to be respected. Men have no problem in respecting laws which they understand, which they can see are for their own good, helping them to restrain their own weaknesses. As long as men are weak, they can be protected by restraints. Laws do have a protective side, but this has little meaning in a human community if the link is lost between the external and the internal. Any stated law may be scrutinized in the light of reason. Anyone can ask, "Why is there this law?" There is also the question, "Why ought I to obey this law?" If the law cannot accommodate honest questioning and honorable disobedience by individuals like Antigone and Socrates, who are proudly willing to accept the consequences, that law will come to earn the moral contempt of the community.

In classical Greece, the term *nomos* had to do with measure. As early as Sophocles, *agraphos nomos,* the unwritten law, had divine sanction, and with the later Stoics it was grounded in nature (*physis*) as the immanent *logos*. *Nous* for Anaxagoras was both a cosmological principle as the source of all motion, and an immanent principle in all living beings. Diogenes qualified the principle, which he denominated *aer-nous,* by replacing mechanistic interpretations with the view that its activity is intelligent and forms the best possible *kosmos,* and it is expressed in the operation of a principle of measure among all things. In the later writings of Plato, *kosmos noetos,* the intelligible universe, is both produced and ordered by *nous,* which is inherent in all men. Plotinus drew the implication that *nous* is transcendent as the cause of *kosmos noetos* and is immanent in human beings, each of whom is, therefore, a *kosmos noetos*. The Stoics concluded that the human *nous* is a manifestation of cosmic *nous*. *Nous* represents a binding together of human minds as rays from one central source of cosmic intelligence. If every human mind is a participant in the thinking of all humanity, if every human being has access to the potential wisdom within and beyond nature, then there is a parapolitical majesty to law. But its grandeur can only be imperfectly transferred to the concretized laws of any social system. This view places man-made laws in the impersonal context of the natural order rather than of arbitrary custom and social prejudice. Rational beliefs may find in intelligent and intelligible nature those persisting laws which convey cosmic justice and apportion its minimal recognition among all moral agents. Yet, even if there are books in running brooks, nature is neither constant nor transparent in its unwritten revelation of law to ordinary men and women. How then do we clearly separate out those natural phenomena which give ethical direction from those which do not? Unless one dogmatically assigns a rigid teleology to nature, the principle of selection will always admit differing interpretations of phenomena. And even if the vast majority of men were to recognize the same laws as supported by and reflecting the *logos* in *physis,* what in nature allows them to compel the unconvinced minority to accept them?

The coercive element in positive law is its seeming source of strength but also its main source of moral weakness and practical inadequacy in the long run. As long as there is no internal sense of voluntary assent to the obligations prescribed by positive law, the attempts at successfully evading them will leave individuals guiltless to a greater or lesser extent under the politics of self-preservation. A man will despise himself more for violating standards he sets himself than those which he feels are imposed upon him or instituted without his tacit consent. Similarly, men are often judged more by the standards they set themselves than by those set by external agencies over which they have little or no control. Self-legislation, grounded in self-awareness, may rest upon, as well as induce, a deeper sense of obligation than could be evoked by external restraints. Thus the seeming weakness of Natural Law is, in fact, its real source of moral strength and significance. Its operative force depends very much upon the extent of self-awareness and the degree of humanity which men show themselves capable of and seek to attain in a given community.

In the modern age, the link has been broken between the internality of voluntary response by rational moral agents and the externality of events and consequences. To negate legal positivism is to increase the meaningfulness of law and at the same time to diminish the excessive worship of concretized law which claims too much. This is important to politics because it has a bearing on the sovereign state and the larger community. To see beyond legal positivism is to assert the ceaseless relevance of moral principles and rational assessment. We also need to see beyond existing legal systems. No logical system can be confirmed or interpreted from within itself. If any logical system is applied to social life or extracted from legal structures, it can only be applied by human beings through their exercise of voluntary thinking, reasonable interpretation, and seeing relevance in relation to examples, variables, and features in complex situations. Further, social norms may not be seen wholly in terms of any one simple view of how they are acquired, whether through developmental ethics, mechanistic sociology, or behavioristic psychology. The argument that the concept of Natural Law is empty of precise connotation rests upon the view that the terms used in Natural Law assertions are too ambiguous to be capable of authoritative and agreed interpretations. It is true that the concept has been formulated at different times in a variety of ways, and that it has been put to contrasted and contradictory uses in the course of history. However, empirical terms may have an open texture, especially terms like "coercion" and "compliance," which are critical to positive law. No doubt, the concept of Natural Law has a considerable degree of open texture as do most political and social concepts. The difference is one of degree rather than of kind. It is not possible to lay down in advance the limits to human self-awareness or to the enrichment and articulation of man's images either of his own true nature or the cosmic order of which he is an integral part.

It could be argued that even if there is a Natural Law, there is no reason to assume that man is capable of knowing it. And if we could never be certain in our knowledge of Natural Law, it cannot be relevant to our formulation and enforcement of positive law. The argument is plausible but it fails to distinguish between logical and epistemological concerns. The conceptual question, "What is justice?" is doubtless different from the epistemological question, "How do we know what is just in a given set of circumstances?" And yet, the two must be drawn together by thinking beings. It is this very difficulty that the concept of Natural Law attempts to meet. Whatever comprehensible attribute we predicate of both nature and of law must also be incorporated into our very notion of self. We must assume that man is a liberty-loving being, a justice-seeking creature, a being capable of love and truth and concord, if we are meaningfully to declare the values of liberty, justice, love, truth, and concord as universifiable and relevant to the human condition. The concept of Natural Law is designed to bridge the gap between man and nature by showing that they are consubstantial at least in certain respects, that human ends may be inserted into our conception of natural order, and that "ought" implies "can." It may be that the reason why the "is-ought" problem seems so intractable in complex structures is that traditional moral precepts are recognized more in the breach than in the observance. On the other hand, in Hopi culture, for example, ethical norms and kinship rules fit together so neatly that there is no striking "is-ought" problem, even though a comparative lack of alternative choices and contrary prescriptions may restrict the possibilities for moral self-consciousness or the search for universality.

The argument that the concept of Natural Law is devoid of contemporary relevance could take several forms, most plausibly that the metaphysical and religious presuppositions underlying the concept are no longer meaningful to man or part of his everyday vocabulary or taken for granted within any particular polity. It is true that the modern conception of Natural Law arose in the context of vast social change and tended to justify the revolutionary reconstitution of politics. As a "higher law," it could negate the privileges of tyrants while affirming individual rights within a liberated and enlightened collectivity. In the twentieth century, Natural Law is sometimes invoked to condone the complacent indifference of the intelligentsia and the bourgeoisie to the suffering of humanity. Nevertheless, the argument about contemporary relevance misses the point of the concept of Natural Law, which is concerned with the moral basis of rational consensus regarding the essential nature of man, to which appeals may be made regardless of the amoral beliefs and insensitive attitudes of some people in different societies and at different times. Since the eighteenth century we have come to place considerable if diminishing reliance upon the capacity of man to master nature and to transform society, upon the power of human reason to devise rules for conduct, criteria of conscious planning, and blueprints for society. The ideas have also taken root that if we grasp historical, social, and psychological laws, there is little or no room for praise and blame, and that impersonal institutions and processes are not to be assessed by the moral criteria applicable to personal conduct.

There have been several subtle attempts to incorporate nature into the very processes of history and society and even politics. To assert that a phenomenon is inevitable is apparently to show that it is irresistible, beyond criticism or amelioration, and even somehow right or fitting. We see such tendencies in Sorel's view that the use of force is natural; in Hegel's view that the State is a natural entity; in the earlier Machiavellian notion that it is natural (normal, inevitable, right) to put primary emphasis upon individual self-preservation and *raison d'état;* in Max Weber's conception of a rational-scientific ordering of society under a centralized bureaucracy in a sovereign nation-state; in the late-nineteenth-century view of automatic, unilinear, irreversible progress through technology; and in vulgar contemporary notions of modernization and of politicization. The most extreme example of this determinist tendency is the

Marxist "discovery" of historical laws as the sole basis of scientific socialism. Such doctrines involve attempts, whether calculated or innocent, to subsume the value judgments of particular social and political theories under the aegis of the objective and independent operations of nature. They seek both justification for the theories and a practical impetus for the programs which the theories promote. Rather than reducing the importance of Natural Law, these doctrines are actually debased or disguised versions of the appeal to fact inherent in Natural Law. As a result of all such theories and tendencies, many are led to assume that the abstract language of traditional moral theory is largely irrelevant in the study of politics and society. This is true only if pedants expect that the mere use of words is really going to change anything. Today the retributivist theory of punishment is fortunately losing its past dominance. In general, if social scientists think they can trace the impersonal causes of the psychological and social roots of deviant and criminal conduct, they are apt to conclude that individual offenders cannot help their actions and may not therefore be held morally culpable, even if they have to be dealt with by means of legal sanctions as a deterrent to others. But it is very difficult for human beings to dispense altogether with some notion of free will. Even if we wish to be agnostic about human nature, even if we are quite willing to suspend judgment about whether Eichmann, in a larger and deeper sense, could have acted differently, we must assume that he could have if we are to regard him as a member of the same human species as ourselves.

The costly consequence of the pervasive deflation of moral language is that we have no words with which to condemn the enormities of evil that our century has witnessed. Even if we no longer believe in human goodness and perfectibility, we seem to wish to retain our concept of human potentiality by pointing to the unlimited capacity for evil of insignificant individuals. It does not seem as if we can entirely dispense with the concept of Natural Law. Apart from anything else, we find today a growing distrust of all man-made laws, of the sovereignty of the State, traditional theories of political legitimacy, accepted modes of political legitimation, and conventional methods of political action. There is also the persisting quest for a world community, for a new order and law among nations, and even for a world authority and world law. We seem to be on the threshold of a profounder definition of man, enclosing greater possibilities for good and evil than earlier rationalists assumed, and of a fresh formulation of the concept of Natural Law which could make easier a more effective communication between morally sensitive individuals in all parts of the globe. While we may no longer believe in the constancy of human nature, an open view of human nature does not reduce the need for reflection upon what it means to be human, upon how the distinction between essentials and non-essentials may be drawn, or upon how our conception of human growth and possibilities may be enriched.

The real point of the concept of Natural Law is that it places the burden of proof squarely upon those who wish to justify murder or torture or untruth or inequality, rather than upon those who wish to invoke the sacred right to life, to liberty, to truth, and to a measure of equal respect. If contemporary proponents of Natural Law wish to avoid the moral dangers of theological casuistry, they must continue to deny that circumstances automatically alter cases. While circumstances may mitigate our moral judgments of persons, the laws upon which moral judgments of acts are based could be derived from the unchanging uniformities of the natural order. Although Natural Law *eo ipso* cannot be properly viewed as "a law of variable content," there is indeed a logical openness to the concept of Natural Law, a logically inescapable incompleteness in all formulations of Natural Law. There is a continual need to preserve a critical distance from each and every formulation. If the concept of Natural Law is empty, this is only another way of saying that the concepts of man, nature, and obligation are empty. All of these are capable of being packed with such moral significance and content as men choose to endow them in their quest for consensus. There is no finality in the attempt. There is ample room for discussion and even disagreement. But if the attempt itself were to be abandoned, our legal conventions, our images of the world, and our ideas of human dignity and growth would be emptied of moral worth and shrink in significance.

4
TOLERANCE AND CIVILITY

Our virtues should be touched with a certain nobleness, our morals with a certain freedom, our manners with a certain politeness. The virtues exhibited are always less what one owes to others than what one owes to oneself. MONTESQUIEU

The core of tolerance is the conviction that conflicts can and should be settled by reason, not by force, and this belief may often be founded on faith in the eventual vindication of truth. Civility, the virtue of the citizen, fosters the sense of fellowship felt by individuals with the society to which they belong. Tolerance makes possible the coexistence of competing forms of partisanship, while civility shows the willingness to transcend partisanship in the pursuit of the common good. Tolerance and civility alike point to the limitations of human powers, the folly of dogmatism and the futility of violence, and the common search for truth by responsible citizens in the service of the parapolitical Agathon. This provides the basis of protection for the inalienable freedom and the fundamental equality of all citizens united in their concern for truth and peace. To hold an opinion deeply is no doubt to throw feeling into it, but an awareness of fallibility can support a sufficiently strong sense of critical distance to prevent personal feelings from overriding the sense of human solidarity. Tolerance could be an act of faith in the ultimate victory of truth, or it may be a mere expedient to avoid the inconveniences of intolerance. Civility could spring from a profound sense of social obligation or it may arise out of a prudent awareness of the costs of violence and discord. Tolerance may degenerate into indifference, and passivity masquerade as civility. The more deeply founded is tolerance, the more meaningful and reliable civility becomes. The stronger the roots of civility, the richer the fruits of tolerance. Thus tolerance and civility constitute the minimal foundations as well as the mature graces of the good society.

Both concepts have evolved in the sacred and secular spheres of the world's great civilizations, finding their way into the parapolitical ideals and visions of all peoples. As the attainment of salvation in the Kingdom of Heaven lying beyond death requires suffering and penance, so too securing salvation in any earthly kingdom requires individuals to love and suffer each other as equally errant truth-seekers. As the pursuit of transcendental truth demands the strength to suffer the ordeals of the quest, so too the collective pursuit of truth in the midst of society and politics calls for the readiness to suffer for their convictions among those anxious to propagate their relative truths against the errors of implacable opponents and the apathy of the indifferent. The earnest seeker of truth in the social and political sphere soon arrives at a recognition of the need for tolerance and civility in the midst of those who wish to coerce others into compliance with their half-truths and exaggerated claims. In Platonic thought, *sophrosyne*–temperance, harmony, and self-mastery–is the essential civic virtue in the polis. In ancient Indian thought the idea of *satya* or truth meant far more than mere tolerance: it presupposed faith rather than skepticism. *Satya* was bound up with the conviction that it is possible for all men to progress through their experiments with relative truths toward the transcendental goal of *SAT* or Absolute Truth. Similarly, the modern doctrine of *ahimsa* or non-injury is concerned with far more than civility, presupposing not merely the conviction that coercion is futile but also the positive faith that non-violence could convert opponents into co-seekers, effectively resist injustice, remove untruth, and protect the weak against the strong.

In Europe, the ideals of tolerance and civility emerged from the protracted struggles of the sixteenth and seventeenth centuries, but it would be a mistake to think they were entirely new. In the ancient world tolerance came to be taken for granted within polytheistic societies and syncretistic civilizations. Quintus Symmachus gave succinct expression to the tolerance that was born from the coexistence of the multitude of cults and religions: "The heart of so great a mystery [as that of the Divine] cannot ever be reached by following one road only." The problem of tolerance becomes acute whenever an individual or group claims for itself an exclusive vision of absolute truth or the possession of a unique revelation embodied in a single scripture or system of beliefs. It is natural for fanatics to feel that they have the solemn duty of making the truth prevail by persuasion if possible, by force if necessary. Intolerance in the Old Testament arose whenever men thought themselves to be executing the will of Jehovah. For the early Jewish people and the prophet Elijah, there was no midway between God and Baal. History was a unique and universal drama moving inexorably toward its predetermined climax, and faith in religious truth meant trust in the ultimate victory of God as the Lord of history. Man belongs either to God or Satan and those fortunate to be on God's side must fight those who have thrown in their lot with the Enemy. Callous intolerance was the besetting sin of most apocalyptic theology, Jewish, Christian, and Islamic. Christian writers from Anselm to Calvin depicted the bliss of the righteous as the greater because of the spectacle of the tortures of the damned. The revengeful eschatology in apocalyptic literature since the Book of Enoch, the sharp division of men into good and evil, and the harsh judgment of the wicked and the unbeliever are repellent to us today. But it was natural for the medieval Church to persecute heretics because it believed itself to be in sole possession of the complete truth.

In both Judaism and Christianity there was a clear, continuous alternative to intolerance and incivility. While there was no place for tolerance within the theocracy of the Jewish people as conceived by the Torah, the Mosaic religion showed remarkable consideration toward those it regarded as heathens, a point repeatedly stressed in the tracts of Christians pleading for religious toleration during the sixteenth and seventeenth centuries. In the Bible itself, Elijah is rebuked for his excessive zeal and Abraham pleads for God's mercy and forgiveness. Later, Rabbi Joshua's doctrine of tolerance was powerfully reinforced by the notion of Natural Law which Judaism, along with Islam and Christianity, inherited from Greek philosophy, notably Stoicism. Christianity continued the earlier tradition of Hellenic Judaism, particularly of Philo, and eventually made its peace with the pagan world. However, the modern doctrine of toleration arose only with the emergence of religious individualism, the idea that every man has his own separate "wire to eternity," the claim to freedom of conscience.

The Reformation by itself did not result in religious liberty, but proclaimed the principle *cujus regio ejus religio* so that in each nation or regional unit the effective government determined which of the rival systems of Catholicism and Protestantism was to prevail. The confrontation between two exclusive forms of Christianity, each claiming to be the sole custodian of truth and denigrating the other as a diabolical perversion, led to some of the most bitter violence in modern history. It was analogous in some ways to the ideological conflict of today, the apparent absolute logical impasse between competing doctrines that can never meet—mutually exclusive systems, neither of which seems secure unless the other is undermined. In the post-Reformation period there were practical considerations that induced *politiques* in France to launch their direct assault on religious intolerance and to plead that the bloodshed must be brought to an end. Toleration was at first only a *pis aller,* the only feasible policy that remained when it proved impossible to go on fighting any longer. The Socinians were willing to tolerate any differences of opinion because of their indifference to matters of doctrine. But there were also those who pressed the case for freedom of conscience precisely on religious grounds. Religion was seen to be too important for one man to thrust upon another; even an entire society could not impose it upon an individual. The decisive moment came when the man who thought his religion absolute realized that he must grant this right to another's claim to his religion as absolute. Reverence for the superhuman cannot exclude a minimum respect for every human.

Although the notions of tolerance and civility found political expression only in the modern era of individualism and nationalism, the connection between truth and goodness was affirmed by early Christian as well as by Renaissance thinkers. Saint Augustine had distinguished between *ratio scientiae* and *ratio sapientiae,* human reason and the grace of God, wisdom and faith. Saint Thomas sought in the *Summa* to identify goodness, the object of will, with truth, the object of reason. Truth and good include one another; for truth is something good, or otherwise it would not be desirable; and good is something true or it would not be intelligible. The intellectual and moral virtues are subsumed by the indispensable virtue of prudence, equated with *recta ratio gibilium,* "right reason about things to be done." This *recta ratio,* derived partly from Stoic sources, is that immutable coalescence of truth and goodness whose source is divine and whose formative cosmic function is revealed in all the workings of nature. The Stoic concept of right reason is based upon the assumption, with affinities to Socratic thought, that knowledge and virtue are in their ideal state one and the same. For Epictetus, good and evil lie entirely within the control of man's will. The power of judgment which belongs to the soul implies by its very nature the will to right action as long as there is the desire to know the truth. Just as it is the nature of every soul to assent to what is true, dissent from what is false, and withhold judgment in what is uncertain, so it is its nature to be moved by the will to obtain good and the will to avoid evil. This philosophical conception lies at the heart of Renaissance optimism and recurs in Milton, who tried to ground truth in morality, and show that to think right is to do right, both truth and goodness being intelligible to the faculties that belong to man *qua* man. Erasmus, too, and Christian humanists in general, believed that ideally all man's faculties may be fused in the pursuit of that goodness which constitutes the highest truth.

With the breakdown of traditional religious authority, the vacuum was filled by the postulation of a law of nature which represented those moral absolutes that are binding on human conduct. In Hooker's theocratic universe all forms of knowledge are modes of goodness in that they derive from the wisdom of God. For Hooker as for Socrates knowledge is virtue, for in doing evil "we prefer a less good before a greater, the greatness whereof is by reason investigable and may be known."[1] With neo-Stoicism and the growth of Deism we find the increasing secularization of this religious conception of the correspondence of reason and piety. Both movements represent the search for those approachable absolutes—metaphysical, epistemological, and moral—which the accretions of time and error had obscured. Jeremy Taylor declared that all violence is an enemy to reason and counsel. The Cambridge Platonists asserted the validity of the human quest for religious truth and sought to subordinate the doctrinal struggles of their age to a sim-

1. Richard Hooker, *Of the Laws of Ecclesiastical Polity,* New York, E. P. Dutton, 1907, I. vii. 7.

ple morality of charity and toleration. The dignity of man consists in the fusion of truth and goodness, the manifestation of the latter being the first fruit of the successful pursuit of the former. He knows most, who does best.

The belief in the connection between truth and goodness was based upon a metaphysical certainty and a secure optimism that might lead men to cherish the virtues of tolerance and civility. They could also, however, be derived from philosophical skepticism and a humbling awareness of the limits rather than the potentialities of human faculties. We find this typically expressed in Montaigne's *"Que sais-je?"* and Cromwell's "I beseech you, in the bowels of Christ, think it possible you may be mistaken." The skeptic is aware of the human propensity for the static and his emphasis is more upon the means to arrive at a decision than upon the decision itself. It is better to begin in doubts than in certainties, to care for processes rather than for results. The seeker after truth is involved in a ceaseless struggle with himself and is, therefore, more likely to tolerate than to coerce others. He is both humble and open-minded, and willing to question from a critical distance those features of society that others regard as sacrosanct. His confidence in the power of truth is matched by his conviction that he has not yet apprehended it.

Renaissance skepticism found its fruition in the seventeenth century, marked by a passion for the pursuit of truth and a steady movement toward tolerance. If truth is one, equally available but also equally elusive to all men, it seems unreasonable to make a serious issue of creedal differences and go to war over them. A theory of progressive revelation was evolved and there was a positive confidence, as in the *Areopagitica,* that truth is armed with sufficient power to overthrow all error. There was a shift in emphasis from speculation to conduct, from contemplation to action. What men do is vastly more important than what they think they know. The road to truth can be traversed only by a soul which through right action has been rendered pure. Richard Baxter said:

> Truth is absolute, knowledge relative. Truth in itself one and entire, is reflected diversely in a myriad of facets in the reasons of men. . . . Pride then stops the process of search and discovery, or distinguishing the true from the false, by

> which knowledge grows, while we go about extirpating not error, which is always with us, but our opponents, who may be wiser than we.[2]

Falkland similarly recommended a skeptical humility, a search for truth which would absorb every man and leave him disposed to permit to every other man the same freedom. There was an increasing reluctance to accept blindly any traditional authority. Truth must be sought, not prescribed. Thus in Europe the powerful and prolonged impact of messianic and missionary religions had made it inevitable that minimal notions of tolerance and civility should acquire a distinct importance at a time of religious doubt and skepticism, when men were sick of civil wars in the name of religion.

In India, on the other hand, the Emperor Asoka in 250 B.C. was not only the first-known sovereign to exalt the virtues of tolerance and civility but also the first to enact religious toleration. Hinduism, which was someimes messianic but never missionary until recent times, had been confronted by Buddhist religion, which was missionary but not messianic. Asoka's Twelfth Major Rock Edict was an earnest and thoughtful plea for toleration among the various sects of the day. Toleration was not passive sufferance but an active search for dialogue and concord, based upon the conviction that in the honoring of other sects lies the welfare and honor of one's own. An individual or a group is enhanced by the display of active tolerance and genuine fellow feeling. Concord was regarded as universally meritorious and it was required that all sects should learn and benefit from each other. The Twelfth Edict declared:

> On each occasion one should honour another man's sect, for by doing so one increases the influence of one's own sect and benefits that of the other man. . . . Again, whosoever honours his own sect or disparages that of another man, wholly out of devotion to his own, with a view to showing it in a favourable light, harms his own sect even more seriously. Therefore, concord is to be commended, so that men may hear one another's principles and obey them.[3]

2. William Haller, *The Rise of Puritanism,* New York, Columbia University Press, 1938, p. 189.
3. Romila Thapar, *Asoka and the Decline of the Mauryas,* Oxford, Oxford University Press, 1961, p. 255.

In the long course of Indian history since the time of Asoka, during centuries of alien rule, tolerance had become a misnomer for complacency and indifference, and fatalistic passivity was passed off for meekness. Hypocrisy and cowardice coexisted with contempt and cruelty, often in a latent form. Genuine seekers after truth retreated to the solitude of the cave. Gandhi, drawing upon the Jain tradition, infused new meaning into salvation and suffering, tolerance and civility, in the context of political and social activity. In Jain thought, the doctrines of *anekantavada* and *syadvada* espouse the view essential to parapolitics that many apparently conflicting judgments are possible about any subject and each gives only a partial truth as everything has multiple facets or aspects. *Anekant* logic both validates man's capacity to know the truth and provides him with criteria by which to test the relativity and the extent of error in his knowledge. Everything may be seen differently by different people and in different spatio-temporal contexts. On the other hand, the doctrine of *syadvada* is based upon the belief that everything in the universe is related to everything else and hence we ought not to narrow our vision by taking account of only one set of facets or relations. To do so is to generate not merely a variety of conflicting dogmas but also personal bitterness and destructive conflict. The greater our sympathy with others and our imaginative identification with their particular situations, the less constricted is our parapolitical vision and the less partial our perception of the truth.

The portion of truth we possess is authenticated by the extent of empathy we display toward others who differ from us. This in turn is a function of the critical distance we maintain toward our own beliefs. Bitterness is all too often the cause, and not merely the consequence, of bias and intolerance. The distrust which men everywhere display toward their adversaries, at all stages of historical development, may be regarded as the immediate precursor of the notion of ideology. When this distrust of man toward man becomes explicit, conflicting groups detect an ideological taint in the utterances of each other. The notion of ideology, according to Karl Mannheim, "refers to a sphere of errors, psychological in nature, which, unlike deliberate deception, are not intentional, but follow inevitably and unwittingly from certain causal determinants."[4] In the past, when vital beliefs were passionately held by some and meant nothing to others, the charge was often made by the former against the latter that their dissent or apathy was willful. Heretics have been persecuted not only for holding views that were not orthodox but also for their obstinacy in refusing to abandon them. This intrusion of the will into matters of belief was called by Pico della Mirandola in the fifteenth century *actus tyrannicus voluntatis,* a tyrannical act of the will, which could arise within a church or against it. These tyrannical acts of the will need not, however, be confined to external pressures, as our will sometimes interferes internally with our recognition of the truth. A man who is full of violence is normally unable and unwilling to give up a theory or an intellectual position to which he has become attached or which seems to be in his interest to maintain. But if a man holds to truth without any violence or any egotistic concern, then no external pressure on his will can affect his inward conviction.

If we are dogmatic only to the extent of the inadequacy of our experience, then we may become more tolerant as we gain the wisdom of experience through "truth in action." A political judgment is made true only when it works satisfactorily in experience. Values without action are barren; action without values is blind. A society is tolerant and open insofar as free choice is maximized and the use of pressure to enforce social norms is minimized. The habit of philosophical doubt does not justify lack of commitment in fundamental matters of social action. Every sovereign principle, other than that of truth, every ideology that pretends that it must never be put in doubt, in the interests of society or civilization or something else, becomes the natural basis for dogmatism or fanaticism. In Socratic terms, all *logos* must be submitted by its author or follower to critical examination, with the same sincere will to understand the criticism of others and, if necessary, to proceed to the requested corrections and adjustments of views which the other participants in the dialogue are expected to show. Such a common pursuit is impossible except in a community which ac-

4. Karl Mannheim, *Ideology and Utopia,* London, Routledge & Kegan Paul, 1960, p. 54.

cepts the need for civility. The fact that a truth-seeker sees no error in his relative truth obliges him to pursue it actively in the midst of society. The possibility that he may be in error obliges him not to inflict harm upon others.

In an age when civility has been reduced to little more than adherence to mechanical social conventions and tolerance has been debased as impotent resignation to the presence of a welter of competing cults, systems, movements, and dogmas, the classical ideal of *sophrosyne* deserves careful reconsideration. Tolerance and civility can be derived naturally enough from perception of moral diversity in the world and our awareness of other sentient beings deserving sympathetic and just consideration, but as passive virtues they degenerate into shams. In the classical world *arete,* excellence or virtue, was not a passive or static mode of response to a homeostatic *physis* or a well-ordered polis. The virtues were strengths, and were truly meant to be cultivated in active response to the music of the spheres and a macrocosmic order. The polis was a microcosmic whole, the structure and growth of which depended upon the *arete* of its citizens. Man may be distinguished but never separated from nature, and human inventiveness is a mirroring of the demiurgic impulse in the cosmos, which when turned against nature will destroy the offender. Hence *sophrosyne* was the crucial political virtue. It was conspicuously absent in Homeric heroes like Achilles and Ajax, who exemplified *megalo psychos* or high-mindedness without the saving grace of *sophrosyne.* Such tragic heroes are doomed when the *Moirae* reckon their strengths and weaknesses, for they are fatally flawed at some point in the critical juncture of mind and nature, thought and action. Sophocles contrasts Ajax with Odysseus to highlight the tension between *agathos* and *sophron,* between the heroic and the sober, the high-spirited and the self-restrained. Odysseus may have suffered far longer than Ajax, but Odysseus survives and contributes to the rectification of a world which men's competitive passions have deranged.

Plato renders *sophrosyne,* soundness of mind, in social terms as balance, proportionality, and judiciousness in action. His daring insistence on seeing the cardinal forms of *arete*—courage, sobriety, justice, and wisdom—in terms of thought, feeling, speech, and action in all classes of citizens, converts individual graces into civic virtues, parapolitical requirements for any healthy polis. *Sophrosyne* can no more be a mere cautious reaction to events than tolerance can be indifference or civility can be moral cowardice. When in *Charmides* the whole of Athens is celebrating the *sophrosyne* and beauty of Charmides, Socrates remains adamantly agnostic. Admired and adored by many, Charmides can either use his natural endowments to exalt himself at the expense of the polis, or he can become an effective leader in public service. For Socrates the supposed *sophrosyne* of Charmides is merely the mannerliness and civility of a shy youth who has yet to realize the range and limitations of his own powers. There is nothing simple or spontaneous about self-restraint and balance. *Sophrosyne* requires rigorous mental training and the consummate mastery of skill in action. Critias goes so far as to maintain that the Delphic injunction "Know thyself" is the strict equivalent of "Be temperate (*sophrosyne*)." Since Socrates sums up his whole life as an attempt to plumb the depth of meaning in the Delphic imperative, his own life and activities, as portrayed by Plato, may be seen as a search for wisdom through the calm cultivation of *sophrosyne*.

Sophrosyne, as a parapolitical virtue, is the elusive precondition for the ethical continuity of a developing moral community. Visibly, it is doing one's work, fulfilling one's duty with cheerfulness and role-precision. For Plato the dialectic of interior growth cannot be separated from the civic activity of the "social self." The creative performance of duty is essential to the well-being of the polis and is also the way to self-knowledge. Ethically, *sophrosyne* is bound up with realizing the good in social encounters. While Aristotle reduced *sophrosyne* to a fluctuating mean (*meson*) between pleasures and pains, an arithmetic formula for effective survival and maximizing fulfillment, the Platonic concept was a geometric aid to continual growth. Doing what is good is bound up with the progressive discovery of the Agathon in and through its myriad reflections. Later the Stoics rendered *sophrosyne* as actual knowledge of the good to be chosen and the evil to be avoided. Plotinus made this mode of knowing an integral part of the mystical self-purgation required for the self-conscious return to primordial Unity. Moral sincerity is critical to *sophrosyne* and if it is absent—or worse, if its simulacrum is used as a mask for manipulation and indulgence–self-deception will be the result. The existentialist concern with *mauvaise foi* is a natural response to the prevailing hypocrisy of seeking selfish ends by employing ethical language. Socrates warned that if one pursued this course to the point of no longer being able to distinguish between sincere efforts and self-centered ruses, one is plunged into Tartarus, where redemption from disintegration is impossible. One has cut oneself off from the nascent sense of perfectibility which is the original plank of salvation for individuals and societies. If, however, moral earnestness is devoid of ever-expanding eros, it obscures the possibilities of self-cultivation in the social context of an imperfect community of fallible human beings, and in time results in moral bankruptcy.

Sophrosyne is a subtle balance of self-development and concern with the growth of the whole, self-restraint and willing generosity in the judgment of all others, sound perspective and social flexibility, and a constant awareness of the interdependence of individual and collective aspirations and fulfillment. *Sophrosyne* is the basis of continual endeavor toward the greater good, ceaseless perfection in act and intention, progressive self-knowledge and wisdom in conduct, and *harmonia* in the Pythagorean sense. It is guided by that toward which it aspires, and elevates and transforms all who would cultivate it. *Sophrosyne* is rooted in the harmony archetypally exemplified in nature, and provides the parapolitical foundation of the common quest for *dikaiosune* in the polis. The cultivation of *sophrosyne* transcends every set of finite goals and may be seen as the fusion of relative truth and partial love which individuals are able to attain at any given time. If we are constant and consistent in our quest for truth, and show *sophrosyne,* we come closer to others. But, unless we are initially prepared to treat our fellow men with some respect and sympathy, the common pursuit of truth in society cannot commence. Truth needs no violence for its diffusion; it is, in fact, obscured by violence. Violence is a symptom of insecurity and incomplete conviction–it makes victory more important than truth, distorts the truth, and renders its free acceptance more difficult. No one can be forced to become free or to see the truth. Partial truth, blindly held and imposed on others against their will, thrives temporarily on violence and pins its faith on immediate results, formal assent, and illusory triumphs.

The attainment of truth is the parapolitical goal of all men, but the practice of civility and self-restraint is the immediate test. Men may legitimately disagree about the truth while they are still engaged in this unending quest, but they must agree at all times about the need for agnosticism. Tolerance presupposes civility. Stimulated by the enthusiasm of eros, tempered by civility, and refined by *sophrosyne,* the tolerant pursuit of truth can become an entire way of life for individuals and an ethical prerequisite for communities.

5
EQUALITY IN THEORY AND PRACTICE

"In all such theories," said he,
"One fixed exception there must be.
That is, the Present Company."
LEWIS CARROLL

Is it possible to find an unequivocal if minimal formulation of the principle of equality that could be accepted by people with very different presuppositions about the world and about human nature, with very different convictions about political methods and the political process itself? Secondly, does the difficulty in addressing this question connect in any way with the ideological and practical quandary of the democratic Left in a Welfare State? By simple and familiar moves, we can push the analysis of the abstract concept of equality to the point where the practical argument can be generated, while revealing the ideological impasse in the protracted debate between the Left and the Right of the spectrum of partisan politics. Political dialogues about equality are sometimes irrelevantly involved with the question of whether men are or are not equal, or in what senses they are equal and in what senses they are not. Crude political controversy has focused on this issue because it seems a testable matter, to which empirical and statistical evidence is relevant. We cannot, however, conclusively decide on the basis of empirical evidence alone whether men are or are not equal, and therefore we are left with dubious assertions rather than compelling evidence. Even if we take a variant of the question, going back to Rousseau's *Discourse,* and distinguish between natural and conventional inequalities, we are still faced with the difficulty that we cannot draw any sharp and decisive distinction without common or convergent presuppositions about nature and man, conventional structures and the causal processes at work in society.

Belief in equality–the view that unless there is a reason recognized as sufficient by some identifiable criterion, no man should be preferred to another–is a deep-rooted principle in human thought. It is also a deceptive palliative to self-regard, untempered by critical distance. It has been assimilated into utilitarianism, theories of natural right, and diverse religious doctrines. Yet it can be isolated from all of them because it has entered them less by way of logical connection than by psychological affinity, stemming from a craving for symmetry and unity that is at the root of all such theories. In its extreme form egalitarianism requires the minimization of all differences between men, the obliteration of the maximum number of distinctions, the greatest possible degree of uniformity and assimilation to a single pattern. For all differences are capable of leading to irregularities of treatment. If this strict ideal is, on the whole, rejected in actual political doctrines, this is mainly due to the fact that it conflicts with other ideals with which it cannot be wholly reconciled. Indeed most ethical and political views are forms of more or less uneasy compromise between divergent principles of equality which in their extreme form cannot coexist. Considering the issue from the representative standpoints of the Left and the Right in a democratic Welfare State, we may inquire: Upon what does the debate on equality really turn? Is it the factual equality of persons as rational agents, a proposition taken for granted by some thinkers of the Enlightenment? Or is it equality in moral capacity and creative potentiality, an untestable assumption held by a few humanists of the Renaissance? This kind of discussion is completely irrelevant to the main practical issues, but the Left is occasionally forced to play into the hands of the Right by talking as though the crucial issue is about whether people are or are not equal. The question is not whether they are or are not equal, but how they should be treated–whether it makes sense to say that all persons are deserving of equal consideration or all persons are equally deserving of due consideration as human beings. For, indeed, if all persons were equal in every single respect, they would no longer be persons. There would be the kind of identity or equivalence that would make irrelevant any moral principle of equality. It is part of any meaningful conception of man that each is uniquely different from other men. This must necessarily be so, if man is not a thing, a machine, an animal, or an angel. It is precisely because we know that persons are plainly unequal in a variety of ways that we wish to consider the relevance of the imperative, "Treat every man as man," or of the principle, "All persons are equally deserving of consideration."

But what could be the point of saying something so vague and general? In ethics, the principle of universalizability declares that we cannot draw different moral conclusions about similiar cases. While universalizability is plagued by the philosophical problem of relevant similarity and the practical problem of significant versus superficial appearances of similarity, abandonment of the principle would destroy moral judgments in favor of expressions of attitudes, desires, intentions, or inclinations. The principle of universalizability suggests formal grounds for the concept of impartiality–the notion that people in similar situations should be treated similarly. Although the universalizability principle cannot preempt the question of relevant characteristics of cases, the impartiality principle presumes that all human beings are relevantly similar. In this sense, the impartiality principle is more than a formal principle derived from universalizability. It forms the foundation of the egalitarian imperative, which affirms the fundamental solidarity of humanity.

In politics and in society we classify persons in a variety of ways for different purposes. This is why the realm of political discourse is apparently so different from that of morals, where one considers man *qua* man as a member of the widest conceivable class, i.e., humanity. However, there is the significantly recurring need in political discourse to look at the citizen not merely as a member of a polity or a class, a vocational or functional or ethnic or territorial group, but also as nothing less than a member of humanity. The simplest Natural Law formulation of equality–"All men are equally deserving of due consideration"–means that everyone who is biologically human is deserving of the same consideration that is owing to any man solely by virtue of his being a moral agent. There is sad confusion when some egalitarians fail to distinguish a descriptive claim about what men are from a normative recommendation about how they ought to be treated. One who believes in equality need not insist that all individuals, races, or ethnic groups are exactly alike in every way; nor that all discernible differences have a biological or environmental explanation. Human beings could be dissimilar in some of their biological characteristics and cultural proclivities without undermining our commitment to equality as a moral ideal. If we do not say this, we are going to incur terminological problems. The supporter of apartheid, for instance, could be a sincere believer in equality. He simply defines man in a special way, assigning race priority over removable distinctions. "Treat every man as man" implies that no man can *a priori* claim a special status or privileged position, let alone a superhuman authority over any other human being, or any kind of authority that would mitigate or diminish the moral autonomy of any or every other man. More pertinently, the imperative implies that no man is to be treated as less than man, as less than a moral or rational agent, as a being not endowed with free will or self-awareness.

This general formulation makes sense, despite its necessary abstractness and vagueness, and it certainly would not be repudiated at this level by any true liberal, genuine socialist, or enlightened conservative. The above formulation is compatible not only with "natural" inequalities (whatever they may be) but also with functional as well as irrational or conventional inequalities—in income, property, and social status. The landed artistocrat or the factory owner in the nineteenth century could have sincerely thought that he was treating those he employed on his estate or in his factory as men, even if he did not recognize any minimal standards or basic rights in regard to income or hours of work. What we mean by consideration for every man as a man plainly depends upon what our image of man is and what we think men are obliged to accept as their own evident responsibility toward their fellow men. Hence, there is really no way of enlarging the practical force and ethical content of the imperative, "*Treat every man as man*" (Principle I), other than by revising one's own image or definition of man. This imperative could be made the basis of some minimum level of Natural Law in politics and society, a minimum which all persons could justify and apply in different ways. Equality in a polity would be enhanced to the extent that functional and conventional inequalities are set aside in favor of the neutral features presumably attributable to all men. We could regard all men merely as rational agents or as creatures of a single creator or God, or as sentient beings endowed with the divine spark of creativity, or simply as persons capable of some measure of free will and self-awareness.

Even before the nineteenth century, people had come to accept the notion of equality before the law. Beginning in the third decade of the nineteenth century, many people came to accept that treating all men with due consideration involves granting to all certain minimum political and civil rights, especially the right to vote. By 1914 people came to see that treating persons with proper consideration involves accepting the obligation by the State and by private parties to make available to all members of society minimum compulsory education. All these concrete applications, for which liberals and conservatives alike claim credit, are quite compatible with numerous differences and social inequalities. From the standpoint of the Left, extensions of equality could regrettably be made compatible with the right to inheritance. Locke ingeniously argued that rejection of the right to inheritance would mean that a man's property would fall into the hands of the State, which is a retroactive abrogation of his own right to property while he is alive. Since the State has no legitimate claim, his nearest descendant is morally entitled to appropriate the property. This will clearly not do for the Left, and so it has to invoke a stronger formulation of the principle of equality. The Left accepts the first formulation, "Treat every man as man." But it argues that even to attain this, a number of concrete measures are needed that can only be justified under a stronger formulation of the principle of equality. Thus the full-blooded egalitarians appeal to a stronger imperative, "*Treat every man as one,*" as one unit, no more and no less (Principle II). It is not enough to regard all men as equally deserving of due consideration; it is necessary to regard them as deserving equal consideration. This means not merely equality before the law, but also equal access to the law. To the extent to which the stronger version of equality contains a Benthamite element, this means recognizing every man's right to happiness, to his own interest, and the equal right to have his interests and his happiness safeguarded or promoted by the State. The Left argued after 1945 that if a man has equality before the law without equal access to the law, in fact there is no equality before the law. It would be like saying that all men are equally entitled to go to the Hilton when only a few can afford to do so. In other words, the Left has, in effect, refused to accept the Hobbesian distinction between right and power as naturally and even divinely ordained.

Hobbes had argued that man, unlike God, is a weak creature—afraid of death, motivated by self-interest, and driven by covetousness. Man does not have the necessary power to back up the natural right to which he could lay claim. Therein lies his predicament. This necessitates allegiance to a sovereign authority to a degree sufficient to enable it to secure for all men the right to self-preservation. But if we argue, against Hobbes, that we cannot in practice make this firm distinction between right and power, we could then further assert that *any* right that does not have at least a measure of power to back it is not a "right" at all. So by invoking the stronger formulation, the Left is able to ask for the abolition of the right to inheritance: death duties and capital taxes are legitimate. The Left is entitled under the stronger principle to ask for the removal of every kind of social pressure and inherited status which militates against equal access to the voting process and the most vital resources of society, invoking the notion of equal opportunities. Thus, we also get the ascription of responsibility to the State in regard to full employment, health insurance, and grants to make universal education possible. In short, the State must recognize the rights derived from presumed natural equalities by using every means at its disposal to empower individuals to exercise those rights. It is at this point that the difficulty appears which throws light on the present predicament of the Left in the Welfare State.

All the concrete gains that can be justified under the stronger formulation (Principle II) can be smuggled back under the earlier formulation (Principle I). If "Treat every man as one" means that every man is entitled to education, to full employment, to minimum social security, and so on, all these concrete gains which the

Left achieved by promising them to the greater portion of the electorate in a democratic system can then be retrospectively endorsed by the Right. If in a Welfare State all parties have broadened their notion of what is owing to man, treating every man as man comes to mean universal education, full employment, and social security for all. Hence we do not now seem to need the further principle, "Treat every man as one." This looks like the stealing by the Right of the clothes of the Left but there need be nothing heinous about this. If the Left truly believes in its own arguments, and because it does accept Principle I, and if it wants Principle II only as a way of ensuring Principle I, clearly it cannot complain if a good deal of what may be achieved by invoking Principle II can now be quite legitimately subsumed under Principle I through broadening the notion of the minimum standards of human existence. Principle II is the lever for moving parties to interpret broadly Principle I. Nevertheless, this seemingly innocuous reincorporation of the gains made through invoking the stronger principle under the umbrella of the weaker creates a host of problems for the Left. Why does the Right not wish to go any further? Why does it want to stick to the first formulation alone? To the Left it looks as if there is something nefarious about this, in the sense in which Bentham spoke of "sinister interests." Owing to the very nature and structure of capitalist society, although the upper classes are prepared to part with a measure of their income or power in a democratic system and are even willing to broaden the notion of what is owing to every man, they will not go beyond minima because they are determined to maintain their own position of privilege, and thus to protect the continuance of something called "the Establishment." There is presumably an invisible fortress in which hide sinister persons who effectively prevent society from making further moves toward equalization because they are extremely cunning. They are able to persuade working men in conditions of precarious full employment and deceptive affluence that the centrist politicians can more effectively deliver the goods than the extremists, and that they do not now need to turn to the old-fashioned Left merely to extend benefits to old-age pensioners, unskilled immigrants, or underprivileged foreigners.

Now, while this looks perfidious and brazen to the old-style

Left, from the standpoint of the Right there is something odious about the boring insistence of the Leftists of the present in wanting to go further than Principle I. To the Right it looks as if the Left simply will not accept the limitations of the political process, especially in an overstrained Welfare State. The Left is bedeviled by the absurd notion that all men *are* in fact equal, even if it is only talking about how all men *ought* to be treated. To the Right, it looks as though the Left wants to do too much within the program of any responsible government in an essentially two-party democratic system. It wants too much taxation; it wants to overextend the democratic process; it will not learn from the lessons of nationalized industry; it is still hoping for a change in human nature merely through social engineering, through tinkering with social institutions, instead of coming to terms with the fact of the relative constancy and fragility of human nature, and the limits of planned social change in conditions of freedom. There is a dangerous impasse and the temptation of brinkmanship. At this point various assertions are made on the Right which the Left counters by using arguments that turn upon contingent or empirical matters. Such arguments obliterate critical distance by converting a moral principle into the ideological basis of endless political controversy with regard to policy formulation.

First of all, there is the familiar argument from scarcity and productivity. If one says, "Treat every man as one," and seeks to equalize the access of all men to the goods of society, one will find that owing to the necessary limitation upon the resources of any society, there is the endemic danger of reducing the rate of productivity of the entire system. By vitiating the best use of the available goods, the net result will be to give so minute a portion of whatever good one seeks to distribute equally that the social consequences are not conducive to happiness or to any tangible advantage. To this, of course, the Left has its hoary answer–that by better State planning, by greater concentration of control over the key industries, the experts can indeed do more for productivity than is possible at present. This seems tedious simply because some measure of it is now accepted as implicit in the smooth functioning of the modern State, and the question is whether one can have more planning (justified purely in terms of equity and efficiency) without sacrificing something that is included in Principle I.

This leads to the second argument, the traditional argument from freedom. Freedom for the Right and for the Left means very different things. The Right contends that in wanting to equalize further, the Left risks violating the freedom of individuals to dispose of their incomes and properties, to seek the work they wish and to promote themselves on the job, and to send their children to the best schools. They are thus flouting "negative liberty," the most precious inheritance and the fundamental right of every man —liberty construed as freedom from undue external interference. The Left replies in terms of some notion of "positive liberty." Liberty is not to be understood merely as freedom from external restraints but also as freedom from costly ignorance, acquisitive greed, and anti-social snobbery. Enlightened intervention on behalf of the larger community or one's better self is socially justified if not always acceptable to the few, and therefore the Welfare State has a legitimate kind of educative or protective role. More specifically, the Right also produces arguments connected with equality and involving freedom. In the argument from scarcity, it points out that if equality means in practice equal access to the law, we still could not ensure that the best lawyers, with the highest fees, could be made equally available to both sides of a dispute. By definition, there is a scarcity of the "best" in this field, as in others. There may be one top lawyer who is so specialized or so experienced or so effective in his field that he is pretty well guaranteed to win a case. One cannot make him available equally to both sides or make him available to the poorer man without being "unfair" to the other side, or without denying the freedom of the richer man to secure the best services or the freedom of the lawyer to gain the best remuneration. This example is complicated by the possibility that a lawyer might sometimes prefer to take up the case of the poorer man. But this only confirms the point that there is no mechanical guarantee of effective equality before the law.

A more important problem is that of the British public schools, which raises difficult issues and confusion on all sides. The Right says, in effect, to the Left: "Now that we have a vast network of State and county grants for education at universities and grammar schools, and various versions of qualifying examinations enabling the brightest children, regardless of social status and income, to get to grammar school and even the best universities, why is it necessary to disturb the public schools? To do this is merely to interfere with the freedom of people to send their children to the schools of their choice, not only the freedom of the very rich but that of the not-so-rich middle-class professionals who care to save their money in order to send their children to public schools. How is equality promoted by a denial of this precious freedom?" The advocates of the abolition of public schools usually argue that these institutions are antiquarian social relics, baronial bastions of privilege which perpetuate false social (or anti-social) values. They have got to go, being bad in themselves. Other abolitionists, who are either "products" or admirers of the visible advantages of a school like Eton (where each boy has a room to himself), say that they want these advantages to be available to all. This means raising the level of all schools as speedily as possible to the relative excellence of Eton. If this argument is also applied to Oxford and Cambridge, the immense practical problem becomes even clearer. Already, a considerable proportion of the boys who do well and who go up to Oxbridge are from "humbler" homes. They are carefully chosen for their demonstrable merit and they all secure State grants. But, as there is an unavoidable and somewhat arbitrary limitation of places for all people, regardless of class, the unanswerable question arises as to how many other universities can be endowed, let alone established, with the highly expensive and "élitist" tutorial system that Oxford and Cambridge have inherited from the age of medieval monasticism and the era of Victorian Platonism. Already these are precariously maintained in an industrial society which needs meritocratic professionalism rather than the vanishing breed of gifted and gentlemanly amateurs.

The argument of the Right can appeal not only to ontological scarcity and to negative liberty but also to mounting injustice, bureaucratic inefficiency, and increasing coercion. To equalize indefinitely in these directions is to move toward a self-contradictory solution. It means an increasing inequality between a managerial class of harassed civil servants and the average citizen. The more equal access is desired, the more rules are needed–preferably non-arbitrary rules, although all general rules would be arbitrary to some extent. Those who lose under the rules of the game are going to perceive the rules as not adequately fair, while those who win have a vested interest in assuming that the rules are pretty nearly foolproof. In any event, the people who implement the rules have far more power than ever before–the power of sanctions and the reinforcing power of winners over losers. The bureaucracy is more powerful, more complacent, and possibly more careless, if not carefree. A variant of this is the argument from deprivation, the universal dependence and distribution of mediocrity in a meritocracy. When almost everyone is benefiting from State aid, people tend to become, or to be treated as, cogs in a mechanistic system that maximizes mutual dependence while minimizing mutual respect.

But the most crucial argument that the Right produces, to which the Left finds it very difficult to give a compelling answer, is the argument from greater psychological inequality. The knock-down argument the Right claims to have against the stronger formulation and which makes it complacently adhere to Principle I is that under Principle II, in the name of equalization, the sense of inequality is effectively increased in practice. To illustrate this graphically, the boy who fails to qualify for entrance to a university and goes off to work is much worse off and feels wholly rejected, haunted by a crippling sense of failure. Earlier, the boy who joined the labor market did not suffer so acutely because he knew it was no one's fault in particular, not his father's, not his own; that was life and he made the best of his bad luck to survive in a world which reflected the apparent or innate injustice of the universe, the weird whims of a cosmic overlord. But to fail in a meritocratic society that claims to be egalitarian is to be rejected at any early age under a set of rules that can never be wholly free from some sting of arbitrariness. The losers may theoretically and potentially have other chances but their lives may have been altered irreversibly and without a reliable hope of redemption. The tragedy of self-defeat is made intolerable by the knowledge or the feeling that other people are constantly looking down on him or away from him, whether in fact they do or not. This may generate the most noxious vicious circles, and a hopeless exacerbation of class conflict. The more hallowed the simpler and stabler class structure, the more frustrating and subtly oppressive the covert class antagonism becomes in a meritocratic society. If there is no collectivized victory in sight or faith in the logic of its inevitability, the alternative course of retreat to a point of sufficient social withdrawal may be impossible to adopt in conditions of overcrowded space and working time.

The Left has its conventional answers to the arguments of the Right, but they have less and less appeal in a meritocratic Welfare State. The argument from scarcity is met by the appeal to more and better planning. The argument from negative liberty is met by some broader notion of positive freedom. The arguments about the managerial class or about universal degradation are countered by the stock reply that we simply need better civil servants, more comprehensive structural reforms, and nationalized industries with better management, the spread of a new concept of social service. The difficulty with any appeal to ceaseless tinkering with the social structure and the educational and political systems is that there is no decisive way of proving or disproving in advance that the Left could and would carry out its claims, promises, and intentions. When all is said and done, it amounts to an ultimate historical act of faith which looks forward to the Second Coming of the Enlightenment–faith in the theoretical and actual possibility of removing all social abuses through legislation, rules, codes, pledges, and through the extension of the quantity and quality of education.

As to the argument about greater psychological inequality, what answer can the Left give? It can merely say that this problem exists solely because of the false social values embedded in the capitalist system. Thus it has to decry the system as a whole, turn on the heat of resentment, and raise the temperature of the politics of attack and confrontation. Are there other arguments that the Left could employ, arguments that would be adequate to buttress Principle II? The most potent is still the argument from exploitation, derived from Marx. If equalization is not a ceaseless process, a few will increasingly exploit the rest. Exploitation is built into the system and will aggravate inequalities. The position will get perpetually worse until revolution is inevitable. The only way (if there is one) to avoid the revolution, under any democratic system, is continually to combat exploitation through budgetary measures, through State education, and through new and evolving forms of social controls, checks, and inducements. The argument from exploitation is pertinent in conditions of extreme poverty, when people are markedly underprivileged, but not when the poor are too demoralized to believe that their sole hope of redemption lies in responding to any call, however irrationally messianic, that seems to address itself to their immediate needs as well as their deep-rooted predicament.

The argument from exploitation can be too easily overemployed by the democratic Left. Such arguments are not only less and less convincing for most of the electorate, but less and less feasible in that they entail a rejection of the whole system. There is a vested interest on the part of most people to avoid a revolution in a society which has so far escaped one. Even if some stringent sacrifices are required of a few citizens of the polity, they may be acceptable if benefits to the polity require relatively small sacrifices from the citizenry as a whole. Though disliked, a minority may give up much to avoid the uncertainties and insecurities of revolution. But the electorate may come to suspect—not only on the Right but also on the Left—that some of the most strident supporters of the argument from exploitation are simply venting their personal grievances, that they trade in the debased ideological coinage of disgruntled intellectuals. Do these disgruntled intellectuals merely want power for its own sake? Are they seeking social expression for private frustrations?

Another argument that the Left has used is the argument from eternal vigilance. As eternal vigilance is the price of freedom, so also it is the price of equality. We must continue "equalizing the unequal." No doubt we will never achieve a perfectly egalitarian system, just as we will not achieve a perfectly libertarian system, but we must go on ceaselessly equalizing the unequal if we are not to freeze the system at any given level of arbitrary and self-perpetuating social inequalities. But such arguments no longer secure votes, and do not seem as credible as they once did. They do not carry conviction because ultimately they are connected to the idea of changing human nature through education, and unfortunately, the extension of educational opportunities creates new classes of men who are intent on seeking promotion in a meritocratic society but who do not necessarily feel that they have any responsibility toward or continuing ties with those they left behind. This is indeed the practical predicament of the Left in relation to its socialist conscience and to a cynical electorate.

The debate about equality reaches a point where we are confronted not just with arguments from evidence and factual disagreement, but also with fundamental differences of presupposition. The Right cannot readily abandon its obsessive belief in the severe limitation of human capacities and of political and social change through State action. However much we can change society, we cannot ignore certain facts of nature (including human nature) with which in the end we must come to terms. The Left, of course, clings to the rather naïve hope of the eighteenth century that we can change everything by social and political action, by well-conceived and vigorous State policies. But one can argue–and it has often been argued–that fundamental social evils are not seriously affected by educational, welfare, and legislative programs because they are powerfully linked with the structure of capitalism itself. Thus the affirmation of Principle II is, in fact, an advocacy of revolution.

The crux of the matter is easily seen when we project this argument onto the international plane. The Left rejects the premises and arguments of the Right within the domestic sector but adopts a similar position in world politics against Russian or Chinese Communists. On the global plane the Left does not talk about strict egalitarianism but rather about short-term aid to developing countries, minimal levels of assistance to the poor. To respect every man is to do something to raise the minimum standards of vast masses of human beings. Ethically, the principle of equality, "Treat every man as man," must apply not only to any nation, but also on a world level. But some on the Left say, "All that we can do as one nation for the vast mass of underprivileged peoples is to aid developing countries to help them get on their feet, to remove poverty, hunger, and so forth. We are not required or in a position to advocate a redistribution of world income." Thus the Left uses the arguments of its domestic opponents on the world plane–it appeals to Principle I and not Principle II. On the other hand, the

Chinese Communists have some influence on the global plane through the persistent use of the argument from exploitation in world affairs. They take Lenin's argument and direct it against Big Power chauvinism. They plead that in the global context we must go on fighting the exploitation of the poor by the rich nations. We find echoes of this argument especially in countries that are preoccupied with neo-colonialism. This makes the predicament of the democratic Left in the Welfare State a very real one. Does the democratic socialist believe in the equalization of incomes on a world level? If he does, how convinced is he that he can eventually carry a majority of the national electorate with him? What proportion of the national income does he want to be assigned to aid, because the proportions mentioned by socialists–1 or 2 per cent–are clearly too small. They are as incompatible even with Principle I as the appeal to the charity of the rich in the nineteenth century.

Is there a theoretical answer to the Left's practical quandary? How many socialists are courageous and heretical enough to see that the earlier democratic socialists who secularized Christianity took certain arguments and weapons from Marx that are inadequate or irrelevant today? Instead of either ignoring or adopting Marx's view of the utopian socialists, the Levellers, and of early Christianity, socialists today should rethink their assumptions and strategies. They also might ask themselves whether their debate with the Left is not simply between Principle I and Principle II but really about how to interpret Principle I. To treat man as man requires not so much the acceptance of the equal potentialities of all men, let alone the infinite potentialities of all men, but rather the acceptance of the unknown potentialities of all human beings. We cannot say in advance that all men's potentialities are equal unless we are being metaphysical. If we appeal to the fact that all men have unknown potentialities, we can understand the concern with that symbolic figure of the forgotten man cited by so many anarchists–the dustman. It is precisely because we cannot determine in advance a dustman's potentialities that it is important to provide the opportunities in society to enable him, if he wants, to play the cello or to send his daughter to ballet school. And not because the dustman is necessarily going to become a great cellist, but simply because he may want to, and if so, it should be available for him. Must this necessarily be done through the State as in the Soviet Union? Given scarce resources and the limits of productivity and of taxable income, there are definitely limits to what the State can do. But is there any reason why voluntary associations should not be entrusted with the task of extending the avenues of opportunity available to the disinherited? The socialist could argue that by an indefinite extension of opportunities (not always requiring State action) and by changing not only the structure but the entire ethos and moral tone of society, new social values could slowly emerge and usher in an era in which men show mutual respect which is not based on skills and promotions, rank and status.

At this point the socialist's faith as well as his integrity are tested, and so are his ultimate premises. Does he believe in perfectibility or in original sin? If, like Condorcet, he believes that the historical process and the progress of humanity involve an increasing equality among nations, equality within nations, and the perfectibility of man, how much emphasis does it put on human growth and perfectibility rather than on inherent flaws and weaknesses? If, like Richard Crossman in his introduction to *New Fabian Essays,* he is a reluctant believer in original sin, then the onus is put on the socialist in theory and practice and the practical advantage is on the side of the Right. In a society of original sinners, why should civil servants be so free from original sin that they can deliver the goods? The argument is all too familiar. But if committed socialists are not imbued with original sin, if they hold to an open view of human nature, then they could adopt a different parapolitical standpoint. They could say that it is because they believe in the unknown possibilities of every human being that they are concerned to extend the notion of human excellence to a point where external social distinctions do not matter so much or have a predominant influence on public opinion. Commitment to a clear and fundamental principle is logically and psychologically compatible with a critical distance from specific policies and practices. We require rational rules for applying an immutable principle in ever-changing contexts. One can believe in the principle and lower one's sights in practice, not hypocritically, but from an awareness that the achievement of any given time, place, and context will imperfectly reflect a worthy ideal. Pure equality is necessarily unattainable and, for that very reason, asymptotes are all-important. If one has trouble maintaining Principle II in a democratic Welfare State, supporting it on the global plane may well seem futile. But if no one stands for strong and universal egalitarianism, no one will take responsibility for the dismal failure to move toward it. One cannot uphold a principle without applying it universally. Those of the Left who think of themselves as belonging to the best socialist tradition must carry their revolutionary program beyond national boundaries, and this means being a revolutionary in the fullest measure.

It is more plausible to accept that human beings at birth are equal in reference to moral virtues than in regard to intellectual or other functional skills. At least we have no way of knowing which of many babies will show heroism and courage. And if in a society valuations are ultimately based upon these heroic virtues, upon integrity through individuation, and upon conscience and the moral excellences, there is no predicting which person is going to achieve them. Teachers in all schools could stress these virtues, the heroic possibilities in ordinary men and women. Persons would come to be judged not by status or property or income if there were enough individuals in society who make all of these irrelevant by actualizing such qualities as heroism and excellence in a variety of ways. These persons will be the heroes of society, and among such individuals would also be found the exemplars, the unofficial leaders of society. How can a democratic Welfare State contribute something to a recovery of the heroism that historically seems to have been married in the modern age to a cheerless, austere Puritanism? Is this anything more than a theoretical possibility? It could be more than that only if the Left is willing to take a stand against the Right by its insistence that they do not share the same image of man and cannot concede that human respect is the same for both sides. Of course, there is still no guarantee that the Left is going to win an election on the basis of full-blooded egalitarianism. But perhaps those courageous, sincere socialists who are not so bothered about winning elections could do worse than recapture the vision of the early socialists and experiment in new ways with the setting up of miniature communities, secular monasteries in which young men and women could learn socialist values and how to exercise them in society.

This requires a tremendous act of faith. Equality has now become a mere political formula, a way of justifying the existing or emerging power positions of people in terms of values that all persons seem to accept. If equality is to be more than that, then we have to reconsider the old saying that socialism is not only about the poor but also about the rich, not only about poverty but also about property. It is not solely a doctrine of protest against the exploitation by the rich. It is also not, like social reform, exclusively concerned with the poor. It is ultimately concerned with a new mode of politics wherein all the artificial contrivances of the political process do not negate but rather subserve the large goals and ideals which were in the minds of the Tawneys of an earlier era. Those pioneers believed that it was possible to give a new and elevating parapolitical image of man to the whole of society. The existing hard-and-fast distinctions, even of a democratic society, could pale into insignificance and individuals confident of their shared humanity could say of each other what Burke said of institutions: "We must venerate where we cannot understand."

6
INDIVIDUATION

What are numbers knit
By force or custom? Man who man would be
Must rule the empire of himself; in it
Must be supreme, establishing his throne
On vanquished will, quelling the anarchy
Of hopes and fears, being himself alone.
PERCY BYSSHE SHELLEY

Contemporary concern with individuation and self-actualization arose with the rejection by humanistic psychologists of the pathological emphasis of a great deal of psychoanalytic literature since Freud. It is only when we see this model from a philosophical, and not merely from a psychological, standpoint that its affinities with classical antecedents become clearer. The distinction between the philosophical and psychological standpoints is important and must be grasped at the very outset. The philosophical standpoint is concerned explicitly with the clarification of ideas and the removal of muddles. It seeks to restore a more direct and lucid awareness of elements in reality or in our statements about reality or in what initially seems to be a mixed bundle of confused opinions about the world. It is by sorting out the inessential and irrelevant that we are able to notice what is all too often overlooked. The philosopher is willing to upset familiar notions that constitute the stock in trade of our observations and opinions about the world. By upsetting these notions he hopes to gain more insight into the object of investigation, independent of the inertia that enters into our use of language and our ways of thinking. By giving himself the shock of shattering the mind's immediate, conventional, and uncritical reactions, the philosopher seeks to become clearer about what can be said and what cannot even be formulated.

Most of our statements are intelligible and meaningful to the extent to which we presuppose certain distinctions that are basic to all thinking, knowledge, and language. Although these distinctions are basic because they involve the logical status of different kinds of assertions, their implications are a matter for disagreement among philosophers. By discriminating finer points and nuances that are obscured by the conceptual boxes into which we fit a vast world of particulars, the philosopher alters our notion of what is necessary to the structure of language, if not of reality. However, as Cornford pointed out in *The Unwritten Philosophy,* all philosophers are inescapably influenced by deep-rooted presuppositions of their own, of which they are unaware or which they are unwilling to make explicit. The philosopher makes novel discriminations for the sake of dissolving conventional distinctions. And yet, what he does not formulate–what he ultimately assumes but cannot demonstrate within his own framework–is more crucial than is generally recognized. Whether it be at the starting point of his thinking or at the terminus, the unformulated basis is that by which he lives in a state of philosophical wonderment about the world.

Our statement of the philosophical standpoint refers to knowledge as the object of thought but also to the mind as the knower, the being that experiences the act of cognition and mode of awareness that accompanies the process of thinking. The mind falls into grooves, and clasps uncriticized reactions to the world in the form of a bundle of borrowed ideas and automatic responses. At the same time, it is the mind in which clarification and resolution are to be sought through the disciplined exercise of critical distance. In the very attempt to seek clarification through new discriminations, the mind reaches a point where it empties itself or cannot proceed any further. It might also experience a joyous release from the very recognition of the fullness of an enterprise that necessarily leads to a limiting frontier. Philosophical activity, at its best, might be characterized as a patient inching of one's way. It requires a repeated redrawing of mental maps, step by step. It is most effectively pursued through a continuing dialogue among a few who respect themselves and each other enough to be able to say, "You're a fool," occasionally and to have it said of oneself. Such men and women must become impersonal by refusing to hold on to any limiting view of the self and by refraining from playing the games of personalities caught in emotional victories and defeats. Only by becoming impersonal in the best sense is one ready to enjoy a collective exploration in which there are many points of view representing relative truths, in which all formulations are inconclusive, and in which the activity itself is continually absorbing and worthwhile.

Whereas the philosophical standpoint is concerned with knowledge and perception, with clarity and comprehension, the psychological standpoint requires us to talk in terms of freedom and fulfillment, of release, and of integration. Psychologically speaking, a man's feeling that he is freer than before is deeply important to him. This condition involves a sense of being more fulfilled than he expected to be in the present in relation to his memories of the past and also in relation to his anticipations of the future. Since this experience is bound up with his self-image, the psychological standpoint must always preserve an element of self-reference. The psychological breadth and depth of this self-reference depend upon the measure of critical distance a person can maintain in the midst of pressing preoccupations. A man's false reactions or wrong ideas are important to him psychologically in a way that they would not be philosophically. Regardless of whether they are good or bad, a man's reactions to the world are a part of himself. If he were to surrender them lightly he would be engaged in some sort of pretense; he might be conniving at some distortion or truncation of his personality. It may sound odd to plead in this way for the psychological importance of our self-image, because we tend to think we are crippled by a self-image that is generated by an awareness of our defects and limitations. Still, we know from our intimate relationships that to think of a person close to us in an idealized manner that excludes all his weaknesses and failings is an evasion of authenticity, possibly even a form of self-love. No mental projection on a love object can be as meaningful as a vibrant if disturbing encounter with a living human being. To be human is to be involved in a complex and painful but necessary awareness of limitations and defects, of muddles, of borrowed and distorting preconceptions, of antithetical and ambiguous reactions, and much else. If we are to recognize and live with such an awareness, we cannot afford to surrender our sense of self–even if intellectually we could notice the falsity of many elements in our perceptions of ourselves and others.

The distinction between the philosophical and the psychological standpoints may be put this way: whereas a philosopher is committed to an exacting and elusive conception of truth, the psychologist is concerned with the maximum measure of honesty in the existing context. Of course, we cannot maintain honesty without some standard of truth, some stable reference point from which we derive criteria applicable at any given time. On the other hand, we cannot be truly sincere and determined in the pursuit of philosophical truth without being honest in our adherence to chosen methods and agreed procedures of analysis. Clearly, philosophy and psychology are interconnected and illustrate two dimensions of critical distance. In the earlier Eastern and Pythagorean tradition, the pursuit of wisdom and self-knowledge were merely two aspects of a single quest. Since the seventeenth century, the impact of experimental science and the obsession with objectivity and certainty have sharpened the separation between impersonal knowledge about the external world and the subjective experiences of self-awareness. The latter have often been excluded in the psychologist's concern with the constants and common variables in human behavior. Nonetheless, the psychologist has not been able to ignore the individual's need for security and his feeling of self-esteem. And certainly, in the psychoanalytic concern with honesty, which Freud exemplified *par excellence,* the element of feeling is extremely important independent of any cognitive criteria. To feel authenticity, to feel honesty, to feel fulfillment, each is integral to the psychological standpoint. To dispense with such personal feelings and to see with the utmost intellectual objectivity are crucial to the philosophical enterprise, although the very term "philosopher" as originally coined by Pythagoras contained, and even to this day retains, an impersonal element of *eros.*

Our contemporary condition may be characterized both from the philosophical and the psychological standpoints. In terms of the most exacting conception of the philosophical enterprise, modern man is singularly ill-suited for it. Most men and women do not have the time, the energy, the level of capacity, or even the will to think for themselves, let alone to think through a problem to its fundamentals. Even professional philosophers are not immune to our common afflictions–the appalling lack of time for leisurely reflection, the pace and pressures of living, the overpowering rush of sensory stimuli. In our own affluent society, the struggle for existence is so intense that (as in Looking-Glass Land) it takes all the running we can to keep in the same place. Our nerves, our raw sense of selfhood, are constantly exposed to the tensions and frustrations of other people, and our state of being is continually threatened by this exposure because we find our very identity at stake. In these circumstances, it is not surprising to find that most thinking is adaptive and instrumental. The activity of the mind is largely preoccupied with the promotion of material ends or the consolidation of social status, the gaining of some token, external, symbolic sense of achievement that is readily communicable among men. The suggestion of Camus that we must visualize Sisyphus as smiling sounds remote. A great deal of contemporary thinking is *ad hoc* and superficial. What is the chief consequence of so much shallow thinking? For those few willing to question everything, take nothing for granted, and think through an idea to its logical limits, it is truly difficult to function in an environment in which the emphasis is on what seems safe because it is widely acceptable. The pressure to think acceptable thoughts is double-barreled, for our thoughts may be deemed acceptable in terms of standards that are already allowed as exclusively acceptable. Acceptability is the decisive hallmark of much of the thinking of our society, and critical distance is seen as either anti-social or ineffective. Most of the time people are so anxious about how they appear to others when they think aloud that they cannot even imagine the intensity of *dianoia,* of thinking things through in the classical mode. To do this fully, regardless of how anyone's "image" will come out, requires a courage that is today conspicuous by its absence.

Philosophically, thinking things through as demanded by the Platonic-Socratic dialectic is bound up with that form of fearlessness which is decisively tested by one's attitude to death. Most people are burdened by a feeling of pervasive futility, an acute sense of mortality, an awful fear that looms larger and paralyzes us though with no recognizable object–a fear of being nothing, a fear of annihilation, a fear of loss of identity, a perpetual proneness to breakdown and disintegration. Thus, it is enormously difficult for people to give credibility in their minds to, let alone recognize, any authentic approximations to that state of fearlessness which dissolves all sense of time and makes a mockery of mortality. And yet this remote possibility was itself grounded by classical philosophers in the capacity of the mind to think through an idea or problem in any direction, and at the same time to value the activity of thinking so much that in relation to it death and all that pertains to the sense of finality and incompleteness become irrelevant. Contemporary culture is marked not merely by a shrinking of the individual sense of having some control over his or her life and environment, but also by an increasing loss of allegiance to the collectivist notions of control transmitted by the political and social philosophies of the eighteenth and nineteenth centuries. Psychologically, the present age may be seen as the historical culmination of man's progressive inability to take refuge from his own sense of vulnerability in some compensatory collective identity. If a person in contemporary society really feels that he cannot take hold of his life, that he has no sense of direction, that he has not enough time for looking back and looking ahead, and that all around him is rather meaningless, then it is small comfort for him to be told that as a citizen of his country or as a member of the human race, he can exult in the collective conquest over natural resources. The repeated ideological efforts to reinforce such a sense of vicarious satisfaction are more and more self-defeating.

From a philosophical standpoint, the present age is impoverished by the inability of men to find the conditions in which autonomous and fundamental thinking can take place. From a psychological standpoint, the social situation facilitates rather than hinders the widespread fragmentation of consciousness. In the daily lives of most people in complex urban societies, the flux of fleeting sensations is so overpowering that they are often forced to cope with it by reducing the intensity of their involvement with sensory data. All the senses become relatively dulled. The fact that men and women seem to manage at some level may simply confirm the extraordinary adaptive nature of the human organism. The key to our survival at a more self-conscious level may be the development of a new cunning and a resilience in the capacity for selection. Although people do not notice most things while driving on a freeway, they display a timely awareness of that which threatens them. Their consciousness, though fragmented, may be sharpened in ways that are necessary for sheer survival. The really serious consequence here is in regard to interpersonal encounters and relationships. In present-day society, it is evident how very difficult it is for even the most conscientious to retain a full awareness of their fellow citizens as individual agents, as persons who suffer pain and are caught up in unique sets of complexities. How much more difficult to see others, even if strangers, as persons with capacities and inner moral struggles that go beyond visible manifestations, as individuals who are more than the sum of all their external reactions and roles. People enter into most of their relationships on the basis of role specialization, and are thereby driven, more than they wish, in their most primary affective encounters, by calculations of advantage or by fears of invasion and attack. Dr. George Bach, a psychologist from Beverly Hills, has suggested that marital relationships are becoming increasingly difficult to sustain because of the cumulative pressure of collective tension. Even though a loving couple may live together on the basis of shared memories, unspoken commitments, and mutual intimacy, their relationship may be unable to carry the burden of a host of social frustrations and milling anxieties that come from outside but which they cannot help turning against each other.

Given the sad predicament of the individual in contemporary society, it is hardly surprising to find various earnest-minded men vying with each other to diagnose our prevailing sickness, thereby adding to the collective gloom. Many of these diagnoses are identified with psychological and psychoanalytic approaches and are colored by a preoccupation with the pathological. In the context of this majoritarian pessimism, pioneered by Freud himself, it required a large measure of cool courage for a small band of humanistic psychologists to initiate an alternative mode of viewing the human situation. They have not evaded the stark facts of our present malaise, but they have dared to provide a democratized, plebeianized version of a model that is humanistic and optimistic. In place of earlier concepts of the well-adjusted man, they offer the model of a man who, although (and rightly) not adjusted to existing conditions, is capable of exemplifying, releasing, and living out what is truly important to him as an individual. Even though humanistic psychology has been launched with the fanfare of a revolutionary movement, it has actually filled a vacuum created by the monotony attendant on much so-called scientific psychology. Whatever else may be said about the behavioristic, reductionist, and mechanistic models of man, they are undeniably dull and unexciting. The boredom is pervasive. If one is so unfortunate as to surrender wholly to these current versions of secular fundamentalism, life loses its savor and luster. As one critic has suggested, the worst thing about these depressing models of human behavior is not that they claim to be true but that they might become true. Ernest Becker makes a similar observation:

> If we accept to think in Freudian terms, we can analyze our lives in those terms–we can shape ourselves into those terms. And it "works"–but it also risks driving us crazy, as any extreme and unreal fetishization will. Use a paranoid vocabulary and you become paranoid, as our political leaders are teaching us today. Use a sexual vocabulary and you can live and feel and act out your life on sexual terms, as most of us have done at certain times. The deeper question is, what is the nature of reality and what are our real desires? And this question is harder to answer.[1]

It is significant that a crucial point of departure for the humanistic approach came from a man, Viktor Frankl, who was not merely reacting against current orthodoxy on intellectualist grounds. The necessity of a new way of looking at the human condition came to Frankl out of the depths of authentic suffering–out of the intense pain and mental anguish he experienced in a Nazi concentration camp. Indeed, many of the existentialist and phenomenological modes of thought fashionable in America today originated in postwar Europe. Then as now, the stern moral philos-

1. Ernest Becker, *Angel in Armor,* New York, George Braziller, 1969, p. 172.

ophy and psychology of a few savants was widely discredited by the behavior of the lunatic fringe of the movement. Frankl's is the uncommon case of a therapist who can write with compelling conviction about man's search for meaning. Faced with the most meaningless and unbearable forms of suffering, Frankl saw the profound significance for some prisoners of a deliberate mental defiance of the absurdity of their condition, and the dignity of an individual restoration of meaning as a mode of psychological survival. Frankl was, therefore, able to see after the war why many of his patients were unwilling to be treated as malfunctioning machines or as anxiety-driven bundles of inhibitions and neuroses. It was much more important for them to engage in the supremely private and uniquely individual act of assigning meaning to their own condition. Frankl then took the unorthodox step of reinforcing his discovery by making a pointed reference to the classical tradition. The emphasis on the noetic (from *nous*) in man is fundamental to what has come to be called logotherapy.

The classical concept of noetic insight could be explained in a variety of ways. A simple and very relevant rendering of the Platonic concept of insight is that it enables one person to learn from a single experience what another will not learn from a lifetime of similar experiences. In their capacity to extract meaning and significance out of a pattern or medley of recurrent experiences, human beings are markedly different from each other. Such differences between persons are acutely apparent at a time when "experience for its own sake" has become the slogan of an entire generation. The refusal to evaluate experiences by reference to any and all criteria is the sign of a deep-seated form of decadence. The rejection by the young of the imposed and restrictive criteria offered them by their parents and teachers is understandable, but, unfortunately, it leads many to surrender to mind-annihilating passivity. In the classical tradition, the notion of noetic insight was exemplified in an aristocratic form. The wise and truly free man was one who had so fully mastered the meaning-experience equation that he had wholly overcome his fear of death and thereby gained a conscious awareness of immortality. His comprehension of the whole of nature, of society, and of his own self in terms of their essential meanings placed him in an exalted position of freedom from the conditioning categories of time, space, and causality. As employed by contemporary humanistic psychologists, the notion of insight is democratized into a basic need for survival–into a desperate and ubiquitous concern on the part of struggling human beings to grapple somehow with their chaotic and painful experiences so as to extract a minimal amount of meaning.

Is a human being, incarcerated in Plato's Cave, with all his limitations, his ignorance and indolence, his illusions and delusions, capable of knowing what is good for himself? This is much less than knowing the good of all, which is beyond formulation and yet meaningful for those concerned with contemplating it. We might say that it is in one's interest at any given time to do that which earlier one had decided to do for the sake of a specific aim. There is a specificity in the language of interest, and that helps a human being to become rational, to be able to control his limited resources, to formulate choices, and to make the most of his decisions and commitments. A man who knows what is in his own interest can be clear about what he wants to do. But given human fickleness as well as growth, a person cannot in general answer the question of what is in his own interest at any specific time without knowing something about the connection between different parts of himself, the relation between his unknown potential and the known actuality, as well as the complex variables of social interaction and of decision making by others. The language of interest has the advantage of specificity, which is why the marketplace operates with considerable precision. Yet when transplanted from theoretical utilitarianism into personal lives, it tends to break down. Individual happiness, like meaningfulness, is a notion that involves self-definition. It is not merely a sum of units of happiness that can be translated into specific goods. Thus, in talking the language of self-interest, one cannot avoid at some point asking oneself, Who am I? and What do I really want?

Bentham assumed that most people come to know their interests when they find that they cannot do exactly what they want, and they quickly learn this in a political society. But when the majority is trapped in pseudo-objectivity, looking for formulas and for certainty, yet nervously preoccupied with interests, those who do not think about self-interest will make those who do uncomfortable.

Those who do have made hypocrisy into a way of life and moral cowardice into a virtue, for such people assume with Walpole that every man has a price. The language of interests, like a banking system, rests upon confidence. Hume thought that this confidence was a trick, though so successful and complex that no one could pull the rug from under it. He was convinced that the whole of political society was built upon opinion and that opinion in turn was purportedly connected with interests. Everyone believes that his interests are such and such because public interests are purportedly the summation of private interests. And Hume felt that most people believed this out of fear or habit most of the time. In general, the language of interests fails to convince because it attempts to construct a parapolitical ethic out of a hedonist calculus in which *arete* or *virtu* is effectively replaced by a concept of happiness indistinguishable from pleasure. Plato held that the citizen individuated within a polity and simultaneously contributed to its growth and preservation by developing moral powers–virtues–and especially *sophrosyne* and wisdom. True happiness consists in the mastery of one's chaotic desires, fears, and irrational tendencies in a manner which enhances the well-being of all. The ideal state, on the other hand, would strive for a justice and harmony which set the best conditions for individuation. Socratic individuation might involve a rebellion against the static structures and hypocritical façades, but many in the Greek polis could understand and at least minimally sympathize with it. To some extent, individual psychological needs received general social recognition and even support.

In contemporary society the needed measure of support has been withdrawn. As personal needs were divorced from positive contributions to the whole, states turned from the support of human growth to management and regulation by manipulation and coercion. It is difficult to pursue a classical or contemporary model of self-actualization in a paranoid social environment. A real sense of liberty based on self-guidance and equality based on human dignity and potential cannot be easily cultivated in an acquisitive and competitive society. The criteria any society uses to assure identity to individuals have a profound bearing upon psychological freedom and the nature of choices made. Such criteria are instrumental in the formulation of internal restraints, and the degree of freedom attained by a person is dependent upon his understanding of the logic of restraints. Equality in such a view suggests the blending of role specialization (demanded by the social structure) and role flexibility (to exercise creative psychological freedom). The positive or negative effect of social support or restraint of interests depends upon the individual's capacity to transcend personal interests and merge his interests within the ecology of human interests in general. Freedom and equality cannot be understood purely in terms of the individual in societies prone to alienation without the logic and politics of participation to bridge the gap between freedom and equality and the necessities of the social structure. Nor can we expect to catalogue all the restraints inherent or expressed in a social system, for that might mislead us into thinking the list is exhaustive, and this could block the realization of freedom and equality.

A parapolitical perspective, with rich conceptions of psychological and social time and space, is essential for individuating beings in dynamic social systems. A psychological sense of temporal expansion allows for a broadening perception of alternatives critical to role flexibility. Creation of psychological space can confirm that no social system is able to exhaust social space. When the multiplicity of possible social forms is seen, men may recognize the infinite plasticity of social expression. Self-actualization within a context of social restraints and psychological plenitude must imply self-transcendence. Self-actualization requires something more than preoccupation with interest, fear of loss, and the constant identification of advantages. It involves a continual extension of opportunity within the structure of a society. Self-transcendence involves asking questions and seeing beyond oneself and accepting the fact that one's life will cease to be meaningless only when one enjoys the truth that one is not the only being on earth, that the universe is not entirely for one's personal convenience, that the world can be a fascinating place, and there is nothing threatening about self-forgetfulness. Any principle of transcendence, however, must be accompanied by a principle of negation to make it practically effective so that men and women have the opportunity, the right, and the requirement of self-definition. Transcendence of interests cast in an externalized language of norms, expectation, and acceptability allows for an ecology of interests which intimates the classical ideal without being bound by it.

In the writings of Abraham Maslow we are provided with a portrait of individuation in a manner that is accessible to all and yet reminiscent of the classical models of perfectibility. He investigated the attitudes of a fair sample of people who displayed uncommon characteristics in relation to the way they regarded the world and themselves, despite their differences in regard to age, sex, social status, profession, and other external conditions. From his empirical observations, he tried to derive the identifying marks of "a self-actualizing man." He drew the tentative conclusion that only about 1 per cent of any sample of the population of contemporary Americans are examples of self-actualizing men and women. This is not to suggest that in our contemporary culture only 1 per cent are *capable* of becoming self-actualizing persons. Presumably the proportion would increase with a greater awareness of what is involved. In fact, the figure of 1 per cent is ten times higher than Thoreau's estimate that one in a thousand is a real man. Maslow suggested a simple but crucial distinction between deficiency needs and being needs. Human beings function a great deal of the time out of a sense of inadequacy. They seek to supply what they think they lack from the external world. This sense of incompleteness will be intensified by the experience of frustration in repeated attempts to repair the initial feeling of deficiency. But there is also in all persons a sense of something within which seeks to express itself, and is fulfilled when it finds appropriate articulation. One of the important features of this distinction between deficiency needs and being needs is that the same need could function at different times as an expression of a sense of deficiency or of a sense of being. It is in his manner of coping with both his sense of deficiency and his sense of being that the self-actualizing person reveals his enormous capacity for self-dependence. Maslow attempted to give an exhaustive list of characteristics of the self-actualizing man. A few seem particularly significant in the context of parapolitics. Although people can see increments of individuation at certain moments in their lives, they might come to know them better through their opposites.

An essential mark of the self-actualizing man is his capacity for acceptance. He accepts himself and the world. Although he may reject certain elements of the world around him, he finds sufficient reasons to accept the world as a whole. The world he accepts includes the social realm and extends into the realm of nature. This cheerful acceptance of the world is possible precisely because he has accepted himself. His self-knowledge may be incomplete, and there may be elements in himself which he dislikes or wishes to discard. Yet he finds meaning in the fundamental act of self-acceptance with all his limitations. If the act of acceptance is authentic, it will be strong enough to withstand all threats from the external world. The self-actualizing person is aware of particular and partial rejections from external sources, but he can never give up on himself or on others. His essential acceptance enables him to perceive reality more clearly. He sees human nature as it is, not as he would prefer it to be. He will not shut out portions of the world that are unpleasant or that are not consonant with his own preferences and predilections. He is willing to see those aspects of reality that remain hidden to other men to the extent to which they conflict with their own prejudices. This fundamental acceptance also involves a negation. His critical distance negates the distortion implicit in his immediate sensory responses to the world and in the exaggerated inferences derived from them.

A second characteristic of the self-actualizing man is his spontaneity. He is simple, direct, and decisive in his action. He is not burdened by the anxiety of cunning calculation or the fatigue of tortuous rationalization and self-justification. He can make an appropriate yet spontaneous response in many contexts–not every time, but often enough to see beyond conventionalities. In everyday human encounters, many opportunities are forfeited because of the habit of mutual suspicion. The self-actualizing man is able to negate the usual signs and symbols because he is not obsessed with social acceptance. He is not trapped by the totemistic worship of token gestures that restrict meaningful involvement. He is thereby less vulnerable to collective modes of manipulation. Consequently, he loses his sense of striving. He continues to grow through his mistakes and failures, but he grows without anxiety and without an oppressive awareness of the opinions of others or the crude criteria of success and failure. An authentic sense of freedom is released by his act of acceptance and by the spontaneity of his responses to the world.

A third characteristic is his transcendence of self-concern. He can center his attention on non-personal issues that cannot be grasped at the level of egotistical encounters. He is aware of the needs of others, in interpersonal relations and in society. He does not view the problems of human beings in terms of the mere interaction of overstraining wills. He is not exempt from the tendency to ego assertion, but he refuses to participate in the collective reinforcement of ego sickness. When the ever-lengthening shadow of the ego provides a substitute world of wish-fulfillment, it leaves a man with no sense of the breadth or depth of the reality of the transpersonal core of human problems. By seeing beyond personalities, the self-actualizing man gives himself opportunities to extend his mental horizon and re-create his picture of the world. He can move freely between larger and more limited perspectives, thereby attaining a clearer perception in relation to any problem. With this enlarged perspective there emerges a capacity for cool detachment and an enjoyment of privacy. A man cannot attain to true freedom if he is incapable of enjoying his own company. Many people today have become cringingly dependent on the need to interact with others to the point of psychic exhaustion. Men and women are so involved in their projections of themselves in familiar surroundings that they are unable to stand back and view their activities free of egocentrism. The self-actualizing person appreciates the need for self-examination. He knows that in order to meet this need he must provide space within his time for solitude, privacy, and quiet reflection. He thereby enhances his sense of self-respect and maintains it even when he finds himself in undignified surroundings or in demeaning conditions. He places his valuation of being human in a fundamental ground of being that goes beyond the levels at which he interacts with others.

Attainment of a high level of authentic impersonality strengthens his independence of culture and environment. A fourth characteristic of the self-actualizing man is his very real enjoyment of a sense of autonomy. He participates, however modestly, in the politics of perfectibility. The notion of autonomy is a part of our inheritance from the Socratic concept of the individual, and has been transmitted since the seventeenth century in modern presuppositions concerning man as a rational moral agent. But although this notion is embedded in the vocabulary of liberal, democratic theory, it has been considerably undermined by the prevailing tendency to see men as intersubstitutable, to view most acts as predictable, and to explain most human responses mechanistically in terms of instinctual drives or the functioning of systems and subsystems. It is therefore against very great odds that the self-actualizing person gives existential authenticity to the abstract notion of individual autonomy as an agent, knower, and actor. He has a sharp sense of his own individuality and of the boundaries of himself. Boundaries are essential to the notion of individuation, but these boundaries will not coincide with the contours of selfhood reflected in the totality of culture-bound responses. The self-actualizing man may choose to express his individuality in the language and symbols provided by his cultural and social context, but these modes of expression will not obscure his sense of transcendence of his environment. This sense of inner space enables him to recognize more alternatives than appear on the surface and to feel himself capable of choosing meaningfully among them. He is aware of an openness within his mind and his personality that helps him to be open to the world outside him. This awareness shows itself in the freshness that he brings to his appreciation of persons and situations and of particular moments. This quality of freshness is all too rare in our everyday encounters. Particularly in a highly fragmented and competitive society, people are starved from a lack of generous appreciation of each other.

The self-actualizing man is self-confident enough to give unqualified appreciation and praise to other people. This does not mean that he is incapable of discrimination. The more he discovers some new and subtle facet of life that draws out his rich and free-ranging appreciation, the more he is able to introduce freshness and joy to every situation. The enthusiasm that goes with freshness generates a sense of self-expansion that accompanies Freud's "oceanic feeling" and Maslow's "peak experience." It is a sense of losing oneself in the vastness and richness of the world around us. The true individual is, paradoxically, so secure in his efforts to find himself that he is also able to forget himself. He becomes a universal man who emancipates himself from the constricting prison of his personality and enters into the spacious kingdom of mankind. The more he actualizes himself, the more he can transcend himself. In place of being acculturated in stifling parochial and provincial allegiances, the self-actualizing man experiences the exhilaration of being truly human. This has a profound bearing on all his relationships. He can relate to many different sorts of persons and react to a wide variety of situations with humor and compassion. He displays a shrewd perception of the relation between means and ends. His creativity enables him to recognize opportunities where other men see only limitations. He is so absorbed in what has yet to be tried and yet to be accomplished that he will have no time to brood over his past achievements and failures. He lives in that dimension of the present which points to the future.

Given this portrait or model of individuation, we might ask how this differs from the classical ideal of the man who has attained to the fullness of self-knowledge. In Platonic thought, the attainment of this ideal involved a deliberate mastery of the dialectic. In the classical Indian tradition, the ideal of spiritual freedom could not be reached without a deliberate voiding of all limited identifications and allegiances, a persistent endeavor to recapture the self-sustaining activity of an unconditioned consciousness. For the mystical quest, this means the recovery of an inward center which is full of creative potential but around which there are fluctuating boundaries. Such a rebirth is impossible without a continual process of dying, a dissolution of the sense of false identity, and the gaining of confidence in a new mode of awareness, as Saint Paul so uncompromisingly stated in his doctrine of the new man. The distinction between a separate knower and an external world to be known is gradually weakened, without sinking back into a state of mindlessness.

It would be appropriate here to consider two statements of the classical ideal. The Stoic philosopher Marcus Aurelius wrote:

> This, then, remains: Remember to retire into this little territory of thy own, and above all do not distract or strain thyself, but be free, and look at things as a man, as a human being, as a citizen, as a mortal. But among the things readiest

> to thy hand to which thou shalt turn, let there be these, which are two. One is that things do not touch the soul, for they are external and remain immovable; but our perturbations come only from the opinion which is within. The other is that all these things, which thou seest, change immediately and will no longer be; and constantly bear in mind how many of these changes thou hast already witnessed. The universe is transformation: life is opinion.[2]

In the classical Indian text on self-knowledge, *Atmabodha,* the true nature of the Self is depicted by Shankara in the following way:

> I am without attributes and action, eternal and pure, free from stain and desire, changeless and formless, and always free. . . . I fill all things, inside and out, like the ether. Changeless and the same in all, I am pure, unattached, stainless and immutable.[3]

The concept of self-sufficiency offered by Marcus Aurelius presupposes a particular theory about the mental processes through which the eternal transformations of the universe are reduced to static opinions. This theory is linked to a certain view of the relation between the distorting mind and the indwelling soul, both of which are consubstantial with different dimensions of cosmic reality. Without deliberate reflection on such premises, a man cannot become a true philosopher or attain a fundamental equanimity of soul. On the other hand, our contemporary humanistic psychologists do not concern themselves with presuppositions about human nature. They do not hold any definite or formulated concepts about human essence and human potentiality or the processes involved in attaining any stated goal of human perfectibility. Instead, it is assumed that human beings act out what they think they are and thereby find out more about themselves. Similarly, we can readily sense the vast difference in conceptual content between the contemporary model of individuation and the classical formulation in

2. Marcus Aurelius, *The Meditations,* IV, 3, trans. George Long, Harvard Classics, vol. 2, New York, P. F. Collier and Sons, 1909, p. 214.
3. Shankara, *Atmabodha,* trans. Swami Nikhilananda, New York, Ramakrishna-Vivekananda Centre, 1970, pp. 148-49.

Atmabodha of supreme self-affirmation. There are several complex abstract presuppositions implicit in building a mental framework which enables a man to feel that he is essentially without attributes and beyond all conditions. If the contemporary model of the self-actualizing person seems to be conceptually less demanding, this is merely because it is assimilated to our everyday picture of psychological health as the absence of known forms of pathology. Humanistic psychologists do not wish to pronounce about how the process of individuation takes place, partly because it could happen in many more ways than could be put in a single paradigmatic scheme. It is important to protect this diversity of paths and to maintain the greatest possible tolerance in regard to the processes of human growth so as to preserve a necessary agnosticism.

The model of the self-actualizing man or woman should not be seen as a static textbook typology with which we can readily identify and thereby gain some form of vicarious atonement. Nor should we mistake it for a model that could be elaborated simply by more empirical research. There is, in fact, no substitute either for the philosophical task of confronting alternative presuppositions or for the practical endeavor of singling out visible examples of maturity in the quest for self-awareness. The former is needed to stimulate our intellectual imagination, and the latter is indispensable in stirring our emotions and channeling them in a worthwhile direction. The two functions are interrelated to a greater extent than we may suppose. By daring to unravel our presuppositions and to confront them with those derived from the classical philosophical and mystical traditions, we are in a better position to find an underpinning for that continuity of consciousness which is essential to the exemplification of a critical but benign distance in our day-to-day encounters with the world around us.

In our attempts to move away from the treadmill of conformity and all that is unnatural in contemporary society, the model of self-actualization could be a valuable starting point in formulating a feasible parapolitical ideal for ourselves. The self-actualizing person knows what to do now, and at the same time sees sufficiently beyond the present to enjoy a wider sweep, a larger perspective than we ordinarily use. The most pathological suffer from either a fixed stare or a wandering gaze, whereas a person who uses both eyes steadily is, by contrast, wholesome and healthy. In the light of Boehme's distinction between the eye of time and the eye of eternity, the individuated man employs both eyes "to see life steadily and as a whole." He may awaken the more distant "mysterious eye of the soul" and develop the synthesizing vision of a sage. He uses both the eye of time and the eye of eternity with facility and freedom. He does not become so infatuated with his image of the ideal that he loses contact with the concerns of other people, who may need the illusions to which they cling at any given time.

We could honor classical paradigms without devaluing the contemporary model of individuation. Is the difference between them a divergence of belief, or a matter of technique? Or does it pertain to levels and modes of awareness? Without proposing here to examine such questions, it is in the hope that the model of a self-actualizing person will not become merely another modish fad that it has been put in the broader perspective of an ancient tradition that we have still to recover. We are now in the early stages of a long exploration that cannot be charted at present. What is surely more important is that as many as possible must share in the first step of the journey inward so that they may enrich each other and respond with sympathy to those who seek their support.

II
COSTS OF COMMITMENT

We find that important parts of goodness are at variance with one another and that they set at variance the men in whom they predominate. ELEATIC STRANGER

7
THE REVOLUTIONARY'S BURDEN

Who could foresee that from so much evil would come so much good, and from so much good, so much evil? From so much indifference such a crisis and from such a crisis so much indifference? Who today could answer for humanity, who could answer for a people, who could answer for a man? Who will answer for tomorrow? CHARLES PÉGUY

There is a fine line between disillusionment and despair, a slender but indestructible thread of hope to which men must cling for survival with a bare minimum of self-respect. Perhaps this is why the wisdom of hindsight and the contagion of cynicism have not wholly deprived the term "revolution" of its irreducible core of moral connotation. Even when it is used as an entirely descriptive epithet, it evokes the response, however dubious ethically, that it is only right to appreciate and to accept that which is unavoidable. The term "reactionary," however, has become in our time so ineradicably pejorative that it reflects a deeper skepticism about the intentions, shibboleths, and achievements of leaders and martyrs in particular revolutions in all parts of the world. But it is still dire heresy, almost anathema, to decry revolution as such, either on *a priori* grounds or as a matter of principle. There seems to be an almost theological element of moral retribution in a revolution that succeeds even partially; there is a residual flavor of moral grandeur and pathos in a revolution that fails to fulfill its high expectations; and there is an inextinguishable longing for a more perfect revolution than our forefathers conceived or brought into being. We have tasted the apple, and no return to pre-revolutionary "innocence" is possible.

Paradoxically, the minimum moral connotation that is now inherent in revolution, as a term and as a concept, obscures the large theoretical issues and practical moral dilemmas implicit in the ethics of revolution. If social and political thinkers before the seventeenth century often tended to overlook ethical and moral complexities in regard to the concepts of "authority," "order," "*raison d'état,*" and "civic obedience," moderns may be apt to do the same in regard to "revolution" and cognate concepts. The difficulty is heightened by the series of major and minor "revolutions" that have taken place in meta-morals. We do not share, in any society, a single set of basic premises about human nature and human ends, cosmology and the course of history, sociology and psychology, much less the relations between them. Even the central terms of meta-morals are matters of acute disagreement, quite apart from the traditional and continuing disputes concerning alternate theories of moral cognition, moral psychology, and moral conduct. We have achieved enough sophistication to be uncomfortably uncertain about answers to questions of ethical evaluation, justification, and obligation, involving clusters of terms in ordinary language connected with the concepts of "good," "right," and "ought." The ethics of revolution raises theoretically difficult and practically perplexing questions such as:

1. What is involved in appraising revolutions as "good" or "bad," "better" or "worse"?
2. How do we decide that political revolutions, or particular revolutionary acts of individuals and groups, are "right" or "wrong"?
3. Is one ever obliged to initiate, participate, or involve others in a revolution?
4. How do we assign responsibility for the intentions, acts, and consequences of a revolution?

These questions should neither be confused with nor reduced to more familiar and manageable questions concerning individual resistance. The concept of revolution is much more far-reaching than that of individual resistance and rebellion. Even in its narrowest political usage, the term "revolution" refers to nothing less than the unconstitutional and usually violent overthrow of an existing regime. In its broader and more characteristic usage, revolution is the conscious, systematic, and even total disruption of the established order and its replacement by a structural reorganization of society with new foundations, new institutions, and new relationships. Revolution, in the narrower sense, does not entail an upheaval in social relationships or even a change in the political system—it may merely refer to the capture of political power by a new set of rulers. It is the broader usage and totalistic character of revolution that is distinctively modern, peculiarly ideological, pseudo-religious and pseudo-scientific, and ethically so explosive that it tends in practice, and often in theory, toward moral nihilism. Herzen was the first to notice that revolution, in this larger sense, is contained in the general notion of palingenesis. He wrote to Ogarev in 1833:

> We feel that the world is waiting for a renewal; that the revolution of '89 is broken, and that a new era must be brought about through palingenesis. European society must be given new foundations, based more firmly on right, on morality and on culture. This is the actual meaning of our experiences—this is Saint-Simonism.[1]

But the sad feature of Saint-Simonism was that the harbingers of revolutionary renewal, in their search for new foundations, were necessarily mere apprentices, at best groping pioneers, in the use of the new vocabulary of moral discourse. "Right," "morality," and "culture" could no longer be viewed independently of the theories, practical aims, and the endlessly debatable outcome of the Revolution.

Despite this difficulty, nowhere more evident than in Marxist thought, the advocates and originators of particular revolutions were naturally affected by the moral climate in which they were reared. They appealed to the prevailing language of moral and political philosophy, even when they did not feel bound by it, being committed to transcending it and judging themselves in terms of the moral values of the post-revolutionary epoch. The ethical justification of actual revolutions was and is a mixture of very different types of claims and arguments. For the purpose of

1. Franco Venturi, *Roots of Revolution,* London, Weidenfeld and Nicolson, 1960, p. 10.

clarification of a complex debate, we may distinguish the different types of characteristic claims.

1. There is the appeal to the values enshrined in abstract terms like "freedom," "justice," "equality," "solidarity," and "community" for the purpose of launching a moral indictment against a particular regime or system (The Natural Law Argument).
2. There is the appeal to the innate right of individuals to engineer the overthrow of the Establishment under certain conditions (The Natural Rights Argument).
3. There is the appeal to the popular will, popular consent, popular sovereignty, and to collective self-determination (The Democratic Argument).
4. There is the appeal to the consequences of the Revolution, pitted in some form of rational calculus against the prevailing amount and distribution of happiness or welfare (The Utilitarian Argument).
5. There is the appeal to the glaring and growing gap (to a degree intolerable for morally self-respecting citizens) between the ethical professions and moral pretensions of a regime or system and its actual performance and behavior (The Argument from Incurable Moral Corruption).
6. There is the appeal to the values of other societies, to historical precedents and analogies, to the wider audience of humanity or posterity (The Argument from Universal History).
7. There is the appeal to the moral force of a utopian vision of an ideal society, together with the claim that the correct identification and immediate removal of the Enemy or the Obstacle would bring us closer to Utopia (The Imminent Utopia Argument).
8. There is the appeal to the notion of a state of emergency (comparable to wartime, a state of nature, or a massive civil disruption), which entitles us to withhold the application of "normally" relevant moral values, standards, and criteria (The Moral Breakdown Argument).

Ethically, the weakest arguments are the Argument from Universal History, the Imminent Utopia Argument, and the Moral Breakdown Argument. The most effective argument, ethically and practically, is the Argument from Incurable Moral Corruption. The most plausible and fashionable is the Utilitarian Argument. The most morally appealing arguments are the Natural Law Argument and the Democratic Argument—especially when combined. The Natural Rights Argument, or some variant of it, seems to be a necessary condition for the application of any theory of revolution, but it can never serve as a sufficient condition. Every one of these arguments, even in its most sophisticated form, raises a number of difficult moral questions. There are theoretical problems in combining any two, let alone all, of these arguments. But the crux of the matter is that none of these arguments, nor any combination of them, is adequate to provide clear, conclusive, and compelling answers to the four questions previously raised.

All the arguments rest upon ethical presuppositions and political premises that are disputable not merely in themselves, but even more so in their interpretation and application in particular circumstances. They cannot convince or convert those who do not share the presuppositions or their interpretations. At the extreme, there is a failure of communication between the advocates of "Left-wing" and "Right-wing" revolutions, even when they adopt the same types of arguments. None can provide firm criteria for particular revolutionary acts, nor can they give clear moral guidance to the revolutionaries as to the appropriate course of action. It is natural for revolutionaries, once they have accepted any one or more of the arguments as valid and adequate to justify a revolution, to view the conduct and strategy of the revolution as chiefly a matter of technique—the most efficient or feasible means available. The rightness of a revolutionary act is seen as a matter of efficacy rather than of morality, or rather it invokes only one—the ethic of expediency. Even if this is adequate in the eyes of revolutionaries and their contemporaries, it cannot dispose of the question of whether a particular revolution is good and what makes it so. Why should ethical appraisals of revolutions be concerned only with the validity of the justification given in advance of a revolution, or with the intentions, claims, and moral presuppositions of revolutionaries? Ethically, it would be appropriate to include an appraisal of the methods adopted in a successful revolution in terms of different criteria from those put forward by the revolutionaries. Furthermore, none of the above arguments disposes of the question of whether we are ever (and if so, when) morally obliged to bring about a revolution, or how we should view those who are morally committed to set aside the obligations that others accept for themselves. Even among those who share a sense of moral obligation for a revolution, there is the unresolved question as to how much sacrifice the revolutionaries are entitled to expect of each other and of their converts and followers.

If the ethics of revolution involves many complex considerations, why is this so readily overlooked by the advocates of revolution? An obvious reason is that a preoccupation with complex moral issues may easily become an excuse for inaction. Such complexities are usually analyzed by moral philosophers from the standpoint of the individual as a moral agent, rather than in the context of social interaction between persons with differing moral sensitivities, roles, and responsibilities. There is also a critical sense in which ethics has a vested interest in order. It presupposes the existence of a civil society in which individuals may be seen and may see themselves as morally autonomous persons. For revolutionaries like Lenin and Mao, however, ethical ideas and ideals are essentially an expression of social consciousness, a veiled reflection of class interests and the ideological props of those in authority. Revolutionaries also tend to be trapped by emotions, however righteous, that are hardly conducive to the perception of morally complex issues. At the extreme, the complete revolutionary may be as obsessed as the nihilistic figure depicted by Bakunin and Nechaev in their Revolutionary Catechism:

> The revolutionary is a lost man; he has no interests of his own, no cause of his own, no feelings, no habits, no belongings; he does not even have a name. Everything in him is absorbed by a single, exclusive interest, a single thought, a single passion–the revolution.
>
> In the very depths of his being, not just in words but in deed, he has broken every tie with the civil order, with the educated world and all laws, conventions and generally accepted conditions, and with the ethics of this world. He will be an implacable enemy of this world, and if he continues to live in it, that will only be so as to destroy it more effec-

> tively. The revolutionary despises all doctrinairism. He has rejected the science of the world, leaving it to the next generation; he knows only one science, that of destruction.
>
> He despises public opinion; he despises and hates the existing social ethic in all its demands and expressions; for him, everything that allows the triumph of the revolution is moral, and everything that stands in its way is immoral.
>
> The revolutionary is a lost man; with no pity for the State and for the privileged and educated world in general, he must himself expect no pity. Every day he must be prepared for death. He must be prepared to bear torture.
>
> Hard with himself, he must be hard towards others. All the tender feelings of family life, of friendship, love, gratitude and even honour must be stifled in him by a single cold passion for the revolutionary cause. For him there is only one pleasure, one consolation, one reward, and one satisfaction—the success of the revolution. Day and night he must have one single thought, one single purpose: merciless destruction. With this aim in view, tirelessly and in cold blood, he must always be prepared to die and to kill with his own hands anyone who stands in the way of achieving it.
>
> The character of the true revolutionary has no place for any romanticism, sentimentality, enthusiasm or seduction. Nor has it any place for private hatred or revenge. The revolutionary passion which in him becomes a daily, hourly passion, must be combined with cold calculation. Always and everywhere he must become not what his own personal inclination would have him become, but what the general interest of the revolution demands.[2]

This terrifying portrait depicts the revolutionary as a moral nihilist who is wholly appropriated by an impersonal and amoral force for social necessity. A more attractive picture, though just as much a theoretical simplification, was given by Tkachev. He saw true revolutionaries as "neither ascetics nor egoists nor heroes," but outwardly ordinary men who were inspired by one single idea:

> Their distinctive badge lies in the fact that all their activity, their whole way of life is dominated by one ambition, one passionate idea: to make the majority of men happy and

2. *Ibid.*, pp. 365-66.

> to invite as many as possible to the banquet of life. The bringing about of this idea becomes the only purpose of their activity, because this idea is completely fused into their conception of personal happiness. Everything is subordinated to this idea, everything sacrificed–if one can even use the word sacrifice.[3]

The solution of moral problems demands the use of reason to overcome or at least check the passions. The man of passion, as Spinoza showed, is himself unfree. The wise man is the only man of true action, and all his acts are underwritten by the rational *conatus*. Men enslaved by their revolutionary passion are in no position to engage in a moral dialogue with those who do not share their premises, their diagnoses, or their dedication to a single, supreme goal and ideological system.

The revolutionary, by definition, is concerned with results. This has two consequences, both of which distract his attention from the complexities involved in the ethics of revolution. First of all, it is natural for a thinking man of action, who sets himself the most exacting conception of success in the collectivist terms of revolution, to seek theoretical assurances that time is on his side, that the course of history guarantees the success of a movement which is more than the product of individual wills, that he is merely hastening the inevitable, and that what is inevitable is also irreversible. If the modern concept of revolution has an innate moral connotation, it has also a built-in element of historical necessity and secular fatalism. This is as much a hindrance to moral analysis as was the theistic determinism which Socrates saw in *Euthyphro* as a threat to the dignity and responsibility of man as a moral agent. The element of necessitarianism has been inherent in the dialectics of revolution since the eighteenth century. Few saw this more clearly than Proudhon, who pointed out that the revolutionary process is a necessary phenomenon, a development that can be no more avoided than such natural events as birth, growth, and death.

> A revolution is a force against which no other force, be it human or divine, can prevail. By its nature it gains strength and grows through the very opposition it encounters. . . .

3. *Ibid.*, p. 408.

> The more you repress it, the more you are tightening its spring, and the more irresistible you are making its action; so much so that for an idea to be successful it is quite immaterial whether it be persecuted, harassed or suppressed when it first appears, or whether it develops and spreads without hindrance. Like Nemesis of old, whom neither entreaty nor threats could move, revolution advances with inevitable and menacing tread on the flowers strewn before it by its devotees, through the blood of its defenders and over the corpses of its enemies.[4]

Secondly, it is not only revolutionaries, but also the theoretical champions, as well as critics, of revolutions and revolutionary acts, who see the ethical issues in essentially utilitarian and historicist terms. Although contemporary moral philosophers are largely in agreement about the notorious theoretical flaws in utilitarianism and historicism, these doctrines are exceedingly difficult to discard in theoretical and practical thinking about revolution. The very notion of revolution involves what Simone Weil called "a catastrophic view of history." When its consequences are so sweeping, what is more natural than to judge a revolution in terms of the inconclusive evidence concerning its consequences? If a revolutionary, by definition, is concerned with results, is it surprising that he and his acts, his aims and his programs, should be assessed by their perceptible consequences? The ethics of revolution cannot avoid a predominant concern with results, even if the ethics of individual life could. But, equally, the appeal to results cannot answer the complex and difficult questions involved in the ethics of revolution.

Perhaps no advocates of revolution saw this more clearly than Tkachev in the nineteenth century and Camus in our own time. Tkachev recognized that the attempt to apply the methods of the exact sciences to the study of society could be not only theoretically misleading, but also morally and politically harmful. He wrote in 1865:

> One can take up an objective, indifferent attitude towards the phenomena of nature. But with the phenomena of social life, one must take up a critical attitude. The phenomena of

4. Stewart Edwards, ed., *Selected Writings of P. J. Proudhon,* trans. Elizabeth Fraser, New York, Doubleday, 1969, p. 159.

> nature can be reduced to general rules and more or less certain laws; but the phenomena of contemporary life, social phenomena, cannot and must not be reduced to laws; doing this implies justifying a number of absurdities which are transformed into principles.
>
> The laws of organic and inorganic development are eternal, uniform and cannot be modified or avoided; organic and inorganic bodies can exist only on condition that they submit blindly and continuously to them. But, on the contrary, the laws which govern society do not have a single one of these distinctive characteristics; they are always the product of society itself, i.e., the results of human will and human calculation.[5]

Comtean positivism, Spencerian organicism, and Social Darwinism reinforced false analogies between nature and history–analogies that misled thinkers on the Left as well as on the Right. The idea of the struggle for existence, once it was made the basis of a specious analogy between natural and historical selection, could lead only to a justification and not to a criticism of events. Even Edgar Quinet, "an eternal worshipper of freedom and irreconcilable enemy of despotism," was led by this theory to defend the idea that "Babylon had defeated Jerusalem."[6]

Nonetheless, Tkachev's opposition to social determinism in particular forms did not prevent him from adhering to an economic materialism that moved in the same direction. Camus in our own time has shown how historicism in the modern concept of revolution could easily lead to moral nihilism.

> Those who rush blindly to history in the name of the irrational, proclaiming that it is meaningless, encounter servitude and terror and finally emerge into the universe of concentration camps. Fascism wants to establish the advent of the Nietzschean superman. . . . If man wants to become God, he arrogates to himself the power of life or death over others. The rational revolution, on its part, wants to realize the total man described by Marx. The logic of history, from the moment that it is totally accepted, gradually leads it, against

5. Venturi, *op. cit.*, pp. 392-93.
6. *Ibid.*

> its most passionate convictions, to mutilate man more and more, and to transform itself into objective crime. It is not legitimate to identify the ends of fascism with the ends of Russian Communism. . . . The former never dreamed of liberating all men, but only of liberating a few by subjugating the rest. The latter, in its most profound principle, aims at liberating all men by provisionally enslaving them all.
>
> But, on the other hand, it is legitimate to identify the means employed by both with political cynicism which they have drawn from the same source, moral nihilism . . . history alone offers no hope. It is not a source of values, but it is still a source of nihilism. Can one, at least, create values in defiance of history, if only on the level of a philosophy based on eternity? That comes to the same as ratifying historical injustice and the sufferings of man. To slander the world leads to the nihilism defined by Nietzsche.
>
> Thought which is derived from history alone, like thought which rejects history completely, deprives man of the means and the reason for living. The former drives him to the extreme decadence of "why live?" the latter to "how to live?" History, necessary but not sufficient, is therefore only an occasional cause. It is not the absence of values. It is one occasion, among others, for man to prove the still confused existence of a value which allows him to judge history.[7]

Marx and Engels devalued politics while their appeal to historicism evaded the toughest problems. The gap between ideas, events, and persons is concealed by the notion of an impersonal dialectic working without the intervention of men. Because there is no commitment to a clear conception of human nature or ethics, it looks as if the Marxist appeal to historic necessity–similar to the Hegelian appeal to cosmic necessity–dissolves all moral problems, and that a supreme amorality supervenes. The revolution is all; the end justifies the means. All ways are permitted. Just as Dostoevsky declared that if nothing is true everything is permitted, these men argued that for the death of a corrupt order and the birth of the communist society of the future anything is justifiable. Among the victims of such nihilism was the vulnerable daughter of Karl Marx.

7. Albert Camus, *The Rebel,* trans. Anthony Bower, New York, Vintage Books, 1958, pp. 246-50.

Late in Marx's life, she was approached by Aveling, a seductive, hypocritical, and ruthless arch-manipulator who spoke the language of Marxism and appeared to be a dedicated communist. He constantly preyed upon her mind and eventually drove her to suicide. When Lenin heard of it, he wanted to call it immoral, but he had no language of ethical appraisal with which to deplore Aveling's conduct.

Sorel contended that politicians merely manipulate illusions, pandering to the desires of the many for the sake of their own ends. In a democratic system pseudo-representatives pretend that there is genuine democracy. Revolutionaries speak in terms of class struggle, but get others to do the sacrificing and enjoy a vicarious thrill. They are usually sad and lonely people. For Sorel, the problem was to find persons who are "monkish revolutionaries," capable of a commitment lacking in armchair radicals. There is no guarantee in practice that such exemplars could be found. The gap between *theoria* and *praxis* in politics becomes the gap between abstract and actual commitments. Appeal to necessity can convince men for a while, but it cannot motivate them to make sacrifices that involve themselves and not other people. Who is to lead the masses? How are they to be organized? All these questions preoccupied the aristocratic anarchist Bakunin for a large part of his life.

We seem to be faced with a formidable dilemma. Any examination of all the complexities of the ethics of revolution could become a mere academic exercise, an excuse for cynicism in regard to the concrete predicament of revolutionaries, an alibi for inaction. To be morally sensitive may be to ask for the ideal revolution and for pure revolutionaries, to retreat from the realm of historical realities into the empyrean of theoretical and formal ethics, to play into the hands of all the hypocritical, mean-minded, and narrow-hearted opponents of all revolutionary changes in the affairs of men. The recognition of the complexities in the ethics of revolution, especially concerning the means as well as the ends of revolution, may put the revolutionary in the position of invoking a higher moral code than that which his opponents violate with impunity, placing a moral burden on revolutionaries that minimizes the chances of a successful revolution against a smugly complacent, unctuously self-righteous, and callously repressive regime.

On the other hand, the appeal to history as the ultimate basis of justification and vindication of revolution is dangerous in that it could lead to moral nihilism. It also shows a naïve failure to learn the lessons of modern and contemporary history. The mere appeal to the intended results of a revolution cannot give any moral guidance as to the immediate course of action. Even if it can be conclusively demonstrated that there is a necessary connection between any historical revolution and the social good that resulted, let alone that if *A* and *B* are adopted now, *X* and *Y* will necessarily follow tomorrow, the gap between "is" and "ought" will remain. It can no more be closed by "must" (except metaphysically, i.e., for those who are immune to appeals to evidence independently of their already-held beliefs in a closed system) than the gap between "is" and "must" can be closed by a mere appeal to the facts. To fail to see this is to be blind to the logic of law-statements and of formal imperatives. Such ignorance may be pardonable and an advantage in terms of the effectiveness of political proselytism, but that ignorance cannot be invoked as an excuse from responsibility for acts and sacrifices (with sweeping consequences) exacted from other men in the name of revolutionary goals. If the revolutionary is a hater of moral cowardice, he cannot acquiesce in the intellectual cowardice of refusing to see the complexities of revolutionary ethics. He carries an awesome burden of responsibility, even though it may be only partly chosen and is often thrust upon him by his immersion in the social and intellectual milieu of his time.

8
MEANS AND ENDS

Before it move, hold it,
Before it go wrong, mould it,
Drain off water in winter before it freeze,
Before weeds grow, sow them to the breeze.
You can deal with what has not happened, can foresee
Harmful events and not allow them to be.
Though—as naturally as a seed becomes a tree of armwide girth—
There can rise a nine-tiered tower from a man's handful of earth
Or here at your feet a thousand-mile journey have birth,
Quick action bruises,
Quick grasping loses.
Therefore a sane man's care is not to exert
One move that can miss, one move that can hurt.
Most people who miss, after almost winning,
Should have "known the end from the beginning."

LAO TSU

Parapolitics requires a radical rethinking of the relations and relative weights of submerged moral and political concepts—sincerity, tolerance, truth, civility, empathy, and non-violence. If we believe that we possess truth in full measure, we risk becoming intolerant or despotic and may foster the delusion that truth is readily discovered or enthroned. On the other hand, to abandon the quest for truth altogether is to invite technological usurpation of our ethical prerogative. Mere sincerity without earned truth could result in the moral collapse of a permissive society and so encourage the dangerous inroads of messianic authoritarianism. In a time of crisis, even an open democracy can be destroyed by massive voting for a totalitarian government. The philosophical balance required to discriminate and deploy such concepts as sincerity and civility is reflected in the *sophrosyne* necessary to rediscover the elusive connection between means and ends. Most political and social thinkers, however, have been primarily concerned with the desirable or necessary goals of a political system, or with the common and competing ends men actually seek, and then pragmatically considered the means available to rulers and citizens. Even those who have sought a single, general, and sovereign criterion of decision making have postulated the ultimate ends and then shown more concern with the probable costs and consequences of social and political acts than with consistent application of standards of intrinsic value. It has become almost a sacred dogma in this age of apathy that politics, centered on power and conflict and the quest for legitimacy and consensus, is essentially a study in expediency. It is viewed as a tortuous discovery of makeshift compromises that can reconcile contrary claims and secure a common if minimal goal or, at least, provide conditions in which different ends could be freely or collectively pursued.

Liberal thinkers have sought to show that it is possible for each individual to be used as a means for another to achieve his ends without undue coercion and to his own distinct advantage. This occurs not by conscious cooperation or by a deliberate pursuit of a common end, but by each person's pursuing diverse ends in accordance with the "law" of the natural identity of interests–a "law" justified, if not guaranteed, in terms of metaphysical, economic, or biological "truth." Authoritarian thinkers, on the other hand, support coercion for the sake of a mandatory common end, the attainment of which cannot be left to the chaotic interplay of innumerable wills. The end may simply be the preservation of a traditional order, the recovery of a bygone age of glory, or the ruthless reconstruction of society from the top to secure some spectacular consummation in the future. A sharp dichotomy between ends and means is common to most schools of thought. It is a distinction deeply embedded in our ethical, political, and psychological vocabulary, and rooted in rigid presuppositions regarding the nature of human action. In the *Nicomachean Ethics,* Aristotle defined action as the choice of means most likely to achieve a predetermined end.

Distinctions have since been repeatedly made between immediate and ultimate, short-term and long-term, diverse and common, individual and social, essential and desirable ends, and also between attainable and utopian goals. Discussion about means has not entirely ignored questions about their moral implications and ethical propriety, or about the extent of their theoretical and contingent compatibility with desired ends or widely shared values. But, despite all these reservations, the dangerous doctrine that the end wholly justifies the means is merely an extreme version of the commonly uncriticized belief that moral considerations cannot apply to the means except in relation to ends. The latter always have moral priority in teleological systems and in those deontological theories which exalt "duty for its own sake" as the supreme end of moral agents.

It is possible to conceive of all human ends as ultimately subserving a single end such as happiness in the *Nicomachean Ethics* or the Agathon in the *Republic*. We can thus postulate ends as given rather than chosen. Socrates in the *Meno* asserts that no one willingly chooses evil and that disputes concerning courses of action arise because of ignorance and misperception. If the end justifies the means and the end is always the same, the means equally must be predetermined. Without precluding the possibility of an ontological unity of all ends, we nevertheless can recognize a variety of partial ends or shorter-term goals which can be meaningfully pursued. Even if from a theistic standpoint it may be true that God is the ultimate cause of every event in the cosmos, stating that God caused the car to break down is useless and uninformative because if the car had not broken down, God would have caused that as well. For practical guidance, we need to know the specific chains of causation, whatever our metaphysical or theological standpoint. Similarly, we need to appraise recognizable ends and the best means of achieving them, whether or not all ends ultimately resolve into one supreme end. Following this assumption, Aristotle proceeded to give a plausible account of the manner in which means are selected. One begins with the ultimate or chief end and methodically works back from the necessary condition for its fulfillment to the next previous condition, and so on, until one comes to some requirement presently within one's power of achievement.

One can then go forward fulfilling each subsequent condition until the desired end is achieved, as far as is possible. But apart from this failing to take into account the variety of ways in which ends are chosen, this explanation fails to consider that several different means may equally lead to the same end. This raises the question of the relative worth of different means.

If alternative means seem to lead to the same end, we can inquire about the moral and social costs of each. Some means may extort a price so high that they impoverish the ends, while others may be morally worthy in themselves. Doing one's duty consists in wisely choosing ends and just as wisely choosing the best means to them, even if this is easier said than done. Conscious exertion toward ends presupposes a minimum ontological commitment, even if it is no more than the existentialist faith in the equal absurdity of every act. The value of ends in this ultimate sense lies outside the historical and temporal order, and even acts which were historical failures or misfirings may still be viewed as noble and worthwhile. Means must fit ends whether we believe that ends fully justify the means or that means have intrinsic worth. Means may take on an atemporal character in virtue of their connection with ends. Outside of the temporal sequence, however, means and ends cannot necessarily be separated in terms of temporal priority. Translated into the realm of action, the ontological connection between means and ends can be best expressed in the language of simultaneity: to choose any means is to choose the ends. One's duty lies in the realm of exertion and choice of means is critical to the end. Rather than letting the means take care of themselves, one's moral conscientiousness is bound up with the choice of means. Whether or not all ends are one, integrity is found in the selection of appropriate means and the fidelity of commitment to them.

The radical moralization of the means-end model could alter the situation by summoning a constellation of concepts intimately bound up with individual psychology, ethics, and behavior. The means-end model may be construed in terms of motives and ends, as in the classical Buddhist teaching that motives color actions and tincture their results. The acceptance of any goal requires the recognition of the means to it as well as the potentials of individuals who may attain it. The mental posture of those aspiring toward some goal, the attitudes they show toward themselves and each other and also to the end in view, may affect and even restrict the means which they can adopt. The chasm between means and ends is bridged by these concepts with the resultant possibility of harmonizing an unconditional loyalty to ultimate ends with an explicit political responsibility in relation to every means. This suggests the possibility of finding ethical solutions to the fundamental problems of politics. Gandhi seems to stand almost alone among social and political thinkers in his firm rejection of a rigid dichotomy between ends and means and in his moral preoccupation with the means to the extent that they provide the standard of reference rather than the ends. He was led to this position by his early acceptance of truth and non-violence as twin moral absolutes, and by his consistent view of their close relationship. In *Hind Swaraj* he wrote that even great men who have been considered religious have committed grievous crimes through the mistaken belief that there is no moral connection or interdependence between the means and the end. The means may be likened to a seed, the end to a tree, and there is just the same inviolable connection between the means and the end as there is between the seed and the tree. Violence and non-violence are not merely alternative means toward the same end. As they are morally different in quality and essence, they must necessarily achieve different results. The customary dichotomy between means and ends originates in, and reinforces, the views that they are two entirely different categories of action, that their relationship is mainly a technical matter to be settled by considering what will be effective and possible in a given situation. The ethical problem of choice is reduced to an initial decision regarding the desired end, leading to obligatory acceptance of whatever steps seem necessary or likely to secure it. Gandhi, however, was led by his faith in the law of karma–the law of ethical causation or moral retribution linking all the acts of interdependent individuals–to the conviction that the relationship between means and ends is organic, the moral quality of the ends being causally dependent upon that of the means.

The psychology of human action in a morally indivisible community of apparently isolated units demands that the means-end relationship be seen in terms of consistent growth in moral awareness of individuals and communities and not in relation to the mechanical division of time into arbitrary and discrete intervals. If there is no fundamental wall of separation between means and ends, this is because in politics–as in all spheres of human action–we reap exactly what we sow. A clear formulation of the means-end relationship may be derived from the following statements of Gandhi, which overlap and yet express several distinct ideas:

1. It is enough to know the means. Means and ends are convertible terms.
2. We always have control over the means but not over the end.
3. Our progress toward the goal will be in exact proportion to the purity of our means.
4. Instead of saying that means are after all means, we should affirm that means are after all everything. As the means so the end.

The first statement rejects the notion that in our actual conduct we can make a firm and decisive distinction between means and ends. Any psychology of action requires this rejection of the conventional conceptual habit which makes us ascribe to ourselves greater knowledge and assurance than we actually possess. We can know, at least potentially, the means available in a way we cannot know the elusive end. Recognition of the interdependence of ends and means implies that we have some knowledge of the moral and political quality of the chosen end, whatever the complex consequences turn out to be. The second statement asserts, as a contingent truth about the extent and limit of our free will, that the individual's capacity to determine what he can do in any specific situation at any given time is much greater than his powers of anticipation, prediction, or control over the consequences of his actions. The third statement expresses the faith in the law of karma, under which there is an exact causal connection between the extent of the moral purity (detachment, disinterestedness, and the degree of moral awareness) of an act and the measure of individual effectiveness in promoting or pursuing and securing a morally worthy end over a period of time. The moral law of karma has its analogues in the Moirae and Nemesis of the ancient Greeks, the Nornor of Scandinavian mythology, the sense of fate in the Icelandic

Saga, and in all religious traditions. "As ye sow, so shall ye reap." This spiritual conviction cannot conclusively be verified or falsified empirically. The fourth statement is a practical recommendation that we must be primarily or even wholly concerned with the immediate adoption of what we regard as a morally worthy or intrinsically justifiable means. This recommendation may be accepted by those who subscribe to the second statement but it is mandatory for those who share the conviction implicit in the third statement.

The closest approximation to this formulation of the means-end relationship was that of Jacques Maritain, who viewed the problem of ends and means as the basic problem in political philosophy. He declared that there are two opposite ways of understanding the "rationalization of political life." There is the easier way of "technical rationalization" through means external to man, and the more exacting way of "moral rationalization" through means which are man himself, his freedom and virtue. It was a universal and inviolable axiom for Maritain, an obvious primary principle, that "means must be proportioned and appropriate to the end, since they are ways to the end and, so to speak, the end itself in its very process of coming into existence. So that applying intrinsically evil means to attain an intrinsically good end is sheer nonsense and gross error."[1] If Maritain and Gandhi had no use for the easier way of "technical rationalization" or for piecemeal "social engineering," this was not simply because of their rejection of a utilitarian in favor of an absolutist (or non-naturalistic) ethic. It was also the result of their forthright repudiation of the so-called pragmatist view of politics and the dominant doctrine of "double standards" which requires a sharp separation between the moral considerations applicable to individual conduct and those regarded as relevant to political action. Gandhi's own view of the morally legitimate means to be employed in furthering political ends was deeply affected by the doctrine of dispassionate action in the *Bhagavad Gita.* Intense concentration upon the task at hand can and must be combined with a degree of detachment, a freedom from anxiety about future consequences. If we are sure of the purity of the means we employ,

1. Jacques Maritain, *Man and the State,* London, Hollis and Carter, 1954, p. 50.

we shall be guided by faith, before which all fear and trembling melt away.

Unconcern with results does not mean that we may dispense with a clear conception of the end in view. But while the cause has to be as just and clear as the means, it is even more important to recognize that impure means must result in an impure end, that we cannot attain to any truth through untruthful means, that we cannot secure justice through unjust means, freedom through tyrannical acts, socialism through enmity and coercion, or enduring peace through war. The man who wields force does not scruple much about the means and yet unwisely imagines that this will make no difference to the end he seeks. Gandhi explicitly rejected the doctrine that the end justifies the means, and went as far as to assert that a moral means is almost an end in itself because virtue is its own reward. In his conceptual scheme, the end is *satya* or truth, which requires no justification, and the means (*ahimsa* or non-violence) must be justified not merely with reference to the end but also in itself. Every act must be independently justified in terms of individual integrity and non-coercion. It is, therefore, neither permissible nor possible to justify a single act of untruth or violence by appealing to the past or future possession of truth or love, though no man can wholly avoid an element of dishonesty or hostility, or claim to embody completely absolute truth and universal love. Weakness and error are ubiquitous and inescapable, but their justification and rationalization make all the difference to our personal and political integrity. We cannot condone our untruthfulness in the present on the ground that we shall be truthful tomorrow when we are stronger or conditions are more favorable. A violent revolution cannot lead (and may not be justified on the ground that it is expected to lead) to a non-violent society in the fullness of time. Further, it is not sometimes but always, that the end necessarily changes in character as a result of the means adopted toward its attainment. The Gandhian rejection of unethical means is based upon the conviction that the whole world is governed by the law of karma or moral retribution, that there is a moral order at the heart of the cosmos. Those who do not share this conviction may well think that a lesser evil could lead to a greater good. This belief, more provable than the former, is taken for granted by many contemporary intellectuals, power-holders, leaders of organizations, and evangelists (whether theological teleologists or secular historicists). It is hardly surprising that religious and social reformers have stressed the moral alienation of narrowly based classes of intellectuals and power-seekers from the toiling masses who derive some strength from the maxim that as a man soweth, so shall he reap.

The doctrine that the end justifies the means goes as far back as Kautilya and Machiavelli, the connected notions of self-preservation at all costs and *raison d'état* and the ideological faith in the attainment of a secular millennium through revolutionary action. The doctrine was implicit in *Killing No Murder,* Colonel Sexby's incitement to political assassination published in 1657. He argued that tyrants accomplish their ends much more by fraud than by force, and that if they are not eliminated by force citizens would be degraded into deceitful, perfidious flatterers. It is only lawful and even glorious to kill a tyrant, and indeed everything is lawful against him that is lawful against an open enemy, whom every private man has a right to kill. It is no doubt possible to justify tyrannicide without going so far as to say that a worthy end legitimizes any and every means. The difficulty, however, is that few practitioners would admit to holding to the maxim in an unqualified and unconditional form. It was Aristotle who coined the phrase "a just war," but this gained its greatest historical importance when the Emperor Constantine transformed Christianity from a minor sect into the religion of the ruling establishment, and the previously pacifist Christians were summoned to defend the Holy Empire from barbarian invasion. It then fell to Saint Augustine to construct the criteria for the religious concept of the just war. It has been argued repeatedly that any means is legitimate when indispensable for internal security or in defense of society against its external enemies. The sole reason for restricting the choice of means is expediency rather than principle, prudence rather than (non-utilitarian) morality.

It is often taken for granted that cunning and force must unite in the exercise of power. Power may be justified as a means to a higher end, but in the attempt to employ any and every means to secure and maintain power, it becomes an end in itself. The idea that one is serving some higher entity which rises far above individual life, and that one is no longer serving oneself, makes one no less insensitive to the morality of the means employed than the flagrant pursuit of naked self-interest. Alternatively, we have the straightforward Machiavellian notion that the individual agent cannot escape the nature he is born with, that as *fortuna* is malicious so *virtu* must always be malicious when there is no other way open. If *virtu* is the vital power in men which creates and maintains States, *necessitas* is the causal pressure required to bring the sluggish masses into line with *virtu*. If there is a moral law, it must be flouted in the practice of politics and this infringement can be justified by the plea of unavoidable necessity. Such reasoning is sometimes couched in such specious or emotive language that in moments of crisis many people are hardly aware of the wider implications of a doctrine easily invoked for special pleading in what seem to be exceptional situations. Hume thought that this doctrine is so widely practiced that it is safer in politics to assume that men are scoundrels even if we do not believe that all men are knaves.

Machiavelli and Bentham have sometimes been rather unfairly accused of actually holding that there is an end justifying *all* means. Bentham said only that happiness is the end justifying all means, which is more an empty than a pernicious doctrine. Again, Machiavelli never said that power justifies all means to it, but merely that the gaining of power often involves committing some very nasty crimes. A similar defense could also be made on behalf of Kautilya. The important point, however, is less the precise formulations of Bentham, Machiavelli, or Kautilya, than the dangerous uses to which their doctrines could be put. Just as Benthamites, Machiavellians, and followers of Kautilya could be charged with ruthlessness (even more than their teachers), so too Gandhians also could be accused of coercive tactics ("non-violent" only in a very nominal sense) in the pursuit of worthy ends. Nevertheless it would be much easier to challenge such Gandhians in terms of Gandhi's fundamental tenets than to appeal to the writings of Machiavelli or Bentham against die-hard Machiavellians or Benthamite planners. The doctrine that the end justifies the means does not even require any special justification for the Marxist who accepts no suprahistoric morality, no categorical imperative, religious or secular. Engels declared in his letter to Herson Trier in 1889 that any means that leads to the aim suited him as a revolutionary, whether the most violent or that which appeared to be most peaceable. In his pamphlet on *Socialism and War,* Lenin said that Marxists differed both from pacifists and anarchists in their belief that the justification of each war must be seen individually in relationship to its historical role and its consequences. "There have been many wars in history which, notwithstanding all the horrors, cruelties, miseries and tortures, inevitably connected with every war, had a progressive character, i.e., they served in the development of mankind, aiding in the destruction of extremely pernicious and reactionary institutions . . . or helping to remove the most barbarous despotism in Europe."[2] Whether an action is justifiable or not apparently depends on what historical end it serves.

Unlike Engels and Lenin, Trotsky stressed what he called the dialectical interdependence of means and ends. He argued that the means chosen must be shown to be really likely to lead to the liberation of mankind. "Precisely from this it follows that not all means are permissible. When we say that the end justifies the means then for us the conclusion follows that the great revolutionary end spurns those base means and ways which set one part of the working class against the others, or attempt to make the masses happy without their participation; or lower the faith of the masses in themselves and their organization, replacing it by worship of the leaders" (*Their Morals and Ours*).[3] This is an improvement on Lenin, in that it at least provides a criterion by which a collectivist regime or revolutionary leaders could be criticized for pushing an exclusively utilitarian creed to ruthless extremes in perpetuating a monopoly on power and privilege. Although Trotsky denied that the end justifies any and every means, he still insisted that a means can be justified only by its end, which for him is the increase of the power of man over nature and the abolition of the power of man over man. To formulate the end in this way invites abuses. While the end is human liberation, it must be sought through many subordinate ends having to do with the increase of power. Corrupt means can lead to the subordinate end but effectively remove it

2. Vladimir Il'ich Lenin, *Socialism and War,* New York, International Publishers, 1915, p. 9.
3. *The Basic Writings of Trotsky,* New York, Schocken Books, 1973, p. 378.

from its place in the larger end. Thus the subordinate end may seem to justify the means even when those means vitiate the broader purpose of the subordinate end itself. If the doctrine that the end justifies the means is invoked in the realization of the good society through a single, violent revolution, it could equally justify repression in the aftermath of revolution.

In Abram Tertz's *The Trial Begins* we have the following dialogue between Rabinovich and Globov. Rabinovich holds that "every decent End consumes itself. You kill yourself trying to reach it and by the time you get there, it's been turned inside out. These Jesuits of yours made a miscalculation, they slipped up." Globov answers: "They were right. Every educated person knows that the end justifies the means. You can either believe it openly or secretly but you can't get anywhere without it. If the enemy does not surrender, he must be destroyed. Isn't that so? And since all means are good you must choose the most effective. Don't spare God himself in the name of God. . . . And as soon as one End is done with, another bobs up on the stage of history."[4] Similarly, when Rubashov in *Darkness at Noon* points out that violence starts a chain of cumulative consequences, Ivanov replies that no battalion commander can stick to the principles that the individual is sacrosanct, that the world has permanently been in an abnormal state since the invention of the steam engine, and that the principle that the end justifies the means remains the only valid rule of political ethics. Ironically, while this doctrine is increasingly taken for granted by some Benthamite planners and Kautilyan diplomats, it has been openly questioned in the most powerful society that has adopted Marxism as a State religion. The Russian poet Yevgeny Yevtushenko pointed out that Stalin was forgiven much in his lifetime because Soviet citizens were led to think that his acts were necessary for some higher purpose:

> They steadily impressed upon us that the end justified the means. A great pain gives birth to a great "flow of energy," as Stalin once declared. But even as we lamented him, many of us recalled our kin and our friends who had perished in

4. Abram Tertz, *The Trial Begins,* London, Collins and Harvill, 1960, pp. 74-75.

> the prisons. Naturally, to lock up such an enormous number of people required a truly prodigious amount of "energy." But people did not ponder on the fact that the aim itself may cease to be great, if one strives after it only with great energy and without paying much attention to the means. We realized that the means must be worthy of the end. This is an axiom, but an axiom that has been proved through much suffering.[5]

The majority of Russian Populists were horrified by the advocacy of Machiavellian tactics and thought that no end, however good, could fail to be destroyed by the adoption of monstrous means. Ivan starkly portrays this dilemma in *The Brothers Karamazov:*

> Imagine that you are creating a fabric of human destiny with the object of making men happy in the end, giving them peace and rest at last, but that it was essential and inevitable to torture to death only one tiny creature–that baby beating its breast with its fist, for instance–and to found that edifice on its unavenged tears, would you consent to be the architect on those conditions? . . . And can you admit the idea that men for whom you are building it would agree to accept their happiness on the foundation of the unexpiated blood of a little victim? And accepting it would remain happy forever?[6]

In the most affluent society, which has almost elevated pragmatism to a State religion, the American President drew a major moral lesson in a national broadcast on the Watergate scandal:

> I have been in public life for more than a quarter of a century. . . . I know that it can be very easy, under the intensive pressures of a campaign, for even well-intentioned people to fall into shady tactics–to rationalize this on the grounds that what is at stake is of such importance to the nation that the end justifies the means. . . . In recent years, however, the campaign excesses that have occurred on all sides have provided a sobering demonstration of how far this false doctrine can take us. The lesson is clear: America,

5. *The Observer,* London, May 27, 1962.
6. Fydor Dostoevsky, *The Brothers Karamazov,* trans. Constance Garnett, New York, Random House, 1950, pp. 254-55.

> in its political campaigns, must not again fall into the trap of letting the end, however great that end is, justify the means.[7]

In general, when the means-end model allows the justification of means in terms of ends, it is often mistakenly assumed that the moral life of evolving societies and persons can be defined in terms of precise and unambiguous goals. Alternatively, we may unquestioningly accept some utilitarian doctrine that the moral life exists to promote happiness whereas it fundamentally enjoins the fulfillment of obligations. Furthermore, the model may falsely imply that it is the same end which is reached by different means. The cleavage between means and ends can become so sharp that the articulation of any theoretical solution does little to alter the psychology of restless striving. On the other hand, when reflective moral integrity is recognized at the heart of the means-end relationship, the model may be transformed at the parapolitical level with radical implications for both individual and political action. An integrative view of ends and means demands more than a pious faith in the moral law or a theoretical clarification of the necessary and contingent connection between truth and non-violence, tolerance and civility. It is essential to replace or modify the moral model underlying the sharp dichotomy between ends and means. If moral life is not mainly a matter of achieving specific objectives, politics cannot be like a field game in which a concrete ideological or technological objective is given in advance and known to all. Even if truth may be regarded as the supreme common end for all men, its content cannot be known in advance. Truth at best refers to the highest human activity rather than an imposed and predetermined target. Individuals could evolve a parapolitical ethic in terms of a theory of action under which conduct can be corrected and justified by continual reference to the indefinable Agathon and manifest *sophrosyne*. It is for the sake of moral excellence–in order that as much of it as possible may at any time exist in the world of moral persons–that anyone can feel justified in inserting himself into the social or political sphere. The *raison d'être* of virtue and excellence, the ultimate test of human endeavor, and the sovereign criterion of social progress must lie beyond the political order.

7. *New York Times,* May 1, 1973.

In rejecting the sharp dichotomy between ends and means, it is obviously not suggested that the distinction is entirely false and useless. It is undeniable that it is often possible and useful to distinguish between ends and means. The distinction is most easily made when we are considering some particular purpose a man might have in mind before embarking on a specific course of action. However, when this is generalized into an overarching paradigm for political *praxis,* we may be seriously misled by the analogous grammars of abstract and concrete terms. But if, like Bentham, we say that what a man wants is to gain or to maximize happiness, then it becomes much more difficult to make a clear distinction between the end (the greatest happiness) and the sum-total of varied means that are sought. A man's conception of happiness depends largely upon his desiring the things said to be means to it. The values commonly viewed as the supreme ends of human endeavor (happiness, freedom, welfare, etc.) are empty, apart from their apparent means. We must distinguish between men's goals and their accepted principles or rules. Sometimes, their goal is to inculcate a principle, to observe it themselves, or to communicate it to others. It seems more realistic to postulate a range of specifiable goals of varying importance than a single, supreme goal to which all others are subordinate. The distinction between ends and means becomes misleading and dangerous when we dogmatize that there is a single supreme good (or even a fixed hierarchy of goods) which can be fully formulated in an Aristotelian or utilitarian sense. Equally narrow psychoanalytic or technocratic categorizations of human needs and wants could impoverish our conception of human social fulfillment, and rationalize the adoption of political means seemingly unavoidable in the light of a somber diagnosis of the human condition. Even if everyone lived in a monolithic society with a monistic and universally accepted end, it would be difficult to make concepts such as "happiness" and "suffering" operational, quantifiable, and the indisputable basis of social consensus.

One could argue from the proposition that all men have some idea of truth but no adequate conception of Absolute Truth to the prescription that society should regard the pursuit of truth as a common end. Gandhi held that in seeking the truth, we cannot help being true to our "real" nature (identical with that of all others) and exemplifying a measure of non-violence in our attitudes and relations. It is possible if questionable to argue that the unhappiness of some is required to maximize collective happiness, that individual citizens have to be coerced for the sake of general freedom, and that the maintenance of public virtue sometimes requires subjects to choose or support a privately corrupt but efficient and outwardly respectable ruler. It would, however, be difficult to contend that the collective pursuit of truth is compatible with the adoption of dishonest devices or the condoning of untruth. This could be advanced only if a preordained, collectivist conception of truth were imposed on the members of a society, a dogmatic ideology propagated by dishonest and ruthless methods. Since none can speak convincingly in the name of Absolute Truth, all are entitled to their relative truths and each must necessarily see truth differently at any given time. Truth in this sense is identical with integrity or fidelity to one's own conscience, and no man can pursue greater integrity while sacrificing his existing integrity. The test of immediate moral integrity is authenticity in the active pursuit of truth, and this requires a high degree of non-violence. If we understand the concept of relative truth and accept its pursuit as a common end, we cannot make a hard-and-fast distinction between this end and the means toward it. On the other hand, if we particularly regard the promotion of happiness as the whole duty of man, we may in the name of efficiency become careless about the means and violate the laws of morality. The polis is essentially the domain in which all persons are free to gain skill in the art of action and learn how to exemplify commitments to truth and non-violence; the arena in which the individual quest could be furthered and the social virtues displayed among masses of citizens in a climate of tolerance and civility. A morally progressive community is one in which neither the State nor any social organization is allowed to flout with impunity the sacred principle that every man is entitled to his relative truth, and no one can claim the right to coerce another, to treat him as a means to his own end.

9
TECHNOLOGY AND POLITICS

Great things may be accomplished in our days, great discoveries, great enterprises; but these do not give greatness to our epoch. Greatness shows itself tellingly by its point of departure, by its flexibility, by its thought.

CHARLES SAINTE-BEUVE

The technological society was portrayed by Jacques Ellul, over twenty years ago, as a vast and murky labyrinth through which prowls the Minotaur of modern technology, and from which there is no escape, for either monster or mankind. Long before this, Mary Shelley conjured the powerful images of Dr. Frankenstein and his dim-witted but dangerous creation–another monster, often conflated in popular conception with Dr. Frankenstein himself. Even earlier, Dean Swift had recounted Gulliver's visit to the Academy of Lagado, where scientists sought to extract sun-beams from cucumbers, convert calcine ice into gunpowder, and prevent the growth of wool upon two young lambs, so that they might "propagate a Breed of naked Sheep all over the Kingdom." Goethe had written of the proud Dr. Faustus and his fateful pact with the Devil. Technology has often been depicted as a clumsy monster, threatening inadvertently to cripple or destroy the social and political order. We may shrink from such portraits and derisively dismiss them, but there remain too many recognizable features for our liking. We may doubtless sharpen our logical tools, point to contradictions and ambiguities in contemporary accounts of technology, and dispose of the monster by analytical skill. It is easy to quarrel with Ellul's use of selective evidence both on factual and evaluative grounds, to adduce a variety of counter-examples, and also to be too literal in responding to rhetorical devices. Nonetheless, the basic point must not be ignored if the mythified phenomenon is anything but a paper tiger.

It would be a failure in imagination to neglect Bacon's intention in retelling the ancient fable of Daedalus and Minotaur. In Ellul's treatise[1] we cannot expect Daedalus, who constructed the monster and its labyrinthine abode, to provide the crucial clue. No tyrant, thinker, or innovator can be held responsible. The fable warns us that his son Icarus destroyed himself through presumption, a danger for mankind. Our psychology of doom cannot, however, be blamed on the monster. This would be to excuse indifference to the heroism of Theseus and the wisdom of Ariadne which could presumably restore the justice and civility of the primordial order identified with Minos, even though we cannot return to the Golden Age of Kronos, the paradisiac phase of our innocence.

Today, we are confronted with a spate of writing ironically reminiscent of the fanciful flights of the *philosophes,* of prosaic and familiar passages from Weber and Lenin which supplement each other, and of the proliferating literary and philosophical treatments of alienation. The approach is that of the hedgehog rather than the fox, closer in spirit to Marx than to Pareto, yet capable of absorbing élitist theories, accounts of the mass society, doctrines of legal positivism, a Sorelian view of political myths, warnings against the police state, sociological as well as psychological simplifications of human behavior, angry exposures of democratic and authoritarian societies, as well as the neo-scholastic abstractions of numerous political scientists. Although many have provisionally ventured to develop a truly integrative theory showing (by its absorptive power) the angularity of all these approaches, none has succeeded. Ellul himself betrays a relentlessly obsessive concern to subordinate every contemporary mode of social change and activity to the causal primacy and constant sovereignty of technique (in several different senses as well as in his reified usage), a concern often criticized as needlessly monolithic. But his provocatively original argument pinpoints the relation of *la technique* and the State. Ellul

1. Jacques Ellul, *The Technological Society,* trans. John Wilkinson, New York, Knopf, 1964.

has put his finger, or perhaps his thumb, upon a formidable, still unperceived and unsolved problem.

Is it possible, in principle or in practice, for the political order to control or command the technological revolution? If not, is this because of anything intrinsic to technology itself? Has the technological revolution completely undermined every classical conception of political wisdom as well as the daring vision associated with the rise of technology in the Enlightenment, the doctrinal hope that noetic politics is capable of serving as a means to the total transformation of society? Is all of this entirely out of date? Such questions involve the significance of political rationality today, not whether men were mistaken for several centuries in construing politics in exclusively rationalist terms. By the seventeenth century, technological breakthroughs had revolutionized navigation and cartography, nurtured a renewed interest in mathematics, and filled palace gardens and theaters with water organs and mechanical swans. This enthusiasm for gadgetry masked a deeper concern to discover the principles of mechanics, which underlie modern technology and promote the rationalist faith that the interdependence of man and nature could be the basis of a new ordering of society. The parapolitical milieu found secular powers challenging the traditional dogmas of the Church, and envisaging the possibility that the scientific method might facilitate the conquest of nature and the freedom of man. The secular challenge found expression through an emerging class of entrepreneurs and financiers who exchanged land for a variety of negotiable values. By supporting an economic system of political patronage they effectively controlled every technological development–often in the direction of increasingly sophisticated armaments. The revolt against ecclesiastical feudalism was a war against priestly authority rather than divine wisdom, and the early developments in technology were not attended by philosophical materialism or scientific dogmatism. The chief figures of the Anglo-Teutonic Rosicrucian enlightenment elaborated the mysticism of the medieval alchemists in the language of Pythagorean mathematics, and a century later Newton could still contend that his sole aim in studying physics and astronomy was to comprehend better the operation of Deity in nature.

The eighteenth century witnessed the rise of a widespread recognition of the intimate connection between individual dignity and the institutional structure of society and politics. By the time the prophetic maxim *Liberté, Égalité, Fraternité* was violently appropriated by the French Revolution, incipient technology was pressed into the service of a broader stratum of society. The foreshortened sense of fraternity which stirred revolutionary France and stimulated the American experiment, harnessed the technological potential as a means of catering to the expanding demand for material goods. Unable to meet the new wants of the industrial class, the political apparatus of an increasingly complex social structure aroused mounting discontent. By the nineteenth century, however, as the Industrial Revolution transformed the managerial functions of social and political institutions, the growing bourgeoisie was sufficiently enamored of technological innovations to embrace the credo of mechanistic science crystallized into the myth of indefinite material progress. Yet, new modes of coercion emerged and emboldened power élites to propagate delusions of grandeur in relation to industrial and military strength. Technological ability allegedly gave proof of national and even racial superiority while furnishing the means for a more complacent and illiberal imperialism. Bizarre varieties of Social Darwinism were invoked to support the élitist and colonial mentality of political regimes in industrial societies. The utilitarian ethic became the basis of new dogmas of political expediency. The ideological collusion of politics and technology in the exploitation of peoples abroad found its reflection in the exploitation of the masses at home. The undeniable connection between the control of the means of production and the grossly unequal distribution of economic resources was stressed by Marx and strengthened the case for a social and political revolution which would enlist technology in the service of all mankind. As the dependency of social structures upon technological means of support has enormously increased, the impotence of political systems has become manifest in the twentieth century, and the managerial problems of modern society became acute in the 1970s.

The terms "politics" and "technology" are undeniably ambiguous. Not only is there no consensus about the meaning of the political, but there are many irreconcilable and competing conceptions of politics, ranging from the minimal–concerned chiefly with security, preservation of order, and maintenance of social equilibrium—to the maximal, where politics is identified with every social and individual goal. At this extreme, politics becomes the sole agent for social transformation, fostering different versions of messianism. There are also intermediate notions such as the politics of prevention, the view that politics is essentially an arena in which conflicts arise and are resolved, in which there are no solutions, but only settlements. In some theories this is the inherently provisional and temporizing character of the political process itself. The etymology of 'technology" is connected with *techne,* which suggests skill and art, wedded in applied science or craft. For Plato *techne* meant any disciplined activity or creative skill as opposed to *tyche,* chance, or to *physis,* natural ability, tendency, or instinct. Aristotle stressed that *techne* refers specifically to production rather than action, involving a knowledge of causes, though distinct from *theoria.* In general, technology comprises the study, use, and mastery of applied principles of production, and "technique" is any distinguishable mode of application. This could conceivably cover the entire ensemble of all practices, procedures, and methods, the totality of means available to secure all possible ends. But if we take so broad a view of technique or technology, we are faced with critical questions. Is there a technique for coordinating, synthesizing, and supervising all these techniques; if so, is that really a technique or even a meta-technique? Normally, we understand by the word "technique" the performance by men or machines of standardized tasks previously delineated in such detail that the work-agents may be regarded as intersubstitutable. Is the same true also of politics? Is politics merely specialized activity, with its own techniques? Does talk about "the routinization of politics" require us to deny any significant role to individuals or any real differences between political actors, let alone between political regimes?

Many contemporary observers contend that there is an entirely unprecedented conjunction of the State and *la technique* in modern history. Ellul calls this the most important phenomenon in history and expresses astonishment that political theorists have not only failed to notice its ramifications, but have blithely continued with more traditional approaches. Daniel Bell has referred to scientists, mathematicians, economists, and "the engineers of the new intellectual technology" as the "new men" of post-industrial society, possessing the theoretical knowledge that is the primary resource for organizational and policy decisions.[2] Systems analysts see this optimistically as an entry into an era of global self-regulation in which the political direction of social processes may be exercised through engineered devices depending upon a computerized flow of reliable technical information. Somewhat less sanguine, Victor Ferkiss depicts a vast ecological and existential revolution erupting from the impact of technology on industrial society, but argues that a new order, based upon technology and relying upon rational calculation and maximum social discipline, could be established. Ellul's observations convey two major points: first of all, a conjunction has taken place of the State and *la technique,* which is far-reaching, fundamental, and certainly more complete than was envisioned during the Enlightenment; secondly, the technical fact explains, or could be used to explain, most if not all major political events. The latter proposition simply relies upon one single explanation for all political phenomena, dissolving differences between political actors and between political regimes, and reducing all contemporary social and political phenomena to a shadowy realm of residual notions from a traditional past of grandiose political rationalizations. It obscures by exaggeration the main problem arising from the alarming fact of technological dominance. Very few go so far as to advance any comprehensive thesis about the technological imperative. Yet many of the specific features which they stress are clearly recognizable characteristics of totalitarian as well as of contemporary democratic societies.

The first point–that the conjunction of State and technique has reached a degree that is wholly unprecedented–is important and undeniable. The State increasingly invades domains that it ignored before. It has the technical resources and the power to do so, and is to some extent required to do so by the exigencies of planning. Respect for privacy has so much diminished that planners hardly attach any significance in practice to the notion of the autonomy of the individual. Consequently, moralistic critiques of political action

2. Daniel Bell, *The Coming of Post-Industrial Society,* New York, Basic Books, 1973, p. 344.

become increasingly heavy-handed and irrelevant, or are inflated by anomic social movements of anarchic and symbolic protest. They cannot in fact be focused upon a rational dialogue, and this confirms the decline of fruitful political dialogue. We may readily recognize that the State alone has the resources to mobilize research in directions which cannot be pursued by private organizations. Furthermore, because of the technical process itself and the emergence of large faceless corporations, the State is the sole available check. But this is no longer effective. With the dead weight of a complex defense establishment (and here we have the horrendous specter of the Garrison State), the problem is not only national but global. Many of our makeshift solutions on the international plane—dominated by technological considerations which seem realistic and rational—do not address themselves to the political realities of our time, which are governed by the growing interdependence of the different regimes, societies, and peoples of the world. Democratic societies, for the very reason that they are more inefficient than autocratic or authoritarian societies, though at the same time needing to defend themselves against these societies, must to some extent imitate their political antagonists.

Today, more than ever before, because of technological developments, the State must coordinate and supervise a medley of technical decisions by Benthamite planners, and support or restrain them with its own familiar sanctions. The State is not only more important than ever before, but even totalistic in mentality, if not totalitarian. Increments in technological sophistication do not, however, entail automatic increments in concentration of political power. The State is less effective because the politician has evolved a specialized political technique to win elections. The politician may masquerade as a super-technician, but he is patently incompetent, usually knowing little of advanced technology and less of genuine science. This gives rise to a parapolitical dilemma. The politician may become overtly and effectively a super-technician, attempting to coordinate all techniques, only to become a prisoner of his own political technique and of all the techniques which he attempts to coordinate. Alternatively, the politician becomes increasingly less important, inevitably more amateurish, and pathetically irrelevant to the social scene. He may continue to talk the language of political tradition or of political rationality, but this is only a smoke screen. Political doctrines are always to some extent rationalizations, but the decline in the effective importance of traditional politics actually makes these rationalizations dangerous distractions. Certainly they become hazardous when transformed into rigid political ideologies sharply contrasting different political regimes. Given this persisting dilemma, the capacity of the political order to inflate popular expectations of significant change, and its increasing inability to fulfill these expectations, combine to produce an explosive instability in technological society. This gap can never be completely closed, though there may be various means of obscuring and concealing it. Politics can continue to pursue its familiar function of maintaining "the deception of the people," but at some critical point the deception will be ruptured. More and more people will come to see this, though they will be largely unable to do anything about it. The massive ineptitude of contemporary politics is reflected in a randomness in its disposal and use of technical resources. This further undermines political effectiveness, while rendering technology, at least for the present, a clumsy monster. Old-style politicians are far from extinct, and the distinction between them and the technocrats is sufficiently sharp to merit the statement that "only God can make a tree as yet, but ordinarily it takes a government to make a park."[3] The staggering implications of DNA research may eventually falsify the first part of this conjunction, but will not necessarily negate the second. The possibilities of centralizing and mismanaging political power increase with technological sophistication, so that the monster can grow increasingly opportunistic.

Industrialized societies tend to display a schizoid attitude toward technology. The social implications of technological innovation are not easily or immediately seen beyond their initial impact and apparent use. Social and environmental myopia fosters a form of technological salvationism whereby any breakthrough or novelty is greeted with open arms. There is, however, an inbred resistance to social change and political experimentation. In consequence, so-

3. Victor C. Ferkiss, *Technological Man: The Myth and the Reality,* New York, George Braziller, 1969, p. 195.

cial structures and political institutions are increasingly eroded by the impact of technological innovation which they cannot reject, regulate, or commit themselves to absorb. Executive and legislative branches of government seem impotent in the face of conflicting and powerful interest groups who do battle against the backdrop of social and ecological disaster. Courts are clogged with civil suits and class actions based upon environmental issues. Many see the problem, yet alleviation seems impossible. While knowledge alone can never resolve clear conflicts of interest, political decision makers, who deal rather in piecemeal improvements than radical rearrangements, are saddled with the application of technological knowledge that has far outstripped their understanding of social systems and of long-term changes. This new access to power might be used to further desirable goals, such as a greater sense of autonomy in jobs and the enrichment of social relations, but the criteria for the right use of new knowledge are lacking. All too often the creation of fresh opportunities by policy decisions merely aggravates a general sense of frustration and estrangement because they are co-opted by various unenlightened entrepreneurs rather than harnessed in the service of the community.

Can political rationality, concerned with the relationship between means and ends, still cope with the overwhelming impact of modern technology? If so, can political institutions bear the cost of commitment to rational ends? To a very great extent political disagreement concerns itself with penultimate and intermediate means to desired ends. Even if universal agreement in regard to one or a few ends were achieved, there would still be disagreement about the actual means to be adopted in relation to those ends. No one would predict that all such political disagreement will cease. The persisting challenge is to refine ways by which the dissent and divergences that will always be a part of politics can be resolved by rational procedures. When the technological advances of the twentieth century promise a social and material utopia and also threaten us with the prospect of a *1984,* the preservation of political rationality requires us to confront some issues squarely. Government must justify, not merely excuse, the use of increasingly sophisticated technological means of coercion as instruments of foreign policy and domestic social control. The mindless tendency toward unlimited technological expansion calls for attention to some global principle of limitation to growth in reference to space, rate, cost, and distribution. The yearning for universal fulfillment of human needs–articulated during the Enlightenment–needs to be matched by a sufficient awareness of the critical distinction between genuine needs and rationalized greed. We cannot entrust electronics to restructure the world in the image of a global village. Nor can blatantly political decisions be disguised as pseudo-scientific, technological imperatives. Technological policy decisions cannot be solely entrusted either to an unsophisticated electorate or to a credentialed élite. These are demanding problems; to borrow an analogy from classical Sankhya philosophy, those who think they see answers often have no legs, and those who have legs often see no answers.

For Condorcet, the improvement in our technical means was necessarily connected with the improvement of human capacities and social organizations. His optimistic vision is unusually comprehensive and indeed rather difficult to understand today, for it was systematically constricted by his immediate successors. In Saint-Simon we find the belief that the old notion of politics, rooted in some kind of will-to-power in men, will automatically decline as men externalize this will-to-power in the collective desire to gain greater power over nature and over the social environment. Saint-Simon held that politics would increasingly be replaced by administration, that all citizens would become spontaneous collaborators in rational dialogue and in associations united for social welfare, and that there would be less and less room for the "old-style" politics which seeks power over man. This has not yet transpired. If it has emerged at all, it is in ways totally different from Saint-Simon's anticipations. Optimism has been submerged under mounting gloom. The Comtean view of an automatic parallelism between intellectual growth and technical development has powerfully affected us only in the Marxist version in which this parallelism is itself subsumed under a sharper theory of economic and social determinism. But for Marx, politics preoccupied with the will-to-power is a compensatory illusion for politicians who are unwilling or unable to alter the social structure, and when the fundamental problem of social transformation is permanently solved by revolutionary leadership, the politics of the past will become wholly irrelevant.

Owing to the atrophy of political wisdom, it seems as if we must either talk in terms of administration and accede to rationalization, or passively accept that we are confronted with the evil enormities of irrational individuals like Hitler and Stalin, capable of using the vast technical apparatus of the State effectively to ruin their own societies and the incipient world order. Seemingly transfixed between political amorality and administrative rationalization, we are far removed from both classical and modern conceptions of political wisdom, and they may seem to have little relevance to the facts. The liberal ideal of political education has been substantially perverted and almost destroyed by new modes of political propaganda in an era when all education increasingly becomes a kind of brainwashing, a manipulation of wills and opinions. There is neither any real sense of rational participation (even in a democracy), nor a truly democratic education. Far more important than any gap in technological expertise, it is the rationality gap between rulers and ruled which is being evaded. Arguing for a fresh examination of the relationship between individual rights and public responsibilities, Emmanuel Mesthene concludes that the political challenge of technology may be met by reassessment of fundamental commitments:

> Given the inadequacy of old formulas, it may be that inquiry into the problem of human choice and effective citizenship in a technological society is more fruitfully conducted in terms of the kinds of commitment that individuals living in such a society are called upon to make. As at once individuals and social beings, all of us eventually come to some balance, appropriate to each of us, between the relative degree of commitment we are prepared to make to private and to public goals and values. Each of us must achieve a symbiotic relationship between our private and public selves. . . .[4]

Altogether, Ellul's deceptively plausible diagnosis carried with it a strong anti-theoretical, anti-intellectual presupposition: political ideas are apparently not as important as we think, and they never were so important. Now we are told that they have become obsolescent, that we must choose between anachronisms and modernity. Such a dichotomy, however, is as deceptive as it is intriguing. Tra-

4. Emmanuel G. Mesthene, *Technological Change,* New York, Mentor, 1970, p. 88.

ditional political goals have always required restatements to be applied to altered conditions. The renewal of their relevance on a global plane could secure the rational cooperation of constructive thinkers in all societies. Crystallized political concepts need to be freshly formulated through a rethinking of past illusions and doctrines, inherited versions of secular and sacred utopias, in order to be translated into a conception of political rationality that can serve the future. The dilemma supposedly created by the technological imperative may be yet another gloomy illustration of the logic of the Cartesian method, which excels only to destroy itself. Perhaps the Comtean doctrine of automatic secular progress directed by a benign sacred presence is merely being replaced by an equally irresponsible historicist doctrine of automatic regression dictated by some unspecified eschatology. The fatalistic denial of effective rationality merely ratifies in advance the conclusion that politics can neither control nor soothe the technological monster. Rather than succumb to the soporific theology of a technocratic apocalypse, we could choose to dissociate from the persisting temptation to delineate human possibilities solely in terms of external forces. Rather than regret the demise of a romanticist notion of freedom, we could, with Spinoza, affirm that knowledge of natural necessity is the beginning of genuine freedom. In a recent statement, sociologist Raymond Boudon concluded from his study of perverse effects in the cumulative process of social interaction:

> In my view the time has come to bridge the rather absurd gulf between the image of man as a rational being and master of his destiny–an image inherited from the Enlightenment and reinforced by economic theory–and that of man as a passive being flung about at the mercy of the elements, which sociology propounds. I am convinced that man's real image is different. I see it as a cross between the limitations of individual circumstance and the possibilities opened up by free will.[5]

The Enlightenment ideal of a unified science of man is still far from realization, and, no doubt, will never emerge in the form sought after by Comte or anticipated by Carnapian positivism. But

5. Raymond Boudon, "The Law of Perverse Effects," *Atlas,* vol. 25, no. 4, April 1978, pp. 23-24.

when rationality in its modern dress dethrones and denies classical reason, it wraps itself in a technocratic cleverness that becomes irrationality itself. The technological society is not threatened by the inescapable conflict of technology and politics, but rather by an avoidable conflation of technique and shallow rationality. The promise and performance of technique compels the technological society to face profounder issues of parapolitics. Reason in the service of technique, employing only the categories and conceptions of conventional politics, is indeed inept; technique in the service of reason, when wedded to a parapolitical awareness of existential scarcity and ontological plenty, is central to the classical conception of politics as an art. As architects of societies, human beings can accept parameters while assigning priorities that are consonant with cherished values. The possibility of success in any endeavor implies the contingency of failure, but to insist upon certainty even before the effort is made is to be unduly insecure and to forfeit rational initiative. The monster of technology, as the Japanese cinema repeatedly reminds us, is a massive projection of our own ignorance of ourselves. Rather than becoming hypnotized by an irrational fear of the future as we helplessly cringe before a nightmare monster, we must confidently retract the self-reproducing projections of our technology to their source and dispel the shadow of collective impotence. In seeking a fresh and feasible vision of man and nature, we dare not dispense with a fearless recognition of the social costs of all commitments to the practical use of human knowledge, with its limits and possibilities.

10

CIVITAS DEI AND THE CLASSLESS SOCIETY

Thousands of people may live in the world but we cannot call it a fellowship until they know themselves and feel sympathy for each other. A true community is a place where truth and wisdom are its light, where the people know and trust one another, where they have things in common, and where there is a harmonious organization. Harmony is its life, its happiness and its meaning. GAUTAMA BUDDHA

It would be churlish to contest sincere proclamations about the need for mutual understanding among those Christians and Marxists who still dream of *Civitas Dei* or the Classless Society. But there is a crucial credibility problem which we must not evade. Is any genuine dialogue feasible at all? Are there any terms on which dialogue between Christians and Marxists would leave inviolate the intellectual integrity of both, would avoid a *dialogue des sourds,* and would allow them to coexist in the forums of *Civitas Humana?* In facing the central issue, it would be helpful to distinguish between three levels of confrontation. In an essay written in the eighteen-forties, Marx observed that members of a civil society are not godlike egoists but merely egotistic men. A contemporary corollary to his statement is the sad fact that godless atheists and presumably God-fearing "true believers" are equally enmeshed in the complex structure of a technological society. They are alike inhibited by the routinized roles and compensatory delusions of an atomized, impersonal, industrial civilization militantly defended by the inflated ideologies of competing nation-states. A contemporary psychoanalyst might deplore the fact that the leading spokesmen of these ideologies are not even egotistic men but rather undeveloped adults with a strong infantile tendency to indulge in guilt-ridden fantasies and anxiety-laden wish-fulfillment. This state of mind seems to be obsessional, sustained by escalating fear based upon almost insurmountable ignorance. On this level of consciousness the concern with dialogue could itself be a version of wish-fulfillment, an unfalsifiable myth promising that as the capitalist and socialist systems settle down in an uneasy yet unavoidable opposition, their increasing interaction and partial convergence will force undeveloped adults to grow into mature persons beyond auto- and hetero-stereotypes. This is no basis for an authentic dialogue in the imminent future.

There is a second level of encounter, on which Marxists and Christians who know themselves as egotistic men (in contrast with undeveloped adults) can conduct an honest and meaningful dialogue. They could come together with the inward recognition that they are intellectually conditioned by a particular social system, with a distinctive culture and social history. They are motivated by apocalyptic faith (couched in the vocabulary of a closed system of concepts and beliefs) representing a plausible though incomplete version of universalization. Despite this initial and persisting limitation, each Marxist or Christian has his or her own inimitable life-history as a human being. Philosophically, each one is, in a Leibnizian sense, a monad with a necessary viewpoint–an ineradicable and distinctively angular view–logically independent of his Marxist or Christian belief system. The cost of commitment to dialogue is the surrender of methodological imperialism, the cultivation of doctrinal tolerance and linguistic civility, and the keen perception, behind the systemic bias of Marxists or Christians, of a rich diversity in the peculiar life-bias of individuals. A standpoint such as this can be accommodated within either Marxism or Christianity by sophisticated adherents. In conditions of inescapable interaction, paranoid self-centeredness produces a poor caricature of dialogue. Only strenuous self-correction can provide the basis for a genuine beginning.

But what is the hope for a third and higher level of intellectual and ethical confrontation? Can sensitive and humane Marxists and Christians come together as "godlike egoists"? Can Christians as well as contemporary Marxists see themselves and each other as members of a *human,* not merely a civil, society? In order to move in this direction, we could borrow from evolutionary biology the demonstrable assertion of the collective capacity of men to transcend their environment, however imperfectly. The critical leap is to the assumption that the individual too has the inherent ability partially to transcend his environment. To the Marxist it might seem that this assumption regresses toward a romantic fallacy, and a Christian thinker might concede that he too does not want to deny sociological interaction–he also knows that no man is an island. However, the individual's capacity for partial transcendence does not require total detachment from collective history, social determination, or contemporary culture, either for the individual Christian or for the individual Marxist. Neither would find it easy to hold seriously an assumption which both might agree to make the basis of a developing dialogue but which is not the existential truth by which they live. They have alike learned only too well to defer to external authority, and to a metaphysical belief in the rightness and necessity of such deference to an omnipotent sovereign outside themselves, whether located wholly in history or partly beyond it.

Neither Marxist nor Christian can readily conceive what it would be like for a man to seek to be godlike. A perceptive philosopher from the pre-Christian era of classical antiquity, or from a non-Christian culture, might identify at least three specific components of a godlike state: self-determination in its fullest sense and in the universal context of creative imagination; a transpersonal level of self-consciousness characterized by the capacity to internalize logically prior and empirically evident laws of nature; and, more concretely, the virtual absence of any volitional gap between intention and result, image and event, thought and act. This is an exacting and elusive ideal, metaphysically, mythically, and metaphorically. Going back to Pythagoras, who first coined the term "philosopher" and laid the methodological basis of exact science, as well as the ethical paradigm of intentional communities, it is part of the Socratic-Platonic inheritance. It cannot be congenially accommodated within Christian culture, modern capitalism, or Marxist communism. Today it seems fortunate for the new nations, and indeed for the world at large, that the Christian and Marxist milieus cannot produce leaders who can conceive such a godlike state even as a logical possibility. There is an acute gap between intention and result, and just as well, for our inhumanity is hindered by our fallibility and relative impotence. Nietzsche observed that "not their love of men but the impotence of their love of men keeps the Christians of today from–burning us."[1] At the same time, our humanness is threatened today by the intolerable growth of the gap between thought and act, the ubiquitous paralysis of will, the glaring absence of creative imagination and forward-looking vision in leaders throughout the world.

The minimal transcendence of partisanship needed for a fruitful dialogue eludes Christians and Marxists alike. The critical breakthrough from being egotistic men to becoming godlike egoists–let alone a transcendence of egoism–has been made by very few. It is easy enough, in a formal sense, to see the individual as a moral agent in a Kantian model, and also possible, with Shelley, to envisage the poetic ideal of the free man:

> The loathsome mask has fallen, the man remains
> Sceptreless, free, uncircumscribed, but man
> Equal, classless, tribeless, and nationless,
> Exempt from awe, worship, degree . . .
> *Prometheus Unbound*

It is much more challenging to imagine the coming together of even a few Marxists and Christians able and willing to enter the entirety of the human enterprise, rising to a parapolitical vision of human solidarity and world history. Once free from the neurotic need to make unique claims on behalf of their own camp, once immune from the preoccupation with collectivist self-flattery, they could be sensitive to the present historical moment, focusing upon the primary needs of the world's disinherited billions. They must speak and act within the larger context of diverse religions and political creeds, rather than masquerade as messiahs with mandates for global leadership. Many Marxists and Christians might insist that to abandon their messianic mantle is tantamount to forfeiting their

1. Friedrich Nietzsche, *Beyond Good and Evil,* trans. Walter Kaufman, New York, Random House, 1966, p. 84.

intellectual integrity. However, it is not logically incompatible with the doctrinal demands of soteriological allegiance to secure preliminary agreement to several propositions, both theoretical and historical.

Sophisticated Christians and Marxists could agree that there is no neutrally acceptable cosmic or historic guarantee in Christ or Marx, Christianity or Marxism, capitalist democracy or communist socialism, and that the gap between theory and practice, between ideal and reality, can never be wholly closed by Church, State, or Party. This is not to deny any role to Church, State, or Party. Historically and at present, the most intractable controversies (and the biggest waste of time and energy) revolve around the presumed and actual capacity of any particular human or social institution to speak and act as the acceptably unique bearer of a messianic mandate for universal salvation–whether a mondialistic Church, a monolithic Marxist International, or a monopolistic World State. No such mandate can be accepted by all humanity. Sophisticated Marxists and Christians recognize this and are now willing to shed the messianic mantle. Indeed, they sometimes insist that their respective belief systems require as much.

The Church once perceived itself as a concrete society, the new Israel which anticipated the Kingdom of God. Under Origen's influence in the third century, the Church was seen instead as the guardian of *gnosis,* the divine wisdom which leads the soul from time to eternity. Origen envisioned a *Civitas Dei* showing more affinities with the Invisible Church and the Stoic Commonwealth than with the tribal Kingdom of God. Augustine was more concerned to base his *Civitas Dei* upon scriptural canon. He could regard neither the Roman Empire as wholly bad nor the visible Church as wholly good. For him the contrasting *Civitas Dei* and *Civitas Terrena* were ideal conceptions which could not be fully represented in space and time. Though Augustine posits the equation *Civitas Dei* = Kingdom of Heaven = Church, he himself undermines it. As Bishop J. W. C. Wand perceptively remarks:

> As there is no one material "Rome" or "Babylon" that can be completely identified with the earthly city, so there is no one organization, not even the Church, that can be com-

> pletely identified with the City of God. Perhaps the nearest equivalent to the City of God is to be found in that notion of an "Invisible Church" which loomed so large in Reformation theology, and made it impossible to recapture an adequate notion of the visible Church until our own day.[2]

The Pauline epistles depicted the Kingdom of Heaven as a *politeuma,* a celestial polis, including those righteous citizens of *Civitas Terrena* who are also fellow citizens (*sympolitai*) with the saints in heaven.

Augustine encountered difficulties in concretely identifying the place of the Church in relation to *Civitas Dei.*

> The Kingdom by etymology must consist solely of those in whose hearts God's rule is acknowledged; its limits are known only to God, but it is to be found in every sphere, secular or ecclesiastical, where men are seeking conscientiously to carry out God's will. The city, however, like the Church, includes both saints and sinners. We may conclude then that the City is an ideal conception not strictly identical with either the Church or the Kingdom of God but having affinities with both.[3]

Augustine's *Civitas Dei* exercised a profound influence both on subsequent Christian tradition and on reactions to it. The *philosophes* examined Christian philosophy harshly and demythologized the scriptures, yet they dismantled *Civitas Dei* only to rebuild it as *Civitas Humana,* in which salvation is found not in an extra-cosmic God but in man himself, and through the efforts of successive generations of men. *Amor Dei* was given a practical meaning in *amor humanitas,* and the doctrine of vicarious atonement transmuted into that of the progressive perfectibility of man. *Civitas Humana* was seen as a fact for those who self-consciously chose to be its citizens and an ideal for the whole of future humanity.

Among Marxists one finds a similar recognition concerning the relation of the Party or the Socialist State to the ideal of the Classless Society, and the dangers inherent in attempts to absolutize any

2. J. W. C. Wand, ed., *St. Augustine's City of God,* New York, Oxford University Press, 1963, pp. xvi-xvii.
3. *Ibid.*, pp. xviii-xix.

instantiation of the former in the name of the latter. Trotsky observed that the completion of the socialist revolution is impossible within national limits. Although it may begin in the national arena, it must assume the nature of a permanent revolution eventuating in a new society extending over the entire planet.[4] He criticized as pedantic and lifeless the classifications of socialist ideologues of the Comintern who sought to consolidate national communism at the expense of global revolution. The doctrine of socialism in one country and the theory of permanent revolution are mutually exclusive. Permanent revolution alone will produce fundamental human changes. As to the intellectual integrity of communism itself, Lenin warned of the dangers of not perfecting the mind through the critical assimilation of principal facts and the "knowledge of all the treasures created by mankind." A steady but undigested diet of Party tracts will clearly not suffice:

> If a Communist took it into his head to boast about his communism because of the ready-made conclusions he had absorbed, without putting in a great deal of serious and hard work, without understanding the facts which he must examine critically, he would be a very sorry Communist. Such superficiality would be decidedly fatal. If I know that I know little, I shall strive to learn more; but if a man says that he is a Communist and that he need know nothing thoroughly, he will never be anything like a Communist.[5]

In addition to muting the messianic trumpets, Christians and Marxists could concur, without any loss of integrity, in legitimating the right of each individual to be a Christian or Marxist in his own unique way, acting in a manner compatible with the present historical moment. In responding to whatever is outside and beyond him in a mode that expresses his personal and moral autonomy, he is establishing his integrity as an individual Christian or Marxist as well as asserting an essential element in his species nature as a human being. Since Marx borrowed this telling phrase from Feuer-

4. Leon Trotsky, *The Permanent Revolution,* New York, New Park Publishers, 1962, p. 157.
5. Vladimir Il'ich Lenin, "Address at Congress of Russian Young Communist League," *The Young Generation,* New York, International Publishers, 1940, pp. 28-32.

bach, a contemporary Marxist might well restore some of the richness in Feuerbach's conception without altogether abandoning Marx's own use of it. Such a standpoint rules out not only the waspish and cowardly backbiting that shadows the conferences of intellectuals, but equally the clannish get-together and ganging up of smug though insecure groups of Christians and Marxists. None of these tendencies have any place in the universal and humanist visions underlying Marxism and Christianity. Marx urged each individual, in his everyday life, in his work and his relationships, to recognize and organize his own powers as social powers, and to refrain from conceiving them as politically alienated from his species being. For Marx, communism is the restoration and normalization of man's authentic humanity–discovered only in his social capacity to assimilate all previous human development in the light of collective possibilities.

> Let us assume man to be man, and his relation to the world to be a human one. Then love can only be exchanged for love, trust for trust, etc. If you wish to enjoy art you must be an artistically cultivated person; if you wish to influence other people you must be a person who really has a stimulating and encouraging effect upon others. Every one of your relations to man and to nature must be a specific expression, corresponding to the object of your will, of your real individual life. If you love without evoking love in return, i.e., if you are not able, by the manifestation of yourself as a loving person, to make yourself a beloved person, then your love is impotent and a misfortune.[6]

The principle that the revolutionary movement toward the Classless Society must proceed through association and organized action was for Marx and Engels less a statement of means than recognition of the permanent relevance of the community of free men as an end. Since cultivation of the individual can occur only in the community, personal freedom is possible only within the social context. Mutual association and human solidarity are the founda-

6. T. B. Bottomore, ed., *Early Writings of Marx* [1848], London, Watts, 1963, p. 194.

tion stones of positive individual freedom. But these fundamental insights offer no justification for a few Party loyalists to dictate the ideologically acceptable means of realization to the proletariat, much less to ask the mass of men to suppress their own ideas until the official revolution is secure. Similarly, Christians might profitably note the melancholy but persistent humanism of Augustine in the exposition of *Civitas Terrena.* Despite natural human bonds, mankind the world over appears to be divided against itself. Marxists may prefer the complementary Rousseauite formulation that man is born free but is everywhere in chains, yet both Christians and Marxists are agreed on the universal plight of man. Augustine distinguishes *Civitas Dei* and *Civitas Terrena* not in terms of factors alien to man, but in terms of the opposed qualities of human will and love: "Two loves built two Cities–the earthly, which is built up by the love of self to the contempt of God, and the heavenly, which is built up by the love of God to the contempt of self."[7] Nevertheless, the two cities ". . . have been running their course mingling one with the other through all the changes of time from the beginning of the human race, and shall so move on together until the end of the world."[8] While regretting cupidity and human weakness, Augustine holds that the frustrated desire for fellowship and peace is central to life in *Civitas Terrena.* To alleviate the grinding selfishness which had vitiated the *Pax Romana,* destroying its courage and probity, its law and justice, and leaving only an oppressive but empty form, Augustine proposed the ideal of the *Civitas Dei.* "Its citizens were a truly united family, each member of which sought the good of the whole, while all together sought the good of each individual."[9] After suggesting that the historical failures of the Church were due to common human weaknesses, Bishop Wand pleads that the important possibilities of the future lie within man himself, that we need to interpret anew the signs of the times to unearth human dignity and hope.

In conjunction with the recognition of human potentials, Christians and Marxists alike must explicitly renew their deepest recognition of the ineradicable gap between the "deterministic" working

7. *De Vivitate Dei,* XIV, 2.
8. *De Catechizandis Rundibus,* XXI, 37.
9. Wand, *op. cit.,* pp. xxi-xxii.

of the dialectic–whether divine or historic–in the collective life of mankind and the capacity of imaginative individuals to initiate their own dialectical transition between theory and practice. The recognition of this ever-present gap naturally raises the vexing issues of assigning responsibility and making appraisals in regard to the historical misdeeds of Christian cultures and Marxist societies. An affirmation is needed on both sides that the larger ideals of a developing dialectic cannot be assigned to an edited version of history or an expedient doctrine of the importance or insignificance of individuals. Christians who deplore the possibility of progress cannot appeal to Augustine as a sanction for their pessimism. Although Augustine might seem to dismiss secular history as intrinsically unprogressive, he did not create a static contrast between the two cities. Far from locating the responsibility for the human condition in factors beyond alteration, Augustine could even be taken to advocate concerted action to seek some earthly justice, founded upon a common will. Society as a whole will be judged by the nature of its affections, so that individual morality and the communal ethic converge, the latter being the sum of the former. The whole conception of *Civitas Dei* was intended to provide the individual with a basis for the transcendence of crippling material existence and for the freedom of full moral responsibility. Although Marxists may disavow the religious ideals of an Augustine, they cannot reject the function of human initiative in the process of history. Some Marxists have been concerned to make the processes of history fully self-conscious and hold that history is less experienced than constructed. It is actively wrought from the play of oppositional forces.

Engels extolled the emergence of man into truly human conditions of existence, stressing the Marxist doctrine of the superiority of man to history:

> Man's own social organization, hitherto confronting him as a necessity imposed by Nature and history, now becomes the result of his own free action. The extraneous objective forces that have hitherto governed history pass under the control of man himself. Only from that time will man himself, more and more consciously, make his own history–only from that time will the social causes set in movement by him have, in the main and in a constantly growing measure, the results

> intended by him. It is the ascent of man from the kingdom of necessity to the kingdom of freedom.[10]

In one of his most remarkable passages, Marx himself espoused the fundamental Promethean standpoint against all cowardly determinisms and orthodoxies:

> Prometheus's admission: "In sooth all gods I hate" [Aeschylus, *Prometheus Bound*] is its own admission, its own motto against all gods, heavenly and earthly, who do not acknowledge the consciousness of man as the supreme divinity. There must be no god on a level with it.
>
> And to the wretched March hares who exult over the apparent deterioration of philosophy's social position it again answers, as Prometheus did to Hermes, the messenger of the gods: "I shall never exchange my fetters for slavish servility. 'Tis better to be chained to the rock than bound to the service of Zeus."
>
> Prometheus is the noblest of saints and martyrs in the calendar of philosophy.[11]

We have too often witnessed the adroitness with which intellectual apologists can incorporate persecuted heretics of the past into their own currently respectable and streamlined versions of history. This will be irresistibly tempting so long as questions about past purges, persecutions, and pogroms are unavoidable in dialogues between Marxists and Christians. It is important and necessary, therefore, for both to concede that individual Marxists and Christians today need not carry the burden of blame for historical atrocities. That a man is a Marxist does not require him to be accountable for the Stalinist purges; every Christian does not have to be held personally responsible for the Inquisition or for every papal or clerical pronouncement on Nazism and fascism. One's accountability should be restricted to the practices that one's own beliefs and

10. "Socialism: Utopian and Scientific" [1880], in Marx-Engels, *Selected Works,* vol. II, Moscow, Foreign Languages Publishing House, 1962, pp. 150-53.

11. Karl Marx, "Foreword to Thesis: The Difference between the Natural Philosophy of Democritus and the Natural Philosophy of Epicurus" [1841], in Karl Marx and Friedrich Engels, *On Religion,* New York, Schocken Books, 1964, p. 15.

commitments entail, not to the excesses of others. Such thorny issues center upon the delicate question of ideological and doctrinal purity. Intellectuals often tend to deplore the lack of a "pure" religion or revolution. Though this concern may be understandable, perhaps reflecting an inextinguishable longing in the human heart, it only too often results in a crop of diehard intellectualist errors. The deeper difficulty and the graver wrong arise when intellectuals are willing to pass off the patently impure as "pure" in some sense and surreptitiously import their own version of historical progress or the whitewash of pseudo-history. It is pertinent here to recall Shaw's telling remark that the council that rehabilitated Saint Joan was even more culpable than that which condemned her. Intellectuals, and not only professional apologists (ecclesiastical or party hacks), are today peculiarly vulnerable to corruption in this connection. "Impurities" involving injustice and bloodshed are evaded as mere imperfections grounded in human nature or the human condition, in original sin or a unique historical context. These modes of self-justification subvert the creative dynamism inherent in *Civitas Humana,* leaving Christians with an unbridgeable chasm between *Civitas Dei* and *Civitas Terrena* and Marxists with a *Civitas Terrena* which will be redeemed automatically. The dehumanization inherent in dialogue on this basis is only too apparent to those outside it. Marxists and Christians could, however, agree that any discussion about degrees of "impurity" within either system of thought and practice could be deferred until there is a more civil and common understanding of the present historical moment in relation to the foreseeable future.

The most profitable dialogue will require a convergence of different modes of transcendence, legitimated differently by Christians and by Marxists, a convergence that enables them to gain credibility with each other and to test their responses to the common needs of mankind in our time. The historical moment has arrived when the Biblical "curse of the poor" and the Marxist self-consciousness of the world's proletariat are pressing upon us from all sides. Dialogue between Christians and Marxists is no longer merely a matter of mutual credibility (though that, heaven knows and Marx knew, is difficult enough). It cannot avoid the global audience that awaits it, an audience increasingly dominated by angry young men and women who cannot wait upon the pre-*Götterdämmerung* wisdom of their morally bankrupt elders. Even sensitive Marxists and contrite Christians may not resolve the unanswered questions of history. But their dialogue dare not ignore completely, except at the cost of falsity and emptiness, the untidy muddles bequeathed this generation by its deferential predecessors. We are the inheritors of a vast and awful burden of historical memories generated by rival mandates, sacred and secular. These mandates–dubiously derived, perhaps, from the healing words of great spiritual teachers–came to be territorially restricted by institutional defenders of religious "isms," so that a variety of walls were erected between "true believers," non-believers, and heretics beyond the pale. This legacy, still present, will require something more revolutionary than the most fervent ecumenism to resolve the hostilities and hatreds bred by past betrayals and tragedies which have left wounds. We are also the legatees of a more recent and ill-shared global inheritance, a prospectus for universal human progress and freedom issued by the *philosophes* and theophilanthropists of the eighteenth century. This mandate has also come to be territorially restricted by successive rival bands of revolutionaries. More walls have been erected between *soi disant* radicals and reactionaries in rich and poor nations alike.

These historical burdens–the burden of memories of betrayal that have their roots in ancient and medieval history, and the burden of extravagant but unfulfilled promises associated with the Enlightenment and subsequent revolutions–provoke us to confront questions that can no longer be ignored. How revolutionary can the sincere but insufficient ecumenism of our time make all our religious leaders? Will they stand aside from contemporary and prospective revolutions, or will they try to subvert them, temper them with honeyed words, or consecrate them with holy oil as expediency dictates? Or will they sympathize with their aims and seek to soften the harsh intensity of hasty and desperate methods? On the other side, how ecumenical will the rival revolutionaries of today become, including the apostles of technological and sociological revolutions in the affluent countries, the social revolutions already frustrated in the poorer new nations, and the political revolutions occurring or still to be initiated in the oppressed regions of the earth? Clearly, Christians and Marxists as well as advocates of other faiths have much unfinished, even undiscussed business on the world's agenda before coexistence and civility can become more than fraudulent slogans of convenience. The most persistent problem will remain with us, perhaps until the end of the century, though some would say forever. It was raised by both Buddha and Christ, and as recently as the social revolution stirred by Marx and the ethical revolution initiated by Gandhi. It was memorably formulated by a Russian populist in the last century: *Shall we admit all men into the banquet of life?* To refuse to consider this question is to be deaf to the cry of human suffering, to forget to ask whether I am my brother's keeper, to care nothing for whether the wretched of the earth can lose their chains. Which affluent man, nation, or church sufficiently wants a redistribution of the world's income and resources to relinquish a significant measure of wealth, power, and competitive status? How many can generate what the Quakers call a "concern" for other men, an active force that arises "through the motion of love," not through what persons think they ought to do or would merely like to do?

Such questions are so difficult that answers must be tentative. The very attempt to raise them holds out the possibility of a minimal transcendence of human egotism and even of godlike egoism. The spirit of fearless honesty, uncalculating self-examination, and unqualified empathy may still seem a luxury to an older generation of intellectuals. But it is seen by more and more restless youth in many countries as a necessary basis for a new and revolutionary way of life which wholly repudiates the System as an insupportable state of mind. In their desperate alienation from a world in which they see so little meaning or joyous vitality, they are unwilling to settle for sophistical formulations. The disinherited young of the more affluent and powerful nations of the world often show an effortless sympathy for the dispossessed and the underprivileged.

It is natural for some Europeans–Christian, Marxist, and diverse combinations of the two–to hope that world leadership might emerge from a closer *rapprochement* between Christian and Marxist intellectuals, even if cynical non-Europeans might construe this as an ideological cover for collusion. Such cynicism need not deter Christian and Marxist intellectuals from seeking ways of reflecting and reinforcing latent moral solidarity on a global plane. If nothing else, Christians and Marxists aspiring to the highest level of dialogue could come into close and fruitful contact with creative minorities of other creeds who care deeply for the universal brotherhood of man. Concentration upon concrete human needs and the societies of the future will surely demand the utmost integrity and constructive imagination of Christians and Marxists alike. If concerned Christians and Marxists are to draw a circle large enough to accommodate each other, they will need to meet both as individuals and as self-tested citizens of the world. If they can do this, they might draw an even larger circle to include those, neither Christian nor Marxist, who can readily acknowledge Christ and Marx as ill-served benefactors of humanity.

11

DEMOCRACY AND LIBERTY IN EMERGING POLITIES

True democracy begins
With free confession of our sins
In this alone are all the same,
All are so weak that none dare claim
"I have the right to govern," or
"Behold in me the Moral Law":
And all real unity commences
In consciousness of differences
That all have wants to satisfy
And each a power to supply.
W. H. AUDEN

I

Political democracy and public liberties need rethinking as well as strengthening in emerging polities precisely because they are less securely grounded than the original founders could have possibly anticipated. The experience of the past decades has sadly been extremely unfavorable to the short-term prospects of democratic government in meeting the demands of economic growth and social transformation. And yet, there is nothing in the conditions and problems of emerging polities that is inherently contrary to the intentions of democratic development or incompatible with commitment to its unrelenting pursuit. Democracy is neither a parochial parlor game nor a peculiar national sport, despite the claims of some democrats. Liberty is neither an exotic plant suited only to special soils nor a disembodied spirit that deigns to take possession of chosen peoples, despite the pretensions of some libertarians. Both democracy and liberty are universifiable, although different traditions and new needs present formidable challenges to our conventional conceptions and demand high costs of commitment. The deficiencies and defects of the structure of political democracy and public liberties in the older States are enormously pertinent to those emerging polities which truly wish to profit from the lessons and illusions of traditional democratic development. There is ample room for radical reform in the older States, and at least some of their problems are common to the new States. There is no problem facing the new democracies that has been wholly solved in the older States. In tackling common as well as special problems, the emerging polities in which have survived ancient communities and civilizations should avail themselves of their own time-tested philosophies and cultural traditions, thus enriching the concepts as well as the structure of democratic government and liberal society in unexpected ways in the coming decades. The practical implications of these propositions are most important. Pessimism of a persisting nature about the costs of commitment to democracy and liberty in emerging polities may result in a total abandonment of the quest that would be tragic. Similarly, a naïve imitativeness in the emerging polities fostered by the defensive self-complacency of the older democracies may result in a dangerous distortion of the universal quest for liberty and equality.

Every profound political idea casts its ideological shadow. Every successful political system is caught to some degree in the glamour of its own propaganda and in the costly unreality of its own mythology. Among democrats and libertarians there are three illusions that die hard and have culminated in corresponding myths. There is first of all the illusion of political arithmetic, the modern belief in the magic of universal suffrage, the élitist reliance upon statistical notions of the normal and the average and the standard deviations therefrom. This is the classifier's attempt to reduce all democracies to a single scale, the academic urge to quantify that which is qualitative and to predict the path of movement of ever-changing institutions and individuals. The corresponding myth is that appropriate machinery may be devised to make democracy secure and to maintain it by the automatic operation of mechanical procedures and that this machinery may be exported wholesale to any country that desires to become democratic and free. Even Mill, who has often misled democrats by his deceptive simplicity and confident tone of voice, recognized this illusion which leads many to look upon representative government as they would upon a "steam plough or a threshing machine." Secondly, there is the illusion of political algebra, the mystique of certain political equations and functional relationships, the reliance upon certain tendencies as constants of human nature, the readiness to regard individuals as interchangeable once the conditions of determinate equilibrium are known, and the endless obsession with the entire process. The corresponding myth is that democracy and liberty rest upon political doctrines concerning the separation of powers, checks and balances, the rule of law, and a panoply of cautionary devices to prevent hasty decisions. Thirdly, there is the illusion of political geometry, the belief in the sanctity of certain constitutional patterns and political forms, the reliance upon certain fulcrum points in the system, the attempt to reduce as much as possible to a definite and final shape, and the concern with the ideal harmony of the whole. The corresponding myth is that democracy and liberty are secured through skill in constitution making and streamlining the political structure, that the new democracies need constitutional experts and libertarian missionaries.

Democracy and liberty, like all political concepts, have a high degree of open-endedness and inevitable imprecision, but they are conspicuous for their enormous emotive flavor and hortatory function. There are two paradigmatic misuses of these terms, two fashionable ways of stretching their meanings, one practical, the other theoretical. The former is familiar enough, the blasphemous application of "democracy" and even of "freedom" by Hitler and Mussolini, Stalin and Salazar to what we rightly regard as their very opposites. This massacre of concepts that are no longer innocent is not confined to totalitarian Herods but has become subtly absorbed into the political language of double-think and double-talk of decent people in the older as well as the emerging polities, in imperialist as well as progressive circles. Even at the time of the American Civil War, the term "democracy" was brandished on both sides, by Calhoun as well as Lincoln. The other systematic misuse of words consists in defining liberty and democracy negatively in relation to despotism and dictatorship. In its simplest form this goes as far back as Alcibiades: "All that is opposed to despotic power has the name of democracy." These concepts are made to connote chiefly the traditional safeguards against tyranny and totalitarianism. Thus they lose their deeper meaning as much by inflation or deflation as by inversion. Their richness and vitality are lost if they are analyzed only in terms of their antithetical counterparts. That this is done at all is an indication of the strange unsureness of democrats and libertarians in their defensive roles and polemical postures.

II

Democracy may be viewed as an ideal, a method, and a process. From all three standpoints, it has a fundamental purpose which gives it a value of its own that makes it seem–like liberty–an end in itself. This purpose is political education in the widest and best sense, a strong commitment to training the populace in the arts of individual citizenship and collective coexistence. As an ideal, it is a system of self-rule that makes no distinction between the government and the governed on the personal, local, or national planes of decision making. This ideal being unattainable on a large scale or at the existing level of individual development, pure democracy remains a logical construction, a notional norm, a conceptual model. The reconciliation of this remote yet powerful frame of reference with existing realities has necessitated popular myths and political fictions as well as a host of pragmatic devices and social conventions. The myth of popular sovereignty, the fiction of the general will, the device of representative government, and the convention that distinguishes the State from the government, are obvious examples.

As a method, democracy is a peaceful mode of securing agreement through free discussion, of settling disputes through various types of arbitration, and of civilizing the procedures of expressing and maintaining disagreement in an atmosphere of amiable tolerance, self-restraint, and mutual respect between persons, parties, and groups. As this method is elusive and subtle, there has been in practice a fetishistic tendency toward formalism, toward the exaltation of conventional procedures and known precedents. As a process of political activity, democracy is a system of popular consent as well as responsible government, of dialogue and dialectic. To use the language of Lenin, it is a talking-shop as well as a working-shop. The dialogue is open to all, ceaseless in operation, and assumes a variety of forms and channels as well as periodic opportunities for the articulation of the wishes and will of the populace. The dialectic provides for the periodical replacement as well as the perpetual replaceability of the existing rulers, while at the same time enabling them during their tenure to exercise power effectively on behalf of their electors. This process contains within itself its own contradictions and consequent tensions, as it is not easy for any government to remain both responsive and responsible to those who brought it into existence as well as those who desire its downfall. How to secure intelligent popular participation and to safeguard against indifference and inertia, how to preserve freedom and to prevent anarchy, how to obtain strong and popular leadership and to avoid demagogic or despotic tendencies–these problems face every democracy in the context of its own internal contradictions and inner tensions. It is helpful to remember that democracy, in its present form, is of relatively recent origin and is frequently in a state of internal crisis, or of emergency caused by external forces. Democracy in wartime or under the stress of an economic crisis or national emergency, in the face of bankruptcy or breakdown, demands so many restraints on itself as a process or as a method that it remains chiefly an ideal that lives by the faith of votaries in itself, its past, and its future. Thus democracy may be seen as a faith as much as anything else. It presupposes faith in the possibility of securing responsible government through representative institutions, of reducing arbitrary action and achieving equity and equality through legislative and judicial means, and of inducing voluntary cooperation and popular support in a free society. Democracy has its own distinctive approach to the three crucial problems of politics, centered on social power and human wisdom–the problem of authority, the problem of law, and the problem of obligation. The democratic approach must be governed by genuinely democratic conceptions of welfare, justice, and freedom.

The essential elements in the everyday concept of political democracy must be appreciated if we are to lay down the minimally necessary institutional conditions.

1. Even if all cannot govern, all citizens must be allowed to choose who can govern.
2. Those who are chosen as eligible to govern must represent those who cannot govern.
3. Those who are eligible must in turn choose[1] those who will govern.
4. Those who do govern must be responsive and responsible to the people through their representatives and also behave as if they were themselves the foremost trustees and representatives of the people, including those who are opposed to their policies and position.
5. All citizens must be allowed to replace or re-elect those who may and those who do govern.
6. Those who are chosen as eligible to govern must be able to remove or replace those who do govern when they no longer enjoy their confidence or the support of the people.
7. There must be adequate opportunities for all these choices to be made and to be realized, as also for the enlargements of the area of choice and the capacity to choose, thus tending to equalize the chances of all to secure their choices and to be chosen as representatives or as rulers.

These essential requirements of the concept of democracy can only be realized through appropriate institutions and arrangements. Power must be diffused as widely as possible and not concentrated in a few centers if democracy is to secure unity without loss of freedom, equality without mediocrity, variety without sacrificing unity, progress without endangering either unity or liberty.

If democracy is viewed mainly as a social theory, there is a natural tendency to think of it in terms of a metaphysical, sociological, or psychological archetype, abstracted from a historical and cultural context. In fact, democracy is a system of government which is determined not only by minimal institutional conditions but also by varying constellations of supporting and sufficient conditions. A

1. If the word "choose" here is taken literally, the entire model would only be applicable to parliamentary democracy. If taken in a looser sense to apply widely to all those who fulfill important political roles, the model can cover many types of democracy.

democratic society, like a developed economy, has its own infrastructure conducive to political democracy as to economic development. It is not feasible to describe exhaustively the elements in this infrastructure, or even to decide definitely which are necessary and which are sufficient conditions. Mill mentioned two necessary conditions–the popular willingness to receive, defend, and preserve democracy, and to discharge the functions it imposes on its supporters. Tocqueville pointed to a variety of factors that supported and reinforced democracy: the application of the federal principle; the vitality of local institutions; the strength and scope of judicial power; the role of a healthy religious spirit in a secular polity; social equality; expanding opportunities; a restless, enterprising, and independent temper; the quality of and capacity for self-legislation; the existence of numerous non-governmental associations; and a variety of avenues of social cooperation. Three others are stressed by James Bryce: the reforming zeal of citizens and their readiness to assume responsibility for public institutions; the role of intellectual and cultural élites in the formation of opinion and the stimulation of thinking on public questions; and the prevailing sentiment of national unity. These conditions were viewed by Tocqueville and Bryce as remedies rather than as prerequisites for democracy.

There are many more stabilizing factors and dynamic forces favorable to democracy, some so obvious that they are mistakenly assumed to be universally necessary, others so subtle and intangible that they are often overlooked. The latter include the following factors, which can only be listed here: the existence of independent institutions respected for their integrity and fearlessness in the face of the State; the ability of people in general to distinguish between the men in power and the System; a nationwide structure of democratic education; the adoption of democratic methods within non-political bodies wherever possible; sufficient diversity of desires and expectations to reduce the stress and strain of competition; intellectual resilience, cultural flexibility, and social mobility; the continual narrowing of gaps between privileged and weaker groups so as to reduce the intensity of conflicts of interests in society; the ability of leaders to influence and be influenced by the widest possible range of public opinion; the sense of responsibility and the self-denying role of élites; a steady rise in the ethical and cultural level of the community; a spirit of trusteeship and a capacity for admitting and correcting errors among those who constitute the administration; a climate of thought and conduct that fosters intellectual honesty and individual initiative. It is only the essentials—conceptual and institutional—of democracy that can help us identify a democratic regime, although its evolution cannot be understood except in terms of the infrastructure of the society in which it functions. Much intellectual and practical harm has been caused by ignoring these caveats.

While the concept of freedom is both broader and deeper than that of democracy, the concept of liberty is narrower but by no means less significant. Although it has positive as well as negative aspects, it means, strictly and etymologically, exemption from tutelage and tyranny, from external restraint and arbitrary power. Every notable instance of such an exemption is called from medieval times a liberty, or, in more modern jargon, the establishment of a claim or right. Some of these are often seen as natural or fundamental and implicit in the definition of man. While these and other rights may be sanctified by notions of natural law, they are safeguarded by sanctions of man-made law. Liberty is the product rather than the sum of particular liberties; it stands for a system rather than a set of rights, as the interrelations of all affect the implications of each. These liberties may be seen as pertaining to different spheres of activity—religious, civil, political, and personal; or to various human functions—thought, conscience, speech, movement, association; or the other things most men value—life, education, happiness, property, power, reputation, convictions, intellectual and social intercourse; or to institutions and organizations—schools, trade unions, parties, the courts, local bodies, reform societies, vocational groups, business firms, the media. Individual liberty seems always to have to run faster to keep in the same place, despite the nostalgia for a simpler and purer world of the past.

The essential elements in the concept of liberty remain unaffected by its ever-extending application to an expanding social universe. There has always been a commitment to fewer restraints, wider choices, and greater self-determination, although these have been differently viewed in the varied historical struggles for liberties by master and slave, feudal lord and serf, the rural aristocracy and the urban bourgeoisie, worker and peasant, producer and consumer, landlord and tenant, the intelligentsia and the proletariat, the imperialist and the revolutionary, the haves and the have-nots in every sphere. In Athens the idea of liberty was incarnated into particular forms such as *isegoria* or equality of speech, *isonomia* or equality before the law, *isocratia* or political equality, and *parrhesia* or equality and freedom of speech. It is no doubt a far cry from the claims and concessions of the Magna Carta to William Blackstone's statement in the eighteenth century concerning the absolute rights that belong to every citizen under a system of laws which reduced the natural liberty but increased "the civil liberty of mankind." Today we can see more clearly and state more explicitly the essential elements in the idea of liberty:

1. All men are equally entitled to liberty, for liberty without equality of rights is meaningless in the social context.
2. Liberty for all means equal restrictions and reciprocal obligations for all. There is a contractual as well as an egalitarian element in the idea of public liberty.
3. The restrictions imposed on citizens by the laws of the State must be laid down specifically so that they may never be increased without adequate justification in the eyes of those subjected to them.
4. Certain liberties are regarded as inviolable but they need to be supplemented by new liberties.
5. These liberties must be guaranteed by constitutional or statutory law and safeguarded by impartial courts of justice.
6. It must be possible to effect changes in the social and political system to increase the amount of liberty available to all classes of people as well as to secure a better implementation of existing liberties.
7. There must be adequate means to prevent the overthrow or exploitation of the system by the internal and external enemies of liberty.

Implementation of these essential elements in the concept of liberty through suitable institutional and constitutional devices is not enough for a liberal society. There must also emerge an awareness of their rights among all the members of a community, together with a deep-seated respect for the dignity and worth of the individual. There must be free legal aid and equal access to the law. Every citizen must be competent to claim his own rights and have adequate opportunities to claim and maintain his liberties. This implies a commitment to a minimum standard of social and economic security as well as basic and civic education.

The immediate implications of liberty must be seen in the context of a constellation of factors favorable to the maintenance of a system of liberties. These pertain to a free country, a free society, and a free people in contrast with an enslaved country, an authoritarian society, and a powerless people. Some favorable factors are readily seen and could be easily listed—the existence of a non-political civil service and a non-military police, the former mainly and the latter entirely an instrument of law rather than of policy; checks on delegated legislation and delegated jurisdiction; a considerable area of autonomy for individuals and organizations, with evident exemption from central control or pressure; a tolerance of novelty and a willingness to experiment; intellectual objectivity and a critical spirit; safeguards against conformity, dogmatism, and persecution; adequate avenues for the development of individual talents and capacities; the fearless performance of civic and personal duties; the criticism and correction of existing social institutions, traditions, and conventions; widespread concern for the promotion of tolerance and moderation, plurality, and flexibility in communal life; the general acceptance of rules to regulate competition between individuals and groups, within and between parties and other power-centers; the role of the State in hindering hindrances to the enjoyment of liberties by the weaker sections of society.

Other factors are more controversial. For example, some believe that a liberal society must necessarily possess a liberal economy, that liberties are best protected by a propertied middle class, thrifty and prudent, counting the costs of State activity and not carried away by loyalist or egalitarian emotions. It is less arguable that liberty needs its leading champions, conscientious trouble-makers who care deeply about the infringement of the rights of their fellow men, who become involved in test cases and set valuable precedents, who are the creators and custodians of the public conscience.

Liberty cannot, however, be made to depend solely upon heroic libertarians. The prevalent climate of thought and conduct must be such that most people come to believe in the sacredness of liberty and the sanctity of a system of liberties under law. Historically, liberties become the foundation of liberty, although liberty is not merely the fortuitous concurrence of liberties. Liberty can only thrive in an atmosphere of creative activity in which there are reasonable restraints on individual judgment so that all moral failures do not become legal crimes, and in which the power of self-determination and freedom of choice are sufficiently cherished for the individual to function as a person and a citizen, not as a mere subject or as a slave except in name. It is not always noticed by libertarians, all too conscious of the bitter struggles that led to formal liberties and their social sanctions, that real liberty, like true democracy, is inimical to any form of intimidation, manipulation, or coercion even to secure the most exalted ends.

There are conceptual elements and institutional conditions common to both democracy and liberty. Similarly, some of their underlying assumptions are the same. This is not surprising, for we would naturally expect the ideals of self-determination and self-development to merge into each other and to be causally connected. In fact, they are quite distinct from each other in strict theory and in actual practice, although it is possible to define either in terms of the other. Democracy without liberty is easier to imagine than liberty without democracy. Social activity may stifle individual self-expression, but the latter cannot easily be conceived in isolation from the former. It is true that the doctrine of liberty is usually regarded as an integral part of the theory of democracy. They have been jointly invoked by many who refused to look upon the existing social structure as fixed and final. Historically, however, the struggle for liberty preceded the movement toward democracy. Democracy itself was at first viewed as an extension of liberty, as a reaction against the absolute power of certain classes of society. While the concept of liberty was positive and dominant, the idea of democracy was negative and even derivative. As democracy became more and more positive, liberty tended to become negative to the point of neglect. As democracy became more a theory of government than a theory of consent or a doctrine of protest, the centrality of freedom was often left to be stressed by backward-looking conservatives and forward-looking anarchists.

Liberty is endangered by the democratic idea that power can be transferred and that the people may be represented by their chosen deputies, for at best this idea is more favorable to welfare than to freedom. There was a dangerous transition from the idea of a government of limited powers over citizens with inalienable rights to the idea of the unlimited sovereignty and the material welfare of the majority. It is an easy step from here to the perilous position reached by most democracies today, in which individual liberties are violated in the name of national security and prestige at home and abroad, in which the mute and the meek are often sacrificed at the altars of public utility and political necessity. It is not surprising that the world has not yet been made safe for democracy when we recognize that there is not yet a single country that has been made entirely safe for liberty. In totalitarian countries the Leviathan has almost swallowed up the right of the individual to his own soul, *habeas animum,* while in democratic countries there has been a growing tendency for the small man, *habeas homunculum,* to be sacrificed to *raison d'état.*

Despite this ever-present danger, which demonstrates that liberty is more precious and more elusive than democracy, there is no doubt that democracy is more conducive to liberty than any other system of government yet devised. It provides the necessary link between liberty and equality, though a democratic government is sometimes required by the people at large to promote equality even at the expense of liberty. Bergson assigned to democracy the role of the reconciler between *égalité* and *liberté* under the banner of *fraternité.* Historically, the struggle for liberty, the quest for equality, and the movement toward fraternity have been stressed as almost successive phases in the development of democracy. Equality has been secured to the detriment of liberty and there is the danger of forcing the pace toward fraternity before equality has been fully established and made compatible with the maximum amount of liberty. Ideally, a proper democratic system can be effectively established only in a society of equals in which every citizen has the full liberty to realize his own ends and the moral responsibility to serve the purposes of the community. This being unattainable at present, we must consider the extent of freedom from executive restraint as the test of democratic efficiency and rely on various forms of voluntary association to safeguard liberty in a democracy. We can secure neither democratic ends through undemocratic means nor liberal aims through illiberal methods. If this is understood, it will be easier to see why democratic ends cannot be secured through illiberal means and why liberal aims cannot be achieved by undemocratic methods. Those who postpone or destroy present liberties in the name of future freedoms are the friends of neither liberty nor democracy. The same is sadly true of those who resort to doubtful devices to preserve and defend democracy.

It is necessary to note the assumptions underlying the traditional models and modern systems of democracy and liberty. Both these concepts were conditioned by the intellectual climate of early scientific metaphysics, the ethical flavor of secularized religious values, and the social and economic context of expanding industrial capitalism, as well as the noble but somewhat naïve optimism and enthusiasm of the *philosophes* and revolutionaries. We cannot trace the details here of the lineage and background of these concepts, but merely indicate a few of the more fundamental assumptions. Political power is assumed to be a finite quantity of storable and distributable force which resides in individuals or in the social system. When it is evenly divided among the crucial agencies of decision making or when its concentration at a single point is prevented by a complicated machinery of checks and balances, the stable equilibrium of the system is achieved. Individuals are motivated by the attractions and repulsions of self-interest. Given an atomistic view of actions, interests, and individuals, the pulls and pressures in different directions throughout the system can be seen as reconcilable only in terms of a central harmony carried over from the ancient world into a mechanistic picture of nature and the finite universe. The stress in politics as in science is on regularity, predictability, and manufacturability. This simple model was modified and generalized into a doctrine of political pluralism and interplay of autonomous centers in our own century.

The pace of change should be slow, measured, and self-regulating, except for inevitable explosions in the system at infrequent intervals. The needs of social life and of State action are generally not so compelling or immediate as to require rapid legislation or even a very strong and expanding government and administration. There should be opportunities for revision and readjustments at all levels of activity, so that the number of irrevocable changes in the system is reduced to a minimum. A purely utilitarian but cautious conception of government may be combined with a contractual and relatively static picture of society. There is presumed to be a majestic movement in history toward better democracy and greater freedom, toward spontaneous social progress. The struggles of the past–between Church and State, Society and State, Government and State, the King and his Barons, King and Parliament and the Courts, Government and the Courts, the aristocracy and the bourgeoisie, the bourgeoisie and the proletariat–have all been regarded as essential and ordered phases in a grand sequence, aspects of the folklore of the political odyssey of liberal democracy. The notion of sovereignty, theories of the State, and many other preoccupations of the political theorists of democracy and liberty were doubtless stimulated by factors such as the bitter struggle between Church and State, which has no parallel in the history of many of the emerging polities of today. The acceptance of the System by all classes and groups through a series of struggles resulted in considerable cultural homogeneity and a common political consciousness. The dissolution of traditional loyalties and local bonds led to a general concern for common rights and wider loyalties. The growth of a civic spirit and of social solidarity thus came to be taken for granted.

A crucial assumption is the unique efficiency of a competitive mechanism of politics, open to all and regulated by its own code, marked by considerable mobility between rival groups and the equalization of risks if not of rewards, destined to maximize general satisfaction. Organized minorities, unashamed of their ambitions and jealous of their internal cohesion, continually clash in their common bid for the unpredictable support of the unorganized majority. The method of arriving at decisions is assumed to be more important than whether the right decision is taken in any situation. It could be contended that the subordination of democratic theory to rationalist ends and utilitarian procedures is not so much the corruption as the culmination of democratic ideas. However, many critics of democracy complain that there is no real competition, that there are non-competing groups and a collusion between different sections of the ruling class, that the élite in power becomes the Establishment by absorbing potential rivals and by alienating the incurably discontented until they are regarded as the common enemies of the entire System. At the worst the System is a social or economic monopoly, and at best it is a form of monopolistic competition in which there are clandestine coteries pulling strings behind the scenes and reaching compromises in the hope of deferred if not immediate profits. Apologists and critics of democratic competition share many common assumptions and play into each other's hands by their respective exaggerations. Mill and Montesquieu as well as Mosca and Marx spoke some truth about democracy and liberty.

An even less pleasant assumption is the uniqueness of particular democratic systems, which fosters a mystical faith in the inevitability and invulnerability of democracy and liberty in a given country and an obstinate belief in the dubiousness of democracy and liberty elsewhere. The greater the prevailing cynicism, the more this assumption has been cherished. The tragedy of democracy and liberty in the older States, like that of religion and culture, has been their prostitution and desecration in the service of individual and national egotism. A less harmful assumption is the magical potency of political ritual, with its ideal as well as symbolic elements, its capacity to bolster up failing morale and to allay persisting anxieties. Like all ritual, it is impersonal, dramatized, and solemn, an equalizer and a tranquilizer, a medium of expression as well as of communication, a substitute for the sense of mystery of the supernatural. When ritual is outmoded and decaying we have democracy at a low temperature. There is, finally, the admirable assumption that political freedom and responsibility could be developed through exercise; that rational policies could emerge through rational discussion; that all social problems are soluble by the good sense of every citizen; that every individual is endowed with integrity, conscience, and reason; that the potentialities of individuals are more important than their present capacities; that it is better to reform society than to accept or reject it; that people have the power of grading loyalties as well as being moved by them; that the citizen knows when to resist and how to compromise; that the leader knows how to listen and when to lead; that, in short, it is better to trust than to fear others and ourselves.

III

This analysis has at least shown the complexity of the concepts of democracy and liberty, the variety of concrete conditions, and the specificity of theoretical assumptions upon which they are usually based. It is also necessary to see some of the telling features and immediate problems of the emerging polities, their sources of weakness and strength, in the light of which alone we can formulate the fundamental challenge to democracy and liberty in these countries. By recognizing the costs and consequences, we are in a position to suggest ways in which a commitment to meeting this challenge might be carried forward. The emerging polities are not all new countries or new democracies or even newly independent entities. There are very ancient and even universal elements in the concepts of democracy and liberty, for they relate to ethical values inherent to all human beings and common to the main religious and cultural streams that have flowed through the recorded history of humanity. There are liberal as well as illiberal, democratic and undemocratic trends in the cultural traditions of all States. A larger proportion of the newer than of the older States found today are committed in principle to democratic and liberal ideals. Even among older States that cherish democracy and liberty, there are those that are at present less democratic and less free than a few of the emerging polities, and among the older democracies the relatively newer ones seem to have made greater progress toward fuller democracy. It is too early to say anything decisive about the relative positions of rapidly changing countries, but it would be risky to assume that the older the State, the safer the prospects of democracy and liberty. The distinction between the emerging and the older States should not be pressed to a point where we lose sight of the significant diversities within either category. This is especially important because of the proliferation of emerging polities in an era of effete imperialism and effervescent nationalism. Whether the concept of the nation-state that emerged in Europe has proved so far to be a liability or an asset, the world-wide demand for national self-determination and sovereignty has now become essentially irresistible. Some of the new national boundaries may be irrational but they were once thought to be feasible. The series of events that led to them is irreversible and unalterable, except by international agreement or by world authorities yet to be established.

A polity may be created peacefully in various ways. It may emerge through amicable agreement with an existing sovereign State out of which it is formed. This is very rare, an example being the separation of Norway from Sweden in 1905. A new State may also emerge through the inability of the parent State to prevent its emergence, such as when Rumania and Finland demanded independence. Alternatively, it may arise as the result of external intervention which the State in question is unwilling or unable to resist with force. Thus the independence of Belgium was assured in 1831 by joint intervention of Britain and France and guaranteed by treaty in 1839; similarly, Albania was created in 1913 in consequence of the success of the Balkan League against Turkey. Again, a powerful State may foster or secure the independence of a portion of a weak neighboring State with the object either of maintaining it as a puppet or satellite, or of absorbing it in due course within itself. The United States created Panama for the former purpose and Texas for the latter. Egypt, Iraq, and Syria emerged as States initially for the benefit of Britain and France. The foundation of Liberia and the Congo Free State was at least nominally inspired by the philanthropic intention to benefit the blacks. These are factors that led to the emergence of new nations in an earlier era. In our own times new States have been set up initially through defeat in war and the exigencies of restoring peace, as in the case of West Germany; through imposed agreement on creation out of other States, as in the case of Israel; through secession, as in the case of Pakistan; through federation, as in the case of the Central African Federation which was subsequently split into Zambia, Malawi, and Southern Rhodesia; through internal revolution, as in the case of the United Arab Republic; through revolt against foreign rule, as in the case of Indonesia; and through transfer of power, as in the case of India, Burma, and Ceylon.

None of these States was born without an element of compulsion, and all of them are affected to this day by the background of their birth as well as their prenatal experiences. Some of the emerging polities are heirs to monarchic despotism, and most were victims of imperialist domination. Only a few are entirely new nations, and many are multi-communal (multi-racial, multi-religious, multi-cultural, and even multi-national) countries with long historical records that in some cases include the world's oldest and greatest civilizations. Most of these new States geographically belong to the continents of Asia and Africa, which have given to humanity its chief religions, which now comprise the great majority of the world's people, which have rich resources as well as pressing needs and formidable problems, and which have much in common besides a new energy and thrust that are both exhilarating and terrifying. These emerging polities range from those with relatively small and insecure territories to those with vast spatial dimensions and enormous human and material potential.

Although it is both difficult and dangerous to generalize about these widely diverse States, it is only natural that by virtue of their being new there should be certain distinct tendencies, each of which seems to be true of most, if not all, of them. Most people in the emerging polities tend to assume without question that their countries are caught up in mighty currents of inescapable change, and that time is on their side. The emergence of a new spirit and a new tempo of development throughout Asia and Africa is, in their view, a global fact of Copernican significance. The past is perhaps obscure and largely irrelevant, the present is intensely exciting though dangerously exacting, and the future is full of promise and manifold rewards. This supreme conviction gives rise to an ebullience and a sense of destiny that is sometimes alarming. It dominates their conflicting attitudes, blends their varied aspirations, cancels and even feeds their ever-present frustrations. Among a few of the new States, we can discern a deeper struggle, reflected in every sphere, between the consciousness of being emerging polities released from a nightmare of slavery and the natural pride of inheritance of ancient civilizations able to transcend to some degree the narrower claims of nationalism. This struggle partly takes the form, but goes beyond the problem, of intellectual conflict between the sources of tradition and the forces of change, of ceaseless tension between the towns and the villages. It is not enough, however, for the citizen of a new State, that his own country has found its place in the sun. Every young man and woman wants to find his or her place in the sun, his or her own means of personal fulfillment and sphere of service to the country. Few are satisfied with what they have; almost everyone thinks he or she could do better or that he or she deserves more. Resignation and fatalism have given way to a restless discontent which may sometimes be divine but is all too abject in most people most of the time. Pride, competition, and discontent combine in strange ways and often result in exemplary idealism as well as extreme cynicism. On a national level, there is a tremendous urge for rapid development and a search for short-cuts and panaceas.

Emerging polities are naturally affected by the conditions of their birth. They intensely desire to develop independently, and also to adopt some of the methods used by the older States (democratic as well as authoritarian); to preserve their freedom and their new status by shifting alliances or by adhering to none; to extend their commonality with other new States as well as cherish what they regard as unique to themselves. They tend to have an ambivalent attitude to older States, based on respect and resentment, suspicion and magnanimity. Many emerging polities, partly by necessity and partly by choice, were conceived in liberty and consecrated to democracy. But they are more concerned with the liberty of the nation than of the individual and with development than with democracy. Under imperial rule or foreign domination, the government, the representative assembly, the civil service, the law, and even the judiciary were all suspect. After independence there is a tendency to assume that all these have become sanctified overnight, as if anointed with popular sovereignty, rather like the Marxist illusions about the apparatus of political power before and after the revolution. In this case, however, the consequence is not so much apathy or self-deception as cynicism or naïveté, reinforced by an ever deeper distrust of democratic and libertarian orthodoxy. As long as even a few free countries are also imperialistic, the enemies of liberty and democracy in the emerging polities will be able to exploit the prevailing distaste for fraudulent claims by dishonest democrats, and cast doubt on the very processes and institutions of liberal democracy. The memories of past misdeeds die hard and are easily stirred. Nationalist leaders once quoted Mill and Milton to their imperialist rulers, the communists among them behaving like Roman Catholics in militant Protestant countries, the liberals suffering like Protestants in those Roman Catholic countries that prevent them from even carrying their Bibles. Most classes of malcontents wrongly identify democracy and liberty with particular regimes rather like those who judge Christianity only by the Inquisition, Hinduism merely by untouchability, Islam solely by *jihad,* or Marx by Stalin. This historical legacy is a powerful menace in the emerging polities, even when people try to forget it. It would, however, be dangerous to deny that despite retrospective cynicism, nationalism could be conducive to democracy. As Mazzini realized, nationalism is more than the expression of democratic will: it is the conscience of the people, which, by assigning to them their part in the work of association, their function in humanity, constitutes their mission upon earth, their *individuality,* without which neither liberty nor equality is possible.

Most emerging polities had to struggle against foreign rule rather than an *ancien régime.* The revolutions that brought about their establishment were more like the American than the French Revolution. Tocqueville's remark, "The great advantage of the American is that he has arrived at a stage of democracy without having to endure a democratic revolution and that he is born equal without having to become so," is applicable to most of the emerging polities. Of course, their revolutionary ferment has reached deeper down and has acquired a greater momentum which may give impetus to a series of revolutionary changes. Social disruption is inherent in colonialism and the impact of the older States initially provided the challenge of new ideas and greater dynamism. The present generation in the emerging polities seeks a moral and material revolution that will overthrow a corrupt and decadent social order and usher in powerful forces of economic and social progress. It wishes to move away from the old order, discredited by its association with political slavery and weakness, even if this involves a perilous venture through chaos toward a political dream which must recede further and further with every advance. The initial revolutionary mood was so widespread and so stimulated by a tremendous passion for equality that the political battle in the emerging polities is chiefly between the Center and the Left, just as in aging America it has been mainly between the Center and the Right.

Politics in the emerging polities is almost a religion even to the extent of breeding a race of anti-political, like anti-clerical, leaders. The possibilities of political action are grossly exaggerated or hotly denied. Political issues tend to be fought out within each party and the patriarchal role of political leaders is even greater than in the older democracies. Parties, as an Indonesian once observed, represent "mental and psychological climates" rather than clearly defined political options. There is an ambivalent attitude to political power itself. As a result, some of the best people refuse to be drawn into politics, while some of the worst willingly rush into it. Further, the rank and file, especially in opposition parties, include a large number of the "educated unemployed," while the leadership in the governing party is mainly drawn from the extremely restricted, self-styled, self-perpetuating élite. At the same time, the power of appeals to spiritual loyalties is still considerable in many emerging polities. Islamic, Buddhist, and Hindu influences are to be seen not merely in the persistence of traditional beliefs and attitudes but even more in the secularized versions of values and ideals derived from the living impact of these ancient faiths upon large numbers of people. The coexistence of different religions makes it increasingly necessary to find formulas of compatibility as well as to go beyond the peripheral forms to the vital core of religious experience.

It is not surprising that in many of the emerging polities the word "socialism" has become as pejorative and all-embracing as the words "liberal," "democratic," or "welfare" in the older democracies. Many governments of Asia, Africa, and the Middle East have professed some form of democratic socialism. This concentration of values in the concept of socialism has dangers as well as advantages. Admittedly, many tasks of the emerging polities are connected with the speeding up of timetables of social and economic change by the government in power, and with securing greater equality, social justice, and welfare for the mass of people. There is, however, a vast and complicated process of national transformation to be undertaken which does not even mainly fall within the scope of State power or political action. To use historical analogies, many emerging polities have to compress a great deal into a few decades: the break-up of the Roman Empire, the overthrow of the feudal system, the Renaissance, the Reformation of the established religion, the French and American Revolutions, the Agrarian and Industrial Revolutions, the extension of the franchise and education, the struggle for the rights of women, the class war of the Russian Revolution. All of this must be carried out in the context of a vanishing Bipolar World and the new technology of the Space Age, and be accomplished as promptly and painlessly as possible. Of course, this is a rather simplified model, but it appeals to many people in the emerging polities, and its main lesson is that no one "ism" or incantation–not even "liberal, democratic socialism"–can do the trick like "Open Sesame."

Above all, we must never forget the most obvious feature of the emerging polities, that they are largely rural societies, developing economies, centralized groupings of a considerable variety of poor communities, disintegrated and demoralized under the impact of imperialistic and industrialized Europe and its American heirs, unwilling and unable to regard democracy or liberty as ends in themselves, yet loath to lose sight of them altogether. Nor must we ignore the significant variations among the emerging polities. During the last century there was a real attempt in the Middle East to develop democratic systems, with constitutional government, elected legislatures, and civil rights. Today in much of the Middle East democratic regimes are in a state of collapse or have fallen into serious disrepute, and military intervention in politics is increasing. In some States, like Saudi Arabia or Afghanistan, democratic regimes were never established. In a few, like Turkey and Israel, there is a continuing concern to maintain liberty and develop democracy. In the new African States, there is an almost infinite variety of indigenous political institutions, a collection of centers of power at widely different stages of development. At the same time the educated élite is modernized to a degree disruptive to society, as it is so identified with imported religious beliefs and social values that it is less able to influence the tradition-bound masses than elsewhere. In most of the new States, democratic institutions were imported from abroad on very unfavorable terms of trade and in delayed installments. The vitality of village communities and institutions was undermined but not destroyed, while centralization was accompanied by dissemination of concern for the Rule of Law and the growth of media of communication between the members of a new intelligentsia. Simultaneously, there was the unpleasant legacy of the Preventive Detention Act and a panoply of emergency devices to suspend even the pretence of democracy. Today the independence of the judiciary has been barely preserved in some cases, and elsewhere severely undermined. Freedom of expression and association have been imperiled, with surprisingly few exceptions.

Democracy is tested, not only by its concern for safeguards, but even more by its success in peacefully resolving social conflicts and securing collective participation in a common national endeavor. In this respect it is not surprising that in countries where strong political leadership and a relatively stable political society are combined with adequate liberties, there has been greater social and economic progress than in countries which have been hindered by internal political instability. India has been called the school of Asia rather as Athens was declared by Pericles to be the school of Hellas. In reality, there is no more room for complacency about democracy and liberty in India than in Britain or the United States, although Indian democracy has its roots in its ancient and unique tradition of tolerance and local autonomy just as European democracy has its roots in the critical spirit and the rational temper of the Reformation. In this sense, the current and sometimes precarious Indian experiment in large-scale modern democracy is of special significance to the emerging polities as well as to older countries concerned about the future of democracy and liberty within as well as outside their territories. However, as the common features of emerging polities are more important than regional and national peculiarities, it is easy to see why they have certain major problems that have not yet been wholly solved even in the older democracies.

First of all, how is it possible to achieve rapid economic and social progress while preserving, stabilizing, and operating slow-moving political institutions, legal safeguards, and constitutional procedures? This problem may be seen either as the problem of planning in a democratic society, or as the problem of democracy in a planned economy and ordered society. Without central coordination there is chaos but without private initiative there is stagnation. How can the optimum use of national resources and a steady, rising rate of economic growth and social change be attained without the sacrifice of individual liberty or of the ethical and legal foundations of democracy? How can individuals and small groups remain the ultimate controllers of decisions and the repositories of local authority, while placing in the hands of the central government the powers needed for essential national planning?

Secondly, how is it possible to preserve the democratic spirit and complicated checks and balances in the distribution of political authority and power, while maintaining a strong, stable, and effective government at the center? This is partly similar to the problem of a democracy in wartime, when everything is subordinated to a common national effort, mainly by voluntary means, thus retaining the essentials of democracy and the potential powers of autonomous groups. Even in peacetime the government must be strong enough to overcome sectional interests when there is authentic and unmistakable expression of popular political consciousness. The greater the measure of public support, the less the need for coercion or anything more than moral pressure. But even then there must be a scrupulous respect for the rights of minorities, however small, and the views of heretics, however unpopular. This requires a readiness to allow for large margins of risk, error, and danger in tolerating apparently and even actually unpatriotic opinions.

Thirdly, how can national unity and common loyalties be achieved while encouraging variety and diversity through workable institutions and methods? This is of immense importance to the emerging polities in view of their size, regional variations, and cultural heterogeneity. Here again some analogy may be drawn with the experience of the older States, since the problem is somewhat similar to that of democracy in a federal system. The American experiment, in this as in other ways, has great relevance to the emerging polities, both through its successes and failures. The United States had to start largely from scratch in the creation of a democratic federal system and libertarian society and is much closer to the emerging polities than some politicians are ready to admit. The problem of national unity amidst diversity is doubtless wider in scope and deeper in content in the larger emerging polities than in the United States. In general, new States must profit from the experiences of relatively successful federations, while at the same time they have neither the time nor the need to secure the dangerous conformity fostered in mass society under modern capitalism.

Fourthly, how is it possible to establish and operate new democratic institutions and forms, while also preserving the best elements in national traditions and indigenous ideas? How can traditional concepts be used to further democracy and liberty in the context of borrowed institutions and modern developments? This problem of tradition in a democratic society, or of democracy in a traditional society, has to be faced more squarely by the new States, though it is also present in the older democracies. It is, at the very least, necessary in any democracy or relatively free society to focus the fiercer emotions and irrational sentiments on relatively harmless objects, as well as on the deeper and more lasting loyalties, so that the country is not carried away by a wave of uncontrollable hysteria. Some of these stabilizers are symbolic entities, either pale etiolated shadows of their former power and grandeur, or dim pointers to the distant future. Jingoistic worship of the past is only less dangerous than millennial and messianic fantasies about the hereafter. The hollow glamour of effete monarchies, the celebration of victories in battles of long ago, the myth of national invulnerability, the intoxication of numbers (population or national income, dams or dikes), national hagiography, hero-worship in the present–these are all examples of ways in which popular emotions could be tapped, with trivial or cataclysmic consequences, depending upon the means and media employed. More fundamentally, it is desirable that people take pride in democracy and liberty because they see them in terms of their finest traditions and not their most bitter memories.

Fifthly, how far should the new States tolerate the intolerant opponents of the democratic system who desire to undermine its liberty or even destroy its foundations? This is a very difficult problem, as it involves a delicate appraisal of unquantifiable factors, taking risks on the basis of present expectations, and making decisions involving distinctions of degree rather than of kind. Communal organizations using militant methods and religious slogans, communist cadres with subtle tactics of infiltration and sabotage, terrorist groups of brigands made respectable by their half-romantic disguise, societies of foreign missionaries with political aims–these and other such bodies present their peculiar problems. Sometimes the best way to confound extremists may be to give them ample freedom of expression, bringing them under the searching light of publicity. At the same time there can be no compromise or tolerance on matters of profound principle relating to the spiritual and moral basis of the system. Slavery or racial discrimination in a free society, religious fanaticism in a secular State, political intimidation and violence in a democratic system are all issues calling for courageous leadership. The difficulty arises when the rules of democracy are invoked by those who are totally opposed to them. It is here that an attitude of non-retaliation, combined with caution and courage, is required. It is a measure of progress in a democracy that it can go further than before in tolerating the intolerant without allowing them to prevail. Democracy must defend itself against internal enemies by democratic methods, however tempting other strategies may be when they are advanced in the name of national security or the public interest.

Sixthly, how is it possible to preserve national integrity, independence, and the pace of development without alienating democratic and libertarian forces in the world or strengthening authoritarian and tyrannical tendencies? Alternately, how can democratic regimes and free societies be supported without provoking their international adversaries to adopt even more extreme measures, thus increasing rather than reducing the prospects of democracy and liberty in the world as a whole? This is partly the problem of democratic foreign policy in the context of continuing world tension between the friends and enemies of freedom. Every democracy, old and new, has to face this problem. Inevitably, each has its own conception of both its responsibilities and what constitutes responsibility. Emerging polities are tempted to assume too little, whereas some older democracies tend to take on too much of the burden of making the world safe as well as fit for democracy. There is room for varying views regarding whether it is wiser for the emerging polities to attend primarily to their own internal prospects of democracy, or to the spread of the gospel. Even among the older democracies, there is a strong temptation to preach at the expense of practicing the gospel. Herein we have yet another dilemma facing both new and old States: to preach at the cost of practice is dishonest, whereas to practice at the expense of preaching is shortsighted.

The sources of weakness in the emerging polities are easy to see. Extreme poverty is not conducive to the growth and spread of active concern for democratic methods or to safeguarding civil liberties. Low levels of general education result in continuing concentration of power in the hands of a few, as well as a widening gap between élites and the masses in rural and urban areas. Sectional interests are promoted by persons entrenched in positions of power and are resolved neither equitably nor impersonally. Party programs are unrealistic and artificial, owing to great disparities in status between the heirs to the national movement for independence and their rivals and critics. Cynicism and corruption feed on each other until there is a general loss of confidence in the workability as well as the integrity of the System. Every ruling clique tends to perpetuate itself by any means and to manipulate the rules of democracy to serve its own ends. Vested interests of politicians, businessmen, and military as well as civilian officials become involved in the network of political intrigue. In the emerging polities there are fewer formal and informal safeguards against these tendencies becoming cumulative and explosive. The centralization of government tends to increase beyond the requirements of State action and beyond the safety limits imposed by popular control. There is a growing dependence upon external assistance in moments of crisis. Religious emotions may be exploited by ruthless politicians. Leaders may be misled by oversimplified models of developed democracy that they have been sold. Imitativeness may result in inertia just as inexperience leads to impatience. Excessive reliance may be placed on bureaucratic methods of the past. Local discontent and regional ambitions may find political expression and foster fissiparous tendencies which invite repressive action by the central authority. In short, insecurity and instability decrease the prospects of democratic stability as well as individual security and liberty. Belated discovery of a cumulative chain of regression may result in a total loss of faith in the System and in a desire to overthrow it.

The sources of strength are more elusive, do not necessarily show on the surface, and are parapolitical in origin. Aristotle thought that the best material for democracy is an agricultural population, in which there is no general clamor for political office, and no unhealthy competition for jobs, while at the same time there is a willingness to participate in the choice of leaders, if not always in the process of decision making. Given the Greek fear of demagogy, this faith in the placidity and good sense of the peasantry is easy to understand. It could be held plausibly that the passion for equality results not only in undue dependence on governmental action but also in more exacting and hypercritical attitudes to authority. Also, the prevailing revolutionary mood of self-confidence and fervor may enable the State to initiate far-reaching social and economic changes which would make democracy more workable and freedom more real. Anxiety to start *de novo* in many spheres, and especially the initial faith shown in written constitutions and declarations of rights and principles, may act as a brake against the open betrayal of democratic and liberal ideals. The need to justify deviations and aberrations from high standards may force rival leaders to vie with each other in intellectual acceptance of the sanctity of democracy and liberty. Even attempts to exploit religious sentiments may boomerang on self-seeking politicians as well as induce a readiness to seek the basis for democracy and liberty within the context of national traditions and religious beliefs and ethics. Democracy is inherent, for example, in Buddhist principles and monastic practices. C. N. Parkinson has pointed out that Buddhist procedure was far in advance not only of anything evolved in Athens or Rome, but of British practice as well.[2] Similarly, Islam has always been uniquely egalitarian in theory, even if not entirely so in practice, allowing for a considerable degree of social fluidity. Hinduism has a highly developed tradition of Natural Law. More generally, traditions in the emerging polities have been as fortunate in their powerful notions of Natural Law, embodied in every man and not applied by ecclesiastics, as they have been lacking in sharp formulations of Natural Rights. The stress has been on divine reason in every man, on intuition rather than conscience, on universal fallibility rather than individual intellec-

2. Cyril Northcote Parkinson, *Evolution of Political Thought,* London, University of London Press, 1958, p. 189.

tual dissent. There are rich sources of strength and sympathy in the thought and tradition of the emerging polities that need to be explored and tapped.

The crucial problem of democracy in the emerging polities is to accelerate the speed, while stabilizing the procedures, of peaceful decision making at all levels of the political system. The crucial problem of liberty is to create individual confidence in the integrity and continuity of the system while also inducing voluntary cooperation in a common national effort. The entire country must achieve a revolution by consent with sufficient rapidity and momentum to secure the popular conviction that a democracy can be effective without violating individual liberty. The cumulative effects of vicious circles of causation, inherent in a developing democracy with largely unused liberties, must be curbed and reversed through imaginative and courageous leadership. Society must safeguard democracy from expanding State activity, while the State must safeguard the liberties of citizens from militant demands of mass democracy. The executive has a protective as well as creative role; the legislature has to reflect local grievances as well as transcend sectional interests; the judiciary must be the custodian of the integrity and conscience of the country within limits set by existing laws. There must be active participation from below and planned action from above, self-expression at the periphery and self-restraint at the center. Political unity must be maintained within a framework of maximum pluralism.

The central problem is by no means reducible to a single, simple formula. In his first message to the United States Congress after the outbreak of the Civil War in 1861, Lincoln raised the question: "Is there, in all republics, this inherent and fatal weakness? Must a government, of necessity be too strong for the liberties of its own people, or too weak to maintain its own existence?" It was possible for Washington to declare in 1797, in his Farewell Address: "With me a predominant motive has been to endeavour to gain time for our country to settle and mature its yet recent institutions and to progress without interruption to that degree of strength and consistency which is necessary to give it, humanly speaking, the command of its own fortune." Nehru spoke for the new States when he pleaded in 1950, the year of the founding of the Indian Republic:

"We have suddenly arrived at a stage when we have to run. Walking is not enough–and in running we tumble and fall and we try to get up again. It is no good anybody telling us to walk slowly. . . . It involves risks and dangers but there is no help and no choice for it, for there is a torment in our minds." The new States have emerged from cruder forms of enslavement to face the tyranny of time, with which they must come to terms if they are not to fail woefully. They must equally come to terms with the soul of their own traditions and with the collective limitations of their social soil. It is not enough for liberal democracy to become a source of inspiration and ferment, or even a constant ideal. It must strike deep roots into the contemporary ground and derive fresh life from the air. The new States have before them the strange story of the Russian and the Chinese experience. Marxism was as much an import from Europe as was liberalism. If the latter withered away in favor of the former, if it faded before it blossomed, it was because, as Trotsky once wrote, "It did not find any social soil in which to grow. Manchester ideas could be imported, but the social environment which produces those ideas could not be imported." If emerging polities are determined to discard the economic basis of liberalism as it developed in Europe or America without, at the same time, discerning the spiritual basis of democracy within their own living traditions, their failure will result less from their inability to solve than their incapacity to grasp the crucial problem facing them.

To state the central problem properly is also to suggest the crux of any relevant solution. The celebrated phrase of William James about finding a moral equivalent to war was particularly applicable to the older democracies. In our own time Mahatma Gandhi was more concerned than anyone else in history to find an ethical alternative to violent revolution against an unjust System. If emerging polities are to meet the internal challenge of democracy and liberty, they must find an adequate and constructive successor to the struggle for national independence. Independence for Gandhi was the beginning, not the fulfillment, of *Swaraj* or self-rule. In a partial sense, this was realized by the early leaders like Nehru and U Nu, Sukarno and Nkrumah. To force the pace would be a futile form of bravado, but to banish the original impulse of the quest would be an unforgivable act of betrayal. It is necessary to canalize this awakened energy into constructive channels by extending new opportunities to the masses of citizens, especially in the countryside, by establishing instruments and institutions through which opportunities could be voluntarily utilized for the good of the nation and the betterment of local communities. Families of farmers and workers must be made aware of their own capacity to act together as groups and communities. Each emerging polity will have to strike its own balance at any particular time between liberty and order, central control and private initiative, national planning and local authority. In all cases it is desirable to create popular emotion as well as to foster a commitment to individual liberty while democratically strengthening the hands of national leadership. The government will have to play a vital part in the creation of a social climate that could give rise to non-governmental democratic bodies, powerful local communities, and a variety of autonomous centers of power. State activity and social action must combine to secure deconcentration of economic power, decentralization of political power, and diffusion of social power throughout the "community of communities." Forces of change must be authentically related to the deepest sources of tradition. Deep moral convictions must be combined with flexible political policies. Variety and freedom of experimentation must be encouraged and sustained. The State should be concerned more to remain a symbol of national integrity and unity, an inspirer of collective effort, than to become the authoritarian architect of uniform social patterns. Even democratic socialism at the center must draw strength from social democracy at the base.

IV

It is not possible to strengthen political democracy and public liberties in emerging polities without a thorough understanding of the underlying problem and the various forms it takes. To provide a proper diagnosis is even more difficult than to prescribe a cure. Having thus far analyzed the concepts and implications of democracy and liberty, the conditions and problems of the emerging polities, the nature of the central challenge as well as of the commitment needed to meet it, it is now possible to indicate, briefly and tentatively, what this approach might involve. Do the ideas and institutional conditions of democracy and liberty need to undergo a strengthening and a therapeutic transformation if they are to be applicable to the emerging polities? Are there any conventional ways by which the weaknesses of emerging polities might be overcome? Could any bold new proposals be made that have not been tried properly anywhere as yet? In general, emerging polities have been furnished oversimplified and even false models of older democracies. The impatience to imitate and import these models has been equaled only by the excessive zeal to export and transplant them. It was particularly unfortunate that those who spoke against the value of such export often did so for the wrong reason or were misunderstood in their time. Men like Lord Cromer could not be regarded by anti-imperialists as friends of democracy. Leaders like Gandhi were misconstrued by some followers as not being progressive enough in their attitude to the older democracies. Gandhi deplored, for example, the fact that so many intellectuals, despite their intelligence and education, or maybe because of them, were uncritically slavish in their attitude toward Western institutions. There is a need for nationalists as well as imperialists to undergo "numerous transmigrations of political thought," in Cromer's telling phrase. This is a formidable challenge to all the new States but in very few has there been any real rethinking about democracy and liberty in the ruling classes.

The ideal and the technique of democracy have often been confused. Self-rule presupposes an assembly of citizens, in the Athenian or Rousseauite sense, *or* a representative assembly of the Benthamite kind in which conflict is necessarily bad and even discussion is superfluous, *or* a parliament which values debate in itself, in the Burkean conception, and which is also a means of canalizing the tensions and conflicts within society and presenting them to the government for arbitration. In the older democracies, there are Benthamite and Burkean elements in operation in the system, while lip-service is paid to the first through some notion of popular sovereignty. Pure democracy is modified in practice by aristocratic and monarchical elements, which sometimes take the form of an oligarchic legislature and a republican presidency. The executive is meant to provide for public needs, the judiciary is expected to protect individual rights and liberties, the legislature is required to reflect and balance differing views and rival interests so that a sense of fraternity and the civic virtues may be promoted. The doctrine of separation of powers has become, in practice, a mechanical division of labor and a theory of political pluralism. The notion of liberty has become a means of justifying the removal of obvious external restraints and environmental handicaps. The eighteenth-century theory of consent of the governed has become partly reduced to the twentieth-century practice of engineering consent. The two-party system fails to polarize the subtler shades of opinion in the country. Whereas in Britain the tensions between the executive and the legislature tend to be obscured rather than resolved by a combination of cabinet government, party discipline, and parliamentary sovereignty, in the United States the constitutional checks and balances do not effectively prevent bitter conflicts and compromises from periodically upsetting the stability and continuity of the system. Major conflicts remain basically insoluble within the existing framework since the logical extension of victory by either executive or legislature would destroy its rival. Many ordinary political conflicts become charged with constitutional significance, so that arguments of substance rapidly shift to arguments of constitutional and legal principle. It is difficult for even the best leaders to be equally effective in their dual roles as the head of State and the head of government.

In the emerging polities the Benthamite-Burkean model must be replaced by a Rousseauite-Burkean model at best, or a Rousseauite-Benthamite model as a second best. It is idle to place much reliance on the feasibility of combining leisurely debate with effective majority rule under the conditions of the new States. It would be desirable to strengthen the slow working of democracy at the base, while also facilitating swift and strong action at the center, whether through a parliamentary or a presidential system. The power of intermediate institutions ought to be considerably reduced so they serve primarily as coordinating bodies. It is normal to think of the federation of states as emerging from below, while decentralization of power (devolution of authority or delegation of function) is seen as coming from above. It would be worthwhile for the emerging polities to achieve a closely federated system, which will give enough scope for agreed action at the center based upon widely accepted ends, and for maximum freedom of discussion and disagreement at the local level during the initial period. Later, when the system has become stabilized and has been able to initiate successfully the processes of social and economic change needed, the balance in the system may be gradually reversed, so that central institutions become forums for national discussion and local bodies become instruments of efficient action. Instead of a sharp separation of powers and division of functions, it would be desirable to give greatest importance to the creation of an impartial, powerful judiciary at the center, which would safeguard the integrity of the system, and local judicial bodies, which would administer everyday needs swiftly and cheaply. The executive and legislative functions could be brought closer to each other, even combined where possible, so that the rigidly narrow roles of doers and talkers may give way to a framework which enables the talkers to act and forces the doers to talk to others and respond to their criticisms. The checks and balances in the system should operate mainly between higher-level and lower-level bodies, rather than between higher-level bodies or between lower-level bodies. A higher-level body should be able to restrain any lower-level body when needed, while at the same time lower-level bodies should be able to combine when necessary to restrain any higher-level body. The judiciary should be placed outside this process.

In order to promote liberty, the commitment should be both to increasing the capacity to choose, and to widening the range of choices of individual citizens. The parapolitical aim of educational institutions and processes should be to liberate the individual from internal compulsions as well as from external constraints. Otherwise freedom becomes a farce and liberty degenerates into license, thus inviting tyranny and facilitating despotism. In mass organizations it is desirable to safeguard against adopting methods of manipulation and subtle devices of intimidation masquerading as "powerful persuasion." In the emerging polities an inflexible party system may not emerge at the center and will not be very relevant at the local level. It would be preferable to provide for adequate freedom of discussion within parties and a measure of agreement between them, rather than to foster intense rivalry between them and uniformity of thought within them. The rulers must show proper respect for constitutional forms while their critics must display an awareness of the real problems and formal issues involved in political controversies. There should be a clear distinction between the roles of the head of State and those of the head of government, so that the latter does not claim an exclusive right to speak and act on behalf of the nation and the former does not intervene, except in emergency, in the task of policy formulation.

These are merely indications of the transformation of the ideas of democracy and liberty that may be needed to strengthen and enhance their prospects in the emerging polities. It is naturally more difficult in the newer than the older States to separate political from non-political, public from private, official from non-official considerations. The democratic State has evolved in the older countries, especially England, by "taking everything out of politics except politics." Justice was lifted out of politics in the seventeenth century, administration was taken out of politics in the nineteenth century, the monarchy and the Welfare State have finally been taken out of politics in the twentieth century. Politics has typically not been allowed to enter into the police force or the educational system, and religion has gradually been taken out of politics. National defense has largely been rescued from party politics, especially at times of crisis, and even in foreign policy there has been some basis for bipartisanship in crucial areas of agreement. Public liberties, like political democracy, have helped to put political power at a discount. The Rule of Law checks the ambitious politician in his fight for power and his exercise of it, thus keeping politics in its place. This has led to a widespread lack of sympathy toward professional politicians and the business of politics itself, an animosity that is tempered by apathy. As a result, the defensive postures of the politician are easily understandable and his occasional self-righteousness and self-importance provide amusement rather than anger. In the emerging polities, however, comparable features of politicians and attitudes toward politics are connected with the faith that may repose in democracy itself. It will take some time before the arena of politics, considerably inflated during the struggle for independence, dwindles down to its due significance. It is more important, however, to remove certain fundamental matters from party politics than to take most things out of politics altogether. Extremely high standards are held before politicians, and while politics may be increasingly distrusted, it is also relied upon to deliver the goods in many spheres. Justice, education, the polities as soon as possible, if not at the time of constitution tarian religion must be taken out of politics in all the emerging polities as soon as possible, if not at the time of constitution making. Furthermore, politics itself must become imbued with ethical considerations of the highest order and politicians must be very much more than power-seeking professionals. It is for this supreme reason that the ideas of democracy and liberty need to be transformed. Democracy must work locally–or perish. Liberty must be linked to moral and spiritual values that the people cherish, and not merely vested in legal or constitutional provisions and amenities. Otherwise it will weaken and fade away. Further, an unimaginative reliance upon the exaggerated virtues of a growing middle class will not help emerging polities if the quality of politics is not raised to a higher level than is regarded as safe in the older democracies.

At the institutional level, it is worthwhile to consider the possible evolution of existing political structures within emerging polities into a gradation of republics, with concentric circles of power and loyalty. The larger the State, the greater the number of such circles or tiers and hence the greater the need for a strong center at the apex of the cone. The smaller the State, the greater the possibility of combining the executive and legislative functions in the same body at the center as is practiced in Switzerland or was envisaged by the 1928 Donoughmore Committee Report on the Constitution of Ceylon. This may be the best way to prevent a hegemony of the executive over the legislature which makes nonsense of the doctrine of separation of powers, and which has been exploited by antidemocrats. Such a system could secure a greater level of popular participation, induce parliamentarians to face concrete issues and pressing problems, guarantee that political progress will go hand in hand with administrative knowledge, compensate for the absence of proper parties while avoiding the defects of the party system, dispense with superfluous second chambers that reduce the prestige and effectiveness of the national parliament, make politics at the center less spectacular and at the periphery more vital. It is notable that small democracies that have reduced the intensity and immanence of politics, notably the Scandinavian, have advanced furthest toward a real social and economic equality, considerably diversified the professional backgrounds of parliamentarians (especially Norway), and been least inclined toward imperialist ambitions, international power politics, and futile wars.

It is desirable and possible to increase initially the power of the State, and then use it to nurture a variety of associations to act in virtual independence of it. As Vinoba Bhave has stressed, it is more important that society be free of government than that there be no central government, short of the elusive ideal of a stateless society. The coercive role of government should be increasingly replaced by its advisory role until the former tends to zero. The mythological giant won from the gods the power of reducing to ashes all those on whose heads he placed his hands. He was fortunately persuaded, when he got out of control, to put his hand on his own head. While Bhave optimistically hoped that "the government, like Brahmāsura, will place its hands on its head and wither away," he conceded that the government has a role to fulfill in the long and necessary transition from the nightmare of brute anarchy to the parapolitical dream of the philosophical anarchists. He insisted that the foremost duty of the State and political workers is the task of inspiring fearlessness in the citizen and developing a sense of unity and cooperation in the citizenry. These ideas are not as impractical as they may sound. Mass movements led to the eventual capture and strengthening of the State machine by the party or group representing the majority, but today the State is often the best protector of minority interests, and the only force capable in a progressive democracy of countering mass hysteria by curbing majority pressures. Similarly, the State has been led to create public corporations secured from its own interference. The principle is clear, even if its applications are strenuous. The universities, the arts, trade unions, private and public corporations, and other associations could be helped by the State to get on their feet and assert their independence, provided the appropriate climate of opinion has been fostered. Marxists are ideologically unable to accept this principle's relevance, let alone its practical application, and do not believe in the possibility of impartiality or even the idea of an umpire. Democrats and libertarians are bound to believe in the theoretical possibility of neutrality and impartiality in the administration of laws as well as in the protective role of the State.

This can be carried out in practice only in an atmosphere where people are fearless before the State, willing to change and even challenge the law, where government does not claim to be the State, and where the State is not coeval and coequal with society as a whole. It is the responsibility of both government and society in the new States to create and strengthen such an atmosphere, while the government has the further duty of encouraging associations to claim and cherish their independence of the State. If the leadership in emerging polities is to lead and not drive, to coax and not coerce the citizen to participate in a common national endeavor and the task of social and economic change, it must approach him as a reasonable and responsible person, increasing the avenues and providing the impetus to voluntary cooperation and group action. This would be impossible in the economic sphere if the peasant were looked upon solely as the source of forced capital savings or the instrument of grandiose industrialization. It is essential to ensure that in the process of development, the forces of growth from within are not stifled by attempts to superimpose preconceived patterns of life and activity. The strengthening of these inner forces and the creation of new institutions, especially at the local level, must proceed *pari passu* so that they reinforce each other.

The emerging polities have to actualize their inner potentialities by a commitment to peaceful and tolerant experimentation. The traditional concept of "mixed government" must be combined with the more recent notion of a "mixed economy" in what may be called the mixed society of the emerging polities. It is necessary for the party inheriting the powerful popular appeal of the national movement for independence to convince its rivals and critics that society can develop as an integral whole. The belief must spread that the position which particular classes occupy at any given time, as a result of various historical forces for which none can be blamed, can be altered without recurrence to class hatreds or the use of violence. The government must secure a large measure of agreement in the community from below upward regarding the basic ends of policy. This fundamental unforced unity of purpose could constitute the ultimate sanction behind any national program or plan, give it driving force, and evoke the necessary sacrifices on the part of citizens. To achieve all these ends, appropriate institutions must be established which can associate people of all parties and every significant shade of opinion with the government at every level of decision making. A few examples of such institutions already exist in India, Malaya, Indonesia, and Israel. In the absence of such devices, the only way in which the government could secure support under present conditions is by allowing itself to be influenced by different groups in the body politic through legitimate pressure activity or through some form of unconstitutional pressure and organized resistance. While we may wish that emerging polities would be prepared to transform their present political structures in some of the new ways suggested, the actual forms assumed will depend upon each State. It might be helpful here to note certain familiar modes of tackling the sources of weakness in emerging polities, methods that have their limited uses even under present conditions and are readily adaptable to a variety of structures.

1. Even though the war against poverty will take a long time to win, it is necessary for the State to adopt various measures to reduce the sharp economic inequalities that undermine the working of mass democracy, and to strengthen the organizing power of peasants, artisans, and industrial and clerical workers. In addition to fiscal and monetary measures to reduce income ceilings, it would be desirable to persuade wealthy landlords and industrialists to part with portions of their wealth, property, and earnings as public contributions toward specific local schemes and plans. The more the redistributive process can be extended beyond legal compulsion and political action, the more democracy is strengthened at the social level. The more the State can bring together representatives of richer and poorer groups, stronger and weaker sections of society, in planning local programs, the better it will be for all.

2. Even if the war against illiteracy cannot be won quickly, it may be desirable for the State to invite various educational and social bodies to undertake programs of civic and political education

administered by local authorities on a strictly non-partisan basis. The more such efforts can be initiated without State control, the better for democracy. It is necessary that there emerge a general awareness of the existing political structure, of the legal and judicial system, of the basic values embodied in a written constitution, of the rights and liberties of the citizen, and of the roles of the civil service, police, parliament, and local and regional bodies. The proceedings of parliament must be widely circulated and spread broadcast in a variety of ways—through high schools and colleges, newspapers and television, periodic summaries and local forums.

3. Sectional interests must be induced to work through legitimate public pressure groups and employ recognized methods of petitioning the government, representing their views, and arguing grievances. Irregularities in this sphere and secret collusion with politicians or officials ought to be exposed through the press, within the bounds of reasonable laws of libel rather than through threat of confiscation without explanation by the State. The more the methods of effectively airing sectional or factional grievances are regularized, the better for the public as well as the system as a whole.

4. The inheritors of the mystique of the former national movement must make a special effort to be fair in their dealings with opponents while refusing to encourage trends that may undermine the secular, democratic, and liberal values on which the entire system is based. Only in this way may obscurantist and extremist elements in the country be weakened, while opposition groups are encouraged to become responsible aspirants to political power. A code of honor might be agreed upon and signed by various party leaders in public, thus discouraging personal attacks, false statements, and unfair aspersions. The code itself should never become a source of rival claims by the various parties.

5. A continual effort must be made by the various centers of opinion formation, especially the newspapers, to stress the distinction between the State and the government, the existing rulers and the system as a whole, the availability of alternative leaders and of multiple centers of power at various levels of decision making. Any attempt by the present leadership to identify itself exclusively with the sacred symbols in the system—the constitution, the Founding Fathers of the independence movement, perhaps even the National

Plan—must meet with opposition and discouragement from all articulate groups. Naturally, this is almost impossible to achieve in the early years after independence, but every effort must consciously be made to see that this situation is not perpetuated.

6. Military and civilian officials must be strictly prohibited from involving themselves in national politics while they are in office, or even when resigning after a prescribed period.

7. It should be the aim of the State to spread the load of its administrative system as evenly as possible over the entire country and to prevent the duplication and overlapping of functions between coordinate authorities. To avoid the concentration and overcrowding of the bureaucratic structure in a few centers or in the central and regional capitals, a top-heavy administrative system inherited from the past may have to be radically overhauled and even partially scrapped. This should be a matter of continuing concern, entrusted to a responsible and courageous Commission that has a shrewd insight into the myriad workings of Parkinson's law. Of course, the need may sometimes be in the opposite direction but it would be a mistake to think that the need cannot simultaneously be in both directions.

8. There should be a national audit of public expenditure, especially of the official spending of money received through external aid and international assistance, as an effective check on the demoralizing effects of waste and embezzlement.

9. Magistrates must be empowered and encouraged to take prompt action against any politician, however exalted, who seeks to arouse religious hatred and communal activity on sectarian lines. Political activity by any religious organization must be proscribed and met with official restraint. The more these things can be achieved by social rather than by legal sanctions, the better for liberty. There should, however, be legal prohibitions of non-religious groups organized on a sectarian basis. The State should see that no public funds flow into sectarian schools and colleges. Literature designed to malign any particular religion must be banned, after reasonable criteria have been applied.

10. Scholars, lawyers, and politicians must be encouraged to visit the older democracies to see the actual working of their systems so that they have no residues of illusions or misunderstand-

ings. Comparative studies of institutions in various countries should be facilitated so that popular myths about the uniqueness of particular models may be dispelled. It may be worthwhile to get committees of experts representing various emerging polities to prepare full reports on the working of different democratic as well as authoritarian systems.

11. There must be a deliberate effort to diversify the social, regional, professional, and age composition of the main parties, so that there is at least more than one national party.

12. Political professionalism must be discouraged by widening the range of recruitment from non-political spheres.

13. Social mobility between different regions must be encouraged to overcome the parochialism of local groups and communities.

14. Politicians, businessmen, civil servants, intellectuals, trade union leaders, and rural and social workers should be brought together on many national bodies and local projects. University courses for civil servants, seminars on national development for research scholars, talks to parliamentarians by outsiders–these and similar possibilities might be explored.

15. The efficiency level of the subordinate civil service must be raised, while the excessive prestige of the upper civil service must be reduced.

16. The delicate relations between civil servants and politicians should be governed by a clearly formulated code assigning their relative function and degrees of responsibility. Violations of this code should be brought before an independent body composed of trusted judges, retired civil servants, and experienced politicians who have now become governors. This body should have only advisory and arbitrative functions.

17. The opposition parties must not develop into pressure groups acting on the government. They must be respected as equals by the party in power if they are to become respectable. The system must allow for adequate understanding, cooperation, and peaceful dissent between the various parties and not degenerate into any form of "guided democracy."

18. There must be national research institutes established in the social sciences, genuinely independent of governmental interference and local university politics. These bodies must pay special at-

tention to the objective study of the workings of all aspects of the democratic system, including the liberties and rights of citizens. At a middle level, there is a need for national, non-partisan institutes of public affairs with branches throughout the country. At the widest level, there must be a well-planned program of lectures, seminars, and discussions conducted by a national association for adult education, independent of government influence.

19. Partisan political activity among students may be discouraged, but students must have every opportunity to study and discuss political problems and to question politicians in an academic atmosphere.

20. The growth of a new technocracy must be safeguarded against by giving special importance to the civic and political education of all technical functionaries.

21. Parliament should devise an agreed code of conduct that may be expected of elected representatives. Nepotism, corruption, and sectarianism, interference with the normal machinery of administration and law enforcement, and other code violations must be referred to an independent body, associated with parliament, with recommendatory rather than mandatory duties. At the same time parliamentary privilege must be respected in regard to freedom of debate.

22. A national association for the defense of civil liberties should be set up and have branches throughout the country. It must be supported by various professional groups and by public-spirited men of repute and standing.

23. There should be increasing contact and interchange of ideas between parliamentarians, civil servants, lawyers, and local leaders.

24. Legal associations all over the country should endeavor to make citizens aware of certain legal maxims sacred to a liberal democracy: a man should be tried in the presence of his peers; he should be deemed innocent until he is proved guilty; he should be punished only for proved violations of the existing law; no man is above the law; to none will the courts sell or deny or delay right or justice; every man is entitled to freedom from arbitrary arrest; the regular law is absolutely supreme, excluding the existence of arbitrary or discretionary powers and prerogatives; freedom of speech is unlimited, subject to the laws of slander, blasphemy, or treason.

25. Written constitutions, incorporating fundamental rights as well as common law prerogative writs and orders, must be adopted by all emerging polities. The abuse of emergency provisions at normal times must be safeguarded against by the courts. A narrow interpretation of the constitution must also be avoided as conflicts between various power groups could lead to frequent amendments pushed through by the dominant party, resulting in a waste of energy and loss of morale. At the same time, the reasonableness of restrictions on individual freedom in the public interest must be decided by the judiciary, thus protecting the due process of law. The principle of judicial review must become firmly established, together with the other remedies constitutionally guaranteed for the enforcement of rights.

26. Parliamentary committees should be neither too few nor unrepresentative, nor must they be too large in proportion to total membership. There must not be lack of opportunities for specialization and training due to rapid turnover of membership. Bills should not be given only brief, cursory consideration. As the quality of parliamentary life is improved, there could also be an increase in the use of legislative powers of investigation as a check on actions and policies of the executive branch as well as public corporations and trusts. The more independent members there are on these committees, the better for their prestige and integrity. They must, however, never be allowed to become self-styled vigilantes or custodians of the conscience of the nation.

27. In a few emerging polities there is the danger that comparatively mature local governmental institutions will be tempted to break away from comparatively immature central institutions. Under such conditions federal institutions must be devised to allow considerable autonomy and flexibility of form to local groups and communities.

28. The feeling must be fostered widely that liberty and not State interference is the rule, and that every restriction on liberty needs special and convincing justification. This must also be true of matters such as State patronage of the arts or State intervention in the affairs of universities.

In addition to these rather conventional recommendations, a few bolder and largely untried suggestions may also be made in a context that does not require the radical transformation of the entire system earlier envisaged. Instead of a second chamber meant to give voice and votes to distinguished citizens who will not otherwise be drawn into politics, a unicameral parliament could be established with enhanced prestige, a closer connection with the executive, and a wider basis of representation. This could incorporate the pleas made by the early Fabians and Guild Socialists for vocational representation; Winston Churchill's forgotten proposal, in his Romanes Lectures of 1930, of an Economic Sub-Parliament; and the untried Danish proposal for a single chamber in 1939. A parliament could be elected as one assembly, partly by traditional constituencies and partly by election from national lists of candidates. These lists could be drawn up by the various vocational groups; and, above all, from personalities somewhat detached from the usual political process who–by virtue of their education, character, or some outstanding contribution to science, commerce, rural development, or urban cooperatives–would be able to contribute expert knowledge and the fruits of their own experience to legislative planning. This unicameral parliament could meet in committees as well as in plenary sessions allowing a free vote as often as possible, and encouraging legislation to be initiated by independents as well as by party leaders. It could take a large share of the responsibility of national planning. It could incorporate Mill's proposal of a Legislative Commission entrusted with the task of translating the wishes of parliament into proper legal language, thus preventing parliamentarians from becoming unduly legalistic. In general, this proposal may be useful in raising the prestige and effectiveness of parliament in emerging polities.

The more complicated problems become, the more essential should be the commitment to try to attract into parliament not only men and women who represent local opinions and interests, but also people of intellectual and moral distinction, and persons with specialized knowledge. It is a mistake to believe that parliament can be treated as a kind of jury, required only to say "aye, not guilty" or "nay, guilty" on the basis of documents and schemes placed before it by the executive. The legislative assemblies of the emerging polities must have far more initiative of their own than those of the older democracies since they cannot cash in on the accumulated capital of past prestige. Their ultimate authority must surely suffer in the absence of a creative role in the first phase of their new life. It is hardly enough that emerging polities compensate for the deficiencies of their political structure and process by relying mainly upon social and spiritual movements that operate beyond the pale of politics. They must be committed to bringing their political institutions into closer contact with social movements and moral ideas. They should, especially, draw into parliament some of the best citizens available, just as the government should, at all levels, secure the finest leadership the country can provide.

It is not enough that the emerging polities entrust their supreme courts with the task of protecting the constitution and the liberties of the citizen. There must be safeguards against abuse of power by politicians, civil servants, and ministers, as well as against suppression of local grievances by the bureaucracy and the party in power. Again, Scandinavian experience has much to teach in the matter of dealing with departmental abuses or miscarriages in individual cases. Particularly important is the Swedish institution of the Commissioner for Justice, the *Justitieombudsman,* created in 1809 to protect basic liberties from infringement by the administration as well as the judiciary. This warden or supreme protector of individual rights does not work like a court which pronounces judgment when a case is brought before it. This is a separate, though important function. A *Justitieombudsman* supervises the observance of laws and the constitution by public officials and employees, by the government, and by the courts. He takes action against those who, in the execution of their duties, have through partiality, favoritism, or other unworthy cause, committed any unlawful act or neglected to perform their official duties properly. The independence of this office, its breadth of jurisdiction, its considerable latitude in methods and procedures, as well as its access to all public minutes and records, are essential to its success. Above all, such a Commissioner must be a person of legal acumen and learning, of judicial wisdom and humility, of courage and discretion, and of impeccable integrity. He has a four-year term in Sweden and a three-year term in Finland. He must be assisted by a loyal and competent staff, entirely under his control.

This institution should not be adopted by the new States at the national level lest it rival a powerful supreme court, but it could be created at the local level, where it should be possible for every unit to find one person whom the people trust and can approach freely. If he turns out to be incompetent or prejudiced, he should be replaced when the end of his short term comes. There should, however, be no attempt to link these local protectors of people's rights to each other, to subordinate them to a superior authority, or to introduce any kind of conventional case-law into the process of their investigations and judgments. Otherwise a top-heavy and superfluous hierarchy would be created which would be hampered by official red tape and the stereotyped mentality of second-rate judges, resulting in an odd sort of parallel judiciary. The more this valuable institution can be integrated into the pattern of local authorities, the better will be its working. The recommendations of this kind of official should have moral rather than legal force, so that the right of appeal to a court of law is inappropriate. In practice, it should be impossible for governing bodies to ignore his authority, while at the same time he can assume neither the pontifical infallibility of a medieval monarch holding public audience, nor the impetuous arrogance of a modern Committee of Public Safety.

There could be set up, in addition to a system of legal aid, an arrangement by which legal advice could be freely rendered by authorized persons to all those in need of it. These legal advisers should be appointed by national or regional associations of lawyers rather than by the government. Some may work part-time while others may act as full-time solicitors holding sessions in towns throughout the country. Lawyers could be invited to enter their names on legal advice panels. The aim of this scheme should be to reduce needless and wasteful litigation as well as to make citizens aware of their legal rights and the procedures they could initiate to air legitimate grievances against powerful officials or other citizens. This scheme could be linked to local arbitration councils, and these legal advisers could be represented on such bodies during their semi-judicial sittings, thus making the others aware of the narrower legal implications of the disputes and acts that are being adjudged. This scheme would not only meet the usual objection that the courts are not open to all. It would also carry out the principle that the weak must be so powerfully protected that the strong will not have the temerity to trample on their rights and risk popular censure.

The emerging polities can combat the forces of disunity by creating multi-command (multi-racial or multi-lingual) zones within which power would mainly be vested in local institutions. The principle of self-government can be applied not only at national and local levels, but also regionally, provided these zones have functional rather than emotional significance and that they remain weaker than central and local authorities. The chief commitment embodied in these intermediate arrangements would be to secure peaceful cooperation in what would otherwise be areas of continual tension and petty power politics. This principle might provide an important missing link in the chain of institutions necessary to secure world order out of the present chaos of international politics. The strongest argument in favor of some form of world federal government is that it could make greater and genuine decentralization of political and economic power possible. Centralization as a system is structurally inconsistent with commitment to a truly nonviolent society and inevitably leads to loss of the larger freedoms, regardless of the liberal and democratic intentions of the regime in power. Democracy and centralization are, in essence, as incompatible as freedom and slavery. The role of the government should increasingly be that of protector and arbiter, rather than an unstable combination of parent, landlord, employer, and despot. Democracy as a system of government is not designed to administer universal social services, to supervise great industrial monopolies, or to manage a vast administrative machine and an enormous economic mechanism. These are tasks beyond the powers and limits of any legislative assembly. They involve innumerable decisions that are parapolitical and are not readily amenable to public opinion or popular control.

V

In conclusion, a few general qualifications may be briefly made about the applicability of proposals to strengthen political democracy and public liberties in emerging polities. First of all, it is in the interest of democracy and liberty that they should feel secure against external intervention of every kind; that they should not be induced to assume international obligations they are not yet ready to fulfill; that the chaos of international rivalries should not be extended into their territories to a greater extent than seems unavoidable; that international institutions should be made as democratic as possible; and that the rule of law and the liberties of the individual should receive growing recognition on the international plane even when they conflict with the interests, policies, and dogmas of older democracies. Secondly, in addressing the problems of the emerging polities, there must be a full utilization of the fresh energies released at their founding as well as a toleration of the inevitable delays of democracy. There is already an element of ruthlessness and indifference to the means employed to secure worthy ends in the older as well as the newer States. This would be worsened if the cause of democracy and liberty became identified with any single class or party, any particular racial, religious, or cultural group, or with any section or stratum of society. Maximum support must be secured at the widest level for the basic values of liberal democracy so that people in general begin to believe in their inherent value, even if they regard it as vulnerable and imperfect.

The paramount need of the emerging polities is not for panaceas or short-cuts, or even practical proposals, but rather for the parapolitical commitment to strengthen the foundations and improve the working of liberal democracy despite past blunders. An increasing awareness of the problem is itself the greatest single measure of solution that could be contemplated. Democracies decline and decay through weakness of will more than anything else. It is, therefore, of supreme importance for existing leaders to see the various implications and costs of the crucial problem of commitment in relation to their present efforts in handling what appear to be more pressing and momentous issues. They must be helped in every way to resist the greatest temptation of all–to lose faith in a system or a free society, and merely keep up appearances before an audience that cannot be fooled for long. They must keep alive their allegiance to the fundamental principles they have accepted, for, in the noble words of the First Inaugural of Jefferson, these principles "form the bright constellation which has gone before us, and guided our steps through an age of revolution and reformation. The wisdom of our sages and the blood of our political faith–the text of civil instruction–the touchstone by which we try the services of those we trust; and should we wander from them in moments of error or alarm let us hasten to retrace our steps and to regain the road which alone leads to peace, liberty and safety." It was given to men like Paine, Whitman, and Gandhi to realize that democracy and liberty, like world peace and prosperity, are in the end indivisible. No nation can today be democratic or free in isolation. In every State there is the need and the possibility of securing the fruits of democracy and the blessings of liberty.

12

THE FUNDAMENTAL REVOLUTION: FROM ÉLITISM TO EQUALITY

Our hopes for the future condition of the human species may be reduced to three points: the destruction of inequality between different nations; the progress of equality in one and the same nation; and lastly, the real improvement of man.

MARQUIS DE CONDORCET

The fundamental revolution from élitism to equality is the hidden force within the avalanche of revolutions deluging the modern world. Its irresistible movement eludes any single formula. At one level, it comprises a series of changes in established governments and political institutions everywhere. At another level, and in the specific sense in which the term "revolution" was used in the late eighteenth century, something more fundamental than the collapse of regimes and forms is taking place. It involves profound transformations of entire social structures and economic systems. Revolutions of this type have not occurred anywhere merely through a substitution in political regime, but rather through the internal logic of industrialization and imperialism, or from decisive confrontations of imperialism and capitalism with nationalist and socialist movements. Avowedly communist countries have radically reshaped their economic and social structures, though this is only partly due to displacements of political regimes. There are also contemporary contexts where it is appropriate to use the term "revolution" to refer to major changes in the conceptual frameworks of science and religion, as well as to significant alterations in the modes of technology and communication, culture and community. Yet the fundamental revolution from élitism to equality is not accomplished through a commitment to any finite series of incremental changes. It is ceaseless and perpetual. Both older and more durable than other revolutions and centered upon man's relationship to his fellow man, it is rooted in his self-awareness and his ruling conception of his relations to God and Nature, as well as to the social and political universe.

Appraisals of revolutions generally emphasize man's response to external changes in institutions, structures, and environments, and contain an unstated reference to this more profound revolution, which recurs in ways often submerged once these outer changes are launched. This revolution alters man's inner response to external events and is grounded in his very conception of himself. It depends for its force and direction on the nature, range, and depth of his self-consciousness. It is furthered whenever a man comes to see himself as a creator rather than a creature, as an agent not a victim, as a subject not an object, as a being necessarily involved in the act of defining himself through self-determination, self-expression, self-fulfillment to any degree, and self-actualization in whatever form. Any alteration in this direction allows the individual a measure of self-transcendence. The adoption of such a Promethean view of man constitutes a crucial break with any worldview centered upon a single creator, an anthropomorphic God, a sultan in the sky, some supernatural being or supreme agent at whose mercy lie all the actors and events on the platform of human encounters. Seen from an existential standpoint, this revolution is man's liberation from an arbitrarily restrictive conception of self. Any restriction a man places upon himself is necessarily self-determined, and whatever premises or reasons he advances for that restriction should not be imposed upon others. It is part of the prerogative of being human that no man need accept any other man's conception of the restriction to be placed in advance upon his self-liberation. When others urge their self-limitations upon us, whether in terms of theological revelation, scientific knowledge, or a sacrosanct philosophy of history, they presumably seek to convince us that the acceptance of certain received premises will enable us to see ourselves more correctly. The perspective they command is allegedly the only proper one to adopt in reference to some God-created world, the predetermined course of history, or any single scientific world-picture. Nevertheless, when we subscribe to premises which are neither ours nor integral to our own conception of being human, we are involved in accepting arbitrary and external limitations.

Is it feasible consciously to free oneself from all arbitrariness or restrictiveness in any and every conception held of oneself? Clearly not. A man motivated by fear of the unknown, "the vasty deep," or the external superstructure, is moved by an impersonal force he cannot wholly control or significantly affect in a short time. He cannot even know whether he can expect to overcome this basic limitation over a long period of time. A man is weakened by ignorance of the possibility, whether logical or contingent, of transcending his limitations, though his ignorance is a hindrance to himself which only he can remove. Its eradication will depend upon his conceptual capacity to generate possibilities of transcending limitations which, for all he knows, no one has transcended, or to ascribe meaning and significance to past attempts in history to overcome human limitations. Yet every man is cramped by delusions, arising from his involvement in an external world in which his own acute sense of limitation atrophies his perspective on the future. If we consider the three chief obstacles to man's capacity to free himself from arbitrarily restrictive self-conceptions–fear, ignorance, and delusion–we notice a critical asymmetry between man's overestimation and underestimation of himself. Any man could mistakenly imagine himself as capable of a freedom which he can never exercise effectively or convincingly. Or, he may be wholly deluded about his capacity to convince himself that he is free even in that illusory sense. Nevertheless, if a man is hubristic and overestimates himself, then events–the external world–will ensure the certainty of his downfall or at least some rupture of his inflated conception of himself. In every case, there is the looming certainty of death. A man who stagnates through self-depreciation, however, traps himself through a stifling immunity to falsification. No set of external events could necessarily convince him that his self-depreciation is misplaced. In this asymmetry lies the difference between the ever-present risk of *hubris,* which in principle can be corrected by external forces, and the enormous danger of self-depreciation, which could effectively isolate a person from external reality. At the core of the fundamental revolution lurks this crucial asymmetry.

Man's conscious liberation from any arbitrarily restrictive conception of himself depends directly upon himself, and particularly upon the act and the assertion of being human. The unfinished revolution in self-awareness works through myriad ways in seeking its unknown consummation, and is much older than the eighteenth century. It harks back in recorded history to the profoundly direct and compelling impact of Buddha, Socrates, and Christ, as well as other great teachers of humanity. Buddha demonstrated that each man's attempt to give meaning to events, or to void the finite self, is a vital part of his own response to the external flux in a world of inexplicable suffering and pain. The very attempt to assign meaning to events, and to void false notions of self, is essential to any deliberate and authentic human response to the world. Paradoxically, this implies a credible affirmation of the possibility of self-enlightenment. Buddha taught that all the bonds of human beings are self-created and self-tolerated. "Each man his own prison makes." The individual alone can identify the network of external bonds and distinguish these from his own mental chains. Every effort to shatter the latter uncovers for each person the path of enlightenment and freedom. The exercise of ethical self-correction, and the ever-present possibility for any person to question, examine, and expand his perspective, were similarly fundamental to the Socratic revolution. To grasp these possibilities, especially in regard to the true and plausible, the good and attractive, is to begin the process of self-transformation. Independent of any external paradigms or patterns of conduct, it is always possible for a person to become truly human—a mature and self-moving individual. To proclaim the dignity and the divine estate of man, as Christ did, is to assure every human being that the Kingdom of God is within. If a person only knew how to go within and surrender himself to a transcendent source of divine light, then he could truly become capable of resisting all forms of earthly authority, which are mere pretenses in relation to his inward access to "the light that lighteth up every man that cometh into the world."

These ancient revolutions quintessentially concern the individual quest. They celebrate the possibility for a man, if he chooses, to view himself in a redemptive light, to correct himself, to enlighten himself, to heal himself. In every case nothing is said about the possibility of all persons necessarily achieving this transformation, except in principle. Yet, to say it of man *qua* man is to commit oneself to the proposition that it is true of all men. To make such an assertion about the individual as a human being is logically to entail some minimal equality for all men. It is an equality in possibility and perhaps in potential capacity, but it is not an assured equality in fact. The revolutions inaugurated by Buddha, Socrates, and Christ were naturally dependent for their impact upon the universal relevance of their message and the concrete consequence of arousing, among as many as were willing to listen, the effective possibility of self-enlightenment, self-correction, and self-surrender. The authentic possibility is central to any powerful formulation of the doctrine of self-redemption. No wonder, then, that so much credence must be given in these three revolutions to the incomparable lives of Buddha, Christ, and Socrates. Understanding Buddha is crucial to understanding his message and its compelling relevance to the individual. To understand Christ–whether one views him as a son of God different in kind from oneself, as the supremely human incarnation of a divine presence, or as a sublime exemplar of every man's creative capacities–requires a redemptive relationship to him. Similarly, no technique or mere re-enactment of the style of Socrates could ever recapture the presence in the agora of Athens of a teacher who carried conviction simply by living as he did. His choice of words and examples closed the gap between being and communication, such that all discussions around him could safely be arguments *ad hominem*. This uniqueness encourages us to place teachers like Buddha, Christ, and Socrates in an exceptional category along with precious few others, so historically remote that in time their teachings have become obscured by the indirect transmission of their ideas. What is worse, individuals have repeatedly spoken in the name of Buddha or Christ or Socrates, and claimed the very kind of privileged access which the original teachings were meant to deny, thereby constructing the illusion of some élitist relationship to these exemplary men, while effectively denying the universal and vital relevance of their teaching.

These men appear so removed from our own time that it is natural for us, overwhelmed as we are by the revolutions that took place in and since the seventeenth and eighteenth centuries, to ignore the revolutionary import of what was said, done, and depicted by them. Each individually and uniquely involved himself in opposition to others. Nevertheless, it may seem that we have saved ourselves by salvaging something of their message (in the equivalent or analogous forms in which they have become available to us since the seventeenth century), either with abstract formality or in terms of some credo of collectivist salvation. The Socratic doctrine was reaffirmed formally by Kant, and has become part of the phraseology and rhetoric of liberal democracy. In assuming that man is a moral being, whose agency predicates moral systems and defines the rational, we apparently form an intellectual commitment to the Socratic doctrine of individuation. Yet it has none of the original revolutionary vitality it had when it was pitted against the Sophists or against the Athenian custom of deriving moral inspiration and guidance from mythical figures. Its inspiration is lost in a formal and rationalist reassertion of the Socratic doctrine of the morally autonomous individual. Similarly, the Buddhist message of self-enlightenment loses its dynamism when translated, either into a Lockean doctrine of the autonomy of man in relation to knowledge, or into a Kantian claim that enlightenment requires assumptions about the collective state of mankind. We have been bequeathed a collective doctrine of enlightenment in relation to transferable and borrowed knowledge. Given the certification that we attach to specific methods for gaining reasonable certainty in knowledge, we imagine that the transference of this knowledge will afford us a basis for democratization in the name of science, the humanities, or an enlightenment which goes by the name of "education." Further, Christ's doctrine of freedom or liberation from all external authority–except in relation to a transcendent God which may be contacted within oneself–is replaced, since the French Revolution, by the belief in the collective capacity of large numbers of persons in classes and nations to come together and secure collective freedom by concerted action.

Concrete instances of individuation are relevant to other men, in principle or in practice, according to the reality of the message and the messenger to men in general. The chief advantage of a collective doctrine is that it proceeds by concrete equalization. It assumes that by removing the hindrances to individuation in external conditions, we could remove the inequalities in society, thereby giving more persons the opportunity for enlightenment, freedom, and happiness. We must collectively affirm human powers and potentialities, and this requires some general statement about collective perfectibility or the destiny of mankind in nature and in history. It can justify a doctrine of collective action in the social and political sphere, contending that by equalizing conditions we will enable more men to individuate. To equalize conditions, we will, in fact, require a creed that will secure collective sacrifices and heroic action sufficient to change an entire system. Through further equalization, we can maximize the chances for as many men as possible to gain individual freedom. The doctrine is both simple and familiar, but if we notice the thread that connects it with the earlier revolutions, we could identify the persisting problem in relation to élitism and equality. Two crucial points are needed to translate the earlier revolutions of unusual individuals into the collective revolutions of unusual nations and epochs.

The first is provided by Kant himself in his perceptive statement: "Enlightenment is man's quitting the nonage occasioned by himself." Every man is in a state of nonage, of minority or of tutelage, to some extent because of himself. His understanding depends on the guidance of others; whether young or old, external advice can be made a substitute or hindrance to one's exercise of understanding as a means of freeing oneself from nonage. The individual must wield his power responsibly. The inability to do so is occasioned by oneself, and its cause is not a want of understanding, but of the commitment and courage to use one's understanding without the guidance of another. "Have courage to make use of thine own understanding," is the dictum for him who would become enlightened. What are the common obstacles to using one's understanding? Chiefly, cowardice and laziness. On the Right, it is always necessary to deplore the laziness of those who are in a state of apparent nonage. On the Left, it is always necessary to summon men, who are seen as being in a state of nonage through no fault of their own, to some version of heroic courage that historically has taken the form of sporadic or organized violence. Given this recalcitrant problem, it is difficult for individuals to extricate themselves from the nonage which has become almost natural to them, and only a few have genuinely and bravely emancipated themselves. Because concrete freedom from nonage is so rare, Kant pointed to the political bridge between individual and collective self-determination, thereby envisaging that a whole nation will enlighten itself. In fact, when it has the requisite liberty, movement toward enlightenment is almost inevitable, because the main obstacle to collective enlightenment–to more and more individuals freeing themselves in a fuller sense–is from religious authorities. To that extent, as a stoical figure of the Enlightenment, Kant thought that the main barrier to a man's voicing and using his own understanding was some prior obstruction of his freedom to think freely and boldly. This obstacle has been clothed in appeals to religious revelations by institutions claiming privileged access to these revelations. The historical and religious obstacles to self-awareness entrenched in institutions must be met by collective social action.

The Marquis de Condorcet expressed this logical conclusion as a comprehensive doctrine of collective progress centered upon the progress of the human mind. He voiced a total vision embracing the universalization of the individual's concept of freedom and enlightenment, grounded in human nature itself, and destined to include all humanity. He saw the human race involved in an increasing destruction of inequality between different nations (which were, in this sense, purely arbitrary historical divisions). Progress toward equality within any one nation would arise as men were freed through their understanding of the collective destiny of mankind. They would be freed from taking too seriously the limits to effective equality placed upon them within a nation at any given time–limits capricious and unsanctioned by the evolutionary process. Then, these two factors–destruction of inequality between nations and the progress of equality within each nation–would together produce a real improvement in man. The human species would, in time, effectively progress and eventually fulfill its destiny. Though the grandeur of this vision was sullied by the passions and the frustrations of the French Revolution, we can clearly see today that the program of this revolution is yet largely unfinished. It has been aborted in many ways through the successive narrowing of the original vision, which was intrinsically concordant with the revolutions of Buddha, Socrates, and Christ.

If we wish to discern the elusive nature of this fundamental revolution, renewed in the eighteenth century, but still so psychologically remote from our own time as to seem utopian, then we must look closely at the persisting obstacles. What made a parapolitical revolution take the form of conventional revolutions against regimes and systems, evoking opposition that cannot entirely be overcome, and seemingly requiring an endless struggle against an external enemy, personal or impersonal? There are some hindrances to self-enlightenment, self-correction, and self-surrender inherent in the human condition, the condition of finite beings with perceptible constraints. But these are not the limitations which give a revolutionary dimension to a doctrine of self-enlightenment, self-correction, or self-surrender. What is revolutionary is the assertion that in addition to intrinsic obstacles, there are specific arbitrary restrictions imposed by some men on others, whether deliberately or by mere connivance or even unconsciously. These restrictions are amenable to being changed by human will, and yet more demoralizing and degrading than those constrictions endemic to mankind. Men are differently placed relative to the criteria of self-enlightenment, and to that extent history will always be an untidy story. In any social structure at any given time, the effort to explain on purely rational or genetic grounds the totality of existing differentiations will fail if all persons are not equally abject. The prosperous juggle with alternatives, and a small number tolerate, aid, and inspire others. While these are very few–so exceptional as to become for us almost non-existent ideals–there are many, all too visible, who seize any vantage point to disallow, hinder, and discourage the rest. Discouragement, if it immobilizes, is the worst form of hindering and disallowing. The litmus test for the integrity and continuity of a social system is not its power of co-option, statistically expressed, but rather the confident or reluctant commitment of the privileged to denying themselves some opportunities for the sake of new entrants. As this self-denial is reinforced by the social structure and the prevailing modes of competition and cooperation, so the equality-élite opposition is weakened.

Buddha was a revolutionary because he identified precisely the Brahmins as a sacerdotal caste presuming unchallengeable supremacy by reason of birth. Claiming privileged access to religious and secular learning and therefore immunity to criticism as a caste, their position precluded new entrants and neglected the needs and the possibilities of all other men. Buddha took the battle into an earthly camp, insisting upon a challenge to the very core of Brahminism, and an increase of opportunities for outsiders to gain the freedom that he exemplified. Socrates, too, as a subversive, identified a respectable group–the Sophists–engaged in disallowing, hindering, and discouraging the rest, and who claimed a unique status as teachers of special skills and purveyors of a view of success which depended upon rhetorical persuasion and manipulation. The Sophists exacted fees from the rich in return for transmitting these skills, although, by their very nature, these skills could only be had by very few and still remain effective. When Christ spoke against the Pharisees, he spoke against men who were hypocritically selfish in their ritualistic formality. They claimed to be unique interpreters of the Torah, while bestowing immense importance to "the fences of the Torah"–the external signs and rules of conduct taken as tokens of allegiance to the spirit of the Torah. Some men were more able than others to claim a special moral status and thereby became a threat to the moral life of others.

In all these revolutions an identifiable class or caste of men made peremptory claims about themselves (to which others acquiesced) with the implication that they were superior either innately or by virtue of skill in formal observances. In every case, the existence of such a class logically entailed the inferiority of other men, and when inferiority was partly removable, the removal reinforced the superior status of the élite. In this sense, "élitism" as a term may be characterized by two separate factors: the implicit belief in the right and capacity of the élite to rule over the rest–to assume, secure, or even to maintain, the subordination or the submission of other men; and, secondly, pride, a consciousness of belonging to a supposedly select or favored group. Thus élitism connotes an exclusivity. It also implies coherence and superiority, the status of being chosen and set apart from others. Given these elements, élitism tends toward self-perpetuation and the promotion of further illusions–immutability, permanence, inviolability, invulnerability, and infallibility. As a result, élitism may maintain its position for a period of time determined by the extent to which its illusions do not become destructive to itself, or by the extent to which other men behave for practical purposes as if these illusions remain intact. Keeping them intact in acute cases would be accompanied by an incapacity to see illusions for what they are. Élitism, then, necessarily means exclusiveness–by birth, or some unalterable and irreproducible characteristics–racial, ethnic, or genetic.

In every case the exclusiveness of an élite logically entails inequality in at least one respect which could lead to absolutizing ever-increasing inequality in a variety of respects. This could be irrelevant, in principle, to the actual degree of inequality if the élite were wholly isolated from the rest. However, élitism is a relational and comparative concept, and involves an assumed and maintained acceptance by others. Whether the élite is open or closed is irrelevant to this consequence for equality. Socially, élitism requires an absolute, or at least contingently inviolable, immunity to any criticisms and challenges which would imply a change in the position of the élite relative to the many. Changes in the actual or absolute position of the élite need not affect its survival in relation to the underprivileged and downtrodden. The maintenance of the relative position of an élite would encourage, sometimes require, the emulation of the élite by other men, an emulation doomed from the start. They may imitate the manners of the élite, but would have no rights to membership unless the position of the élite itself was maintained intact. Imitation can never rise above caricature, because the élite invariably reserves some key privilege, symbol, or activity to itself.

The eighteenth century's failure to fulfill expectations of greater equality suggests that changes in historical conditions, relative equalizations, and replacements of one élite by another, do not eliminate élitism. Indeed, the last two centuries have witnessed a growth and proliferation of subtler theories of élitism than was necessary for élitists to propound previously. These theories even justify functioning élites in modern industrial society in the very terms invoked by the *philosophes,* which became the basis of the collective programs of the Revolution. Furthermore, these subtler theories are reinforced by a social determinism shared in some form by élitists (at least in theory) and by many revolutionaries (both in theory and practice). A huge price is paid in the process.

By becoming fatalistic either in relation to evolutionary and biological determinism, or in relation to historical destiny, or by taking a deterministic view of progress, men undermine at the sources their capacity to overcome passivity and cowardice by eroding the very core of individuality. As individuality shrinks, equalization, in turn, becomes increasingly self-defeating. Equality has become a minimal and abstract doctrine combined with collective freedom and producing a poisonous theory of democratic élitism, championed in America and widely practiced elsewhere. It suggests that because an élite is open or because there is a plurality of élites (in free and fair competition), élitism is compatible with and even indispensable to democracy in modern industrial societies. It is a theory officially propounded by men who regard themselves as belonging to an élite of academics, bureaucrats, and entrepreneurs entitled to privilege by virtue of their degrees, offices, and acquisitions. They claim to be authoritative interpreters both of the doctrine itself and of its sources in their versions of science and history. Thus they reinforce determinism sufficiently to exasperate the alienation, anomie, and helplessness of the individual. They purchase the loyalty of enough people to make the system seemingly open and thus capable of disarming otherwise obstreperous critics, and they require in every case that the rules be administered with sufficient rigor to force failures to become total drop-outs. These rejects may mutter in revolutionary language, but are by now so weak that their movement is crippled.

There was something essentially valid in the eighteenth-century revolution still pertinent to many systems, and while all, including the élites, are victims of prevailing doctrines of despair—what is so bad about it? As long as people are reconciled to their own conditions, or at least increase their identification with the successful and powerful, surely the whole process can be made tolerable. We see most clearly, however, on the global plane and increasingly within nations and between individuals, that the ideological propaganda of this insidious form of élitism in the name of democracy and freedom is etiolated and self-defeating when its advocates are not actually backed by political or economic power. Even when they are so buttressed, there is an erosion from within, both because of boredom and because of the conspicuous gulf between profession and practice in men of power. The possibility of communication between the nations, and the emergence of a large part of the world unwilling to adopt one or the other major alternatives, encourage, at least in theory, a freedom to criticize which has rendered ideological propaganda self-destructive. If the Soviet Union or the United States extol themselves sufficiently, then upon visiting either, men become so disillusioned that they revert either to the opposite extreme or to apathy. As long as professional bodies are involved in promoting ideological doctrine, which is bound to become cruder in order to be more immediately plausible to persons ignorant of the conditions, then at least those gulled will soon evince an immunity to propaganda.

Is there then anything that can be said in favor of the existing System? Peter Blau and Otis Duncan reported on extensive statistical indications of changes in the occupational structure in America where the theory of democratic élitism has had ample opportunity to produce its purported benefits. One of their extraordinary conclusions is that, despite the enormous technical and historical changes over the past fifty years, the amount and nature of social mobility have remained remarkably constant.[1] To increase significantly the rate of mobility we must reduce the influence of family background, since it has been found that a child's life-chances depend very much on his capacity and choice, which in turn are largely determined by his early childhood experience. This experience accounts for a quarter of a person's chances of achieving "success." However, what remains elusive is any specification of the effective possibility of ensuring upward mobility and preventing downward mobility, sufficiently to produce a substantial change in the position of groups relative to the élite (according to Paretian criteria). Yet the dream of equality of opportunity persists, and generates incessant demands for new government programs and new social institutions. This will continue so long as people pin their faith upon the State.

Is it possible, nevertheless, to diffuse the revolutionary potential generated among the failures, rebels, and non-starters, by reducing

1. *The American Occupational Structure,* New York, John Wiley & Sons, 1967.

differentials of wealth, income, prestige, and power among occupations in general? Or are we to continue to assert, as the slogan of equality of opportunity implies in its cruder form, that the troubles of the have-nots in prosperous nations are of their own making? The latter cowardly course cannot benefit anyone, not even the élites, because their élitism depends upon the perceived connection between effort and reward. The other alternative–of diffusing the revolutionary potential by reducing economic, social, and political differentials–has still to be considered and seriously discussed. Even if it were possible, can a crippling sense of failure be precluded in spite of the unfalsifiable character of chronic failure? For example, those individuals comprising the poorest 20 per cent in America–the figure varies slightly in other industrialized nations–have become profoundly important to those members of the affluent classes aware of the limitations of the entire system. The poorest are not even on the ladder, but trapped within a vicious circle. For the "welfare mother's" child who goes to high school, the chances of securing a better position on the occupational scale are statistically so much smaller in relation to the rest that there is a negative incentive from the start. Stripped of self-confidence, the sense of foregone defeat produces a refusal to accept the opportunities supposedly available, and reinforces–even weakens–the individual's position, leaving no viable option but degradation. The poor, though outside the System, are a stark reminder to those within it that they themselves may be in danger of experiencing some form of the same phenomenon if they do not enthusiastically embrace the premises of the System. On the other hand, those who totally abandon the System, in the absence of any emergent alternatives, reinforce it by increasing the sense of depredation within it. They cannot, however, attach any significance to the term "failure" which would follow from an internal acceptance of the System, and yet they see themselves as irredeemable failures. Is it possible, then, to abolish failure itself instead of merely trying to ensure that every group gets its fair share? Is it possible to achieve this and also to diffuse the revolutionary potential? To abolish failure itself requires a fundamental change in the social structure. But the feasibility of this social transformation does not lie in denying the judgments of others, but rather in regarding them as partially relevant though in no sense compelling. Individuals can commit themselves to increasing their own capacity for self-transcendence of external criteria of differentiation, and thereby attain liberation from the self-perpetuating iniquities and horrors of the System.

Simply to investigate these possibilities, despite the enormous difficulty of their effective realization, is to pioneer a universal route relevant to the fundamental unfinished revolution. But who is to provide the revolutionary program? Not militant leaders who challenge the entire System, creating expectations that cannot be fulfilled and simultaneously producing a matrix of bitterness and hatred. It is possible, however, that increasing numbers of individuals may emerge who voluntarily opt out of the élite, disregard it, and who commit themselves to the service of the weak. They would define for themselves, through inner search and community action, an authentic freedom from external criteria–and thereby from the System–and erode the asymmetry which supports ineradicable failure. They would have to do this sufficiently to give meaning to the entire human enterprise. They must support themselves by the reassurance that what they are doing either is in accordance with an historical movement, that it is in line with evolutionary possibilities, or at least that, however paltry, it will be recognizable by people everywhere as the foundation stone of an initially small but genuine world community. Those who define themselves in this way as individuals accept the totality of the human enterprise, consciously inherit the whole of human history, are willing to draw upon and borrow from it freely, and make their own rich selection from every religion, tradition, philosophy, science, race, and culture. Becoming authentic universalists is a strenuous ideal. It is most difficult of all for people within the System, unless they can psychologically free themselves from its confines, whatever their actual situation in relation to the allocations of wealth and power within the System. A change in the concepts both of activity and courage is necessary to overcome passivity and cowardice. Courage must be detached from violence, and activity must be removed from the self-protective formulations of entrenched élites. This involves rooting new notions of activity, which are creative, playful, and tolerant, and new notions of courage, which are heroic, magnanimous, and civil, in a search for universal self-transcendence. An individual must feel, both abstractly and concretely, a secure sense of joyous eros in fellowship, and a positive sense of involvement with human beings everywhere. He must feel at one with the victims of incomplete revolutions, with the understandably impatient and occasionally mistaken pioneers of great revolutions, and even more with those willing to defy every presumptuous criterion and form of authority which trespasses upon individuality.

All criteria need not be rejected–they arise from human needs. But the ideological froth surrounding existing structures and élites must be firmly dispelled in favor of an existential transcendence, a transcendence rooted either in an open view of immortality or in a form of religious or spiritual belief, and above all devoted to human relations. Given the course of history and its parapolitical logic, if the fundamental revolution is to connect itself with the present moment, it must announce itself in the concrete relationships of particular men and women who stand at a critical distance from a particular society, and who reach out to others by renouncing their own families, classes, or the System as a whole. This universality was part of the original vision of the greatest Americans, who defined themselves more in terms of the freedom and joy of being ordinary men and women, than in terms of greatness or even formal equality. Concerned rather with a new vision of humanity than with embryonic nationalism, theirs was an attempt to create a metaphysic of democracy. It was to have been employed in a markedly different direction from that attempted by later political theorists, especially those of the last fifty years operating under the influence of ersatz Marxists and quasi-Paretians. Unlike self-centered and insecure apologists of democratic élitism, these brave men and women are true descendants of the Enlightenment. They aspire toward that vision of universality so powerfully affirmed by Whitman. In his poem addressed to "Him that was Crucified," he addresses every man who recognizes the limitations of past expectations and who is committed to acting independently of external authorities and institutions:

> My spirit to yours dear brother,
> Do not mind because many sounding your name do not
>   understand you,
> I do not sound your name, but I understand you,

I specify you with joy O my comrade to salute you, and to
salute those who are with you, before and since, and
those to come also
That we all labour together transmitting the same charge and
succession,
We few equals indifferent of lands, indifferent of times,
We enclosers of all continents, all castes, allowers of all
theologies . . .

Here is an appeal to initiate among ordinary men and women the necessarily limited nucleus of unthreatened individuals who will gladly protect the concrete implications of universality and the universal equality of all humanity–living, dead, and unborn. This is an attempt to reproduce in many microcosmic and incipient forms that brotherhood which belongs to the uncrowned "élite" of men like Buddha, Christ, and Socrates, those who return into the Cave, voluntarily identify with the meek, and scorn all earthly authorities. By practicing a new form of effective and unending equality, they exemplify a level of excellence which towers far beyond conventional distinctions and standards. Whitman's vision is reminiscent of Buddha's statement that the gap is great between enlightenment –which few persons have achieved though many have sought it– and the general condition of mankind. In relation to enlightenment, all the distinctions of the world are meaningless. But is this merely a compensatory statement for the poor and the deprived, or can it become the beginning, the basis, and the goal of a way of life? Men and women who recognize it as a crucial beginning may celebrate with Whitman:

Compassionaters, perceivers, rapport of men,
We walk silent among disputes and assertions, but reject not
the disputers nor anything that is asserted,
We hear the bawling and din, we are reach'd at by divisions,
jealousies, recriminations on every side,
They close peremptorily upon us to surround us, my comrade,
Yet we walk upheld, free, the whole earth over, journeying
up and down till we make our ineffaceable mark upon
time and the diverse eras,
Till we saturate time and eras, that the men and women of
races, ages to come, may prove brethren and lovers as
we are.

III

LIMITS AND POSSIBILITIES

We all commend a fair beginning of anything, though the beginning is, in my own opinion, more than half the work, and a fair beginning has never yet been commended to its full merits. ATHENIAN STRANGER

13
GLOBAL POINTERS

Let us join the human race.
W. STRINGFELLOW BARR

Decision makers in all countries are striving to see beyond the psychology of doom and limitation while groping toward a more positive and fraternal philosophy. A constructive vision of the needs and capabilities of humanity could inspire many. As Herzen realized in nineteenth-century Russia, we do not change events in the world by rational demonstrations or by syllogisms, but rather by "dreaming the dreams of men." Most futurologists are methodological captives to the false charms of quasi-dynamic models in the social sciences, mesmerized by systems analysis, computer techniques, and linear extrapolation, seeming to possess an epistemologically ill-founded faith in the sovereignty of such methods. Others speak of the time discount, "the inverted telescope through which humanity looks to the future, estimating the present worth of objects to be enjoyed in the future far below their worth if they could be instantly transferred to the present. This consequent devaluation of the future is generally considered to be an entirely rational response to the uncertainties of life."[1] The problem is further compounded by the fallacy of projection, a common error which makes forecasting the future a mere extension of the status quo. Those involved in projecting often portray phenomena as if they represented a fixed trend, foreclose undisclosed possibilities from altering the shape of the prognosis, and thereby become prisoners of their own predictions. The seeming immutability of cur-

1. Robert L. Heilbroner, *An Inquiry into the Human Prospect,* New York, W. W. Norton, 1974, p. 114.

rent categories all too often generates a built-in bias toward existing structures.

In the long run, apologetics and linear extrapolations will not be enough, especially if we are to outgrow our obsessive concern with the limits of growth and also consider the limits of waste and the limits of wants. A comprehensive parapolitical theory and program of resource optimization would be an invaluable corrective. Over two millennia ago, Pythagoras taught that unless we have a mathematical sense of limit we will not be able to maximize our possibilities in the psychological and social realms. Limits themselves are not limitations but indicate the need for wise choices. Unfortunately, much discussion of the limits to growth does little more than consolidate a non-constructive language of limitations. Before determining whether and how far growth must be stopped, we must define the concept precisely. There are evident in nature two types of growth: one is the indiscriminate growth through which cells reproduce by splitting in two, then into four, in a geometric progression, the multiples being essentially replicas of the original–a purely quantitative and accretive process that is rare in living organisms; the other is differential or organic growth, a process where the cells of an organism are specialized according to principles of harmonious development. Brain cells, for instance, differ from liver cells. Evolution also alters life-forms–some develop, others atrophy–and displays a serendipity that leaves discursive analysis behind. The diversity of the past is sifted through the present moment to create a future whose possibility is then evident, no matter how much obscured it was before.

In observing forms of growth in crystals, cells, animals, individuals, communities, and societies, George Land has identified three distinct patterns:

1. *Accretive growth,* which is an accumulation of sameness, simply extending boundaries and getting larger without changing basic form.

2. *Replicative growth,* which occurs by influencing other things to take on the form of the initiator, and the reverse.

3. *Mutual growth,* which is reciprocal interaction, a two-sided exchange, the equilateral sharing or joining process. It is the culmination of the success of accretive and replicative growth. "The

process of growth continually transforms itself into ever higher levels of organization," Land observes. "The growth of atoms leads to molecules, molecules proceed to cells, cells join to become multicellular, and organisms recapitulate the growth processes at a biological, psychological and cultural level. In every natural phenomenon there is the ubiquitous and irreversible procession from accretive to replicative to mutual growth, at which point, at a new level of organization, the process repeats itself."[2] Mechanistic conceptions of this irreversibility result in costly mistakes in social prediction and planning. There is a common tendency to confuse the conservation of structure through change with the principle of irreversibility itself. In living organisms persistent factors, such as the DNA-RNA scheme of biological transmission and the molecular patterns of energy conversion, function as structural elements superimposed upon increments of variation and change, pervading whole hierarchies of biological organization. They serve as limits which allow the specification of sets of transformations, conceptually uniting change and conservation while showing both systemic determinacy and individual indeterminacy at lower levels. This method presupposes a correspondence rather than an equivalence between the conceptual map and the set of essential relations within life itself. Confronted with the conceptually inexhaustible potential of reality, all cases of structural and transformational conservation must be understood as quasi-invariant, not identical to the irreversibility of life itself. Planners must be willing to see growth as involving the non-conservation of invariance, difficult as this is when faced with pressing decisions. In the absence of such open-mindedness, the temptation is to convert conceptual limits into pseudo-limitations of the social and political process itself, resulting in sincere but inherently irrational pronouncements about deadlines, supposedly irreversible social trends, and the certainty of doom.

Today, when we refer to growth we generally imply accretive growth. Yet if we rule out replicative, much less mutual growth, we would have to stop all growth immediately because at the rate of 5 per cent per year, by the end of the next century the world

2. Barbara Hubbard, "Grow or Die: The Unifying Principle of Transformation," *The Futurist,* February 1975, p. 16.

economy would be about four hundred times its present size, and the earth's natural resources would be exhausted. This type of growth cannot continue indefinitely. Even more important, such growth is inequitably distributed around the globe, proliferating like a cancer in the industrialized world, while condemning billions elsewhere to famine and poverty. The 1976 report to the Club of Rome–*RIO: Reshaping the International Order*–stated that by the early 1970s it had become clear that the cornucopia of economic growth was turning into a Pandora's box, the industrial world having radically widened the disparities between regions of the globe. In 1973, North America, with 6.1 per cent of the world's population, had 30 per cent of the world GNP, while Africa, with 10.2 per cent of the world's population, had 2.4 per cent of the world GNP. Between 1913 and 1957 the per capita income in North America jumped from U.S. $917 to $1,868 (a 103 per cent increase).[3] With the near collapse of the international monetary system established at Bretton Woods near the end of World War II, the current world recession aggravated for industrialized nations by the OPEC increases in crude oil prices, and recurrent instabilities in world weather patterns causing crop failures, the World Bank predicted a per capita growth rate between 1970 and 1980 of a modest 2.6 per cent for developed countries and a tragic 0.2 per cent for low-income developing countries.[4] The enormous gap between rich and poor is alarming, and yet less oppressive than the low spending power of the economically depressed peoples of the world. The real question, as in post-Paretian formulations of social justice, concerns the elevation of the bottom line of the impoverished. Growth *per se* is less the cause of the current crisis than is its anarchic nature.

Unlike living Nature, which effortlessly exhibits orderly organic growth, we have no general scheme for the harmonious development of the world, even though mankind's salvation depends on the possibility of just such a global plan. This is not a matter of merely drawing up a world-wide economic program but rather of finding a pattern of development which respects the regional diversity of

3. Jan Tinbergen, *RIO: Reshaping the International Order,* New York, E. P. Dutton, 1976, pp. 12, 21.
4. *Ibid.*, p. 94.

the planet, a global system of interdependent components, each of which would contribute its economic, cultural, and natural resources to the whole. The pluralistic character of the earth, its plasticity of function, must be preserved. We cannot be theoretically committed to any monistic conception of ontological scarcity or survival for its own sake. The *RIO* report readily recognizes that in attempting to develop a viable plan for restructuring the world economic order, economics as a science is prone to usurp consideration of other factors. Political, social, and cultural changes are also relevant to any new global organization and critically affect the possibility of fundamental economic reform as well as being affected by it.

W. W. Harman attempted a sober formulation of the problem that faces industrialized society, phrasing his analysis in terms of a series of dilemmas intrinsic to the accepted structural paradigm of the System. He distinguished four subordinate dilemmas:

1. *The Growth Dilemma:* The System requires the economic stimulus of growth but cannot afford it socially or environmentally.
2. *The Control Dilemma:* The System both needs and is repelled by control of innovation in technology.
3. *The Distribution Dilemma:* The System can neither envisage nor afford redistribution of wealth but it cannot afford the cost in world stability of neglecting redistribution.
4. *The Work-no-less Dilemma:* The System cannot generate enough productive and fulfilling roles, while fostering expectations indefinitely. All of these are facets of a more fundamental dilemma:

> The basic system goals that have dominated the industrial era and that have been approached through a set of fundamental sub-goals have resulted in processes and states which end up counteracting human ends. The result is a massive and growing challenge to the legitimacy of the basic goals and institutions of the present industrial system.[5]

Although Harman remains agnostic in relation to the future, he concludes that industrialized society will undergo, or has even

5. Willis W. Harman, "The Coming Transformation," *The Futurist,* February 1977, pp. 4-11.

started to undergo, an uncertain but awesome transformation. The hope is that by a sort of evolutionary leap to a transitional society a condition will be reached where there is not only know-how, but "a deeper inner knowledge of what is worth doing." Clearly, such a quantum jump cannot be the result of mere linear extrapolation.

It is conventionally assumed that these dilemmas of growth, and the challenges they pose, arise out of the physical scarcity of resources and commodities. Fred Hirsch, in *Social Limits to Growth,* shows that social scarcity is the more fundamental problem.[6] He reiterates the distinction between oligarchic and democratic consumption, resting upon the intrinsic scarcity of certain commodities and inherent limits to the democratic consumption of services, and concludes that democratic growth must experience a lower level of satiety than oligarchic growth. The traditional measures of welfare associated with economic growth are open to question, and furthermore the pressure of maximization of individual welfare intensifies the distributional struggle in ways that undermine the social legitimacy of the liberal market model. The ethical justification of the system requires that all must eventually benefit from economic growth, but individuals find themselves increasingly caught up in defensive consumption necessary to secure positions of relative welfare. Ever-expanding expenditures on transportation to and from work, and palliative measures against various forms of pollution are examples. This positional competition undermines any simple correlation of genuine welfare with such factors as GNP, average income, and standard of living. Even where partial correlations can be found between these indices and welfare, there is no commensurability from one culture to another in the relation of income to happiness.

Cultural and spiritual elements of welfare are not easily calculable. Individual economic advance is related to systematically scarce positions on a ladder so that performance determines access. Collective advance is measured in the market power of groups, which is largely a function of effective class loyalty. As a result, even if individuals feel inclined to contribute to redistribution, they

6. Fred Hirsch, *Social Limits to Growth,* Cambridge, Mass., Harvard University Press, 1976.

cannot generate it individually, and must surrender the individualistic ethos implicit in the meritocracy of positional competition and in the market system itself. If they do not make this value shift, they must reject the morally legitimating liberal principles of democratization and equalization. At this point it is impossible to sustain either the conviction that the market is guided by benign spontaneity through piecemeal incrementalism, or the assumption that beneficent use of the market system through social planning will occur. The limits to growth make themselves felt through the undermining of social virtues like trust and truthfulness, restraint and mutual acceptance, as well as a sense of fraternal obligation, all of which are essential to individual initiative in a contractual economic system. If such virtues are treated as public goods necessary to universal welfare, then unrestricted individualism faces noticeable limits, lest the social justification and viability of the whole system be destroyed.

The implication of this analysis for global planning is that any reliance upon the trickling down of welfare from higher positions is illusory. Individualistic incentives toward positional superiority involve a progressive hardening of resistance to collective advance, and bear no guarantees of raising the condition of classes of people at the foot of the ladder. The decline in social obligation and civic ethics owing to increased egocentricity is corrosive to social organization and obstructive to any satisfactory individual ethic. C. B. MacPherson goes further in predicting that the time will come when it will no longer be feasible to put acquisition ahead of spiritual values, and that national power will become a function not of market power but of moral stature. Although we have to confront scarcity, emphasis on Hobbesian self-preservation alone is inadequate.

> We need a revolution in democratic consciousness if we are to avoid being caught up ourselves in the backwash of the revolutions in the rest of the world. We need to inquire soberly whether competitive, maximizing behaviour is any longer rational for us, in any ethical sense. . . .[7]

7. C. B. MacPherson, *Democratic Theory,* Oxford, Clarendon Press, 1973, p. 184.

The basic requirement is the parapolitical idea of ontological plenty in spiritual goods and creative potentials. Neurological research indicates that human beings employ only a fraction of their brain potential. As long as people are merely creatures of habit, imitative and adaptive, they will be fear-ridden because of their neurotic concern with scarcity, necessity, and impossibility. They will run around in mazes. Often what looks like a new truth about the world is nothing but the precipitation of cumulative self-doubt. A man for whom everything has gone wrong in his individual life and who has to face the accelerating consequences of his past errors may create a pessimistic theory of the universe as a compensation for his acute sense of futility and his inability to achieve a conceptual breakthrough. This projection of their predicament into a theory about the world seduces experts, groups, and societies painfully confronting the psychological Nemesis of accumulated illusions. E. H. Carr contended that the surfeit of pessimism among historians is essentially a symptom of spatial discontinuities in the locus of the driving impulse of human progress.

> Indeed, if I were addicted to formulating laws of history, one such law could be to the effect that the group—call it a class, a nation, a continent, a civilization, what you will—which plays the leading role in the advance of civilization in one period is unlikely to play a similar role in the next period; and thus for the good reason that it will be too deeply imbued with the traditions, interests, and ideologies of the earlier period to be able to adapt itself to the demands and conditions of the next period. It is significant that almost all our latter day prophets of decline, our sceptics who see no meaning in history and assume that progress is dead, belong to that sector of the world and to that class of society which have triumphantly played a leading and predominant part in the civilization for several generations.[8]

The capacity to envision and initiate the civilization of the future cannot be based upon Aristotelian inferences or any simplistic theory of cycles. More people today than ever before are intuitively aware of the noetic, creative potential which cannot be measured in terms of the logic of the excluded middle, or of closed and

8. *The Listener,* May 18, 1961, p. 871.

mechanistic systems. Not having the concepts as yet, they function intuitively, and are unready to formulate what they feel. The vexing problem for those who are well aware of the intellectual history of the world, for truly original thinkers afraid of nothing, is to provide concepts that can help to underpin the intuitions and dreams of large numbers of people. The psychologically underprivileged in affluent societies can often empathize with the uprooted and the dispossessed everywhere, and sometimes display an unconventional ingenuity which could serve the future. Unfortunately, they lack the conceptual hooking points necessary to put their talents to good use. Many of the intellectual representatives of the so-called Third World are also partly paralyzed by obsolete categories, expressed in terms of statistical indices of the GNP. They can only be distraught or angered by those sophisticated models that suggest that developing countries cannot significantly improve the disproportionate ratio between rich and poor regions of the globe in less than four decades. "The question is of course whether the poor are prepared to wait half a century to attain what is now barely acceptable within the industrialized world."[9] However, behind this angry puzzlement there is a growing awareness that the poor constitute the majority of mankind and that they have the right and the effective possibility to create their own new cultural patterns–a feeling that is perhaps stronger in Africa than in Asia. The Asian, through a long period of intellectual enslavement, has been deceptively successful in partial modernization. The African, on the other hand, in his efforts to modernize, has had to create such an abyss between himself and the great mass of the people, that his innate sense of dignity and self-respect forces him now to ask more fundamental questions and to explore alternative conceptions. In the coming decades the excitement about ideas, in creating a new society and vivifying global brotherhood, is very likely to prosper in many parts of Asia, Africa, and South America.

The course of events will be decisively affected by current developments in China, and emerging possibilities on the Indian subcontinent. These are the two opposite poles, and the pivotal influence could be Japan. The Japanese have now reached the crucial stage

9. Tinbergen, *op. cit.*, p. 94.

where they are both in the forefront of the developed nations of the West and poignantly aware that their past is deeply rooted in the traditions of the East. Many Japanese would like to swing in one direction or the other, while some worry whether this will lead them into developing a split personality, hanging on to the rituals of their old world while at the same time embracing the rites of modernization. This dilemma was first clearly seen by Fukuzawa in the last century, who posed it in terms of a conflict between Newton and Confucius. An apostle of progress, Fukuzawa believed that Japan would eventually advance to a golden age, and that greater scientific knowledge would lead in time to greater virtue as well. The present problem of Japan is one of resuscitation of rituals and forms versus a deeper regeneration or renaissance. Even a Japanese renaissance must be eclectic and somewhat wild, willing to take risks and to invent an entire world of new ideas. As the old thought-patterns, social philosophies, and ideologies of Europe lost their relevance, many people in the Afro-Asian world passed through a phase limited by inherited ideological categories. Initially, they tried to develop Arab socialism, Indonesian socialism, and Indian socialism, but all of these efforts turned into clichés and hollow phrases because authentic political formulations could not be reconciled with the tremendous need for self-definition. This process has begun to affect Japan; its consequences there will progressively interact with Chinese and Indian developments.

For India, the most critical issue involves the current rethinking of Mahatma Gandhi's philosophy. Gandhi said that soon after his death India would bypass and betray his ideas, but that thirty years later India would be compelled to restore them. Events have begun to validate his prophecy, and the trend will accelerate. One could draw a parallel with the Indian national movement. It was only because the liberal intellectuals failed (while the terrorists were equally unsuccessful) that the educated turned to Gandhi, who alone could appeal to the traditional masses. India will be increasingly confronted with a similar situation in regard to its social and economic structure. When India fully accepts that it cannot conceivably emulate Japan without harnessing its own indigenous values and providing new motivations, and when out of necessity its leadership recognizes that it can no longer inflate the token symbols of Gandhi or the facile slogans of socialism, she will be forced to ask more fundamental questions. Only then can the real social revolution emerge, which could have a strong radical base and also borrow from ancient traditions as well as modern movements. While it would be difficult to predict the changes themselves, they will require serious reassessment of Gandhi's questions relating to the quantum of goods needed for a meaningful and fulfilling way of life.

In the United States the pursuit of happiness is integral to a vital strand of the American Dream–the persisting conception of the American nomad, rootless, homeless, and constantly required to define himself. There is a vital impulse behind the American Dream, which has nothing to do with the System and its identification of property with happiness. Americans are unique in history in their insistent if hasty fusion of theory and practice. An American's theory might often falter, and his practices might be immoderate, but he does take ideas seriously. If an idea strikes an American, he immediately wants to explore it. In Europe, and for a long time among the Brahmins in India and Mandarins in China, men flirted with ideas in recurring moods of verbal auto-eroticism. They articulated ideas without any reference to changing patterns of conduct. On the other hand, the close interaction between theory and practice in America is a crucial dimension of its contemporary restiveness. Groping toward role flexibility, rule skepticism, and unconditionality in mutual acceptance, the younger generation is discovering how to relate to one another in ways independent of fixed roles. This seemingly novel attitude, a critical distance toward institutions, is psychologically important and global in its relevance, integrating the detachment of the Stoics and "the politics of shipwreck" described by Ortega y Gasset. More recently, this standpoint has been commended by Manfred Halpern on the basis of a neo-Platonic and Maimonidean theory of emanation.

> In contrast to pre-modern times (a contrast which has been rapidly sharpening even since Marx's time), today everyone's concrete inherited connections are in process of breaking up. Most of us are now becoming ready for transformation, even if it is only apparent in our incoherence–but therefore we are especially susceptible to forms of fascism

> which manipulate and enforce our return to a primitive form of emanation by organizing our fury and our powerlessness. We can therefore no longer confine ourselves to teaching politics as the theory and practice of government, but must teach it as *the theory and practice of creating, nourishing, destroying, and re-creating relationships.*
>
> Thus we must take care not to become attached to any particular moment in its present concrete manifestation—whether it be a particular idea, institution, strategy or person, whether friend or foe. Such attachment can destroy human beings who, when fully alive, participate consciously and creatively in a process which, by its nature, involves encounters from opposing positions, thus producing change.[10]

The older generation still has a conventional faith in institutions. This is partly the legacy of the aftermath of World War II and the search for a megalopolis or some form of world government. This faith is not widely shared among the young, and the present gestation will not express itself in new institutions, for such expressions would subvert it. What is incubating is a revolution in human encounters and life-styles. To understand this philosophically, we must consider the informal logic of human communication—the intangibles we employ with our eyes and gestures, and which cannot wholly be contained in a true-false dichotomy or fed into computers. Margaret Mead spoke of the seventies as the decade of the brain; over the past fifty years we have assimilated more facts about the human brain than in all recorded history, but they are facts divested of a suitable theory and still entangled in seventeenth-century concepts. Today many people in America and Canada are pioneering new modes of creativity and heightened awareness. They engage seriously in contemplation, are experimenting by making mistakes, and so learning the power of creative imagination.

America's odyssey is very relevant to the secret of Japan's success and also to the future of Asia. The Japanese have succeeded not merely by imitating American modes of living and working; they have always possessed a gift for creating images, and are par-

10. Manfred Halpern, "The Politics of Transformation," *Main Currents in Modern Thought,* vol. 31, no. 5, May-June 1975, p. 135.

ticularly skillful in creating images that release the will. No doubt, many Japanese do not do this self-consciously and are confined by illusions of their own. Hence the crucial question arises: Which individuals will emerge anywhere in the world who will exemplify a high level of self-consciousness in the sustained and creative release of internal energies? Intellectually, who can inhabit simultaneously many different metaphysical perspectives? As Immanuel Kant once suggested, there could be as many metaphysical frameworks as there are states of mind (even though this conception does not conform to the rest of Kantian philosophy). The person of tomorrow will be able to see the world not only as a Nietzschean, as a Freudian, and as a Marxist, but in many other modes as well–through Zen, through Shankara, Lao Tzu, and so on. He will learn conceptual flexibility. Those who actually engage in systematic contemplation have an advantage. Since there is no sufficient basis in modern behaviorism for understanding the thread of continuity in the life of a man from birth to death, the thought of the ancient world becomes profoundly relevant. Krishna said in the *Bhagavad Gita* that every man must meditate upon birth, death, sickness, decay, and error, while for Plato man is not a philosopher, a true lover of wisdom, until he overcomes his fear of death. This is becoming a paramount issue in the context of the collective global psychosis, the weakening of the will, the separation between the "living" and the "dead." The question is increasingly about who can self-consciously recover continuity of consciousness amidst the ever-escalating pace of change.

We see this problem most acutely in America, because of the prevailing fragmentation of consciousness and the mass of sensory images which create a context where it becomes a challenge to remember anything about today in the course of tomorrow. Even morality makes little sense, because promises are forgotten within days. People must then discover more fundamental solutions to retain continuity of awareness. Out of sheer necessity, this searching has begun in the post-industrial society of America. In time this activity will fruitfully commingle with the untapped cultural wealth of India, Japan, China, and elsewhere, leading through a dialectic of conservation to some surprising changes everywhere. "Ultimately," as the *RIO* report concludes, "we must aim for decentralized planetary sovereignty with the network of strong international institutions which will make it possible."[11] If such institutions are not to crystallize prematurely, they will have to be created and nurtured by men and women who possess enough credibility as human beings and who have mastered this new consciousness, without reference to external signs and claims. There are still many unconscious traces and structural biases in the human mind. If someone is Japanese, he does not automatically comprehend Zen. An Indian is not necessarily rooted in the culture of India. An atavistic legacy fosters subtle forms of racism, compensatory messianism, and a search for instant salvation or vicarious atonement. But these concepts are increasingly being challenged through the emergence of a new kind of self-reliant human being who is looking for the invisible thread of continuity which the ancient called "the line of life's meditation." It is not founded in the external world of material gain but in inner states of experience. These individuals, while effectively playing their part in society, aspire to a higher level of self-consciousness in the dynamic interdependence of individuation with an ever-increasing breadth of authentic universalization. Such pioneering forerunners can quietly contribute to the parapolitical foundations of the global society of the future.

11. *Op. cit.*, p. 84.

14
THE FUTURE OF EUROPE

The Kingdom is like a man
Who is ignorant of the treasure
Hidden in his field.

THE GOSPEL ACCORDING
TO THOMAS

I

What might be Europe's relations with other continents in *annus* 2000? Is there a parapolitical vision that can provide the basis for viable programs during the coming decades? Do we know what it means to possess the visionary power of *Kriyashakti*—the "faculty divine" intimated in *Phaedrus* and *The Prelude*—associated with "clearest insight, amplitude of mind, and reason in her most exalted mode"? Questions of this magnitude should be explored by a permanent forum of free spirits in the context of a continuing dialogue bound by no limits but those of reason and of relevance. The task calls for an inspired exercise in creative imagination. It is a sad degradation of the term "vision" to apply it to any merely mechanical extrapolation of existing trends, or to narrowly self-flattering images of the future which consolidate current fads and predilections. The present moment may seem unfavorable for a Promethean, let alone a Demiurgic, effort to fashion out of contemporary chaos an architectonic conception of the world of the future and of Europe's role in relation to the vast majority of mankind. To alleviate this pessimism it is important to notice some of the contemporary hindrances to political imagination and creative participation in the politics of vision.

First of all, current conceptions of the future are being molded by technocratic and mechanistic substitutes for political wisdom.

The prevailing view of collective progress is framed in the disembodied language of national economic statistics, having almost lost its last links with the profoundly optimistic faith in universal enlightenment of the *philosophes* of the eighteenth century.

Second, there is a world-wide nervousness about thinking seriously in terms of fundamental global solutions in the political arena. The relative decline of ideological dogmatism has been accompanied by an unrelenting pursuit of short-sighted forms of national self-interest by most political leaders.

Third, the persisting apathy toward the United Nations is rationalized in many ways, but it is rooted in a deep resistance to the logic of democratization on an unprecedented scale.

Fourth, the eyes of the world's intelligentsia are narrowly focused upon the "technetronic" models of the future of a few Americans who have enjoyed a greater influence in Europe than in the United States. At the same time, we find a pervasive cynicism in regard to traditional political and social revolutions. There is little understanding of the contemporary rebellion among the young, especially in America–with its bizarre blend of nihilism, mysticism, utopianism, and hedonism, and its insistence on defying recorded history and institutional solutions.

Fifth, there is an appalling credibility gap between policy makers and intellectuals, as well as between peoples of different races, cultures, and social systems.

Sixth, there is frequent recourse to the rhetoric of doomsday and despair, concerning the supposed inevitability of atomic war, world famine, the population squeeze, and ecological catastrophe. The mood is one of secular fatalism, and its vocabulary that of historical determinism and mechanistic social science, interspersed with moralistic obsessions with universal corruption or particular scapegoats. Even the activity of rationalistic problem solving in futurology seems at times like an escapist form of game playing. Small wonder that many imagine themselves to be in a time of agonizing suspense, a "historic void," in which we can hardly envisage a comprehensible future for "post-historic man."

Despite these hindrances to vision in its noblest sense, it is natural for a few humanitarians to attempt either to predict or invent the future for their own societies, although they cannot claim to discover it. Even while seeking to preserve a necessary agnosticism in regard to human nature with its limits and possibilities, their love of their fellow men dictates a measure of historical optimism. They cannot dispense with the assumption that the future will be benign to the present strivings of the leaders and the peoples of their own societies, if not of all mankind. To have a vision of the future is to grasp the idea that, even in the midst of inertia and hopelessness, our problems are matched by the knowledge, energy, and will needed to make efforts to resolve them. To focus on the year 2000 is to celebrate an act of faith in our immediate descendants even more than in ourselves. The collective act of envisaging the Europe of 2000 is meaningful for the new Europeans only insofar as it can provide a stimulus to constructive political imagination and appropriate political action.

What are the indispensable prerequisites of an authentic European vision of the future? First and foremost, it must be rooted both in current preoccupations and in the legacy and lessons of the past. The future of Europe is seen today mainly in relation to its own progressive integration and internal unity, but as an emergent entity, it is still in search of a new role commensurate with its historic past. The successes and failures of the Enlightenment, of the French Revolution with its incomplete invocation of liberty, equality, and fraternity, and of subsequent extensions of these ideals, are no less relevant than the more spectacular consequences of the recent industrial and technological revolutions. A deeply humane doctrine of universal progress through the spread of knowledge has dwindled to a utilitarian, manipulative, and deterministic formula for secular salvation. The bitter memories of the ignoble failures of nationalistic messianism have begun to fade in the face of the conspicuous successes of the new economic integration of Western Europe. But contemporary Europeans have yet to reappraise and recover the ennobling vision of universal human welfare of their forebears in the eighteenth century. An authentic vision of the Europe of the future would contain a partial promise of its actualization as a parapolitical force acting in the lives of men. There is a variety of images through which men project and transcend themselves, but an essential difference lies between those for whom the fear of an external deity or force is the beginning of an adaptive wisdom, and those who live out their awareness of potentialities that transcend their limitations. The latter are more likely to display the courage that springs from authenticity of vision. Such a vision is sharable among Europeans if based upon a discriminating perception of the promise as well as the perversion of the past.

Any feasible vision of the future must meet a second and more demanding requirement. It can be realized in a world moved by many visions and conceptions only if it is capable of effectively superseding, subsuming, or somehow being compatible with them. The world is characterized by two powerful and contrary tendencies—a widespread concern for parity of esteem and international status seeking, and a growing awareness of the practical demands of global solidarity. An authentic vision of the Europe of the future must reckon with the logic of equalization and the logic of globalization (or mondialism) central to the dialectical politics of welfare and reason. Europe's vision of its future cannot be realized—except on terms repugnant to its deepest values bequeathed by the Enlightenment—unless that vision is compatible with the claims of non-Europeans for their own growth and initiative, as well as with the increasing recognition of common needs which can only be met by global measures and strategies. This second requirement may be called the Universalizability Thesis. It implies a more crucial determinant of the world of the future than the first requirement, which is primarily concerned with the Europe of the future.

The Universalizability Thesis, essential to the politics of reason, has several revolutionary implications. Any vision of Europe relevant to its own future will affect the policies and plans of non-European societies in ways which will have a critical bearing, through a process of feedback, on whether Europe's own prophecies of its future will be self-fulfilling or self-negating. This is an obvious limit imposed by the global interrelation of events and causes. The self-actualization of Europe's long-term vision is dependent upon Europe's capacity to mitigate the glaring lack in its imaginative awareness of problems and possibilities in societies with different perspectives and goals, as well as differing rates of change and degrees of morale. The tougher challenge is that the world's basic needs cannot be met without massive reallocation of resources. This demands a readiness to rethink the categories in which societies have hitherto construed their problems–concepts of scarcity and plenty, development and affluence, psychological and social mobility, time and energy, work and leisure, authority and freedom in education and politics, contemplation and activity, exploitation and harmony, wants and needs, happiness and fulfillment. In meeting this challenge, a therapeutic leap from the inertia of past criteria of appraisal is required, not merely rational reformulation or moral exhortation. Implementation of a truly universalizable vision will require a measure of practical wisdom which eludes even theoretical grasp in societies that have corrupted or abandoned their classical inheritance, and cannot recover it in traditional terms. The dialectical problem is one of timing.

II

Predictions concerning the world in 2000 may tend to focus mainly on what is likely to happen to us, given the limits of the present and the recent past. On the other hand, predictions concerning the possibilities of our own society must also give due weight to what we, collectively and as individuals, determine. The former predictions tend to be inductive, extrapolated from Epimethean hindsight out of an anxious concern to be plausible and safe. In a world changing at exponential rates, we encounter the temptation to seize on what is novel while still thinking in terms of linear continuity. But how much were even the most gifted men able to predict in 1880 about the world of 1910, in 1910 about 1940, or in 1945 about 1975? How much allowance was made for decisive discontinuities, the monstrous "rogue events," or for such beneficent breakthroughs as resulted from the Einsteinian impact on science, the Keynesian movement in economics, the Gandhian modes of action in politics, the ecumenical courage of Pope John, or the revolution in food and agriculture? The theoretical problem presupposes distinctions between parts and wholes, between primary and secondary causes, and questions the validity of assumptions of congruence between factors in analysis and forces in reality. Major leaps in "zigzag" thinking are all too rare, and their implications are apt to be distortingly inflated by solemn dialecticians like Hegel and Marx.

The problem is hardly made easier when it concerns our predictions about ourselves as actors as well as our descendants. The theoretical limit of our success here is a function of our individual and collective self-knowledge and self-consciousness. It is even more dependent upon the extent of our empathy for the contemporary revolution in the mentality of the young, who take for granted the wholesale and irreversible rejection of our institutionalized structure of values. Even Prometheans, who show daring in foresight and planning, have their blind spots and self-supportive illusions. They also experience strenuous limits to their sympathy for those who wish to displace them. Shelley's version of the Aeschylean story may yield a clue to the present-day Prometheans of Europe and the world. While Prometheus lacked the powers and wisdom of Hermes, his credential for survival was his capacity to endure suffering out of compassion, and his mandate for inevitable victory was grounded in a large perspective of long memories. How much do today's Prometheans really care for the lot of the impoverished, and how much are they willing to sacrifice–especially of their self-image–on behalf of the world's proletariat? Further, Europeans would gain by placing the coming thirty years in a variety of time-perspectives–the period that began with Buddha, Pythagoras, and Christ, the epoch opened by the Enlightenment and the French Revolution, as well as the postwar decades with their global *idées fixes* and lost opportunities, and also their fertile seeds that promise a harvest for wise sowers in fields still to be reclaimed.

Even a pinch of theoretical skepticism could help European thinkers and men of action to resist the strange spell cast by the laborious and provocative projections of professional futurologists in America. At a factual level, they may be more misleading than the cold statistical projections of United Nations officials. On a holistic level, they are doubtless valuable as a stimulus to reflection upon the post-industrial society of the future. Phrases like "technetronic society" and "knowledge revolution" are suggestive in the technological milieu of the United States, but are insipid to a significant proportion of its future citizens. Such clichés should not be allowed to obscure the continuing relevance of Sombart's early analysis of "mature capitalism," or of Scheler's careful consideration of the resolution of interrelated dialectical tensions in "the age of adjustment," or of many alternative portraits and anticipations of the future provided by men in the past. This is not to deny that some recent trends in science, technology, and fast-changing social structures are crucially relevant. Given time, modern science and technology can attain an almost limitless capacity to invent if adequately supported by public and private allocations of resources. It might also be that we cannot stop inventing merely because we are riding a tiger. Further, given the new knowledge that is accumulating at a surpassing speed and its immense diffusion via almost instantaneous modes of transmission of information, there could result a profound expansion of human capacities and opportunities. It is even possible that what Keynes said of Newton–that he was "the last of the Magicians"–might be falsified by plebeianizing the term "magician." By 2000 we may see for the first time that almost every man is potentially and practically a magician. In a sober Kantian sense, humanity may truly have emerged from its nonage by the widespread removal of the social and psychological hindrances to universal enlightenment. Seen thus, the prospect is noble and awe-inspiring, pointing to the tapping of the rich resources of human beings rather than to a frightening blend of technological messianism and socio-economic determinism. It is also intriguing to think, like Buckminster Fuller, of the task of global and regional design of the whole environment in a radically new context of matter in relation to a new kind of man. Such optimism is at least a much-needed corrective to the many intimidating threats to human survival before different deadlines.

The central questions regarding the world in 2000 are the most difficult to raise, let alone to answer. They concern the ends and means governing the uses of knowledge in human society; the democratic control of wise and knowledgeable decisions regarding allocations of resources; the agencies for the application of diffused knowledge to the tasks of social transformation; the eliciting of active participation in meeting the common needs rather than the engineering of tacit consent; the rethinking of the relation between *techne* and *arete;* and the protection of the fullest possible freedom and diversity in life-styles. To think boldly yet realistically about 2000 is to explore a radically new type of politics in a profoundly altered social structure (superseding inherited dichotomies such as that contrasting ascriptive with achievement orientations) that may well need to be loosely unified by many versions of a universal civil religion (in Rousseau's phrase). To contemplate this parapolitical possibility on a global plane as well as within different societies and subcultures is perhaps the greatest challenge to our constructive imagination. Its importance at the world level requires great vigilance in protecting the open-ended character of the future of man in 2000, and a consequent refusal to yield to intellectualist and other attempts to impose a controlling set of pseudo-limits upon the events and policies of the next two decades. For Europeans as well as for others, this means new thought and new action in relation to the unfinished business of the unfinished revolution, the recurring tension in every sphere between the forces of equalization and the legions of élitism, the authentic universalization of human growth, welfare, and fulfillment.

Vinoba Bhave has prophesied that in the foreseeable future science and spirituality will replace politics and religion as the dominant forces in society. Perhaps, at the majority level, we may witness both political disengagement and the carefree pursuit of parapolitical values in an atmosphere of economic and material security. This may leave behind a large minority of persons who enjoy bureaucratic tasks and the conventional politics of power. But surely there will also be needed a small minority of persons capable and suited to assume the most onerous roles of responsibility pertaining to architectonic politics, planning, and leadership. Poincaré said of Einstein that he saw all conceivable possibilities when confronted with a physical problem, and that in his mind this was transformed into anticipation of new phenomena that may some day be verified in actual experience. This is tough enough in regard to any single society. In forming a clear, coherent, and plausible picture of the world of 2000, we are confronted with a bewildering array of possibilities. We must also isolate the core factor in analytical forecasting. In order to secure a fruitful simplification, without assigning any core factor with seeming arbitrariness, we need to highlight certain contradictory and provocative features in any picture of the society of 2000 with reference both to already visible trends and to underlying if unseen forces that might attain a massive momentum in the next two decades.

1. We have the prospect of a profound increase in the amount of scientific knowledge, technical innovation, natural wealth, and human energy available. But we also have, in human beings as they are, in existing social structures, and in our childishly competitive modes of action, the self-protective mentality of ontological scarcity. Will the mounting dissatisfaction with our Aristotelian intellectual premises and Darwinian social values, especially among the incurably alienated, the educated unemployed, and the half-hearted drop-outs, result in an iconoclastic movement which will help usher in the new social order of 2000?

2. On the one hand, we are witnessing the cumulative acceleration of all modes of communication–of ideas, men, materials, techniques, and information. On the other hand, we can apprehend the deep-seated and widespread inertia in our institutional structures and styles of rationalization, many of which are incapable of being radically altered by incremental reform. How far may we expect to find entirely new–possibly self-regenerating or at least self-correcting–institutions, and how often will we savor new wine in old bottles and old wine in new bottles? Will there be a truly revolutionary alteration in men's attitudes to and relations with all institutions, a vast enrichment in interpersonal relationships in the context of precise role specialization and creative role flexibility?

3. Will the provision of a Guaranteed Annual Income (in real or monetary value) to every adult within the most affluent societies be accompanied by a progressive redistribution of incomes across as well as within the national, regional, and other frontiers dividing the members of a single family of mankind?

4. Will the spread of a psychology of abundance and the release of a vast reservoir of constructive energy be accompanied by sufficient restraint upon the multiplication of wants to provide the support needed for effective global action in meeting the basic needs of the whole of mankind?

5. Will the planned promotion of ecological balance within societies and regions be accompanied by global mobilization and appropriate reallocation of natural and human resources through the world as a whole?

6. Will the emergence of ethically growth-oriented, materially abundant, and maturely therapeutic societies, which exemplify a

knowledgeable compassion toward the psychologically sick and socially delinquent, also facilitate the effective global control of all armaments and militaristic tendencies, and the consequent release of enormous resources for constructive and peaceful purposes? Will more non-violence at home necessarily mean more non-violence abroad?

Altogether, the most important feature of the world of 2000 may well be–or could be–a radically new formulation of the now explosive ratio of human expectations to human satisfaction. In the classical religious and philosophical systems, the path of wisdom consists in modifying the numerator as well as the denominator of this ratio, and even more in refining each individual's capacity and need for his own parapolitical interpretation of the ratio in temporal affairs. Above all, it consists in maintaining a critical distance from preoccupation with the ratio itself. This would perhaps become more feasible and accessible for all when the monopolistic dominance of monetary values and rigidly narrow notions of self, self-preservation, self-expression, and even self-transcendence are mitigated by time allocations, energy distributions, and non-institutionalized leadership. This makes sense in a world society that is freer, more creative, and less acquisitive than any now conceivable.

III

In the light of the limits and possibilities centrally relevant to the world of 2000, where would and could Europe fit in? To answer this question is, in fact, to request a definition of Europe in 2000. What will the term "Western Europe" include and what will it exclude? What will be the basis of inclusion and the significance of the frontiers of exclusion? Will the European Economic Community expand, and if so, how and how soon? What will be the internal results of irreversible decisions in a variety of possible directions? Within the European Economic Community there is a fundamental cleavage in principle and emphasis between federalists and functionalists, as well as an increased sophistication in awareness of the interrelation between the political problems and the economic structure of the new Europe. However, the practical corollaries for future policies are viewed very differently by the European Economic Community and by the member-states. On the basis of recent studies and current trends, we could point to seven alternative models of Western Europe in the future, including three negative–though unlikely–possibilities and four more likely and positive alternatives.

1. *The United States of Europe*–an independent federal entity supported by a strong paraliament exercising democratic control over a vigorous federal executive. This model, if fully developed by 2000, would represent a unique combination of constitutional and democratic politics, and a degree of economic integration, that are on an unprecedented scale.

2. *The European Economic Community*–a much more powerful, centralized, and integrated version of the present structure, essentially functionalist and administrative rather than federalist and parliamentary. To the extent that, in a Saint-Simonian sense, politics is reduced to administration or largely subordinated to economics, sociology, and law, this model would exemplify in 2000 a distinctive fulfillment of the Benthamite-Comtean theory of benevolent technocratic élitism.

3. *The European Microcosm of World Government*–the widest possible framework of firmly yet loosely integrated states, including the existing Common Market and the other potential applicants for membership, and perhaps eventually some East European and Near Eastern states. Integration on such a scale is bound to make an expanded Europe a powerful nucleus of world government by 2000, depending upon its skill and success in its relations with the major world powers and with the many small nations of other continents.

4. *Europe des États*–a coalition of states strongly linked by a general consensus on political objectives, a more cohesive version of what now exists, but without either an effective European Parliament or a very powerful European Commission.

5. *Fragmented Europe*–with no common structure, split into states tied to the United States of America and states that maintain a fierce independence, but with some remnant of a customs union.

6. *Atlanticized Europe*–which is part of an Atlantic economic structure based on free trade and unrestricted access to markets, essentially an economic equivalent to NATO as originally conceived.

7. *Hobbesian Europe*–in which one nation emerges as so power-

ful that it pushes the rest of Western Europe, through its economic and possibly military dominance, in the direction of a collective autarky and perhaps into the aggressive role in the image of a super-power.

Of these alternatives, *Atlanticized Europe* is the least likely, owing to the lack of a sufficiently strong ideological basis. *Hobbesian Europe* is, fortunately, almost equally unlikely, owing to the brilliant role already played by the smaller countries. Even if *The European Microcosm* materializes, it would have to contend with sufficient suspicion and even hostility from other powers to make it impossible to envisage seriously its development into a genuine nucleus of world government. *Fragmented Europe* is too sad to contemplate, and the odds are now very much against it. *Europe des États* would at best be a commendable example of successful survival. The crucial choice is likely to be between an independent federal *United States of Europe* and a powerful *European Economic Community,* or some mixed version of the two. *The United States of Europe* has the merit of pointing to something more than nineteenth-century nationalism writ large. The *European Economic Community* could demonstrate what harmonization and integration could achieve administratively in a post-industrial society. In either case, the emergence of a strong and stable Europe will help to speed up the process of rationalizing the international economic system and, less obviously, the international political system. In any event, the fate of Europe in 2000 will have been irreversibly determined by its earlier decisions in favor of a "have and hold" outlook or of a "give and receive" standpoint in relation to the rest of the world. The role of Europe in either direction will be functionally limited by the degree of its self-confidence as well as by the life-style and self-image of the New European, with a fundamental allegiance to European rather than sub-European conceptions of culture and solidarity.

Relations between Europe and other continents are at present vitiated by interrelated false assumptions about the United States of America and about the so-called Third World, which ignore the profound internal questioning taking place in contemporary America and the slower but no less decisive reappraisal taking place in the historically immense and geographically vast perspectives of the peoples of the Third World. By correcting these false assumptions of older Europeans today, and by providing a broader and possibly more accurate standpoint, it should be easier to picture a valid and vital role for Europe during the rest of this century.

IV

Several curious paradoxes result from ambivalent attitudes in Europe's relation to America. Hermes was said to be both an old man and a virile youth. This is strikingly true in regard to Europe and America. If America is ethnically and culturally the vigorous and somewhat ruthless son of a Europe which–in del Corral's mythic image–is in dire danger of being raped by the non-European bull, the incestuous element in the mutual attitudes of Europe and America is a fit subject for psychopathology. European integration has been partly motivated by a healthy suspicion of American military and economic power, and its unduly self-righteous and rigid political use and abuse. Americans in turn have shown a condescending if affectionate concern that a divisive band of allies should speedily embark upon a federation inspired by the American experiment which itself was partly influenced by the confederation of five Iroquois Indian nations. In the eyes of some of the New Europeans, America is rather like a young *nouveau riche* whose spectacular success necessitates the response, in American slang, "If you can't beat 'em join 'em." They may of course take for granted that even if they had to emulate the innovative, ultrademocratic, and super-energetic temper of the American, they are bound to attain in time a more sober and sophisticated style of technological success. On the other hand, many successful and self-made Americans cannot help viewing the new Europe as an aging, somewhat venerable matriarch about to undergo a rejuvenation resulting in the vigor of simulated youth, with its attendant preoccupation with self-esteem.

More seriously, in a concrete socio-economic sense America is, as Gertrude Stein reportedly said, the oldest country in the world and the first to enter the twenty-first century. So it is legitimate for Europeans to assert, as did a British economist, that what America does today, Europe will do tomorrow. But there's the rub: the very notion of catching up is demoralizing for Europeans. Could it really provide the motivation, let alone the dynamism, for European economic and social transformation? The analogy here with the plight of the intelligentsia in the so-called Third World in their fast-fading adoration of European affluence, power, and success is painfully suggestive. It could be argued that to "catch up" in the economic rat-race one would have to run faster to remain in the same place, competitively speaking. There is another curious paradox implicit in the possibly self-defeating notion of "catching up." It is ironical that Europeans should so often admire precisely those features of the American socio-economic system—with its staggering productivity in terms of GNP—which are being questioned by older critics of the American System and rejected by many of America's youth. American historians have pointed to the consequences of partial borrowings from European culture in the course of American development. It is possible to contend that the European Enlightenment won a greater victory in America, but at the cost of obscuring the deeper spiritual and intellectual vision of the *philosophes,* even though the vision was shared by some of the Founding Fathers. Hence, the subsequent split in the American psyche between the pull of the American Dream and the pressures of the American System. It is possible that, in a tragic instance of role reversal, the New Europeans may succumb to the fatal fascination exercised by the American technological system, rationalizing this bewitchment in sophisticated ideological language which invokes the inevitability of trends pointing toward 2000. They would thereby pay the price of effectively casting aside the authentic soul of their complex inheritance, and then they might fail to match up to the intransigent and distinctive political problems of the coming years. The ushering in of the abundant society of 2000 depends on the richness of our political imagination. Europe has an untapped legacy in this respect, and a potential role of the highest importance. It would be unfortunate for the world, for America, and certainly for Europe itself if its greatest challenge and opportunity were set aside on the basis of a hasty and inadequate grasp of the complexities of technological society and democratic politics in the United States.

To put it in another and traditionally Eastern way, Europeans have something important to learn from the historical and contemporary American experience, but real learning is very different from impetuous imitation. This learning process applies both to the techno-cultural gap and to the counter-culture in America. Upon the effectiveness of this learning and its consequent discriminative wisdom will depend the course of Europe in the coming decades and its collective destiny in the year 2000. The technological gap between Europe and North America became the pivot of much attention in the alarmist account of Jean-Jacques Servan-Schreiber and the more fundamentally global picture provided by Aurelio Peccei. The formidable challenge of American corporations to the member-states of the European Economic Community, the access of American business enterprises to economies resulting both from technical innovations and from production for a much larger market, the American emphasis upon market research, and the willingness to incur considerable selling costs for the sake of significant and recurring profits, the upward mobility in American management hierarchies and their professional as well as religious dedication to the Greater Mysteries of Organization Theory and the Science of Management, and above all, the enormous and ever-increasing investment in Research and Development–these are all familiar, undoubtedly relevant facts for their European competitors and emulators. But even in regard to this narrow meaning of the technological gap, the explanation is to be sought more in the psychology of American business than in the technology of European industry.

Europeans tend to underestimate the extent to which differences between European and American industrial structures are rooted in profound and comprehensive differences in social psychology and political culture. American society is marked not merely by great social mobility but also by a psychological flexibility arising from a combination of self-reliance and self-doubt unparalleled elsewhere. Furthermore, American culture is shaped by widespread public education, by a more pervasive if formal democratization, by a mental egalitarianism and resilience, as well as by an unashamed self-seeking individualism reinforced by an inward ideological conformity such as is scarcely imaginable outside the United States. Indeed, any emancipated and objective world-traveler may well be struck by the extent to which Western Europe and much of the so-called Third World are significantly similar, for good and for ill, by sharp contrast with American society. An entirely psycho-philosophical diagnosis of America considering the logic of externalization implicit in industrialism, and the compelling need for self-individuation–as a condition for sheer survival in a minimal dimension of human dignity–was offered by Richard Müller Freienfels in his neglected essay, "The Americanization of the Soul."[1] He thought that the whole world was headed in the direction of American industrialization, but suggested that at some future date, Americans might be pioneers in a spiritual search for the solution to the ailments of the human psyche in modern technological society. No society is as theoretically and diagnostically self-critical–even to the point of masochism–as that of the United States. Perhaps this is because America has been dominated by psychiatry as other societies have been powerfully molded by political ideology, economic growth, and social stability. Non-American cynics might think this has mainly to do with the magnitude as well as the glamour of affluence in America, plus the appalling burdens of massive military and economic power. But outsiders have yet to appreciate, over and beyond the national pastime of self-diagnosis, the novel significance of the recent assault on all cherished assumptions that has assumed immense proportions among older as well as younger Americans.

Present concerns are particularly focused upon imminent ecological catastrophe, foreshadowed by poignant disasters widely seen to be early warning signals. In a penetrating article, the contemporary biologist, Wayne H. Davis, defines overpopulation by the degree to which a nation destroys the ability of land to support human life. He quickly identifies affluent, technologically monstrous America as the worst offender. The economist and veteran humanist, Kenneth Boulding, argues that whatever type of integration of technology and society is anticipated, if it is not to be a fatal menace to mankind, America faces a far greater intellectual and moral task than it has ever contemplated. One could multiply examples of such grave warnings by Americans, who cannot help thinking in global terms when appraising their national predicament. It is still too soon to know whether such self-critical question-

1. Richard Müller Freienfels, *Mysteries of the Soul,* trans. Bernard Miall, London, George Allen & Unwin, 1929.

ing will be followed by the major revaluations of policy needed from politicians and administrators in the American System. But most Europeans are inadequately aware of the enormous vulnerability of the technological society of America–not so much to an old-style revolution, but to the profound challenges to its basic value structure coming from the young. The intensity and scope of this self-searching makes the rebellion in America different in kind, and not merely in degree, from movements elsewhere. This may be partly due to the peculiar difficulty in launching an effective political revolution in the United States today. On the other hand, recent polls taken in countries like France would suggest that the majority of European youth are mainly concerned with more direct participation in the decisions that affect their lives. The totality and eclecticism in the responses of American youth result from religious and sociological factors embedded in American history as well as the consequences of mass education. American youth draw freely from Marx and Freud, Marcuse and Maslow, the *Bhagavad Gita* and Zen, in bizarre combinations that do not come easily to those nourished within the culturally narrower if intellectually more intensive educational systems of Europe. Even more importantly, the conversion of theoretical standpoints into practical formulas for living is much faster and commoner in the United States than in the more critical and hypocritical atmosphere of European intellectual centers.

Broadly, the future relations between Europe and America will be determined less by current European preoccupations than by the consequences of a better grasp in Europe both of the techno-cultural gap in American society and its emerging counter-culture. The latter is grounded in a persistent and growing anxiety about status and identity, and may become an increasingly important feature of European society as well. The social structure of the future in America will in all likelihood be molded by a psychology of plenty rather than of scarcity, elaborated through an amazing plurality of subcultures and life-styles. However, the mere emergence of even fundamental new trends in the social structure will not tell us much about America in 2000, as the critical questions in the coming decades lie in the arena of American politics, with major changes imminent either in its sacrosanct constitution or at least in the practical working of its political system. In this respect Europe's relations with America may afford an incomparably unique opportunity for radical self-transformation as well as for external contributions of the greatest importance. If America has the technical and economic preconditions, in the largest measure, for the abundant society of the future, and if it also has the ingenuity, eclecticism, and the sense of immediacy to usher in a profoundly new social structure, Europe also has its own legitimate contribution to make, from its wealthy inheritance of political and social philosophies, and its mature grasp of proportionality and scale, the elusive components of *sophrosyne,* the rarest of all personal and social excellences.

Significantly, it was a European biologist who most clearly formulated what may well be the central principle of the social structure of the future. In a far-ranging article written in 1961, Julian Huxley declared:

> The humanist goal must therefore be, not technocracy, nor Theocracy, nor the monolithic and authoritarian State, nor the Welfare State, nor the Consumption Economy, but the Fulfilment Society. By this I mean a society organized in such a way as to give the greatest number of people the fullest opportunities of realizing their potentialities–of achievement and enjoyment, morality and community. It will do so by providing opportunities for education, for adventure and achievement, for cooperating in worthwhile projects, for meditation and withdrawal, for self-development and unselfish action. . . . [It] will uphold the ideal of quality against the assault of mere quantity, of richness and variety against drabness and monotony, and of active, open and continuous development, personal, social and evolutionary, as against static self-complacency or unreal millenary fanaticism. . . . the religious spirit must soon break through from its old framework to a new system of expression, and . . . an evolutionary humanism will inevitably provide the pattern of ideas and beliefs at its core.[2]

There can doubtless be many other valid ways of formulating a vision of the society of the future in terms of the traditions and problems of an evolving European order. The problem, however,

2. "The New Divinity," *The Twentieth Century,* Autumn 1961, pp. 17-18.

is less one of intellectualist formulation than of political will, intensity of vision, breadth of perspective, and truly revolutionary transformation of persisting mental attitudes. A contemporary American poet, William Carlos Williams, remarked: "The mind is the cause of our distresses, but of it we can build anew. . . . A new world is only a new mind." Will Europeans today and tomorrow make the profound changes in mental attitude needed for a constructive, non-incestuous, educational, as well as therapeutic relationship with the America of the future? This question is dependent upon Europe's self-image, which in turn will be shaped even more by its external relations with the peoples, cultures, and societies of the "Third World" than with America.

V

In our attempt to foresee the world of 2000 and the future form of European evolution, especially in relation to a rapidly changing America, we are acutely aware of our ignorance and inadequacy. The task becomes more forbidding when we contemplate the fate of the oft-maligned majority of mankind who suffer the privations of dire poverty in the dual societies of the "Third World." The meek may be blessed, but does anyone anywhere believe that they shall inherit the earth before the end of two decades? Europe's developing relationship to the peoples of the Third World, perhaps the pivot of its own future, is still poisoned by sincere misconceptions, anachronistic criteria of appraisal, myths springing from insupportable illusions, and by reciprocal suspicion. Every term in the phrase "The Third World of Developing Nations" is seriously misleading at present, and certainly in connection with the year 2000. The very semantics in which current attitudes are framed is a blinding barrier to any inspiring vision of the future. Today's Third World will either be the First World in 2000 or nearly synonymous with the One World of the twenty-first century. Could anything else be safely assumed about an area so geographically dispersed, so politically tempestuous, and so economically insecure? At least three presently unchallenged myths might well be absurd in 2000. That these myths are still widely shared by the intelligentsia inside as well as outside the Third World is no warrant for their relevance to long-term realities.

The unhistorical myth of modernization overstresses discontinuities and obscures the deeper historical continuity among peoples, particularly those with an amazing cultural longevity. Although there is a greater recognition now than a decade ago that there is no single, monolithic model of modernity, social scientists are generally unable to see the cultural roots of the spectacular economic success of Japan or the massive social movements in China. The prolonged debate between reformers, revivalists, and others over the last century was markedly different in Russia, China, Japan, India, and the Arab world. A broad historical perspective would suggest that major changes in modes of leadership could occur in the next decades, resulting in a variety of unprecedented modernity. The priorities implicit in capitalistic economics will hinder the understanding of the diversity of cultural and social patterns in the world 2000.

The deterministic myth of economic growth through intensively capitalized industrial development serves to reinforce the categories, the quantitative language, and the narrow assumptions of ontological scarcity. A few bold writers have already begun to point to a new economics of resource mobilization. Essays by Polanyi, Wollman, Buchanan, Schumacher, and Boulding are modest portents of future developments in thought. In *The Age of Discontinuity,* Peter Drucker has hinted at the implications of the emergence of knowledge as the central capital, the cost center, and the crucial resource of a new economics. A small sample of such rethinking cannot render the traditional economics of scarcity irrelevant to the emergent structures of the developing countries. But the year 2000 is remote when seen from the standpoint of possible breakthroughs in our fundamental modes of economic and social thought. In any case, the term "developing" implies a time-lag in the transmission of ideas and skills that is already being foreshortened in conspicuous instances. We might fruitfully reflect upon the perceptive remarks of the biologist C. H. Waddington.

> It is often thought that the "undeveloped" nations have, as their first task, to catch up with the societies which are at present more affluent, but this is only very partially true. The real challenge to them is to leap, in as few jumps as possible, from their present position to where the affluent societies will be in ten or twenty years' time. They do not need to learn

> how to build early twentieth-century industry, but how to develop late twentieth-century society; and that is something which the affluent societies themselves do not know.
>
> What forms can the materially-good life take in a world of automated industry, mechanized agriculture, great mobility of individuals, and widely dispersed supplies of energy? There is need for great creative thinking in the domain which is becoming known as "the science of human settlement," or "ekistics," which is concerned with such questions as the organization of cities, complexes of towns and villages, roads, railways, and other communication networks, different types of land utilization and so on. Again, mankind will have to think out afresh the kinds of economic systems which will work effectively in a world from which the burden of heavy, time-consuming work has been removed. The under-developed nations approach these problems from the starting-point of conditions which differ from those of the affluent countries; but all societies face the same challenge to their ability to create a new type of society. In respect to the past and the present, the various societies of mankind differ widely, and in those differences there is scarcely any basis for a stable world order. It is in respect to the future that all men are equal; and it is only by concentrating their attention on the material future that mankind can discover a community of interest which could serve as an adequate basis for a world order.[3]

It is a great leap from a new economics of resource mobilization and the application of new knowledge—as well as the accumulated wisdom of the ages—to the design of the environment, to the current preoccupations of developing nations. The implications of the dismal science for the unbridgeable Development Gap often emphasized are indeed as depressing as ever, possibly much more so owing to the emphasis itself. More generally, the demand for equalization has become a formidable movement. Its explosive logic is doomed to precipitate a degree of disillusionment that must eventually result in either some form of international conflict on the basis of race and class, or a radical reappraisal of the nature of

3. C. H. Waddington, "The Desire for Material Progress as a World Ordering System," *Daedalus,* Spring 1966, pp. 672-73.

development by the leaders of the Third World, or the adoption as a last resort of the concerted global strategy of "convergent measures" advocated in different ways by specialists like Tinbergen, Prebisch, and Peccei, and by representatives from seventy-seven nations in the historic Charter of Algiers of 1967. Even more radically, we must move toward international application of our increasing acceptance of ethically imperative and diverse methods of income redistribution in favor of the less privileged. A firm criterion for reallocations could be adapted from that given by Bertrand de Jouvenel in his excellent book on the ethics of redistribution.

Paradoxically, the basic problems of the Third World, involving the translation of both legitimate and inordinate economic expectations into genuine political grievances as well as unrealizable political demands, are also obscured by the myth of Third World Solidarity. It is grounded in certain realities–the commonality of the experience of political and economic imperialism, the resistance to ideological polarization in the now outmoded dualism of the Cold War, the need for a concerted stand on inequitable terms of trade and a rigidly self-perpetuating division of labor, the advantages of collective bargaining with richer nations, and, above all, the growing awareness that the universal deliverance from starvation and destitution is entirely feasible through the honest application of knowledge available to all national governments and international agencies. These are facts of considerable importance. Nonetheless, the myth of Third World Solidarity is a costly and ingenuous delusion if it is taken to imply a continuing coherence of economic interests and policies among the significantly unequal and divergent societies lumped and dumped together under epithets like "new states," "developing nations," and the "Third World." The myth is delusive for the nations so grouped, but even more dangerous to all peoples if it distracts from the rising demand for the democratization of all genuinely global institutions. It would serve no long-run purpose for the emerging Europe to imagine that its future relations with the continents of Asia, Africa, and South America could be construed merely in terms of token gestures toward historically selected or economically convenient "representatives" of the Third World.

The tragic failure of the Development Decade has already led to much agonizing reappraisal in many nations. It assumes a peculiarly poignant form when the larger problems of socio-economic development are ignored as a result of focusing upon the Development Gap, which is abysmal relative to the technological gap between Europe and America. A. P. Thirlwall has raised several crucial questions in concluding that for the vast majority of countries an annual rate of growth of per capita income of 8 per cent would be required to match by 2000 the EEC countries, and 10 per cent to match the United States, compared with actual per capita income growth of between 2 and 4 per cent. What are the practical implications of such figures for the whole world, the economic fate of which cannot be detached from that of its many parts? This compassionate economist says:

> The much awaited Pearson Report eschews a precise definition or quantification of the development "gap," but is bold enough to make recommendations which have implications for the future "gap." One is bound to say that the Commission's recommendations are surprisingly unanimous in relation to the present level of world income disparities and likely future trends. Their growth target, for instance, is a mere six per cent per annum. This is only one per cent more than the average achieved so far this decade and, as will be seen, is insufficient to reduce the disparities in absolute per capita income between rich and poor countries in the foreseeable future. With a two per cent rate of population growth, a six per cent growth of national product implies only a four per cent growth of income per head, which even the Report admits would take a century to raise living standards in the average less-developed country to those prevailing in Western Europe today. . . .
>
> In short, the development task is colossal, if it is defined as achieving roughly comparable living standards throughout the world in a relatively short space of time. For most of the less-developed countries a doubling or trebling of per capita income growth would be required over the next three decades, necessitating net investment of between twenty and thirty per cent of national product, even with population growth substantially reduced. Investment ratios of this magnitude, from domestic resources alone, would involve intoler-

> able reductions in consumption and the only hope must lie in a massive infusion of resources from abroad.[4]

The logic of equalization is either absurd and chimerical or dangerously unfulfillable if construed in narrowly economic terms, and in an indefinitely maximal rather than a minimal though progressive form. There is a significant analogy here with the internal problem of Welfare States, but the psychological and political consequences of the international "rat-race" could be extremely costly by 2000. Further, Europeans should be, as already noted, in the best position to appreciate that just as the notion of "catching up" with America is demoralizing, it is even truer that a similar psychology of emulation and envy could not provide the motivating force for enabling the societies of the so-called Third World to accomplish the needed self-transformation. Even more, as Franz Fanon suggests, the idea of "catching up" involves a mutilation and manipulation of coerced individuals, which will not result in fruitful communication and global reciprocity. "Catching up" is certainly a poor substitute for the determination "to develop late twentieth century society" in a creative exploration that could be fruitfully shared by Europeans and non-Europeans alike. Our descendants will not look kindly on the pretences with which we now combine internal criticism of our archaic industrial techniques and structures with an external glorification of them. As long as we emphasize the logic of equalization, the pressure of the past, with its edited memories of discreditable encounters, will continue to dominate the choices we make in the present to the exclusion of the call of a vastly different future. This is abundantly confirmed by even a passing glance at the Charter of Algiers. In its way, it is a moving and passionate plea for justice as we now know it. It is a political exhortation that makes much sense within the context of the existing patterns of international trade, and the current economic practices of the powerful and rich nations. It is, however, doubtful whether such exhortations to the finer instincts and the sense of justice of the more powerful governments of the more prosperous nations will produce the desired results. The Charter

4. A. P. Thirlwall, "The Development 'Gap'," *National Westminster Bank Quarterly Review*, February 1970, pp. 34-35.

of Algiers could, no doubt, serve as a rallying-cry for future political confrontations of the sort implicit in Lin P'iao's historic thesis about the global class conflict, as well as in the encounters between the overprotected and the inadequately enfranchised members of the United Nations and its various international agencies. On the other hand, a few nations of the Third World are already pioneering more modest paths of development that place greater emphasis on self-reliance and self-sufficiency.

The logic of equalization has also led economists like Dudley Seers to consider current measures of international redistribution of income and to explore the possibility of first steps in the direction of world taxation of some sort. He argued that an international fiscal scheme is needed to ensure a more equitable sharing of the burdens of world "development," to reduce international tensions caused by exploitation of the divisions between the rich by poorer nations, and to take the supreme concern to abolish poverty out of the age of charity, in particular the power of the donor over the receiver.[5] The deepest objection to an overemphasis on the logic of equalization is that it consolidates Epimetheanism in the economic policies of all nations, promotes an eventually self-destructive mentality of warfare and retaliation, and limits the emergence of enlightened, Promethean planning on a world scale. It must be balanced not only by the politics of reason, but more significantly by the dialectic of transcendence central to the politics of perfectibility. Europe has little to gain from a short-term preoccupation with token equalization if it is to serve the necessary function of acting as a catalyst for launching significant changes in the global society of 2000.

It is hardly surprising that more and more far-sighted men of compassion are emphasizing an entirely global approach to meeting basic needs, and finding the most beneficent utilization of the diverse resources, of all mankind. The theoretical advantages of such an approach are manifold, but its greatest merits may lie in the following two considerations. First of all, a global approach could help to treat each economic unit (local, national, or regional)

5. Dudley Seers, "International Aid: The Next Steps," *The Journal of Modern African Studies,* vol. 2, no. 4, 1964, pp. 471-89.

as a unique combination of potential resources and pressing needs (with an appropriate scale of priorities), while at the same time bringing to the tasks of resource utilization the best available knowledge and skills from all over the world. Secondly, this approach could promote the common good and collective long-term interest of a more integrated and less wasteful economy. The practical difficulties with the global approach are also considerable. The logic of economic mondialism cannot be disentangled from the equally compelling logic of democratization and consequently from the entire superstructure of a megalopolis with a world federal government. Nor can the fate of the Third World be left merely to the whims and mercies of those who respond voluntarily, pre-eminently out of fear, to its pleas for social justice and more sympathetic consideration. It is also an open question whether the political obstacles to economic mondialism could be overcome more easily than the mental hindrances to pioneering applications of a new economics of resource utilization and the eco-social design of agro-urban communities, especially in the Third World. On the answers to such questions will depend the shape of world society and its degree of diversity as well as unity.

Europe's role in relation to the so-called Third World in 2000, that is, to the majority of mankind, will primarily depend upon its own self-image and political structure. But as that role must gain the credibility of the highly shrewd policy makers and sophisticated planners of the Third World, Europe must learn to accommodate its role both to the logic of equalization and to the logic of mondialization. This implies more equitable economic relations with Third World countries, as well as closer political coordination and cooperation with every move in the direction of mondialization. Such a combination of efforts is by no means beyond the skills, energies, and resilience of the technocrats of the Europe of the future or even of the present; the real problem is to apply as much wisdom, compassion, and foresight as Europe can command to political decision making within Europe itself.

Dr. Henri Rochereau, in an article on the relations between the EEC and the developing countries, displays a remarkable generosity of spirit and an honest recognition of built-in limitations. He contends that in the world-wide dialogue already begun between the rich and the poor, the developing countries consider the EEC as their preferred partner in the debate. Quite apart from the ties formed in the colonial era and the high rank the Community occupies among the "haves," its vital part in international trade makes it singularly eligible to be both the recipient of requests and the target of criticism by less developed countries. Dr. Rochereau is deeply concerned about the special responsibility which the Common Market must assume today with regard to the developing world—especially as it has differential relations with about thirty less-developed countries with a total population of two hundred million. He is also aware of the need for economic assistance in the absence of effective global arrangements.

> There is, all the same, nothing to prevent adaptation of the Association in order to take into account progress made in wider contexts. In other words, steps that have become necessary as a result of the absence or inadequacy of measures taken at a world level could be modified once multilateral arrangements of comparable efficacy have been made. Until then, the aid granted at regional levels remains fully justified even if, by its empirical, down-to-earth approach, it falls short of the more ambitious but unfortunately still theoretical model of systematic organization of the struggle against under development on a world-wide scale. Is it therefore astonishing that the A.S.S.M. should refuse to drop the substance for the shadow? They know only too well that a decline of the Association would lead to a reduction of total aid from outside or at best to increased dependence on national bilateral aid, assuming that such aid came to take the place of the assistance given under the European Development Fund.[6]

Is this a happy portent of the future relation between Europe and the Third World? Whatever the economic advantages of the Association, it has been viewed with mixed feelings in the countries concerned. Dr. Rochereau is himself only too willing to concede that a conflict between the interests of European farmers and those of the developing countries limits the concessions that the EEC

6. Henri Rochereau, "The European Economic Community and the Developing Countries," *Progress,* vol. 53, no. 297, 1968, p. 13.

can make in the field of commercial policy. In any event, decisions of any importance involve a degree of control over its members that is not now possessed by the Commission or the Community.

> Such a control would certainly be easier if the provision of development aid were acknowledged as one of the objectives of the Community. There is no doubt that, here as in other sectors, closer co-ordination of the activities of the individual member states would be fully consistent with the spirit of the Treaty and would be bound to strengthen the Community. But, in view of the intimate connection between development aid and the foreign policy of the member states, it appears questionable whether such progress is possible except through much more comprehensive decisions relating to the aims and the mechanism of a political union of the member states of the Community.[7]

Men like Dr. Rochereau could be helpful to future economic relations between Europe and the Third World. But long before 2000, an almost Copernican change will be needed in the entire approach to the economics of world development, consistent with the legitimate claims of equalization and the larger logic of mondialization.

Clearly, Europe's relation to the majority of mankind by 2000 will be decisively affected by the future internal evolution of Europe, its degree of parapolitical imagination, and genuine capacity for self-transcendence. The fate of the smaller Community may well depend upon the capacity of its leaders, planners, and citizens to show that they can subsume their collective allegiance to the whole of mankind, *Civitas Humana.* The measure of such supreme allegiance will be the critical test of maturity and self-confidence in men and societies in the year 2000. By then the phrase "human solidarity" in the context of "universal unity and causation" will have no meaning except through every practical effort to exemplify it, where it hurts and where it counts. Can this be left to accident or will Europeans now seriously prepare their educational institutions, their technical agencies, their entire social and cultural environment for the concrete exemplification of universal brotherhood?

7. *Ibid.*, p. 14.

VI

The greatest problem in relation to 2000 may well lie in bringing closer together the new world of knowledge and the new institutions of society. This is in part a problem of politics–in the classical sense and in the Enlightenment tradition rather than in the conventional terms of the politics of power molded by a psychology of guilt, and the politics of self-preservation working through the economics of scarcity and competition, and the politics of stability suffocating in the corrupt religiosity of exclusiveness and endless self-justification. In the arena of political innovation, Europe's capacity for effective contribution to the American experiments in social transformation will be determined by its own receptivity to the ancient wisdom and modern traumas of the cultures of the so-called Third World. The more Europe is occupied between now and 2000 with "catching up" with the economic wealth of America, the more the leaders of the Third World will tend to overlook Europe altogether in favor of their own concern to imitate the methods of American prosperity. On the other hand, the more Europe is concerned, in its relations with the Third World, about maintaining the economics, the politics, and the psychology of scarcity, the more she will become insensitive to the consummation of the profound value crisis behind the revolt of American youth. But the problem of a split psyche will not be insoluble for the European therapists of the future.

Europe's greatest test will be its ability to act, at least as a shock absorber, and ideally as a sort of Jacob's ladder, between the Third World and the United States. The terms "heaven" and "earth" must surely be interchangeable in their application according to one's standpoint. In 2000, let us hope, each man will find the heaven of his choice and avoid whatever hell he finds fearful. It could be that Europe's future in 2000 will be earned through the efforts of Europeans to learn, through their sufferings, to forget themselves in the service of the sufferers of all mankind. Europe's rebirth will be determined by exhaustion of its past karma–the consequences of its past follies and errors. A morally bankrupt and spiritually impoverished Europe, strutting in the clothes of the *nouveaux riches* and whoring after the fleshpots of Babylon while claiming to speak with "inside" knowledge about the new Jerusalem–is too sad even to imagine. The new Europe would then mark a total break with everything precious to the cultural heritage of the past, while being competently "managed" by a new breed of Eurocrats. It would compensate by the loudness of its self-praise for the pain of its own inward betrayal. This nightmare has to be faced–if only to be exorcised when its first shadowy outlines appear on the scene. As Heidegger thought, Europe must revert to the beginning, not merely to evoke familiar memories, but to make a new and more radical beginning, bringing with it all that is strange, dark, and uncertain. The European heritage does, however, provide many safeguards, of which only two need be mentioned as peculiarly relevant to the future promise and interim temptation of the new Europe. A tortured but noble soul like Simone Weil wrote prophetically in wartime Europe:

> Enslaved and oppressed Europe will not see better days, when she is liberated, unless spiritual poverty has first taken root in her. . . . The new élite must be a part of the mass and in direct contact with it. And, further, they must do something which is harder than enduring poverty, they must renounce all compensations; in their contacts with the people around them they must sincerely practise the humility of a naturalized citizen in the country that has received them.[8]

While spiritual poverty, exemplified by the noblest of all élites–those who truly love all mankind–may be an antidote to the fatal temptation of self-adoration, the splendid promise of the Europe and the world of 2000 must also involve the kind of mental meditation in a positively universal context that was Condorcet's own consolation while hiding from Robespierre's police in a Paris garret. In his last testament, he spoke of the self-validating joy of merging oneself in a universal vision of the human race in its ceaseless quest for liberation and enlightenment.

> This sentiment is the asylum into which he retires, and to which the memory of his persecutors cannot follow him; he unites himself in imagination with man restored to his rights, delivered from oppression, and proceeding with rapid strides in

8. "War of Religions," *The Twentieth Century,* Autumn 1961, pp. 107-8.

> the path of happiness; he forgets his own misfortunes while his thoughts are thus employed; he lives no longer to adversity, calumny and malice, but becomes the associate of these wiser and more fortunate beings whose enviable condition he so earnestly contributed to produce.[9]

A society of such men could today prepare for the world and the Europe of 2000.

9. Marquis de Condorcet, "Man's Future Progress," in Nicholas Capaldi, ed., *The Enlightenment,* New York, G. P. Putnam's Sons, 1967, pp. 312-13.

15

THE COMMUNITY OF STRANGERS

With the energy of the innocent
They were gathering the tools
They would need to make their journey back to nature
While the sand slipped through the opening
And their hands reached for the golden ring
With their hearts they turned to each other's hearts for refuge.

JACKSON BROWNE

In a time of confusion, constant change, and continual crises, we are ever tempted to elevate our tentative judgments to the status of finalities, closing the door to the future and limiting the possibilities of growth in others and ourselves. The therapist Carl Rogers emphasizes the importance of unconditionality in human relationships, seeing beyond the apparent constants of human nature into that mysterious underground in which the origins of change are found. Can the germs of change–hidden within the depths of human beings–be the basis of communities, communes, conceptions of community, at several levels and in concentric circles, in a new and more intentional sense than any known in recorded history? Can they serve as the seeds of a rich variety of modes of participation in the politics of perfectibility? A community is any collection of human beings, diverse but more or less united, who share an unconditional and continuing commitment to ends, values, and beliefs, or minimally to procedures, who can rely upon each other to render voluntary compliance with accepted obligations, and in some measure affirm their potential for self-correction, self-expression, and self-transcendence. A community is as utopian as the ideal man or the ideal relationship. But every human being is constantly involved in some kind of correction from his external environment, so that he engages in criticism of others (often his own way of criticizing and defining himself). Everyone can see through formal laws and coercive sanctions and recognize some alternatives among friendships for an easier, more natural, trustful context in which one can free oneself and grow. To that extent human life is larger than social structures, and man vaster than all the classifications of man.

The large definition of the community is close to some element in every one of us–an element which cannot be abolished, cannot be annulled, cannot be reduced to laws or institutions, but reaches beyond our parents, our teachers, and our environment, and includes lonely moments of bewilderment before the vastitude and versatility of nature. When a human being apparently seeks to ascend to the top of some social or professional scale, at heart perhaps he only desires to ascend to the top of a mountain. This is an inward journey to some invisible summit from which he can see his life–if not steadily, at least less unsteadily than at other times; if not as a whole, at least sufficiently as a whole to make sense to himself and have self-respect as he approaches the moment of death. We witness today a fragmentation of consciousness, most clearly in the structure of American society, toward which the whole world is tending: an excessive increase of roles, complexities, rules, and pressures of every sort. Even human beings with enormous social mobility cannot meet external challenges because of inadequate psychological mobility. The contemporary revolution is elusive partly because of its insistent stress on flexibility against the rigidity of educational, religious, and political institutions. On the other hand, while we wish to be flexible, open-ended, willing to change, the very pace of change makes us want to do more than merely adapt. We search for a basis of continuity amidst the Heraclitean flux. When fragmentation of consciousness becomes insupportable, persons may seek, either through meditation or music, through silence and solitude, less through traditional forms of worship than through self-created rituals and rites of the sacred, to penetrate the depths of their potential being. They hope to tap latent energy so that they can develop a tangible, ever-existing sense of the unlimited at the very time when limitations are so pressing.

American history, over two hundred years, has not been merely some sort of homogenized search for a national community. There was much more to the American Dream as understood by the so-called successes and even more poignantly by the failures—all the immigrants who set up communes and communities which eventually died. They somewhere felt that their efforts represented something real with a possible meaning for other human beings. More than a hundred communes involving a hundred thousand people flourished in America. Geography bears their marks—Amana, Oneida, New Harmony. A few, like the communities of the Shakers, lasted for more than a century. The Rappites survived almost as long and the Icarians lasted for fifty years, while others still exist on altered terms. The Hutterites have carefully considered the compromises with the larger society necessary to preserve the core of their mode of living and being; the Amish still struggle for their way of life without compromise or modification. But there were many more communes and communities which were meteoric, dying within months of their birth through internal conflict and fragmentation or by absorption into the broader cultural and social context. Through all of them stirred a strong impulse which might have been premature in certain respects, might have been misconceived and mistaken in the narrowness of the basis of allegiance or the degree of reinforcement through controls. But nonetheless they represented a daring, defiant, and sometimes desperate assertion of freedom that is part of the American Dream. So it was that Charles Nordhoff was told by a member of the Icarian commune in 1875: "Deal gently and cautiously with Icaria. The man who sees only the chaotic village and the wooden shoes, and only chronicles those, will commit a serious error. In that village are buried fortunes, noble hopes, and the aspirations of good and great men. . . ."[1]

These social experiments are invariably instructive. They are concrete as well as abstract lessons now being relearned by those who, in the seventies, have attempted every kind of communal, semi-communal, and merely transient and nomadic form of existence. One of the lessons, said Arthur Morgan, looking at early communities, lay in the fact that they were exclusive, not universal.

1. Charles Nordhoff, *The Communistic Societies of the United States,* New York, Harper & Brothers, 1875, p. 339.

Very few people can rise to that ultimate affirmation of the American Dream represented by Buckminster Fuller. At a time when doomsday seers talk in quasi-racist language, and demonstrate the ancient fear of diversity and an acute incapacity to consider the whole, Fuller insists that no utopia will ever be wholly justifiable unless it is democratic and created for every living person. He adds that the resources of the world today are used on behalf of about 44 per cent of the population, that unless and until they can be used for all, there will be no Kingdom of Heaven on earth. Does this mean that any one community, any one communal experiment, must take on the burden of all? Does this mean that there must be a once-and-for-all total change in the social structure? So Burnette Haskell thought when he joined others in attempting to establish a "Fraternal Republic" based on *Co-operative Commonwealth,* Laurence Gronlund's reformulation of Marx's thought in American terms. After the Kaweah Co-operative Commonwealth failed, Haskell wrote without bitterness:

> We were not fit to survive and we died. But there is no bribe money in our pockets; and beaten and ragged as we are, we are not ashamed. . . . And is there no remedy, then, for the evils that oppress the poor? And is there no surety that the day is coming when justice and right shall reign on earth? I do not know; but I believe, and I hope, and I trust.[2]

It was natural for pioneers of communes to expect that they might show the way to others, but they too easily ignored both their predecessors and those yet to come. Upon arrival in America they forgot timeless truths concerning the continuity of human history and of individual life–that birth and growth are inseparable from suffering and death; that all life must accommodate a preparation for the moment of death while welcoming the moment of birth of other human beings; and that there is togetherness in space and community in time. There are many orders of time. At one level time is merely the succession of events; at another level it marks the transmission of ideas that cuts across purely chronological divisions and the historical delimitations of epochs.

2. Burnette G. Haskell, "Kaweah, How and Why the Colony Died," *Out West,* vol. 17, no. 3, September 1902, pp. 303 and 322.

American society began over three hundred years ago, on a vast land of abundance and opportunity into which came sons of the soil, immigrants of every kind from all over the world. These were people without prestige, without inherited property, without political power, and without the experience of the leisurely pastimes of the privileged. They were a sample of the world's proletariat brought together through a commitment to principles embodied as propositions. This beginning is bolder and more glorious than the accounts of historians suggest. It is a story rooted in revolution. The American Revolution was the first in recorded history to be founded in *theoria,* a commitment to theoretical propositions embodied in a Declaration of Independence. These principles were thought to be eternal and universal, applicable to all persons in all climes at all times. The original vision became crudely materialized in a desperate desire for concrete embodiment. Most people crave results quickly. The great mass of men generate an immense pressure in the name of immediate earthly results which they can parade and show. In demanding instant proof and repeated demonstration, they place an insuperable strain upon even the greatest leaders, most of whom fall prey to this temptation. They fear that if they do not, they would lose their following, or they would have to require from their following such an immense pure love of the good, such a profound impersonal conviction of the self-validating nature of the quest, such a long march, and such an overwhelming compassion for others that their followers might not be equal to it. There is a simplistic quality about the minds of the autodidacts, the half-educated, and the poorly educated, who want an immediate and final solution. But does that mean that we should go to the opposite extreme and look for no solutions, posing as existentialists or nihilists? Is the nihilism in today's high schools the only answer young Americans can offer as an alternative? Can they not visualize small solutions within a large vision? They surely can, but sadly too many people merely react and mistake posturing for pioneering.

Thomas Paine, the Theophilanthropist, gave the keynote to American radicalism in his statement that society arises from human wants, while government emerges from human wickedness. Society arises because men need one another. No man can fulfill his many wants except in the company of others; because of the collective wants of human beings, there is validity and value to human societies. But unfortunately, men want to bequeath the burden of finding fulfillment to some external authority. When embodied in imperfect men, whatever the laws, systems, or government, this will gradually license every abomination. For Paine, the ideal society was stateless. But he also knew that to approach the ideal, we must first deglamorize government. Until men are ready for a stateless society, they need to own, though not to worship, a government. Because men in governments have limitations, governments are ceaselessly liable to go wrong. There must be a permanent revolution in society. The story of America is that of the weak inheriting the vision of the strong and encumbering the original dream, so that it has descended from the dialectical politics of perfectibility, reason, and revolution to the unilinear concerns of power, stability, and self-preservation. The old communes strove toward intangible ideals in isolated enclaves. They sought universality, but because of their intense isolation from the greater community–more possible in America than in Europe–they ceased in time to be therapeutically self-critical. Their leaders lacked the ability to be philosophically skeptical about their own roles. There was no principle of negation within the structure of the community sufficient to permit self-transcendence; people were prey to the very same desire ubiquitous in modern society, the concern to settle down and find bourgeois stability and respectability.

California has become a symbol of promise, disappointment, and decadence for much of the world. As early as the nineteenth century, Josiah Royce saw California essentially in terms of social irresponsibility and sloth, sunny indolence, and the scarcity of truly cultivated persevering persons. This sybaritic, hedonistic image of California pervaded other sectors of the United States. There were also those who felt that California was not merely to be assimilated into some Mediterranean mythology, that a richer mixture in a greater ferment was involved, and that it was a logical culmination of the American Dream. After pioneers had reached the limit of physical settlement, another kind of pioneering was involved in another kind of journey. Whitman put this in his characteristic way, broadly and boldly. On visiting California, he asked, "What is it that I started a long time ago, and how can I get back to that?" It is a venture into the interior realms of consciousness, digging into the very depths of one's being, transcending ancestral ties, racial affinities, cultural and social conditions. It is the asking of deeper questions. Others saw this in terms of a mix of North and South, Latin and Anglo-Saxon, Europe and America, East and West–much more evident in our own time.

The recent history of California, perhaps even more than the history of the United States as a whole, is a history of lost opportunities and misfired innovations. It is a history of intellectual and spiritual abortions in a state where there are often nearly as many abortions as births and more divorces than marriages. How, then, in such a California, can people get excited and be credible to each other even in discussing the community of the future? When Plato spoke of *koinonia* he said that a community involves a sharing of pleasures and pains. When Californians are sharing pleasures, for what they are worth, they are quite forgetful of communities. But when they share pains, they experience an immense void. When they experience post-coital sadness, when they experience the pain after every new wave of excitement, when they experience that deep discontent–which may sometimes be less divine than demoniac–they begin to suspect that there is something more to life than they know. A Sufi sage was once asked by a student, "Why is it, O Master, that when people come to you for teaching, saying they really want enlightenment, you merely get them engaged in some activity?" The Master replied, "Very few of those who think they want enlightenment want anything but a new form of engagement. And very few of them will get engaged to the point where they can see through the activities, because they will become so totally consumed that they will have no opportunity to see beyond. But those few who are confident in their engagements know that they do not need to put themselves totally into them and can see limitations. They will talk of 'something beyond.' They do not know what that something beyond is, but they are certain that there is something beyond. And when they are ready to maintain in consciousness that conception of something beyond, then they are ready for those processes of training that might lead to enlightenment."

California is to be characterized not only by triumphs but also by frustrations which prepare it for that ultimate *hubris* which is still the privilege of the American—to think big, to cherish the impossible dream. Whittier may have been more extravagant than misguided when he said that in California there could be a second founding. But this could be a very different kind of "founding" from what can be historically dated or blazoned forth by the national media. This is perhaps the most important lesson to be learned from the failures of the past decade. A few understood at the very beginning of the Hippie movement that, once bombarded with publicity, it would be killed before it flourished. The early "flower children" were instinctively right in regard to the logic of inversion. Society had reached a point of such absurdity that inversion was unavoidable. Teachers were no longer teachers, parents not really parents, scholars usually not scholars. Each was tangled in his ego-game, although none were taken in by phoniness. Many were desperately concerned to find some authentic meaning which could be sustained through trust, openness, and love exchanged in everyday relations. But they could not stay permanently aloof from all institutions, all efforts to capture and formulate. The contemporary revolution is a revolution not in institutions or in men, but in the standpoint of individuals toward institutions, and the relations between human beings. As Socrates observed in *Gorgias,* "Where there is no sense of community, there can be no love."

Recent social experiments could no more overcome the insoluble problem of new entrants than the old communes. Either one closes the community to all immigrants, which results in a boring uniformity of belief and practice as well as intense mutual bitchiness, or one opens the community to new entrants, whereby every fresh wave produces a dilution of what was there in the beginning. This universal problem is peculiarly American because of the logic of assimilation and the logic of homogenization. The constant flow of immigrants is part of America. In that sense, it must always aim at the sky—at universality—for all the tired attempts to limit America to some narrow view of a Judeo-Christian succession to the Roman Empire. Historically and philosophically, America is that country in which every man may continually redefine himself, taking what he needs from the world's heritage, making his own authentic selection out of the entire inheritance of humanity. If he is not helped by his schools or his parents to exercise his privilege of individuation, he must self-consciously negate the conformist culture of Middle America. The first step for many today is to let go, to shake off the hypnotic hold of a constricting structure of transmitted prejudice. This is irreversible and increasing. Even people apparently cozy in their middle-aged, middle-class existence are unavoidably affected through their children. The break with stereotyped values and superficial allegiances is as necessary as it is painful. Inevitably, it has produced a great deal of chaos out of which new forms of consolidation precipitate, though that is no worse than the visible muddle of institutions that proliferate in rules but are inefficient and no longer work fairly or properly. America is curiously less efficient than many countries of the Old World.

Santayana, not an American by birth or at the time of death, reflected deeply on the American experiment and continued to ponder it when he came to California. His America was a contest between the aggressive man and the genteel woman (which sounds strange today, but it is as historically important as it is relevant even now). Again and again men emerged who, though aggressive, were the purveyors of the creativity that is at the center of the American impulse. There were women, from maiden aunts to wives, who sought security, but also wished to become sophisticated, to become what they thought Americans were not. In this tension between the male adventurer and the bourgeois lady lurked a constant peril to the creative drive. A Marxist-Leninist would see this as an inevitable trend toward "the bourgeoisification of the proletariat." Here came the world's proletariat, but as they became "bourgeoisified," they forgot the grander ideal behind the American experiment–not class or status or structure, but the free man. The original impulse became obscured or was perverted into a jingoistic sentiment, a substitute for true feeling, and a flight from real experience of the wide open spaces and their equivalent in the human mind. Santayana thought that California, for the very reasons that others criticized it–its lack of gentility, its crudity, its slothfulness–would not permit maiden aunts and stylish women to set the pace. It was impossible in California for gentility to tyrannize, halting the creative ferment. He also thought that, whereas elsewhere in America people came to exchange the strong Transcendentalism of the early years for a wishy-washy admiration of nature, in California when people went to the Sierras they felt something deeper—a negation of argument, a negation of logic, a sense of the vanity of human life and the absurdity of so many of their structures and relationships. Nature in California made people think beyond America itself. It made them have larger thoughts about human frailty and the fragility of human institutions.

In this context, and with the hindsight of some lessons learned from two hundred years of American history, we can see that the community of the future will require a rethinking of fundamentals—the allocation of space, time, and energy. It will need a macro-perspective and a micro-application. It may relate to old and new institutions, but must essentially see beyond them. Some may drop out, some may cop out, and others will be psychologically at a critical distance from their jobs, schools, and the entire System (psychologically outside though socially inside them). Some will have the imagination and the determination to create with minimum means, often merely by purging excess or juxtaposing otherwise disparate skills, experiments in new kinds of informal institutions. Free from contrast and competition with the System, these fluid experiments can transcend the efforts of Kaweah, Deseret, and all isolationist movements. A long time will pass before we can arrive at self-regenerating institutions. No society has a hidden secret formula in this regard, although other cultures knew something America has still to learn about the secret of institutional longevity. It took great effort by Plato to prepare the foundation for an Academy which lasted nine hundred years. In the thirteenth century, groups of individuals in England set up houses, monasteries, and small colleges which eventually became the University of Oxford and which has lasted for many centuries with some fidelity to its origins. Americans are not unaware of the significance of such facts. Today, when everything appears fragile and transient, Americans are willing, unlike earlier generations, to ponder the fact of death, and also to discuss immortality in philosophical, not merely religious, terms. They are now ready to find ways in which they may self-consciously thread together moments and years in their lives. The search is intense and poignant because there are so many mistakes, so many misfirings—at every point there is a re-enactment and repetition of those problems embedded in the existing structure.

Institutions might be envisaged in terms of a series of concentric circles. The inner circle entertains those who make decisions. We may call it "the Establishment," though fortunately there is no real Establishment that believes in itself in America. Outside that ring is a large number of followers–people often apathetic, who seem blindly to conform, and even think it unpatriotic to question decisions taken by central agencies. Beyond this circle are the negators and the critics. We might call them radicals and they may see themselves as revolutionaries. Essentially they are people more concerned with talk and analysis than with action and example, the victims and agents of the very social structure which they seek to negate and reject. Beyond the negators is the circle of those willing to be quiet for a while, willing to relinquish the limelight and become fully occupied in pioneering new ways of living and new ways of sharing. There are communal householders who beat inflation by sharing their uses of time, space, and money, as there are explorers of energy, and disciples of music and meditation. There are bolder and more ambitious experiments on a larger scale on vast farms and estates. In all these circles, the problem will persist: How is it possible to ensure an unconditional commitment both to shared values and to persons as sacred–an allegiance to the forms and not to the formalities? As McWilliams has written in *The Ideal of Fraternity in America,*

> For a real revolution, a turning back in human affairs away from the needless limitations and threats which liberal modernity has inflicted on mankind, time is needed–a long series of partial moves and shrewd compromises that demands a clear sense of direction. No one need be told, in America, how easy it is for men to lose the way. The only hope for that direction, the only hope too for an end to the "eclipse," lies in the "inner city" in the true sense. Such a fraternal city can exist within an unfraternal polity only if men know the dangers that beset it and the possibilities it offers.[3]

How can we ensure that people will gain such confidence in rules that they will have rule-skepticism built into them because they

3. Wilson Carey McWilliams, *The Ideal of Fraternity in America,* Berkeley, University of California Press, 1973, p. 623.

know that no general rule could ever perfectly fit a unique situation? People might conceivably gain so much confidence in the fulfillment of particular roles that they could also afford to show role flexibility, even role transcendence. To some extent this is a feature of every society; human beings do not have to be told to be informal. They do not have to be told to see beyond law and rules, for otherwise they could not fill up the large areas of life which are unstructured. But where human beings become self-conscious—and this is a function of confidence in one's ability to operate the structure—they combine precision with flexibility, mastery with transcendence. The most crucial factor in individuation is the imminence of death and the readiness to see through the incessant talk of catastrophe to the constant presence of unavoidable suffering. This is crucial to the present and future maturation of the American mind, though it does not involve sacrificing anything quintessential to the American Dream. Indeed, it is a kind of growing up which may for the first time make the vision of the Founding Fathers meaningful, outside the formal apparatus of rules and institutions, and create not islands of instant brotherhood, but new areas of initiative with unprecedented avenues of commonality hospitable to discovery and imagination. This demands a radical repudiation of success and failure and external status, which are so corrosive to human consciousness.

If ever Americans develop a refined culture that is neither a technological civilization nor an imitation of Europe, which does more than doodle with gimmicks and participate in token gestures and symbols, they will have to learn from the sagacious Emerson. His perceptive essay on "Self-Reliance" suggests that creeds are the disease of the mind and prayers the disease of the will. As long as we petition and pray to some outside force for a magical cure, we have rejected true religion on behalf of false religiosity. Arthur Morgan's insight is apposite: "The problem of the community of the future is not to win acceptance, but to deserve acceptance."[4] The future is indeed much larger than the past. If one takes man's age as over eighteen million years and translates it into a twenty-four-hour

4. Arthur E. Morgan, *The Community of the Future,* Yellow Springs, Ohio, Community Service, 1957, p. 54.

scale, six thousand years of recorded history do not amount to half a minute. History is extinct for those who set limits on the future. Many people today are willing to cooperate with the future, unthreatened by the universal extension of the logic of the American Dream to the whole of humanity, willing also, despite past mistakes, to make fresh experiments in the use of space, time, and energy. One day, perhaps in our lifetime, possibly around the year 2000, some may remember these trying times of subtle exploration and say without smugness:

> We dreamers, we derided
> We mad, blind men who see
> We bear ye witness ere ye come
> That ye shall be.

16

AN UNFINISHED DREAM

The solution of the problem of physical maintenance so as to banish care and crime, so far from seeming to us an ultimate attainment, appears but as a preliminary to anything like real human progress. We have but relieved ourselves of an impertinent and needless harassment which hindered our ancestor from undertaking the real ends of existence. We are merely stripped for the race; no more. We are like a child which has just learned to stand upright and to walk.

EDWARD BELLAMY

I

The unfinished American Dream has been historically focused upon the generous and equitable provision of goods and services to vast numbers of disinherited immigrants from the world's proletariat. It is hardly surprising that the utopian proposal of ensuring a guaranteed annual income to every adult should be a recurring topic of controversy since Bellamy wrote *Looking Backward* in 1888. Whether or not this proposal is politically feasible at present, it would be worthwhile to consider some of the drastic implications of the proposal for social theory and contemporary values, and for a daring vision of the future. The proposal to provide a guaranteed annual income (GAI) for all is seen by critics and champions alike as a revolutionary act. Even if nothing else were done, the enactment of such a proposal would in itself be a primary factor in changing the way in which the social structure could give form and direction to the universal human urge for fulfillment. The unprecedented divorce of basic income from work, and of involuntary work from survival, would have significant repercussions on the level of income distribution, attitudes to work, social differentiation, social stratification, occupational ranking, and even the definition of success and failure. It would alter the possibilities of fulfillment in an affluent society with an abundant economy, a mass consumer culture, and a federal system of representative democracy. All these repercussions–economic, social, political, and ethical–would be too chaotic and complex to be adequately handled by computers, master-planners, or committees of social engineers. But it is certain that they would produce a change in the social structure so radical that it could not take place without a transitional period of social disorganization and increased anomie. Even if the eventual outcome were a Golden Age in which there was a new and stable social structure uniquely conducive to universal human fulfillment, it is difficult to weigh the high cost in human suffering, waste, and frustration against the unearned gains to a future generation of inheritors of an unforeseeable utopia.

This statement could be deployed to support an obscurantist refusal either to consider the merits of the GAI proposal or to contemplate the future outcome of present economic and technological trends. Alternatively, the prospect of dislocation could be invoked as an argument for devising a rational and coherent plan for social transformation, a tidy blueprint in which the GAI proposal is incorporated in a relatively unobtrusive manner. It is not necessary to adopt either alternative. That the GAI proposal does not make practical sense on its own merely illustrates an easily forgotten truth: the guarantee of income or of material goods cannot guarantee anything else that we may desire. Nonetheless it draws attention to an array of possibilities which we tend to overlook in conventional appraisals of available means in relation to elusive ends. The more we reflect calmly on the GAI proposal, the more we discern its dual impact upon our minds. It is both dynamite to mental inertia and a stimulus to creative imagination. It heightens our awareness of dangerous trends and illusions already visible in America, and it reminds us of the awesome prospect of the imminence of *1984* in some technocratic blueprints for the day after tomorrow. An automated economy could be an authoritarian nightmare if central control were to fall into the hands of power-hungry experts whose manipulative skills include the art of arousing emotion through the deceptive rhetoric of freedom or welfare, while catering to the insatiable demands of mass consumption in the name of happiness. The nightmare is aggravated by the thought of increasing coercion or pressure in the form of pills and drugs used by social planners to modify the genetic inheritance or emotional responses of human beings.

The nightmare is frightening, and it must be dispelled. It obscures real dangers in a riot of fantasy rooted in irrational fears of individual impotence. What Henry Adams regarded in the late nineteenth century as a great discovery, the law of acceleration in social change, has now become less the basis of millennial expectation than the haunting specter of post-millennial dread. A technological utopia is indeed a denial of freedom if every man is made to carry out the function for which he is best qualified, as determined by some supposedly enlightened despot or a committee of benevolent experts. It may be true, as Samuel Butler warned in *Erewhon,* that the mass of mankind will acquiesce in any arrangement which gives them better food and clothing at a cheaper rate. It is further evident that even if the individual's lot matches his biological needs better after the second industrial revolution than after the first, this would not make the worker any more the master of his job if there is no real change in the conditions in which jobs are created and distributed. The optimum use of individual capacities, much less a purely rationalistic optimization, need not mitigate natural or social inequalities and it could easily sacrifice freedom to efficiency, and augment what Butler derisively dismissed as "man's grovelling preference for his material over his spiritual interests." Above all, the masses who give power to clever technicians (the New Barbarians, as Shaw called them) are in real danger of finding themselves dominated through dependence. Such dangers are possible and even probable in a purely technological cornucopia. But the nightmare misleads us precisely through the feeling that we are helpless, that what is possible and probable is inevitable, that the technological utopia is historically determined and rules out any alternative vision of a feasible future. If we are frightened, of what are we really afraid: the machinations of a few men; the superhuman capacities of man-made machines; the mediocrity, conformity, and materialism of the masses in an affluent society; or the lack of an adequate social philosophy or political wisdom in a representative democracy? Or, are we afraid only of ourselves? Are we convinced that there is nothing we can do about our fears? Do we despair of our capacity to exercise constructive imagination? Are we doubters of dreams and believers in nightmares?

Mechanistic concepts are immensely tempting in an industrial society but we must not allow them to distort our awareness. If all specifiable tasks for human beings can be reduced to routine movements which a machine can perform, engineers may lead us to the *non sequitur* that anything a man can do a machine can do. Computer experts may be able to use the techniques of formal logic, but they do not necessarily think more clearly or less illogically than other men. The cleverest men may overlook an elementary point in modal logic: there is always something beyond their ability. (Either they can tie a knot that they cannot untie, or they cannot. Either way, there is something that they cannot do.) The technologist is neither god nor devil, nor even a man who is the main purveyor of mechanistic concepts. The difficulty is deeper, lying partly in the fact that the image of mechanism also expresses forcefully the necessary hierarchy of the industrializing process. Even Marx saw that mechanistic materialism implies a distinction between those who are manipulated and those who are able to manipulate. He charged Robert Owen with forgetting that it is men who change circumstances and that the educator must himself be educated. Actually, Owen was less forgetful than Marx imagined and Godwin, who influenced Owen, forgot even less than Owen or Marx. There is indeed a tension between the democratic theory of equality–based on an appeal to rational argument–and the tendency under industrialism–dependent on the conversion of science into technology–to subsume the theory and practice of human relations under statistical laws of causal interaction and normatively defined circumstances of effective manipulation among unequals. Nonetheless, as long as the control of the apparatus in modern industrial society (which limits consciousness) requires free agents, rational discourse cannot be wholly eliminated.

If we respond to the GAI proposal merely with negative emotions, with nightmares to the exclusion of noble visions, we may be the reluctant prisoners of secular fatalism and technological determinism. The doctrine of inevitable, unilinear progress has flattered our collective self-image (maintained by nationalistic ideologies, conservative or radical) but flattened our individual ideals of self-fulfillment and unduly limited our perception of human potentialities. A logical gap inevitably separates a descriptive account of the impact of technology on the social structure and an evaluative appraisal of either or both in terms of criteria of human fulfillment. This gap may be bridged in social theory and in human life by assuming in advance that we can know and predict contingent connections between changes in the human condition and changes in human capacities. This is a plausible assumption and the mainspring of much that is admirable in the quest for collective self-improvement. But this assumption is dangerous when it is elevated into a dogma and may blind us to the lessons of contemporary history. There can be no universal method of ensuring that the life of men in society becomes continually better in every way. Just as any scientific or social theory is modifiable, even obsolete, as further observations are made, so any improvement of society may disappear when an advance is made in some other direction. Similarly, since the changing concepts, axioms, and criteria of social theories are themselves products in part of the societies they seek to understand and improve, no permanent insight is possible through them though they maintain a high degree of methodological self-consciousness. However, even if the notion of uniform progress toward a fixed goal is an illusion, it is both illogical and defeatist to cease altogether from thinking of possibilities for improvement. Every proposal for technical change or social improvement must be assessed in terms of criteria of human fulfillment.

Any social structure gives form and continuity to the range of possibilities of human growth and fulfillment. Every social system can be appraised (though such appraisals are not final and infallible judgments) in terms of human growth and fulfillment. Any social structure can promote, retard, or pervert human growth according to internally shared or externally held criteria. It is also a contingent truth that remarkable individuals arise from time to time who transcend the limitations of their social situation and enrich our concept of human excellence. Democratic theory requires us to view any social structure in terms of the opportunities for growth extended to the many rather than the attainments of a few. It is majoritarian and egalitarian (at least in a minimal sense). But there have been high cultures–high in the display of human excellence–which were unashamedly undemocratic. They tended to have stable and hierarchical social structures, in which men could identify with and even profit from the cultural attainments of the few. Modern democratic societies seek to appropriate the excellence of the hierarchical societies and rich cultures of antiquity. This attempt can never wholly succeed and sometimes vulgarizes borrowed standards and concepts of excellence. A culturally developed society may show compassion or contempt for a less mature society that boasts of being more democratic, egalitarian, and affluent. The latter protects itself by caricaturing the former.

Hierarchical social structures are justifiable only in relation to a consensus of belief regarding the structure of reality and of a constant human nature, and the mirroring of a transcendent structure in the social system. Their internal stability depends upon the effective maintenance of shared beliefs and values and the reasonable relevance of role performance to ideal expectations. As this cannot be indefinitely maintained–though the longevity and attainments of some hierarchical societies are amazing–high cultures decay and their hierarchical social systems become ripe for revolution or radical reform if they are to survive at all. Egalitarian social structures can be justified in terms of equality as well as freedom, but they are more difficult to admire in terms of the criteria of human solidarity and human excellence. They may make considerable advance on the basis of a seeming consensus of belief in current theories (scientific in different degrees and senses) regarding the structure of reality and of human nature. But their real strength lies in the extent to which an open view of human nature and diverse world-views and dialogue between men of varied beliefs are maintained. This requires an appropriate social structure and political system.

The argument is often advanced that once the essential attributes of human nature are known, a society will only be tolerable if it is designed to satisfy those overriding needs which can be identified. If we can decide on a hierarchy of needs and values, an egalitarian social structure can be judged both in terms of common and minimal needs as well as by the spread of standards and attainments of human excellence. However, if we agree to be more agnostic about human nature and human possibilities, if we regard human nature as always indeterminate (or our knowledge of its limits as inevitably inconclusive), if we are willing to admit that the range of human needs, and their order of priority, cannot be anticipated or agreed upon beyond a point, then we have a new criterion for appraising changes in the social structure in relation to multiple criteria of human fulfillment. The changes in social structure foreseen in connection with the GAI proposal must be estimated not only in terms of these multiple criteria but also in relation to the actual pursuit of diverse ideals of human growth and excellence. There is no need to think of social progress as the production of some ideal type of man, to be further multiplied like desirable manufactured goods. The important thing about the idea of perfectibility is in the quest for it, its stimulus to indefinite growth. In this sense it can be combined with the uncertainty of nature that is part of our notion of a person and also our view of humanity as a species.

In envisaging a new social structure, we may think of progress chiefly as the continuous extension of the avenues of opportunity for decision, experiment, and fulfillment. Rationality of organization means simply that there should be less waste and better use of human potentials. The egalitarian principle requires us not merely to match rewards with deserts, but also to respect the fact that every man carries an aura of uncertainty and unknown potentialities around him. Since we cannot agree about the end of human development, we have no right to exclude anyone from the opportunity to share in the process, still less from the freedom to determine his own ends and to make his own decisions. Society's judgments of success and failure are pretentious and costly if they are more than provisional. They may even be irrelevant to a man's inward vision of growth and fulfillment. The ideal of fraternity implies the capacity and need in individuals to recognize and identify with the achievements of others, and to empathize with their weaknesses and failures. Education is the unfolding among receptive individuals of the capacity to choose effectively, to set themselves their standards of excellence, to exemplify tolerance and civility in relation to others, to identify with the achievements and failures of those near at hand and of persons everywhere, and to see life as a process of continuous self-education.

II

A social system entirely based on the above considerations is truly utopian, but the justification of its ruling principles is no more difficult than that of the ethical and social principles underlying the GAI proposal. The paradoxical and unpleasant corollary of all this may be that the nation which is economically and technically capable of implementing the GAI proposal is culturally and ethically unprepared for a utopia based on similar principles. Can a conformist, success-oriented, competitive society deserve a sudden jump from mature capitalism to a technocratic and democratic utopia? Is this remarkable society of self-made men and women a distorting mirror of the repressed ambitions and muffled vulgarities of the world's proletariat? Or is it already the logical limit of human development, magically freed from the burden of historical memories, and also the crown of human evolution, displaying the heights attainable in a remote future by the rest of the world? Americans may regard the cultural contempt of many Europeans as motivated by envy. Every conspicuous weakness of this society—the paranoid style, the pervasive profanity, the timidity of men in high places, the almost total displacement of intrinsic by instrumental values, the problem-solving approach to the whole of life, the reduction of everything to a technique—can be and has been explained away in terms of the System, some "ism," a single catchword, the Predicament of Modern Man, or simply as anti-Americanism. The non-American critic's difficulty lies in correctly characterizing a society that he sees as a vast and vulgar caricature of so much that is still sacred to him. In his eyes the sharpest self-criticisms of Americans still stop short of something more fundamental, which they fail to see owing to their predisposed and commendable distaste for talking about anything so amorphous and intangible as national character.

Is it possible to give some impersonal concreteness to the notion of cultural adolescence? This may be attempted by consulting Sombart's portrait of modern values in mature capitalism. He chose to give American examples since "in America . . . this modern tendency may be studied better than anywhere else because there it has reached its greatest perfection, people come to the point at once, and prefix to every commodity its monetary values." Sombart wrote at a time when Europeans chose to give sociological explanations for phenomena which in the post-Freudian era are liable to be explained in psychological terms. There is a connection between sociological and psychological explanations of the same phenomenon, as of yet insufficiently explored by either Marxists or Freudians. Sombart understood cultural adolescence in terms of the following features:

> The child possesses four elementary "values"; four ideals dominate its existence. They are:
>
> (a) Physical bigness, as seen in grown-ups and imagined in giants;
>
> (b) Quick movement–in running, bowling a hoop, riding on a roundabout;
>
> (c) Novelty–it changes its toys very quickly, it begins something and never completes it because another occupation attracts it; and
>
> (d) Sense of power–that is why it pulls out the legs of a fly, makes Towzer stand on his hind legs and beg nicely, and flies a kite as high as it can.
>
> Curious as it may sound, these ideals, and these only will be found in all modern "values."[1]

For Sombart modern values are precisely those implicit in references to the Americanization of Western Europe, which ushered in the modern age. He referred to the tendency to mistake bigness for greatness; the influence on the inner workings of the mind of the quantitative valuation of things, the connection between success, competition, and sheer size; the tendency to regard the speediest achievements as the most valuable ones; the connection between megalomania, mad hurry, and record-breaking; the attraction of novelty; the habit of hyperbole; the love of sensationalism and its effect on journalism; the concern with fashions in ideas as well as clothes; and the consciousness of superiority through a sense of power that is merely an expression of weakness.

1. Werner Sombart, "The Sociology of Capitalism," in Hendrik M. Ruitenbeek, ed., *Varieties of Classic Social Theory,* New York, E. P. Dutton, 1963, p. 184.

Sombart illustrates what he means by modern values and what many in the world have come to associate chiefly with the United States.

> Anyone gifted with true greatness, which is usually inward, will be hardly likely to estimate the outward semblance of power at all highly. Power has no temptation for Siegfried; only a Mime thirsts for it. . . . Moreover, when neither by money nor any other outward force power over mankind is given us, we talk of the conquest of nature. . . . A truly great generation concerned with the deepest problems of life will not be enraptured because it made discoveries in technical science. Power of this sort it will assuredly regard as "superficial." . . .
>
> So long as the needs of the living human being governed economic activities, so long did these have a limit. But with the disappearance of the governing factor, the natural limit fell away. . . . Every minute of the day of the year, nay, of life itself, is devoted to work, and during this working period every power is occupied at highest pressure. Everybody is acquainted with the hard-working man of today. Whether employer or employed, he is constantly on the verge of a breakdown owing to overwork. That he tends to be excited, that he is always on the move, is generally known too. Speed and yet more speed–such is the cry of the age. It rushes onward in one mad race.
>
> The influence of such a life on body and soul is not difficult to gauge. It corrodes the former and fries up the latter. Everything is sacrificed to the Moloch of work; all the higher instincts of heart and mind are crushed out by devotion to business. How much the inner life of modern man has been shattered is best seen if we cast a glance at the kernel of all natural life–the relationship to women. These men have no time for the enjoyment of delicate passions, nor even for gallant flirtations. They seem to be quite incapable of deep erotic emotions. Either they are wholly apathetic so far as love is concerned, or they are content with a brief sensual intoxication. They either do not bother about women at all, or they buy what they require in this respect.[2]

2. *Ibid.*, pp. 186-88.

If cultural adolescence could be ascribed to modern capitalism itself, to the business ethic and the Moloch of work, the mere availability of leisure could not elevate contemporary values. But if cultural adolescence cannot be explained wholly in terms of modern capitalism, any vision of social transformation will require a radical rethinking of the conventional wisdom. The wealthiest and most powerful nation in the world may be the poorest in what was supremely precious to the highest cultures of classical antiquity and the renaissances of world history–the availability of time for thought and contemplation, for relaxation and creative work, for conversation and study, for love and friendship, for the enjoyment of the arts and the beauties of nature, for solitude and communion, for doubts and dreams. There is little room or time for indolence and excellence, for salons and coffeehouses and the market-place, for laughter and tears, for poetry and philosophy, for song and dance and worship, for birds and beasts, for sleep and convalescence, for birth and death; time to live and enough time to dwell on eternity. Can the mere availability of more time teach the most time-saving society in history how to spend time, how to transcend it, and how to appreciate timelessness? If the greatest souls from the largely forgotten cultures of antiquity were suddenly to descend upon the contemporary American scene, they would not begrudge its golden opportunities for ushering in a better future for itself and for mankind. They might freely concede that other societies gave too much to too few and not nearly enough to too many. They might rejoice that this nation has already given more to instruct minds and to nourish bodies in larger numbers than any other country. For this reason alone, the American Republic deserves all its golden opportunities for enriching the lives of its citizens and educating them in varied ways of inspiring and serving the rest of mankind. But, in order to plan and prepare for the future, we must not shrink from calling things in the present by their proper names and learning all we can from the past. We must be deaf to the contemporary voice of America at least for awhile if we are to listen to earlier voices in American history, and learn from the highest cultures of antiquity and from the most primitive societies.

In an interview in *Il Contemporaneo,* Claude Lévi-Strauss contrasted "Western mechanical civilization" and "primitive" societies of preliterate peoples. He commented:

> Viewed in the light of ethnology, the difference between our Western, mechanical civilization and so-called primitive societies strikes me as being a little like the difference between the higher animals and viruses. As you know, a virus is a living organism only to a certain extent; it can move but it cannot reproduce itself outside a living cell, cannot on its own create an organism similar to itself. At bottom it is nothing but the possessor of a certain formula which it injects into living cells, thereby compelling them to reproduce themselves according to a particular model. Then what is a virus really? It is an extremely elementary organism—hardly an animal at all but the most elementary living thing we can conceive of. But without the other more complex animals it depends on, the virus could not exist.
>
> Our civilization seems to me to be a good deal like this since, as we learned with Descartes, its greatest discovery, its essential characteristic, that which constitutes its deepest being, is the fact that it is the possessor of a *method,* just as the virus is but the possessor of its own reproductive formula. We inoculate other cultures with this method in such a way as to force them not so much to perpetuate themselves as to reproduce the same formula, to duplicate the same method and to widen the scope of its application. . . .
>
> Ethnology postulates that an *optimum* of diversity must exist for humanity. If, as seems very likely, our civilization will soon extend over the whole of the inhabited world, then in the very midst of this civilization that would otherwise become monolithic there would reappear those small differentiations which are vital to humanity's existence and development. . . . We are living in an age—a very brief age—in which humanity is coming face to face with itself. . . .
>
> Basically the world of nature, which is the main protagonist in the mythology of "savage" peoples, is a world which we have refined and assimilated by scientific analyses and which therefore offers us nothing more on the mythological level. But for us there exists a world invulnerable to science—or at least to its state today—and that is the world of history, which means to us what nature meant to "primitive" peoples.
>
> In conclusion, I'd say that the myths of "primitive" peoples

> are more than anything else spatial myths. The great problems they pose are those of height and depth, of cardinal points, etc. For when they deal with time they are myths of regular periodicity: of day alternating with night, of season with season, and so on. Our myths, on the other hand, are almost entirely temporal; and they are myths of irreversible time. The central idea which runs through all our mythology is that time flows in one direction only and nothing can reverse its current.[3]

What is the relevance of this profound observation to the social structure of the future? A nation that prides itself on the conquest of nature and is uniquely free from the burden of history naturally looks forward to its future progress and need not sink backwards into the stagnating structures of the past. Is it possible to combine the methodological tools of a mechanistic civilization, sustained by the gospel of secular progress, with a cyclical view of time, a concern with organic solidarity, and a sense of cosmic order transcending a dynamic social structure? Isn't this like squaring the circle? Isn't this asking for the best of all possible worlds? Isn't this even more absurdly daring than expecting the GAI proposal to transform overnight a competitive society into a democratic utopia? The answer to such questions was attempted by a nineteenth-century American, the boldest social prophet of his time, a latter-day child of the Enlightenment and a student of ancient philosophies, a visionary whose chief work was a best-seller for decades, although he is strangely neglected at the time when he is most relevant. A renewed consideration of Edward Bellamy's conjectures is worthwhile, as his philosophical insights and sociological illusions are alike suggestive.

In his remarkable essay on "The Religion of Solidarity" (written at age twenty-four), in his unpublished manuscripts, and in several of his romantic stories Edward Bellamy gave intuitive expression to a philosophy and psychology of man that are worthy of study. His understanding of human nature, of the burden of guilt, the connection between the quality of motive and the degree of fulfillment in human action, and the tension between self-love and self-hate was profounder than that of the *philosophes* of the Enlighten-

3. "Exploring Lévi-Strauss," *Atlas,* vol. 11, no. 4, April 1966, pp. 245-46.

ment. His inversion of Calvinist theology and psychology enabled him to detach the moral appeal of Christianity from the Protestant ethic of capitalism. His view of man found place both for the *vita contemplativa* and the *vita activa* within a larger vision of human fulfillment than that of Marx or Freud. He understood what was overlooked by these titanic iconoclasts but known to the noblest and humblest of men–the divine discontent, the urge for self-transcendence (and not merely the desire for self-annihilation) in human nature. Bellamy saw a deeper restlessness in modern man, a frustration that is behind and beyond the partial truths embodied in the concepts of alienation and repression.

Looking Backward and *Equality* portray a vision of social transformation more daring than that of any modern reformer or utopian dreamer. It is truly more than a plan for social engineering or a program of political action, more than any picture of what society could be like if human nature was ideally different from what it is now. His conception of a future society was not based upon any single social criterion of human fulfillment–social justice, equality, communal welfare, individual freedom, or even human solidarity. He was concerned with all of these and much more because of his acceptance of the complexity, richness, and creativity of human nature, its capacity for self-expression as well as self-transcendence. He cared more for selfless romantic love, for human relationships, and for communion with nature than those modern thinkers who have socialism or anarchism or communism in their brains, but only anger (however righteous), resentment, meanness, pride, or even self-hatred in their hearts. He combined the compassion of English utopian socialists with the stress on a rational reorganization of society that characterized the French *philosophes* and also with the immense concern for individual freedom and human diversity of Constant and Mill. He was a prophet without anger, a thinker without disciples, a dreamer without lunacy, a poetic philanthropist. He was American to the core–adventurous, somewhat plebeian, charmingly naïve at times, an autodidact, forward-looking, a man who deeply cared about the practical realization of universal brotherhood. He was an American in a rather old-fashioned sense, understood by Crèvecoeur and the Founding Fathers: self-confident and generous, not desperately insecure.

The fatal limitation of Bellamy's vision was his blurring of the distinction between reason, in the classical sense, and rationality as a principle of organization; hence his heavy reliance on the machinery and bureaucracy of centralized authority, his emphasis on efficiency and formal regulation, and his belief that ethical criteria provide rules of reasonableness which could be properly applied and justly enforced by institutions. This nineteenth-century conception of public service could not foresee the stark political irrationality of the twentieth century. There is an unresolved gap between his philosophical insights into human nature, emphasizing willing self-transcendence as the key to self-actualization, and his sociological emphasis on external organization and formal regulation, on inducing cooperation in an industrial army, on the externalization of the hierarchical principle in a social system with economic equality and the ethic of solidarity. Even the elevated social norms of such a community can be challenged in terms of criteria of human fulfillment when embodied in a formally hierarchical structure, with a centralized authority empowered to enforce the ethic of solidarity. Despite the central flaw in his detailed picture of social organization (the flaw of most social theories since the Enlightenment), Bellamy has a unique relevance to the American social structure of the future. We can learn from Bellamy's distinctive concern with the correspondence of the social structure (through the universal provision of opportunities) to the spread of new norms which reflect a concept of human nature that seeks external expression as well as inward fulfillment. He sought to divest government of its glamour and reduce it to a service organization, making basic economic needs independent of competitive striving, so that work could become creative rather than burdensome, emulation might be directed toward non-material ends, and all persons find an inward freedom that reinforces social solidarity and also transcends it. His method was parapolitically sound, moving from criteria of human fulfillment to social principles and norms and then visualizing the limits and possibilities of the social structure and the institutional set-up. In one of his notebooks he wrote:

> My mind is not stratified as that of a practical man's should be, I mean, is not divided by horizontal floors; the floors of

> practice and theory, of phenomena and noumena, of physics and metaphysics, of material and psychical. Now your practical man never thinks of commingling these levels. But so it is not with me. The strata with me are like those disjoined commingled strata of rock that puzzle the geologists. . . . I am immensely practical in the sense that no abstract idea is any satisfaction to me till I have realized it concretely.[4]

III

If we are to exercise our imagination in regard to the social structure of the future, we must begin with a complete reversal or radical modification of several assumptions hitherto taken for granted. This will give some of the ruling principles—or rather what Coleridge called "saving principles"—in terms of which we could initiate major institutional changes. Our concern here is with the ruling principles rather than specific institutional changes. The former are more fundamental; while we need to be flexible and pragmatic regarding the latter, we need not rush in where even a Numa or Solon might fear to tread. The three most influential philosopher-legists of history, Plato, Manu, and Confucius, have been the victims of colossal theoretical misrepresentation and corrupt institutional misuse.

Frustration and fulfillment are relative terms. They are largely connected with the gap between expectations and their realization. A person could decrease the gap either by lowering the level of his expectations or his standards of achievement, or both. He could endure the gap by evading it—by deluding himself as to the extent of his achievements, or by becoming indifferent to past expectations or to present and future achievements. He could be humiliated or stirred by the fact of the gap, by his estimate of it at any given time, and by the constancy or growth of the gap. All this depends upon his self-image, his own conception of himself in relation to others, his level of self-awareness, his concern with self-actualization, and his capacity for self-expression and self-transcendance, as well as his powers of self-correction, his spatial and temporal perspective. As society is the mirror in which a man sees himself and

4. Arthur E. Morgan, *The Philosophy of Edward Bellamy,* New York, Kings Crown Press, 1945, p. 28.

as no man lives in a historical or cultural vacuum, the gap itself and the factors affecting it will all be affected by his social situation, his multiple roles, his occupation, his wealth and status, inherited, borrowed, and prevailing concepts of human nature, human excellence, success, and failure. The more he is affected by the factors within his power and determined by himself, the more of an individual a man is. The more varied, flexible, and changing a man's expectations and criteria of achievement, the richer he will be as a person, and the more capable of a variety of meaningful relationships with others. The more he is affected by external factors within his own society, the more he will be conditioned by it and the less capable of transcending it.

The wider a man's vision of human excellence, the greater his access to other cultures in time and in space, the more universal he will be. The less conditioned he is by his own society, the more of an individual he is likely to become. But, in every case, he cannot be indifferent to those around him and to the values and judgments of his own society without becoming anti-social and even anti-human. Social judgments, when reasonably just, must be somewhat relevant to him if he is not to become a total heretic or hermit and risk the danger of becoming egocentric and losing touch with reality (social and human). The more he can modify social values, the more he can maintain and incarnate them, the more heroic, iconoclastic, conservative, or exemplary will be his role as a member of his society. In a mature society (in which the proportion of "individuals" is high and increasing), a man will come to be judged more by the standards he sets himself than those external to him, though there must be some sort of optimal relation between his internal and external standards. Excellence in society is determined by a variety of factors, but it is both shaped by and exemplified in its heroes and saints, its philosophers, artists, and scientists, its craftsmen and innovators, its carriers of creative achievement as well as exemplars in the art of living. A society may be judged not only by its excellence but by the opportunities it affords all men and women to benefit from and to participate in its excellence, the conditions of work it provides, the area and freedom of individual choice, the mitigation of social inequalities, the measure of social sympathy, the peaceful resolution of disagreements, the tolerance of diversity, the treatment of nonconformity in rebels, eccentrics, deviants, and delinquents, the impact of its criteria of success and failure upon the strong and the weak, the restraints on its powerholders, the degree of participation of citizens in policy making, its reliance on persuasion rather than coercion, its stimulus to fulfillment, and its mitigation of the burden of frustration.

Given this very broad perspective, what ruling principles should govern the social structure of the future in a republic that has enacted the GAI proposal? First of all, we must re-examine the established relationships between division of labor, multiple roles, and social differentiation; occupational ranking, distribution of income, property, and power; social stratification, status seeking, and social mobility. Three sets of factors (*alpha, beta,* and *gamma*) determine the social structure through their interrelationship. The *alpha* factors are deeply embedded in the very notion of a complex society and are logically inseparable from the concept of an industrial society. The *beta* factors are institutionalized and self-sustaining (or self-perpetuating) unless modified by deliberate acts of policy and to some extent by private initiative and social interaction. It is possible to give a descriptive account of the *alpha* and *beta* factors. The *gamma* factors introduce a shift from the empirical to the evaluative, although empirical indices could be found for them. They are dependent upon the internalization of social norms and upon individual valuation of these norms, as well as of their external signs and practical consequences. There is no reason, in principle, why the *beta* factors should be seen as the necessary conditions for the maintenance of the *alpha* factors, still less as the sufficient conditions for the determination of the *gamma* factors. The *alpha* factors underline the fact of diversity in society, that individuals are different, do different things, and contribute differently to society. The *beta* factors indicate the inequality of conditions and opportunities available to different individuals. The *gamma* factors result in a more or less rigid, stronger or weaker, form of the hierarchical principle rooted in human tendencies toward externalization.

Durkheim, in his classic treatment of division of labor, pointed out that there exists in the mores of every society an imprecise notion of what the various social functions are worth, the relative remuneration due each of them, and consequently, the degree of comfort appropriate to the average worker in each occupation. The various functions are ranked by public opinion into a sort of hierarchy, and a certain coefficient of welfare is assigned to each according to the place it occupies in the hierarchy. There is, consequently, a set of implicit rules which sets the maximum standard of living each class of functionaries may legitimately seek to attain. The scale changes as the total social income grows or diminishes, and in accordance with the changes which occur in the mores of the society. Under the pressure of social norms, each person in his own orbit takes account in a general way of the extreme limit to which his ambitions may go and he aspires to nothing beyond it. If he respects the social ruling and submits to group authority, he is "well-adjusted" to his station in life and a limit is thus marked out for his desires and wants. He may try to embellish or improve his life, but these attempts may fail without leaving him despondent. The equilibrium of his happiness is stable because it is determinate. However, it would not be sufficient that anyone accept as equitable the hierarchy of functions implied by the mores if he did not also consider equally equitable the manner in which the individuals who are to perform these social functions are recruited. If each person began life with the same resources, if the competitive struggle were joined under conditions of equality, few would consider the results of this struggle unjust. The closer we approach that ideal equality, the less necessary would be social control. But this is only a question of degree as natural endowments are unequal.

Modern industrial societies have shown that the determination of the *gamma* factors by the *beta* factors is not as logical or satisfactory (in terms of equality, equity, and coercion) as Durkheim suggested. The *beta* factors, so far from being merely a secondary consequence of social differentiation, have assumed a primary role in determining the *gamma* factors and distorted the principle of human solidarity that is compatible with the *alpha* factors alone. We further tend to associate inequalities of social rank (a *gamma* factor) with people's income and occupational ranking (a *beta* factor). This correlation could be affected sufficiently by the GAI proposal (if several other things were done), so that the *beta* factors ceased to be the crucial link or intermediate agency between the *alpha* and the *gamma* factors. Furthermore, among the *beta* factors, the importance of occupational ranking as the determinant (through the market value of the required qualification) of the unequal distribution of income, prestige, and power could also be affected by the GAI. By undermining the importance of the *beta* factors (through social policies accompanying GAI, especially in relation to conditions of voluntary work, attitudes to work, and the social norms engendered by education), a revolutionary change could result in the social structure of the future. Social stratification is always a rank order in terms of prestige and not esteem, a rank order of positions which cannot be thought of independently of their individual incumbents. Social norms mediate between individual attitudes (partly governed by sanctions) and the inequality of social position, i.e., the degree of social stratification. The implications of the reversal or modification of these current attitudes will become clearer when we attend to other ruling principles.

The second reversal, or modification, of something we take for granted (in all societies, past and present) is just as revolutionary as the first, though it is less dependent on the GAI proposal as such. We customarily take for granted that human life must be seen as a succession of stages, corresponding to somewhat arbitrary divisions of physical growth and decay, marked by exclusive concentration on distinct activities–education, productivity, and retirement. Education is seen as the preparation for a vocation, especially in an industrial society with increasing specialization. In an action-oriented and success-obsessed culture, retirement is regarded as a state of uselessness, indolence, senility, and loneliness. The accent on youth makes the plight of the aged a generally intolerable and inhuman condition, made more pathetic by nostalgia and the pretense of rejuvenation. Second childhood is not a return to innocence but to that peculiar immaturity displayed by the physically and mentally aged when they pretend to be immature and sometimes make the pretense a reality to others and to themselves. The emphasis on productivity, and its identification with economic activity or some tedious labor, distorts the very meaning of education. It makes alienation less comprehensible to its victims by reducing their conception of their capacities, and by making the notion of leisure as an effortless, relaxed celebration of the highest human potentialities seem an effete or idle anachronism. No wonder there is no meaningful use of leisure but, on the contrary, a dread of solitude, while the emphasis on gregariousness perverts the concepts of play as well as of love and friendship.

The succession principle in regard to human activity was elevated to its highest form as an aid to fulfillment in a few cultures of antiquity. Its defense in modern society as given by Durkheim is questionable:

> Man is destined to fill a special function in the social organism, and, consequently, he must learn, in advance, how to play this role. . . . We do not, however, wish to imply, that it is necessary to rear a child prematurely for some certain profession, but that it is necessary to get him to like the idea of circumscribed tasks and limited horizons. . . .
>
> Why would a mere extensive activity, but more dispersed, be superior to a more concentrated but circumscribed activity? Why would there be more dignity in being complete and mediocre, rather than in living a more specialized but more intense life, particularly if it is thus possible for us to find what we have lost in this specialization, through our association with other beings who have what we lack and who complete us? We take off from the principle that man ought to realize his nature as man . . . as Aristotle said. . . . Among lower peoples the proper duty of man is to resemble his companions, to realize in himself all the traits of the collective type which are then confounded, much more than today, with the human type. But, in more advanced societies, his nature is, in part, to be an organ of society, and his proper duty consequently is to play his role as an organ. . . . To be a person is to be an autonomous source of action. Man acquires this quality only insofar as there is something in him which is his alone and which individualizes him. . . . Individual natures, while specializing, become more complex, and by that are in part freed from collective action and hereditary influences.[5]

Concentration is required by all activity, but is it only the result of specialization or of a separate discipline available to its posses-

5. *The Division of Labour in Society,* Glencoe, Illinois, The Free Press, 1949, pp. 403-44 *passim.*

sors at all times? Reciprocity between men is more effective when their minds are more rounded rather than too angular; the relations between men are not at all like those between the parts of a machine or of an organism. The social differentiation implicit in the *alpha* factors affects the concentration, distribution, and flexible direction of human energies through levels of articulation in a shared system of work. It is possible to rationalize both the coordination and diversification of effort and the general promotion of social order and growth within a theoretically isolated system and homogeneous environment. But however appropriate any entropic/anti-entropic social model may be within these theoretical limits, the logical priority of human nature to theories of human society restricts the universalization of the model. Human interdependence is logically different in kind from mechanical interconnectedness and only similar to organic interdependence analogically, not ontologically.

In place of the succession principle let us take the principle of simultaneity of pursuit of education, work, and leisure during the whole of a person's life in the new society. With the introduction of the GAI, work would become voluntary, training for and enjoyment of leisure a continuous activity based upon a philosophy of life-long education. There must, of course, be differences of emphasis in the kind of education or work or leisure activity and there may also be some flexibility in regard to the proportions of these three modes of activity (though ideally they should merge into each other) in successive biological periods of human life. Paradoxically, the simultaneity principle will better subserve one of Bellamy's philosophical insights than the succession principle, with which he combined it. The latter generates that false continuity through identification with the personal ego, rather than the individualizing self, which Bellamy was concerned to attack on epistemological and on ethical grounds. Bellamy drew important social corollaries from his view that the individual is a composite of many persons–the abandonment of the retributive theory of punishment (which is a welcome contemporary trend) and the danger of a man binding his future selves by pledges and engagements which he is in no position to take (this would be true of some pledges and not of others–a fruitful subject of inquiry).

Thirdly, theories of society, and the social structures implied or recommended by them, have tended to take for granted that there is in every individual man a limited quantum of energy, a finite potential, which must be distributed economically in different directions, possibly according to some marginal principle of diminishing returns (in terms of tangible rewards or psychic satisfactions), or according to some specific theory of balance and integration. This principle dies hard—it is logically connected with a closed view of human nature, which perceives man as an unchanging essence governed by known and knowable laws. This view of the finitude, scarcity, and fixity of human energy and potentiality, of the human being in relation to finite space and finite time, with an unalterably finite mind, is easily used to support the principle of specialization in economic and educational terms and rigid schemes of social differentiation. It makes more plausible the shift to social stratification and the need for a centralized authority responsible for the efficient and equitable allocation of functions. This theory was Aristotelian in origin and was reinforced by the sharp Judeo-Christian contrast between man and God. It was used by Hobbes to justify the subordination of the individual to the State, stated explicitly by the physiologist Bichat, powerfully influenced the social thought of Saint-Simon, and has been revived in the niggardly views of man of some contemporary psychologists. It also makes more plausible the collectivization of the concept of perfectibility, ascribed to the human species and denied to the individual (even in a Godwinian sense). This closed view of man is philosophically vulnerable. Its rejection in a society of abundance can also be justified on psychological, sociological, political, and even pragmatic grounds. It could become increasingly important in a largely automated society, which requires a continual redefinition of the concept of being human as opposed to a computer or machine.

Bichat's physiological doctrine of inequality penetrated the social thought of the nineteenth century and became part of a general conception of man and society. He constructed a trinary division—brain man, sensory man, and motor man—and his vitalist theory allowed for only a given quantum of energy in each individual. In each type one dominant faculty was capable of great development, while the other two were destined to remain feeble, and no person, with the rarest exceptions, could develop all three faculties equally. Men were born limited and physiologically restricted, and vital energy invariably tended to channel itself into one receptacle rather than the other two. This parsimonious, deterministic, and assured view of man has some plausibility; it is vaguely confirmed by common experience in that we do assume that human choice is needed between competing activities, that our time and energy are limited. But time means different things to different people. We have no reason to set advance limits to human creativity or to confine the term "energy" to a purely physical interpretation. William James, in *The Energies of Men,* emphasized that we all tend to use less than our potential energies, a point that is perhaps more meaningful to the American, who in turn possesses an energy that seems unbounded to the European. Even if we simply recognize that no man knows his potential amount of energy, however limited, or its quantitative measure in relation to all expended energies, we are entitled to base the structure of the future society on a rejection, if not reversal, of the static view of human energy, let alone arbitrary classifications of men and women into human types. The amount of energy in a person is at least partly a function of its use, as is confirmed by learning theory. The brain surgeon, Wilder Penfield, has shown that it is just as easy for a child to learn three or even four languages as one, provided they are spoken and taught in appropriate circumstances. The importance of this entire question is considerable in the social structure of the future, in which one of the traditional drives behind the egalitarian principle will be weakened (by the GAI) and in which élitist theories and the dominance of experts could do enormous harm.

Fourthly, a sacrosanct assumption in all social systems needs to be questioned–that it is always possible to find a correlation between individual worth and external criteria such as income, possessions, occupation, prestige, power, conformity to social norms, or conventional morality. We might define a Golden Age as that in which there is a perfect fit between the external role and the expected qualities or virtues of men in society, when kings were really kings, and hierophants and priests and seers and warriors and traders and peasants and all others conformed to the ideal images of their roles. Such a society is unknown to history and belongs to mythology. We have lived, for better or worse, for millennia in the Age of Zeus, in which there is no necessary correlation between role performance and ideal images, and in which there has been an enormous and increasing amount of role confusion. It has been tempting for the young to plunge to the opposite extreme and suggest that there is usually an inverse correlation between entitlement and possession of any position of power or responsibility, especially in the United States, with its conformist nominalism and pervasive abuse of names. This tends, however, to make for so much cynicism that it subverts social sympathy, let alone social solidarity. It is more important to hold that a mature society, like a mature man, will rely upon individual and freely given appreciation or due approval to individuals in different roles rather than upon superficial signs. Externalization is related to conformity rather than to solidarity; it limits the growth of individuality, as Durkheim saw. This modification of a generally held attitude could have several implications for the institutional framework in the social structure of the future. The fewer formal requirements and external honors in such a society, the greater the chance of evolving an ethic of responsibility, a climate of intrinsic values, and the emergence of social norms out of the willing if imperfect recognition by men of their peers and exemplars in a variety of subcultures. This also has a theoretical and practical implication for the emergence of a new type of non-official leadership, the encouragement of voluntary social and political schemes for reform, the devaluation of governmental authority, and the gradual discrediting of coercive methods of regulation.

Fifthly, we might consider the replacement of the simple, crudely competitive, and rather juvenile distinction between winners and losers by the idea that all men are givers and receivers in a variety of ways. Penalizing the winners and compensating the losers does not help to weaken the distinction between winners and losers, nor does an apotheosis of the losers promote community. All rules are inevitably arbitrary and will at any rate be viewed differently by the winners and losers. A rule-bound society will accentuate inequalities, however much equality of opportunity is achieved. As involuntary work gives way to a new concept of work, the classical and conventional religious view of work as a burden could be replaced by the attitude of enjoyment and positive fulfillment in work that emerged in the Renaissance. This is connected with the diminution of the importance attached to competitive and comparative assessments, except in relation to a flexible and ever-enriched view of excellence. The distinction between mature and immature will not disappear in the society of the future, but it may be hoped that the former will set the pace and increasingly hold the initiative, provided that the latter do not seek positions of political power to compensate for their sense of inferiority. It will be difficult to safeguard against this danger without increasing the role of the psychiatrist to a hazardous degree.

Sixthly, an overarching national ideology is no longer needed to maintain the social norms providing stability and continuity to a social structure. The social structure of the future must incorporate within itself the principle of transcendence if a truly free society is to emerge. This change is perhaps the most difficult to see at present, and will only come gradually, but it must come if the idea of a society of abundance is not to become intolerable in a world of misery. The loosening of national ties, consequent upon the dwindling of a national ideology, will be countered by the strengthened foundations of a new society, a community of communities, a confederation of subcultures. The terms "American" and "American Dream" could be redefined and also recover the inspiration attached to their original meanings. The American would be a person of universal culture, as Whitman expressed it, a "compassionater" and "encloser of all continents"–the continent of Humanity. The American Dream would refer to a vast social experiment and an example in practical brotherhood to all men and nations.

Seventhly, there might be appended the principle of synergy. Ruth Benedict distinguished between "high" synergy and "low" synergy in different societies:

> Is there any sociological condition which correlates with strong aggression and any that correlates with low aggression? All our ground plans achieve the one or the other in proportion as their social forms provide areas of mutual advantage and eliminate acts and goals that are at the expense

> of others in the group . . . societies where non-aggression is conspicuous have social orders in which the individual by the same act and at the same time serves his own advantage and that of the group. . . . Non-aggression occurs [in these societies] not because people are unselfish and put social obligations above personal desires, but because social arrangements make these two identical. . . . I shall speak of cultures with low synergy where the social structure provides for acts that are mutually opposed and counter-active, and of cultures with high synergy where it provides for acts which are mutually reinforcing.[6]

Bellamy would have approved of this principle, but there is something unsatisfactory in the idea that virtue pays and that the person who is selfish necessarily benefits other people. This smacks of an invisible hand, harmony of interests, and all that Keynes devastatingly attacked in *The End of Laissez-Faire.* The problem arises out of the notorious ambiguity of the notions of "interest" and "self-interest." But the principle of synergy, needed by the weak in every society, has a profound corollary. Secure, high-synergy societies tend to redistribute wealth equitably, whereas insecure, low-synergy cultures tend to illustrate the maxim that the rich get richer and the poor get poorer. Recognition of the principle of synergy could be the basis of benevolent programs of interchange of materials and personnel between the United States and the rest of the world, provided that "rich" and "poor" are understood in non-material as well as material senses, and that a new concept of voluntary limitation of wants among the maturer members of society emerges as a check against wasteful and conspicuous consumption. It would also involve a fundamental departure from the goal of accumulation of capital and its attendant market concept of scarcity. Keynes in the thirties foresaw a time when customs surrounding the distribution of income would be based on the good, not the useful, and the money-motive would be assessed at its true value, as distasteful and unjust. The social restructuring brought about through the GAI could precipitate this change in values much sooner than Keynes expected.

6. Ruth Benedict, "Synergy," *American Anthropologist,* vol. 72, no. 2, April 1970, pp. 325-26.

The social structure of the future could function on the basis of two sets of social norms, connected with two contrary conceptions of social and individual ethics. On the one hand, the authoritarian, subjectivist, and guilt-engendering theories of a non-naturalistic ethic could be replaced by one which translates the "good" into the vocabulary of mental and psychophysical "health," a Paracelsian view of wholeness and a post-Freudian view of "maturity" as developed by humanistic psychologists. This would enable us to view deviants and delinquents as candidates for compassionate therapy, while recognizing that even the most "mature" may need temporarily to go into retreats to sublimate, or to permissive places to work off their own deviant tendencies. On the other hand, a suprasocial or universally appealing ethic (in Bergson's sense) could evolve on the basis of the superogatory acts of courage and compassion of "heroic" and "saintly" individuals. In this ethic the "good" would be connected with a new concept of honor and chivalry and *noblesse oblige,* which could shame thoughtless individuals into an inward recognition of their neglected moral potentials.

IV

Given these ruling principles, how can we visualize the rules and institutions, the limits and possibilities of the society of the future? How could all of them be fused into a single vision of *Civitas Humana?* These are matters for continuing discussion and practical experimentation, but a critical connecting thread may be pointed out. Consider, for convenience, a distinction between *private* time, *communal* time, and *civic* time in the life of every citizen, corresponding to a similar division in regard to space (that would be the basis for ecological and urban-cum-rural planning), and a similar division in regard to education, work, and leisure. Civic time is what the citizen owes to the government in return for the GAI. Communal time would be divided between voluntary and creative work performed in voluntary professional associations, and leisure-time activities and discussions under the auspices of voluntary clubs and societies of various sorts. Private time would be devoted entirely to contemplative and creative tasks performed in solitude or in small families. There must be the maximum possible flexibility in the proportions of civic, communal, and private time at any point in the life of any citizen. Every person must contribute a minimal share of civic time during the early and middle periods of his or her life. Everyone must be encouraged to have some private time throughout his or her life and be offered a variety of incentives to give some communal time in the neighborhood as well as abroad. Educational facilities could be used during communal time, civic time wherever and whenever possible, and private time if desired. Those who wish to concentrate their energies, for a period, on civic or communal or private time must be allowed to do so, as far as possible. As a result, people would be free to augment their purchasing power (within broad limits determined partly by the supply and demand for goods and services, partly by the investment needs of the economy, and partly by the needs of foreign economies, as also by a ceiling to ensure social justice), their educational equipment, their chosen creative skills, their share of civic responsibilities, their leisure-time activities, their desire for privacy, and their services to their families.

All of this points to a degree of freedom and flexibility quite incompatible with the amount of control that we have come to regard as indispensable to social survival. But in practice our approximation to this model will depend upon the extent to which a substantial number of citizens balance their concern with individual claims to freedom against a willingness to consider the claim of the community upon them. Can even the organization of industry be dominated by the desire to serve, not the desire to be served? Psychologically, the desire to serve a community may be a late development, but the "instinct" to serve persons is as much rooted in the desire for self-expression as the instinct of self-preservation. The impulse to serve persons, first displayed in the family, could develop into the desire to serve a community. But even if the desire to serve is strong enough to dominate self-seeking, several questions arise. Will the free service of those engaged in industry allow sufficient freedom of choice to those who need their services? Will a bureaucracy of industrial organizations rule us for our good but without regard to our own conceptions of what is good? Clearly, we must envisage some control of industry by the persons served, by composite authorities representing both consumers and producers. On the other hand, a special virtue of the above model is its allowance of individual claims to develop in activities not needed by other individuals or communities.

The entire model rests upon the crucial psychological assumption that as citizens mature into individuals, the very process of individuation involves the growing recognition of the claims of other individuals and of communities as well as their concern with transcending themselves and the limits of society. In practice, this requires an emphasis upon the continuance of the family in the future, possibly in an altered form anticipated by present trends. The connection between this psychological assumption and an institution traditionally regarded as natural, but increasingly viewed as wholly social and dispensable, is simple. The strength of the model of the future society lies in the extent to which the principle of voluntariness is enthroned. But, as a great deal depends upon whether this principle will generate the desire to serve the community (to a greater degree than in an acquisitive society of scarcity), the family acquires a new and important role. To call it a natural institution is to stress not only that it fulfills biological needs, but also that a man does not choose his parents and relatives and that he has a psychological bond with his wife and children that is not severed by a formal forfeiture of that bond. As a social institution which need not be an iron cage, the family is an instrument of socialization which enables individuals to gain an awareness of others, and which helps them to choose their many voluntary relationships. This role acquires a new meaning when the economic function and the inescapable character of the family are undermined. But the continuance of the family will require that any distinction between the sexes (on the basis of childbearing and childrearing, apart from other criteria) be relevant to the allocation of private, civic, and communal time, just as the difference between children and adults, and other distinctions (in terms of physical and social handicaps) must also be given due consideration.

A crucial feature of the model is that communal time will be employed not only in creative work but also in informal associations. This is the immense opportunity made possible by the enormous increase in leisure consequent upon the enactment of the GAI. The arts of friendship, participation in new forms of folk activities and play activities, and of conversation and dialogue are casualties of the present industrial society. They are the lost arts which could be vital in the new society, giving it a richer way of life than is now known to Americans, helping to transform a mechanistic "utopia" into a high culture and a true civilization. The great ages of achievement in world history reflected a fortuitous clustering of creative individuals, a high degree of social and especially intellectual mobility, the confrontation and eventual fusion of diverse world-views and personal philosophies, the concentration of common energy on pervasive and transcending themes, the magical release of imagination from the ruts of conformity and effete tradition, the free flow of persons and ideas. The art of conversation requires that each member of a voluntary group be judged by his individual value and not as a member of a class or race or status group. As centers of extended conversation arise, the issues of deepest concern to men—the ultimate questions of life—can be explored with a degree of freedom that organizations with formal and partisan allegiances cannot allow—academic or political, vocational or religious.

In envisioning the social structure of the future, I have tentatively put forward several fundamental ruling or saving principles and suggested the merest hint of a possible model. The principles raise numerous questions of theoretical and practical importance which need to be considered carefully before concrete institutional possibilities could be elaborated. The embryonic outlines of the future social system have been couched in relatively abstract terms so that the logic of one possible model, embodying several unorthodox principles, could be intimated. Many gaps remain, many questions are unanswerable. The vision is utopian. It never has been, it never will be, and it is not intended to be a concrete reality. In the course of pursuing utopias, the dreams of men did not materialize but something materialized which was the consequence of the dreams taking the forms that they did. Only small-minded persons have imagined that the dreams and visions of men and women necessarily turn into nightmares. The consequences of utopias cannot be conclusively established as there is no way of knowing the gap in awareness between those who entertain utopias and those who try to translate them. Idle dreams like those of Gonzalo in *The Tempest* merely reflect the goodness of heart, the childhood longings of the Gonzalos of this world, and may their tribe increase! The prophetic visions of hope represent the triumph of hope over experience. They recognize the forgotten truth in the exclamation of Miranda, "O brave new world, That has such people in it!" These words show nothing less than an act of faith in man, not in societies, still less in institutions.

We have glimpsed the broad outlines of a parapolitical vision of the City of Man of the future. If the suggested model is elaborated, the crucial question will be the relation between the private, communal, and civic sectors. In terms of the premises (some unstated) underlying the model, the communal sector has the highest visible priority, the private sector is causally and invisibly the most important, and the civic sector must wither away in its glamour. In a deeper sense, it is incompatible with the ruling principles of the model to talk in terms of sectors except for convenience. In practice, the major problem of the new society, which must grow out of an unregenerate past, is likely to be in relation to the civic sector. If future rulers are even more unwise than the rulers of our time, this examination will stand as an ineffectual but nonetheless verifiable warning against the danger of subordinating the private and communal sectors to the civic sector while pretending to do the opposite. Present trends suggest that the deception of the people will be increasingly difficult to maintain in the future. As the sense of individual dignity and power of choice strengthens, there will be an augmentation of the force with which self-chosen values are directed against existing structural patterns that frustrate individuals. Many of the institutions of mass society have begun to suffer from the first symptoms of a process of creeping paralysis. There is a loss of stimulus and a failure of response. Neurasthenia has set in, and increasingly energetic minds and stout hearts must turn elsewhere for sustenance and inspiration. It is becoming difficult to fool most people much of the time. If future rulers are no more unwise than at present, they will see the need for a new balance between the private, communal, and civic sectors. But if any society is fortunate to find future rulers wiser than before, they might allow the civic sector less and less priority than the communal and private sectors while appearing to do the opposite or, better still, to do nothing.

The inquisitive might wish to know more about the unstated premises. The answer to such was given by Goethe's Faust:

> Who may dare
> To name things by their real names? The few
> Who did know something, and were weak enough
> To expose their hearts unguarded–to expose
> Their views and feelings to the eyes of men,
> They have been nailed to crosses–thrown to flame.[7]

But this need apply only to the unstatable premises. Several of the unstated premises were articulated a long time ago, and are shrouded in the myths and mists of antiquity, notably in Plato's story in *Protagoras.* In their concern for the preservation of the species of human beings, the gods charged Prometheus and Epimetheus with the task of equipping them and allotting suitable powers to each. Epimetheus begged Prometheus to allow him to make the distribution himself, and he acted on a principle of compensation, being careful by various devices that no species should be destroyed. As Epimetheus was not particularly clever, the task eventually fell to Prometheus, who stole from Hephaestus and Athena the gift of skill in the arts, together with fire (for without fire it was impossible for anyone to possess or use this skill). With these stolen gifts men could survive, but had no political wisdom. Prometheus, therefore, gave to man Hephaestus' art of working with fire, and the art of Athena as well. But as men still lacked the political wisdom to live in communities without injuring one another, Zeus sent Hermes, imparting the qualities of mutual respect and a sense of justice, so as to bring order into cities and create bonds of friendship and union. The gifts of Hermes were distributed to all and not only to a few. What Protagoras omitted to mention was the greatest of all gifts–it was not given and it could not be stolen, but only won by secret striving–the gift of Orpheus. If with Epimethean hindsight and Promethean foresight, we could prepare for the societies of the future, in which the gifts of Hephaestus, Athena, and Hermes are wisely used, Orpheus may well appear again on earth.

7. *Goethe's Faust,* trans. John Anster, New York, Barse and Hopkins, 1894, p. 49.

17
EX CHAOS COSMOPOLIS

If the capacity for Intelligence is common to men, so too is the faculty of Reason, by virtue of which we are rational beings. If that be so, then that part of reason—the practical reason—which tells us what to do and what not to do, is also common. If that be so, so too is Law. If Law is common, we are all fellow citizens; and if that be so, the cosmos is, as it were, one State or city. What other political community is there in which all mankind can be said to share jointly? This is the source—this State or city common to all men from which we draw the capacity of Intelligence, the faculty of Reason, and the gift of Law. MARCUS AURELIUS

All individuals and associations must strive to secure a balance between uniqueness and universality, some abiding basis of union beyond the limitations and differences of finite and transient particulars, if they are to serve any future world community. In classical conceptions of the cosmos, every particle of matter is a manifestation of spirit, unique within its context. In an ever-changing universe, every particle is moved continually in a ceaselessly shifting spatio-temporal context. The continuity that underlies a series of shifting positions of uniqueness represents the universality of motion that enlivens every particle of matter. Duality characterizes all manifestation, the result of the coexistence and cooperation of ideation and image, force and form, spirit and matter, intention and result. Without a universal basis, uniqueness of expression would be impossible to attain; without the latter, the former would be abstract and unrealized. In human society, more a chaos than a cosmos, affirmations of uniqueness and of universality are alike artificial. Genuine cooperation and conscious interdependence can only be founded upon a parapolitical basis of union that binds seemingly independent and imperfectly unique entities in a manner that unearths the universality which ultimately underlies them all, as a fact of nature rather than a result of artifice. Whatever our aims and purposes we cannot dispense with associations in human society. Most associations, however, are at best partial brotherhoods, fraternal in name rather than in fact, and precariously held together by limited and temporary loyalties. Unique claims may be made for their members by virtue of their formal allegiance, but exclusive and extravagant ascriptions generate counteracting currents of opposition, even hostility, from other associations. The centrifugal and centripetal forces of ideological conflict alternately assert themselves in an unending search for homeostatic equilibrium. This familiar phenomenon, competitive and conflict creating, is elevated in sectarian religion to the status of righteous rivalry, and in partisan politics to the level of legitimacy regarded as essential to the political dialogue of a liberal democracy, which in practice is no more than a demagogic oligarchy. The sun of Truth is obscured by the misty revelations of ideology.

The problem is most acute on the global political scene, dominated as it is by the politics of power, stability, and self-preservation. It arises in the relation of a parapolitical world order to its materialization on the visible plane–the connection between the cosmopolis which is metaphysical and mythic, existing already for some though utterly irrelevant for others, and some kind of megalopolis which many would like to see emerge in the realm of political institutions. It is connected with the problem of identity for individuals in all cultures regardless of sex, age, and race, and it is involved in all the feuds of our time–those tensions which cannot be resolved vicariously for the many by a few, however gifted or generous they may be as leaders of thought and opinion. It cannot be resolved for the laity by popes or bishops, swamis or lamas, for it pulsates at the very core of every human being. We face it collectively, in all walks of life, as the problem of organization. Historically, where the most ardent movements emerged in the name of the greatest ideals we find the most hideous nightmares, long shadows cast by large causes, as in the aftermath of the eighteenth century or the syncretist movements in the nineteenth, often succeeded by bizarre forms of separatism. To speak of unity and universality, and to speak more often than one means it or more than it is possible to mean it, is to tempt the adversary in every man and in collective humanity, and to invite more division and disorder. This is an ancient story, which may well explain why some of the most diligent students of the latter-day and overwritten history of the world came to grim and pessimistic conclusions. For Gibbon, history is a story of crimes, follies, and misfortunes; for Hegel, the only lesson men seem to learn from history is that they learn nothing from it.

World politics today is a foul tissue of tragic contradictions, a chaos partly inherited from the past and worsened by the present. This chaos is both obscured by and reflected in the ideological double-talk of all nations and the ineffectual, escapist utopianism of sectarian or millennial solutions. Nation-states with historical inheritances that have resulted in self-perpetuating inequalities of size, power, status, and material welfare compete in a medley of mounting suspicion, fear, prejudice, and hostility. Facts and feelings equally militate against the minimal consensus needed for a world security system, for genuine and effective coexistence, let alone for constructive cooperation toward common needs and common interests. Big Powers and smaller nations are alike unable, separately, jointly, or in any possible combination, to take the first vital step toward world-wide military, economic, or social security, to evolve a feasible philosophy of coexistence, or even to agree on the rules of the game of international politics and on rule-changing procedures. No government today is willing or able to push the existing state of affairs in the direction of any of the goals agreed upon formally in the U.N. Charter. Which national leaders can successfully take the initiative in a frank exchange of views about the central issues that obstruct even the exploration of a workable consensus of collective if limited agreement? The balance of terror limits the ambitions of the two greatest Powers, but also reinforces the parity of distrust that prevents any positive proposal for safety. For a variety of different but familiar reasons, the same atrophy of will is found in Western Europe and among the many non-aligned nations of the developing world. While it was once tempting to treat the emerging Colossus of the Far East as *the* villainous enemy of world order, this is singularly implausible at a time when China faces internal threats to national order and remains psychologically isolated from an international system which delayed so long in including her in its forum.

It is patently clear, without assigning praise or blame, that the nation-states of the globe are bereft not only of any common concept of world order but also of a clear, consistent view of national interest that could apply to anything beyond the contingency of the moment or a perilously short-term time-scale. Yet, paradoxically, it would be false to assert that the national governments of member-states of the United Nations are so irrational or immoral that they do not see and accept the logic of their allegiance to the U.N. Charter. Insofar as its precarious existence represents a minimal identification of long-term national interests with the collective interest of mankind in survival and the prevention of total war, the member-states are imprisoned in a cage of contradictions between the potential morality of abstract principles and the actual conduct made possible by the absence of any of the instruments of effective world community. More specifically, the member-states are implicitly committed to at least a half-hearted recognition of three principles of considerable significance, which help to identify the gap between theory and practice.

There is, first of all, the principle of universal community of interest in physical survival and collective self-preservation. This principle, imperfectly embodied in the Security Council, is ignored except when seriously threatened by brinkmanship, the escalation of conflict to a point of visible common danger. This danger is endemic in world politics today because there is no check to the pretensions of a Big Power, should it adopt policies of military intervention in the name of global goals. Similarly, the members of the U.N. have come to accept–with varying degrees of reluctance and responsibility–the principle of minimal equality of status embodied in the General Assembly, an equality of rights and duties implicit in the Charter, irrespective of wealth, power, or race. This theoretical abstraction is practically inoperative for two reasons. It is contradicted by glaring and irremovable inequalities between Big Powers and small nations, between nuclear and non-nuclear powers, between the "haves" and "have-nots," between the "ex-haves" and "haves," and between the "ex-haves" and "have-nots." There is, further, the seemingly irreconcilable conflict of ideologies in a world increasingly fragmented by contradictory policies based on incompatible conceptions of the nature of world order and by competing demands for the reallocation of world resources. The internal pressures of the prosperous democracies resist the global demand for equalization, undermining any feasible hope for universal liberty and fraternity. The contradiction between the principle of minimal egalitarianism and the fact of growing inequalities results at best in a form of brokerage politics, reflected in the tedious rhetoric of confrontation in U.N. debates and the more insidious pursuits of bilateral bargaining with its tactics of intimidation and subtle blackmail. Such stratagems easily degenerate into abject power politics, a concatenation of coercion and fraud which is peculiarly repugnant as the stakes are often higher in the international context than within the nation-states and the participants are even less representative of the peoples on whose behalf they pretend to speak and act.

Thirdly, the emergence of an inchoate but increasingly vocal body of world opinion has crystallized the principle (implicit in the Charter) that no nation can live, or lay down the law, unto itself or be the judge and arbiter of its own conduct in international affairs, and in internal matters of international importance. It has received elaboration in President Carter's statement that no U.N. member-nation can claim that mistreatment of its citizens is solely its own business. But this principle is invoked by all nations when their interests are not in conflict with it, and is ignored with impunity whenever their short-term national interests or ideological posture requires. All too often the principle is invoked merely to express pious sentiments or to throw a veil over activities that violate the principle. Some would argue that the contradiction here is so embedded in a system of nation-states and the absence of effective world authorities that the principle is non-existent. That it does exist, even in the realm of ineffectual judgment, is shown by the need and concern of all nations to manipulate world opinion in their favor. There is also the confirmatory evidence of the frightening self-righteousness with which nations seek to identify their partisan or sectional interests with the collective good of a non-existent world community. Every nation–even if it might once have claimed to be a custodian of world peace–has blotted its copybook enough to relinquish a credible role as the champion of the world community of the future. At the same time, every nation protects its self-image in world affairs by identifying the concrete ways in which the Enemy–whether communism (Soviet or Chinese), Yankee imperialism, neo-colonialism, nationalism, or racialism (black or white, brown or yellow)–is the root evil, the supreme obstacle to world security and peace.

More neutrally, the threat to the processing of demands, and the question of where support is to be given, which arises in all complex organizations with no clearly authoritative agencies, is critically acute in the global system of world politics. Yet the contradictions inherent in world politics present a challenging problem of theory and practice precisely because there are elements of a visible if frustrated sense of world community, although these elements are glaringly inadequate to support rationalist schemes of a grandiose megalopolis. The development of any institutionalized world order presents enormous difficulties–primarily the resolution of the relationship between the still current concept of State sovereignty and the still begging concept of international law; the determination of a balance between fixed normative rules and authoritative processes of decision making in international law; the development of a basic concept of international solidarity, and international standards of right and wrong specifiable in legal and moral discourse; and the radical rethinking of the internal and external relations of States, their mutual impact upon each other, and the significance of their relative positions of power. Once any progress is made in these directions, it would be possible through the integrative use of geography, geopolitics, economics, ecology, social technology, and political theory to begin to consider feasible architectonic modes of institutionalized international cooperation and new devices for the formal consolidation of world peace in a future megalopolis. This is difficult even to imagine at present.

Nonetheless, the current vague intimations of a sense of world community may possibly be sufficient to provide the bare minimum of an embryonic cosmopolis or *Civitas Humana*. In the global system of world politics today, there are at least some limits on interaction; conduct is neither law-like nor lawless insofar as it is affected by some rules and the inertia of expectations. While articulated and enforceable principles of international law are absent, chaos is moderated by the procedures and customs of diplomacy, randomness is countered by perceived interest, and irresponsibility is inhibited by real and imaginary fears. At the same time, the level of support given to the status quo is critically low; so too is the expectation that it will persist. The crucial variable in the present global system, chaotic and unstable as it may be, is the minimal willingness and ability of the members of the system to maintain it, even if only so that they may continue to form shifting alliances for partisan purposes. There are norms and commitments of some sort, but they may be backed only by military force, economic power, and short-term interest, and they are unreliable brakes on conduct whenever the emotional temperature falls below or rises above the floor of calculation and the ceiling of explosive irrationality. These are features peculiar to a *de facto* system of anarchy composed of members in some sense sovereign. It is anarchical in that there are no central authorities that can be identified, no rules that can be universally and impartially enforced, no allocations of resources that can be turned to global advantage, and no firm guarantees for the territorial integrity or effective independence of national groupings.

The embryonic world community exists already–all nations share a common political fate–but it provides no practical hope of becoming, in the near future, an actual world polity sharing a common and integrated political structure. Regardless of the inherited dissimilarities of traditional religious and secular beliefs and values, or of socio-economic status, nationality, and national power, we may discern the silent members of the invisible world political community. There is an increasing awareness among individuals (among scientists and artists, civil servants, businessmen, and even some politicians, and especially among the disinherited youth) that an invisible but tangible parapolitical community is coming into being. This awareness may well be heightened under the growing pressure of influences for transformation working upon the system of interdependent nation-states. At the least, we have more cosmopolitans in the negative sense in which some of the Cynics and the Stoics spoke of the cosmopolis, men and women with weaker roots in national tradition, more fragile loyalties to national ideologies, alienated from their own impersonal societies, with less hostility if not greater empathy for people abroad. Though few would, like Crates, choose obscurity and penury as their country, there is an undeniable appeal in the self-sufficient Cynic cosmopolitan spirit he expresses:

> No single native tower or roof for me:
> The citadel and house of the whole earth
> Stands ready for us as our dwelling-place.

Despite the fact that "utopia" originally meant "no place," men have nurtured dreams of ideal societies and attached them to particular places. They have desired concrete embodiments of abstract visions and often become deceived by their own creations. This is a perennial temptation. Utopianism becomes a bad word because men with creative imagination become prisoners of the images of their ideal, and expect others to applaud their concretized versions of it. To arrive at a true cosmopolis is even more utopian than to launch a localized utopia. Warren Wagar delineates this tension between utopia, which is presumed to satisfy the desire for creative comfort when achieved, and cosmopolis, which involves a self-surpassing search for the widest community in thought and feeling.[1] According to the French poet Lamartine, "The ideal is only truth at a distance." Without a critical distance from the ideal in our contemplation, we lose it. Thereafter, men mislead others in relation to the ideal, because real and ideal are dialectically equivalent. The dialectic enables us ceaselessly to convert the one into its antithesis.

The less adventurous face a bewildering and intractable problem. We seek a deeper sense of world community at the very time when there is a diminishing sense of community among the nation-states that confront each other in the chaotic arena of world politics. This paradoxical situation is somewhat reminiscent of the period when, owing to the identification of the political sphere with the entire known world, the Hellenes were confronted with the politi-

1. W. Warren Wagar, *City of Man*, Baltimore, Maryland, Penguin Books, 1963, pp. 14-17.

cal inadequacy of any mere integration of the individual with the city-state. Whereas the nation-state today is less and less of a polis in any meaningful sense, the forums and modes of international communication cannot enable a metaphysical, metaphorical, or embryonic cosmopolis to materialize into an actual megalopolis. This is *par excellence* the parapolitical problem of theory and practice which confronts us poignantly in all politics–personal or local, national or continental, and now global. No one expects a universally acceptable answer, but, if there is a dialectical as opposed to a static solution to the problem, where is it to be found, in the Platonic dialectic of transcendence, of ascent and descent, *or* in the Hegelian dialectic of reason–a direct correlation between extending self-consciousness and intensified political integration, a linear extrapolation from the course of recorded history? If the latter, there remains the considerable difficulty of connecting supposedly value-free assessments of history and nature with the conclusion that such scientific judgments are the sole basis for problem solving, while at the same time avoiding a hopeless confusion of rhetorical persuasion with moral exhortation in policy making. Or do we need a Marxist dialectic of revolution–a concept of world revolution at the perfect moment of ripeness coincident with the dissolution of the pseudo-political realm of disguised class interests? And if so, do we invoke the milder version which is compatible with minimally peaceful and militantly competitive coexistence, corresponding to the Leninist notion of the State as the spurious adjudicator which enables the conflict to continue until the righteous side is ready to take over? Or are time and history on the side of the Trotskyite-Maoist doctrine of a permanent world revolution, even in a thermonuclear age when international institutions are not only irrelevant but doomed until the defiantly meek shall inherit the earth? In either case, it is an open question whether Marxist philosophy must defer its own integrity until the establishment of a world communist state. Is there some super-dialectic which can reconcile all alternatives, or do we abandon the dialectical mode for the traditional sort of Augustinian tension affecting the parapolitical realm of world community and the temporal realm of nationalist politics, *Civitas Humana* and *Civitas Terrena?*

Practically, should we work within or without the System? The answer is, no doubt, that we should do both, but even more, that we should act in areas of creative initiative in which the System is neither a positive nor negative frame of reference, but necessarily ineffectual and irrelevant. It is not enough merely to see through some particular linear extrapolation of the chauvinistic history of the past centuries, whose very relevance to the future of the nation-state is questionable, whether elaborated in terms of sovereignty or economic power. We have grown so accustomed to a Weberian analysis that we tend to ignore any alternative. The modern centralization of state-power and national citizenship gave a new meaning to the post-Renaissance notion that society and government are partly interdependent and partly autonomous spheres of social life. There was a historical tension in Western Europe between the forces making for social solidarity independently of government and the forces accounting for the continuous exercise of central authority in the national political community. The high cost of this tension was the diminished solidarity of all "secondary" groups, the emergence of a minimal consensus with such an impersonal quality that it cannot satisfy the persistent craving for fraternity or fellow feeling, the degeneracy of the idea of participation to a purely formal notion, and also fortunately a replacement of parochial obsession in the struggle over the distribution of national product and hence over the policies guiding the administration of centralized governmental functions.

In *Ancient Law,* Sir Henry Maine underlines the illusory nature of territorial states:

> The idea that a number of persons should exercise political rights in common simply because they happen to live within the same topographic limits was utterly strange and monstrous to primitive antiquity. The expedient which in those times commanded favour was that the incoming population should *feign themselves* to be descended from the same stock as the people on whom they were engrafted; and it is precisely the good faith of this fiction, and the closeness with which it seemed to imitate reality, that we cannot now hope to understand. . . . But though all this seems to me to be established with reference to the communities with whose records we are acquainted, the remainder of their history sustains the position before laid down as to the essentially transient and terminable influence of the most powerful Legal Fictions. . . .

> States ceased to recruit themselves by fictitious extensions of consanguinity.[2]

If this contains some core of truth, it has implications for resolving the chaotic forces of explosive politics in an embryonic world community or cosmopolis. We must discover at all levels, but increasingly on a global scale, means of reflecting, representing, and reinforcing the latent social solidarity of the cosmopolis, even before the emergence of centralized authority in existing international institutions, and long before the birth of the minimal structure of a megalopolis (see Figure 4).

Displacing the realism of the Cynics in regard to the pseudo-politics of declining and warring city-states, the Stoics (as well as Skeptics and Epicurians) forged their diverse concepts of the cosmopolis–the polis of the universe, the city of the world. In time it would be called *Civitas Dei* but for these men was *Civitas Humana.* Its antecedents can be traced in the Heraclitean notion that men are united by reason amidst the divisions, diversity, and complexity of the world. An additional dimension emerged in the Socratic idea that men are integrated with each other vertically in their degrees of wisdom, and horizontally through their temporal kinships. In the Panhellenism of Isocrates this hierarchical element was understood in terms of degrees of internal possession of *logos* which could be increased by education (*paideia*) and by the concerned attention of guardians (*epimelia*). Further, since all men were equally helpless before fate, they also bore bonds of sympathy (*philanthropia*) and compassion (*eleos*) toward each other. These ideas coalesced in the detached political vision of the Stoics. For Zeno of Citium, the political ideal crystallized into the portrait of a society based upon wisdom and inhabited by the wise, not a concrete polis but a mental habitation where *sophos,* or inner self-sufficiency, and *ataraxia,* freedom from anxiety, reigned in a Golden Age. This city was the universe and its free men included all truly rational beings–the sages on earth and the stars in heaven. Kropotkin considered Zeno the finest exponent of philosophical anarchism in ancient Greece:

> He repudiated the omnipotence of the State, its intervention and regimentation, and proclaimed the sovereignty of

2. Henry Maine, *Ancient Law,* London, J. Murray, 1905, p. 195.

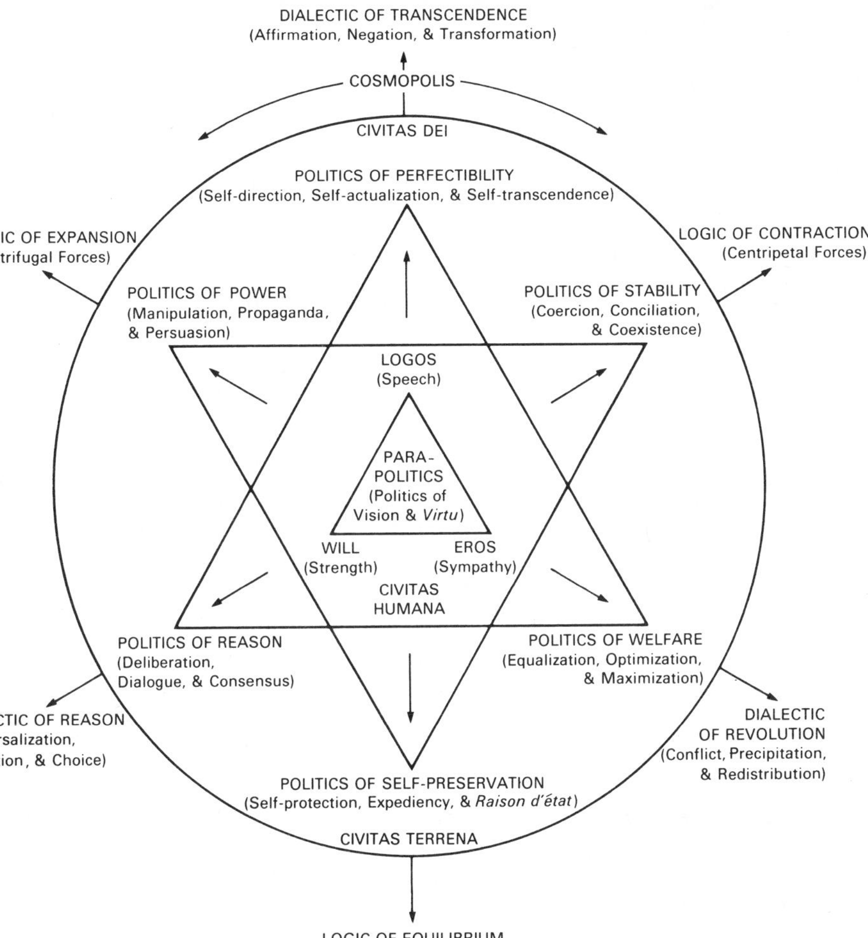

Figure 4. Parapolitics and *Civitas Humana*

> the moral law of the individual–remarking already that, while the necessary instinct of self-preservation leads men to egotism, nature has supplied a corrective to it by providing man with another instinct–that of sociability. When men are reasonable enough to follow their natural instincts, they will unite across the frontiers and constitute the *Cosmos*. They will have no need of law-courts or police, will have no temples and no public worship, and use no money–free gifts taking the place of exchanges.[3]

The translation of this parapolitical conception into temporal affairs followed several lines of influence: only a monarch had authority over a variety of city-states; cosmopolitanism itself indicated a world-state; all men had duties to their fellow men and the duty of the citizen was to work for the common good; since the order of the cosmos was universal reason, true law was a natural law arising from the nature of man *qua* man; the sovereign was the exponent of reason and law, and therefore ruled to benefit the whole. Cicero elaborated this conception of natural law to include the social importance of speech and reason in bringing individuals together in a natural fellowship by means of communication, teaching and learning, discussion and decision making. Antiochus saw the bonds of friendship exfoliating from the family in ever-widening circles until they eventually encompassed even the gods. Later classical expositions of the cosmopolitan ideal ranged from the mystical universalism of Marcus Aurelius through Philo's realistic doctrine of dual citizenship under Two States, to the emphasis of Epictetus upon disinterestedness in the public pursuit of transcendent ends. The Stoics saw man as a micropolis and the polis as a microcosm. Historically, these ideas exercised considerable influence before being deformed by the Augustan compromise between the city-state and the human requirements of a world community. Mason Hammond points to the contemporary relevance of this event:

> The lesson which the ultimate failure of classical civilization in its phase of a world state teaches is that stagnation is inevitable when orthodox political theory fails to progress in

3. *Encyclopaedia Britannica,* 11th ed., vol. I, Cambridge, Cambridge University Press, 1910, p. 915.

> response to changed political conditions. Today national sovereignty dominates political thought as firmly as did the orthodox theory of the city-state with its mixed constitution in the classical world. Only in so far as individuals throughout the world are able to conceive of a citizenship and of political participation on a scale larger than the nation will the "one world" . . . be realized in any fruitful sense. The alternative is that presented by the Roman Empire—a government imposed from above and divorced from the governed. Such a government has historically meant, in Toynbee's terms, stagnation and the decay of civilization.[4]

The emerging cosmopolis is best seen as a challenge to individuals and to non-governmental associations rather than to nations. The Californian poet, Edwin Markham, declared decades ago:

> He drew a circle round him thrice
> "Heretic, rebel, a thing to flout"—he said
> But love and I had the wit to win
> We drew a larger circle and took him in.

Love as well as wit could win the battle between future and past, between the contradictions of international politics and the context provided by the emerging cosmopolis—the love of humanity cannot forever remain in the abstract. It must become a concrete love of persons, involving thoughtful consideration of others, interest in their growth and welfare, and sufficient self-confidence to identify meaningfully with the unhappiness and anxieties of the less secure who crowd the cities of the world. Perhaps we can already witness small portents of the shape of things to come. Indications are positive at present and promising for the future. People of compassion and charity around the world intuitively understand authentic affirmations of fundamental universal propositions. A Yevtushenko could understand and celebrate a Martin Luther King more ardently than most Americans could. It is possible for men in distant places to identify with those rare harbingers of the authentic language of the human race. Many young people for a variety of reasons are afraid to be joiners. Some are seekers, perhaps needing

4. Mason Hammond, *City-State and World State in Greek and Roman Political Theory until Augustus,* London, Biblo and Tannen, 1966, p. 165.

more help than they know. The universal will not limit the capacity to communicate with or reach out to anything outside. The parapolitical revolution (though not equally visible everywhere) envelops the whole world. But what is distinctive to this revolution, which has been gaining momentum every year since the war? As is readily recognizable in the antinomian atmosphere of California, it is not merely intellectual, as was the European Enlightenment of the eighteenth century; nor is it a revolution in the structure of institutions, as in France, the U.S.S.R., or China. Nor is it a revolution in human nature as such, though in many countries there is an evident crisis of credibility, a lack of faith in cultures and philosophies as well as in leadership. In this situation, it is natural for people to react passively to circumstances, compounding the prevailing confusion instead of acting creatively. We need an adjustment on the part of each person in every given situation of the critical distance between the human agent and the limited structures, systems, and ideologies, which he handles as instruments of his human purpose. This readjustment is the contemporary revolution.

Charles Birch, the biologist, has summarized the fourfold chaos experienced by individuals around the globe and most intensely in America:

> 1. Our inner chaos: the inability to live in harmony with oneself, to accept oneself, to discover one's identity, and to let body, feelings, and thought dwell together in friendship.
> 2. Our social chaos: the lack of relatedness to others, the inability to live in harmony with others. . . .
> 3. Our environmental chaos: the green and varied landscape in which man evolved is swiftly being replaced by a polluted wilderness of concrete and steel; not only has this man-created environment produced physical ills but it seems also to be accentuating psychological disease and lack of rapport with our surroundings. . . .
> 4. Our metaphysical chaos: the sense of separation from the "whole scheme of things." . . . [5]

5. Charles H. Birch, "Purpose in the Universe: A Search for Wholeness," *Zygon,* vol. 6, no. 1, March 1971, pp. 4-5.

The hidden promise in the current chaos echoes an old parable. In Plato's *Symposium,* wherever Poros (Plenty, Resource) goes to visit, it is not long before Penia (Need, Lack) comes begging at the door. In the modern context the abundance of Poros is material, whereas the emptiness of Penia is psychological and existential. Poros is intoxicated (perhaps on the wine of Western technological progress), and Penia designs to get a child by him. Their child is Love, who stands midway between lack and plenty, between ignorance and wisdom. Those who stand in this position today have a stake in the cross-pollenization of world politics. Many young people, in America and elsewhere, have shaken off their inherited cultures as backward-looking and have adopted and adapted elements of other philosophies and cultures whose beauty they intuitively understand. They enjoy the freedom and the dignity of making a selection, perhaps erring in that selection, and thence learning from their own mistakes. The age of textual scholarship has been relinquished. The spirit breathing through the great Eastern classics has begun to permeate in the West. Old barriers are rapidly falling everywhere, and the partnership of freedom of thinking and experiment in action casts the pattern of current revolution into clearer focus. Old social structures cannot contain a new fraternal spirit without bursting. The rigidity of institutions has to be dissolved, and this can only be accomplished through inner transformation by informal groups of individuals. Self-definition becomes the key to greater universality. We can test it in terms of our capacity to come closer to, communicate with, and become credible to, more and more human beings wherever they be, whatever their language, their upbringing, or their external labors or labels.

Freedom and flexibility must become powerful allies. This does not happen automatically, but we may strive to realize our individual place within the broader framework of mankind and nature, gradually reaching upward and inward until we can grasp the nature of our duty and destiny. We can begin to instantiate the parapolitical conception of citizenship expressed by Epictetus:

> You are a citizen of the universe (*polites tou kosmou*) and a part thereof, and a part too, which is primary and not [like the animals] auxiliary; for you can understand that it is di-

> vinely governed and you can reason out the results of its being so governed. What, then, is the service to which such a citizen is summoned? It is to take no thought of his own private interest, and never to think and plan as an isolated unit, but to act as a hand or a foot would act if they had reason and could understand the material constitution of the body, and were moved by no impulse or appetite which had no reference to the good of the whole.[6]

While large-scale changes in social structures can only be introduced gradually, the existing social structure must be reformed deftly by each individual and group on a short-term basis, so that violent destruction and individual hardship may be avoided. The person of tomorrow must wield a moral sureness, acting humanely, compassionately, flexibly, and relevantly in complex situations, without violating the broad norms of administrative or social behavior. Men of the future must accept their individuality and their loneliness, must pass in imagination through their death experience, realizing that they are born and will die alone; yet they must live in identity with all mankind rather than with any exclusive group. They must act as individuals, independent of the class or group to which they belong, independent of color, sex, age, or the myriad denominations which obscure their membership in the human family.

To be worthy of embodying the supreme vision of the City of Man will require preparation, deliberation, and meditation. Even now persons might participate in that universal vision through the heart. Love may be the way, but real love is not born immediately, and arises only from mistakes and false anticipations. "Love is the tension between the imperfect soul and the magnetic perfection which is conceived of as lying beyond it."[7] Somewhere in our hearts is the glory of a birth potentially present, of a higher love like light, which can be shared without limit, can provide a model of ontological plenty, and so transcend the zero-sum games of the

6. Ernest Barker, *From Alexander to Constantine,* Oxford, Clarendon Press, 1956, p. 314.
7. Iris Murdoch, *The Sovereignty of Good,* New York, Schocken Books, 1971, p. 103.

logic of scarcity and competition. That is the unwritten logic of the psychology, the ethics and morality, the mysticism and the philosophy of plenty. Reason may harmonize with concern instead of being degraded into rational cunning, which only partially sublimates an illusory sense of power in the name of an equally illusory image of stability. In this way alone can emasculated portraits of perfection be replaced by ever-renewed images of perfectibility, and the seemingly robust but futile impetus toward self-preservation be displaced by a cooler attitude toward temporal persistence. Is there a moral imperative that what is scarce must be more justly and wisely allocated? This is Tolstoy's question in "How Much Land Does a Man Need?"

The sacrificial loneliness of pioneering individuals will find expression in a poignant awareness of mankind and as mature action subserving the welfare of all. They will embody a balance between uniqueness and universality and carry this forward as the basis of their associations with each other, avoiding the parochialism of particulars and the dissociation of empty appeals to the universal. They will be more concerned to generate and participate in a deeper sense of community than with cultivating means of collective escapism. They will not identify themselves with the extremes of Right or Left, indulge in mutual conflict, or tilt at governments. They will recognize the concrete facts both of existing structures and emerging situations and will utilize available material, mental, and spiritual resources. They will, at least, abandon the insecure, weak, and chaotic mass of conflicting doubts which are the incubi of those who seek sacred or secular guarantees of salvation or concretized utopias (though only for themselves). The early pioneers of the emerging cosmopolis will cherish Krishna's teaching that the sovereign test of citizenship in the cosmos is to cease finding fault with one's fellow men. In all human relationships there must be a magical quality of trust–as between mother and child, or between teacher and pupil–more apparent in arenas of moral neutrality, like music, than in our self-righteous social encounters. As a sense of difference spontaneously dissolves, the magic of potential may culminate in the birth of Wisdom.

18

DIANOIA

Men earnestly devoted to becoming good, with all speed, are rare indeed. Hesiod is acknowledged wise for his discovery that the path towards folly is smooth, and, being so short, can be traversed without sweat, whereas before excellence the immortals have set sweat, and the road is long, uphill and rough at the outset although when the summit is reached, the going is easy for all its hardness. ATHENIAN STRANGER

Politics involves the maintenance, transfer, or distribution of power, influence, and authority–among states, groups, or classes of citizens within a state. Parapolitics emphasizes the architectonics of the progressive awakenings and movements of humanity within the ever-shifting relationships of the One and the Many, the whole and the parts. Politics must concern itself with decisions, allocations, and orders applicable to diverse sets of people, but it cannot, with convenience or credibility, allow for endless justification of the primary instrumentalities of policy. Politics, like medicine, often needs the timely application of incomplete knowledge to compelling situations. Political leaders need to think things through, to exercise *dianoia* in seeking reliable and provisional settlements, even if they do not aspire to the *noesis* needed to discover permanent structural solutions. *Dianoia,* as any effective method in logic and mathematics, can work for the solution of a class of problems and for each member of the class, even though it is not possible in practice to follow it as far as is necessary in some–or even any–given case.[1]

Even more than the known limitations of diverse methods, the

1. Geoffrey Hunter, *Metalogic,* Berkeley, University of California Press, 1971, p. 14.

intractable limitation in concretely applying political principles (with weak and strong universalizability) forms the central problem of politics. Individuals cannot be treated as ethically intersubstitutable in the name of loyalty to some contrived scheme of desirable distribution of measurable or identifiable goods. If this is recognized, however, a cruel choice between inertia and imposition seems to confront us, as F. H. Bradley indicated:

> Everybody knows that the setting out, whether in religion, morals, or politics, with the intent to realize an abstraction, is a futile endeavour; and that what it comes to is that either you do nothing at all, or that the particular content which is necessary for action is added to the abstraction by the chance of circumstances of caprice.[2]

But there is a third way suggested by Marsilio Ficino of the Florentine Academy in his essay, "Five Questions Concerning the Mind":

> Just as the single parts of life [of man], that is, deliberations, choices, and abilities, refer to single ends (for any one of these looks towards its own end, as it were, its own good); so in like manner the whole life [of man] looks towards the universal end and good. Now, since the parts of anything serve the whole, it follows that the order which is inherent in them in relation to each other is subordinate to their order in relation to the whole. It follows further that their order in relation to particular ends depends upon a certain common order of the whole—an order which especially contributes to the common end of the whole.[3]

This standpoint underlies the parapolitical quest for multiple approximations to a clear-sighted and inclusive vision of universal welfare in which all individuals and groups may seek their own good without loss of dignity or realism. "Man is not a combination of an impersonal rational thinker and a personal will. He is a unified being who sees, and who desires in accordance with what he

2. Francis Herbert Bradley, *Ethical Studies,* London, Henry S. King & Co., 1876, p. 138.
3. Ernst Cassirer *et al., The Renaissance Philosophy of Man,* Chicago, University of Chicago Press, 1948, p. 197.

sees, and who has some continual slight control over the direction and focus of his vision."[4]

Politics is not autonomous, but must content itself within appropriate circumstances to be a limited means to transcendent ends. These ends cannot be sharply formulated or narrowly appropriated, but their transcendence of available means can work as a palliative to false expectations or sorry disappointments bound up with specific attempts at creative politics. Furthermore, politics as ordinarily understood operates within established structures which draw forth conservative and revolutionary tendencies in participants and observers of the life of the polis. Parapolitically, the needless oscillation between coercive establishment and anti-establishment politics may be avoided by realizing the ever-present possibility of interstitial politics. This encompasses those pivotal points in political structures which reveal that the potential or free space in human encounters is always greater than the bounded, visible arenas of short-term political activity. Paradoxically, institutional limitations might suggest human possibilities when limits (in a Pythagorean or mathematical sense) are properly understood. Critical distance allows perception of vital points and hidden interstices through which individuals may sense the undefined ontological plenty within which defined politics occurs. Great opportunities lie before statesmen and citizens at every turn, but they can only be seen and seized when there is calmness and clarity, nourished by a reasoned conviction of the supreme potential of all men to participate in a truly universal vision.

This conviction is the nerve-current of the dialectic, which involves the raising of questions and progression through a series of approximate answers. But the more questions one raises and answers, the more questions in turn arise. This eventuality, as Plato knew, cannot be accommodated even by the best kind of discussion. It can only mature when an individual creates a life for himself where the internal dialogue is continuous, constructive, and fruitful. Unfortunately, people tend to be inwardly torn in mind and heart, torn above all by borrowed opinions and ideas, as well as by instantly received fleeting impressions from the great flux of

4. Iris Murdoch, *The Sovereignty of Good,* New York, Schocken Books, 1971, p. 40.

sensory phenomena. Rather than succumbing to the turmoil of unresolved priorities and passions, there must be a nobler way. Kayser's suggestion is apposite here:

> Anyone who lives outwardly only, in steady fear of being alone with himself, may imagine he is doing useful things, but he is like a chained dog leashed to a thousand necessities, knowing nothing of freedom, which can be engendered only in the free space of the soul around its own self and the self of others. Man can thrive only in the quiet of a meditative state and only from there will flow a genuine humanity of thought, purpose and feeling.[5]

A man can reformulate for himself the problem of inner conflict. Otherwise, his confusion will only make him a tarnished mirror for the pervasive conflicts of society. The prospects of growth and redemption are severely restricted by the inability of all persons at any given time to do very much about their problems.

There is a natural, perhaps unavoidable, polarity between the architectonic vision of parapolitics and the changing constructions of existential politics. This polarity may yield an electric potential in progressive change and moral growth at the macro-social level, but it is often consolidated into a destructive dichotomy through a failure to honor the fact that ontological priority may not always be equivalent to existential or ethical priority. If time is the moving image of eternity, all political and social systems are necessarily imperfect–local and temporal approximations to some parapolitical order.

> With the necessary descent into instantiation goes a necessary descent into imperfection: the indefinitely numerous, defective and deviant forms which merely fill in the holes and gaps of the eidetic order will be given a new character in the realm of instantiation. We shall have all the irregularities and inexactitudes and conflicting realizations of which the world of instances is full, and which *appear* to give it a being which is cut off from its only source.[6]

5. Hans Kayser, *Akroasis,* Boston, Plowshare Press, 1970, p. 126.
6. J. N. Findlay, *Plato: The Written and Unwritten Doctrines,* London, Routledge & Kegan Paul, 1974, p. 305.

To absolutize any image is to claim for it an ontological status which it cannot bear, and those who recognize this will rebel against conventional fetishism, while those trapped in the dichotomy will be tempted to cloak the polity in the rhetoric of political dogmatism. Self-justification is the chief block to self-transcendence. The greater good is often the enemy of the lesser good, and eternity ever mocks time. This is no excuse for defeatism, much less nihilism; rather it provides the impetus for building within every political system and social structure the basis for further evolution and deliberate transformation in accord with timeless parapolitical ideals. Although the light of the Eternal Sun cannot be seen directly with earthly eyes, could not many a roseate dawn revealed in noumenal light be glimpsed by those who thus look afresh upon existing things?

Negative answers to such questions underlie the failure of institutional liberalism in politics, the moral evasions of Skinnerian social psychology, and the timidity of pluralistic pragmatism. In each, the banners of moral expediency and endemic human weakness are raised to mask the dire need for individual and social renewal and to preclude the restoration of a sense of timelessness and plenitude in human affairs. Owing to their inevitable failure to provide either coherent and comprehensive solutions or functional piecemeal "social engineering," excuses and rationalizations abound for abdication from all striving toward fundamental or far-sighted solutions. If we would cease to cower before the Leviathan of self-imposed limitations and the Lilith of escapist ignorance, we must blend a commitment to non-interference in the moral lives of others with an awareness of our own place in the interdependent ecologies of individual and social relationships. Together they engender a rediscovery of role-precision which can transform the Behemoth of the State into a graceful if imperfect dancer, as in "The Dance of the Hippopotami" in Disney's *Fantasia*. Renewal and restoration are themselves only partially ensured. Commitment to the highest ideals and jejune experiments in their name may range from zero to 100 per cent. Political renewal is possible through the voluntary efforts of individuals toward self-renewal in a context of self-transcendence and fraternal awareness. To demand 100 per cent commitment on the part of others is a moralistic attitude which often tends toward a return of zero per cent. Each individual must be like a mango–hard as the seed toward his own failings, sweet and soft as the pulp toward those of others. The reversal of this standpoint based on honesty and charity is responsible for much of the humbug of social judgmentalism, the harshness of political moralism, and the compulsive intellectualist vivisection of the myths and ideals of the masses, past and present.

To grasp the possibility of growth that is not wholly dependent upon everyone doing the same thing equally in the short run, the process of inner conflict must be converted into a helpful dialogue in which one is able to recognize one's similarities to a variety of other human beings. This fosters sympathy, love, and, most crucially, the ability to put oneself in the position of others. Any citizen who engages in the truly philosophical enterprise–a lifelong love of wisdom–can put himself in the position of his political leaders, in the position of those totally different from him in habits and beliefs, in the place of persons in other cultures, as well as of diverse actors in world history. In time, he could put himself in the position of his enemy, even of someone who became an instrument of evil. This requires mental toughness and moral courage continually underwritten by the willingness to see in oneself elements common to all humanity. The dialectic for Plato involves this dynamic, self-conscious process or activity. Eros is crucial to the ceaseless adventure of discovery and the acceptance of repeated failures in the self-validating quest for wisdom. The dialectic is a way of refusing to settle down. It is a way of rejecting lesser equilibria, thus preventing constriction of a human being or his containment in one or another box. It is a man's determined insistence that as an evolving agent he cannot be contained or fairly judged from outside. Nothing in his life is final. No set of failures tells the whole truth about him or limits his possibilities of further growth. He is secure in the recognition that it is better to travel than to arrive.

Much of the time men live in a state of unconsciousness, semiconsciousness, or incomplete, intermittent awareness. A man who truly begins to take his life into his own hands becomes willing to heighten his awareness of himself, to see himself as others see him, to see himself now as he could see a portrait of himself ten years ago with detachment and without flinching. The heightening and enlargement of self-consciousness is central to the Platonic dialectic. This is stated from the standpoint of the individual. But what begins at the locus of the individual is continually indicated by the interaction of all human beings in society. At the highest level, it involves an interaction with different parts of the universe before returning to the individual through an approximation toward such perfection in human excellence as may be available to men. The concept of perfectibility, which begins in traumatic self-questioning, moves through increasingly effortless self-correction, and at its highest conceivable terminus–though there is no real terminus–is a humbling conception of grandeur gained through that divine manliness which was the original meaning of the word "virtue," and which somehow came to be transferred from manliness to mere chastity. The route of the Platonic dialectic reflects the collective drama of interaction, even in the *Republic,* where the dialectic works at the individual level. Through careful study it will be seen that he employs the dialectic both in the elaboration of his models and also in his refusal to cling to any single model or classification, frustrating as this may be to Aristotelian or Baconian classifiers. Above all, it is evidenced in his unconcern with the instant feasibility of any mode, or the narrow conceptions of purported realism within limited imaginations.

The Platonic dialectic daringly integrates knowing and becoming, man and nature. This process transcends society though it occurs involuntarily in society. It presupposes a living unity at the very core of the universe, a potential unity accessible to all individuals. It also presupposes that the world is an intelligible, rational structure, and that human beings, as part of that world, have a capacity for reasoning which enables them to understand and reflect, even to approximate the structure of the world in concepts, definitions, equations, axioms, and models. But just as the world and nature have a structure, so too does human nature. It is part of, yet apart from, the totality of nature. In human nature there is a representation in the immortal soul, in the pure individuality, of the highest, unmanifest free man struggling to express himself. There is a reflection of unlimited freedom in the universe, beyond nature and represented by the *Nous,* the collective mind or the

Demiurge. Plato did not personify this notion, and held no concept of a personal God. But there is a One that is beyond the Many in nature. For a man to become One in relation to the panoply of elements in society and in himself, he must touch the transcendental core through which he is consubstantial with the One beyond time and space. It is beyond motion in the ordinary sense, beyond causality as we know it, and beyond conventional categories. These distant prospects of the Platonic dialectic begin here and now, but go far beyond the most exalted, albeit still limited, conceptions of space and time, universal motion and matter, nature and knowledge, beyond compromises in the search for equilibrium or the deceptive comfort of stasis–only too often a thin disguise for worldly status.

The Platonic dialectic is articulated differently in its earlier form in the *Republic* and in its later form in the *Statesman,* but both are concerned with the One and the Many. The Many are in the One incompletely through partial participation; the One is in each of the Many but also transcends them because It is without form, color, and limitation. The One becomes the aim of abstract thought. It cannot be simply related to any of the particulars and their parts existing in the world of heterogeneous and differentiated things. In politics, this can help us to understand unity and diversity, universality and particularity; it can help the individual, as an instrument of change, to integrate the differentiated elements in himself, an art exemplified in its highest form by the true philosopher. It may also be elusively enacted by the philosopher as ruler. This is tantalizingly mentioned in the *Republic;* in the *Statesman* many specific definitions of rulership and illustrations of the downward dialectic are presented. There the philosopher as a ruler has a political wisdom which may be expressed in two ways. First, it is a skill in varying control to meet varying needs in changing situations. The statesman knows how much pressure to apply; he knows the potential of the public at all times. In periods of crisis, a statesman can summon enormous reserves and resources that he would not otherwise tap. What the statesman is entitled to demand, and what he can credibly elicit from citizens, varies according to the temperature of the time. Secondly, he wields an architectonic or parapolitical skill that helps him to integrate all roles, knowledge, and arts. He takes those decisions behind which the consensus of the community can be secured, decisions which each individual, as a self-determining agent, could adopt as his own.

The intuitionist criterion of the best decisions is that even if we do not fully grasp them, we hear the echo of their correctness: they look fair or sound right to us. More than that, they are decisions we could live with though made by another, decisions we might as well make ourselves. Recognizing this, we feel no alienation from the decision-making agents. In politics the least wisdom, or the greatest gap, arises from the inability of persons to live with decisions and to carry them out, let alone to regard them as their own. Platonic wisdom rules out passive reliance upon self-declared experts in moral issues. Every man is an apprentice and an expert in the art of living. Every man cannot have the same job but each has a distinct role in relation to the community's needs, the common good, and the public welfare. Every man is entitled by right to have a view, and can, if he chooses, gain as much expertise as is needed and will be helpful. There is no privileged access to expertise in decision making; if there is always a gap between decision makers and those bound by them, there is obviously a theoretical alternative to actual oligarchies. Why not take a different view of knowledge which will validate universal expertise, and why not put the most disarmingly benevolent experts in positions of authority? The choice between ethical excellence and disguised élitism need not be settled always in favor of the latter simply because it can wear the cloak of democratic consensus, dubiously supported by "tacit consent." This ethical alternative implicit in the *Nicomachean Ethics* was worked out blandly but clumsily by Aristotle in the *Politics,* providing the ideological basis for middle-class meritocracy.

The most fascinating feature of the Platonic dialectic is that the standpoint of the philosopher in the *Republic* and of the ruler in the *Statesman* could also be viewed as the standpoint of the rebel and the revolutionary. This is not made explicit in these later dialogues because several earlier Socratic dialogues were already written from the standpoint of the gadfly, the rebel, and the martyr. Where the philosopher is not available, not known, or not in power, or where there is no statesman at the helm, the revolutionary could become, in the age of *anatrope* or inversion, a philosopher or statesman without the trappings of power, a king without regalia in a Hans Christian Andersen world of emperors wearing no clothes. Wittgenstein's enigmatic aside may be relevant: "What I have to do is as it were to describe the office of a king; in doing which, I must never fall into the error of explaining the kingly dignity by the king's usefulness, but I must leave neither his usefulness nor his dignity out of account."[7] The revolutionary can arouse public opinion and gain broad support for ideals or causes that are humane and crucial but overlooked by the upholders of the System. At all levels of the upward and downward dialectic, there is the danger of pseudo-freedom and appeals to pseudo-necessity. It is not easy for the revolutionary to avoid the mistakes responsible for the scarcity of true philosophers and real statesmen. Revolutionaries are vulnerable to the same errors as rulers. They may try to release the will through a temporarily credible formulation, but they may be weak in implementation, or effective implementation may seem to mandate an intolerable imposition of will and force. They may see more alternatives and possibilities than rulers, but they may become dogmatic about what they see. To see more is not to see enough, let alone to see all.

Nonetheless, wisdom in reference to the dialectic, from the standpoint of either philosopher, statesman, or revolutionary, has to do with clear and distinct characteristics: persistence through struggle and pain, through error and imperfection; the willingness to remove misconceptions by self-correction; the seeking of connections between separate facts and an accurate discernment of necessary connections and contingent or empirical connections. This requires flexibility of perspective in the formulation of what is necessary and what may be possible. This also requires detachment. A revolutionary without detachment will be dogmatic; a statesman without detachment may be nearly right, but immense consequences will result from his wrongness and the consequent reactive perspectives of those vainly attempting to dissent from his judgments. A philosopher without detachment is an impossibility. Even more importantly,

7. Quoted in Peter Winch, *Ethics and Action,* London, Routledge & Kegan Paul, 1972, p. 69.

wisdom involves the continual expansion of awareness of alternatives, the development of an eye for essentials. Wisdom is needed to penetrate the core of anything–of a situation, of reality, of a problem. The discriminating eye focuses like a laser beam, so concentrated, intense, and powerful that in penetrating the core it burns out irrelevant obscurations. It removes mental blinders, linking all in a collective awareness. One with such an eye speaks for us all. But how rarely this happens. Most often others address our weaknesses–elements within us which respond to any form of bribery or flattery. Usually men are cowards, afraid of those truths which speak only to their inner strength. *In extremis* and in the ideal context, so rare in public life, when there is a telling formulation that is universifiable and strikes a universal keynote, it finds an echoing resonance in the hearts and minds of many. A very few persons in world history speak about that which is eminently necessary, in a manner other people can readily recognize.

Part of the inimitable charm of the Platonic dialectic is that even though the ideal is remote, individuals may move steadily toward it. These characteristics of wisdom will be developed only by training ourselves in the giving and receiving of reasons. It is often extremely important to perceive motivations. The dialectician will never give the real answer if we are in a challenging or threatening mood. But when he explains to us, we find that we can accept much, though perhaps not all. We can then ask ourselves why we are able to go along with so much and no more. This questioning is itself a constructive and therapeutic act through which we may gain understanding. Most disagreements are failures of communication, and most misunderstandings arise from various contexts with concealed assumptions. In contrast, the Platonic method in the *Statesman* involves exclusion and inclusion, as distinct from excess and deficiency. In the end one tries to evolve a scheme that seems comprehensive, genuinely finding a place for everything. At the same time, each part is so specific and precise that there is no ambiguity. Unambiguous parts in a comprehensive whole form the conceptual strength of the Platonic tree which is not meant to be seen only conceptually. It is relevant in any context and in every dialogue. A person can always draw the larger circle, can always accommodate all points and make them compatible in terms of something more important that each omits.

When a human being begins to exemplify even a small measure of the Platonic dialectic, he evolves. He becomes a minor Initiate in his own company and circle, initiating without strain, with detachment, and without concern for praise and blame. He is concerned that the good ensues, that it be tentatively formulated for the sake of understanding. He is happy when other men care for his ideas, if they are ideas for the good. He loses a sense of mine and thine in the realm of what is good because of his constant pain at the anguish of mankind, the wastage of human resources, and compassion for the world's victims. Because he so much wants the good to happen, to be maximized, he achieves self-transcendence. Without such a motive, he could never handle even one stage of the dialectical process. What one man can accomplish partially, with effort and self-transcendence, within his own sphere, is perhaps a mirroring of what the wisest beings do continuously and invisibly—unseen, unknown, and unacknowledged—for the sake of all. Of them it must be true what Shaw said of Freemasonry and marriage: that those who are outside can know nothing about it. In Plato much is accessible to all but much is beyond each.

We need both eyes—the eye of time and the eye of eternity. We need them especially in politics. The language of the politics of the future cannot be simply the language of the left eye; it must also find place for the right. It cannot participate only in classical reason, different indeed from modern rationality. It must also allow for the encompassing *eros* of unending love. The hidden third eye is the eye of boundless compassion born from pain and struggle, sustained and nourished by growth, heroic efforts, and moral courage, giving birth to an alliance between pain and rapture, at one time called "the mystic marriage" and also *recta ratio.* Right reason is not the monopoly of those who speak in the name of Aquinas, while mystic marriage is not the monopoly of Kabbalistic scholars and alchemical philosophers. No one has privileged access. Each must discover what in the universe is relevant to oneself. Aldous Huxley aptly remarked in 1961:

> Many civilizations have had a real art of living, and I think we are in a position now to be able to understand the art of living much better. We know enough, from a scientific point of view, about what other civilizations have done. I think we are now in a position to be able to develop an art of living of

> a kind which our ancestors could not have developed, because we have these resources at our disposal. . . . What we have to ask is what sort of a social pattern and what sort of a political regime is best calculated to help the individuals within the society to realize the maximum extent of their desirable potentialities. . . . We have it within our power to do extraordinary things if we want to. The question is, do we want to enough? It is not merely a question of will; it is a question of extreme intelligence. We have to use the maximum of intelligence and the maximum of goodwill to solve these problems: we have carefully to think out what is going to happen and then have the desire to do it.[8]

Every person must self-consciously enter the world's heritage, in his or her own way, drawing whatever materials are needed to make a self-tested contribution to the City of Man.

The consciousness of human beings is generally bound up with personalities, conditioned by the influences of this life. Men are all too apt to externalize their internal defects by projecting them upon their own or another race or family, nation or culture. Further, because of the need of the personality to "belong," while evading confrontation with its individuality (which shines by its own light), human beings tend to make sectarian claims on behalf of the group with which they are identified by birth–or by a choice which is more emotional than rational–and thus are caught up in those concretions of thought and feeling that constitute the degradation of every group, religion, and nation. These identifications reinforce false identity, false alibis, narrow attachments, and aversions by invoking the apologetics and distortions of "cunningly made-up History." They lead men to deny their debts to remote ancestors or their share in the iniquities of the past and the injustices of the present. They look outside themselves at fragmentary and distorting portions of history that obscure the continuity and interdependence of the past endeavors and failures of mankind. Handcuffed by current doctrines and modish slogans, they see the past largely in terms flattering to their present predicament. Reacting rebelliously against received notions is little better, and quite different from achieving a true objectivity. We must gradually learn to see that the habit of re-

8. *The Listener,* August 17, 1961, pp. 237-39.

garding everything unpleasant in our collective and individual lives as unjust or fortuitous traps us in time and makes us lose touch with reality. Nature does not move by fits and starts, and there are no "accidents" in history or in our lives; what we cannot comprehend is not intrinsically inexplicable. The dignity of the human soul requires us to look for explanations, not excuses; to seek a heightening rather than a drugging of our sense of responsibility.

Who cares for the fraternity of mankind? If some enlightened beings had not cared for the extension of freedom and had not shown the spirit of fraternity, there would have been no extension of liberty since the eighteenth century. All such extensions of political liberty re-enact parapolitical teachings and movements toward mental, psychological, and spiritual freedom. If some men had not been willing to meet the costs of commitment to extending opportunities to others, the process of equalization would never have begun. Those few who had enough did much for many who had little. A few men worked for the freedom of women; a few who belonged to the ruling nations worked for the freedom of the ruled; a few members of the upper classes, aristocrats or anarchists, worked for the freedom of the very poor. Those who so labored were truly aristocratic in spirit, full of an inner confidence beyond the meanness and narrowness of the bourgeoisie. They appreciated the absurdity of external tokens. The wisest always recognized that *Liberté, Égalité, Fraternité* were sacred, but also saw that while their politicization and secularization in the realm of human limitations was necessary, it was liable to be costly and that many would come to be enormously disappointed with the resulting political infrastructure. That is exactly the point we have reached. We must recover the element of transcendence in every notion so that we can see beyond "isms," institutions, rules, and roles, and especially see beyond the passing panorama of shifting shadows on the wall of the Cave.

Total freedom, complete equality, and the fullest fraternity will never be realized in practice, let alone institutionally guaranteed. But unless human beings consciously sustain an active and constant commitment to exalted ideals, they will descend by default to demeaning rationalizations of individual weakness and collective failure. The gap between the universal ideal and the manifest particulars is inevitable and the sole corrective to apathy or remorse lies in positively celebrating the incremental progress of others as well as of oneself. When we plumb the paradox of the ideal and the manifest to the core, necessity is seen to be based upon spiritual fiber, moral choices, and intellectual honesty. There need be no tension between the transcendental and the temporal; no frustrating hiatus between "is," "ought," "can," and "must"–our nature, obligation, potential, and destiny. The mind may be progressively freed from factious tendencies and partisan perspectives, and begin to enjoy a wider, deeper, and nobler view of the heritage of humanity. Louis Claude, Comte de Saint-Martin, wrote at the time of the French Revolution:

> The society of the world in general appeared to me as a theatre where one is continually passing one's time playing one's role and where there is never a moment to learn. The society of wisdom, on the contrary, is a school where one is continually passing one's time learning one's role and where one waits for the curtain to rise before playing, that is to say, for the veil which covers the universe to disappear. . . . We are only here in order to choose.[9]

9. *Mon portrait historique et philosophique* [1788-1803], Paris, Julliard, 1961, section 117.

INDEX